Teachers of multimedia journalism will love this book. Mindy McAdams has written a refreshingly thoughtful and accessible book about how to create Flash journalism, beginning with introductions to basic drawing tools and building to instructions on how to create photo slideshows with sound and other more advanced techniques. McAdams provides step-by-step directions along with an excellent reference set of first-rate Flash journalism sites.
—Janice Castro, Assistant Dean/Director, Graduate Journalism Programs, Medill School of Journalism, Northwestern University

Flash Journalism: How to Create Multimedia News Packages *fills a technical void in the area of multimedia journalism and mass communication education. There are abundant choices for teaching Flash for beginners and moderate producers, but this book focuses on the tools you will need to produce interactive and visual narratives.* Flash Journalism *will surely be a companion book for my own teaching in the lab and classroom.*
—Andrew DeVigal, Assistant Professor, San Francisco State University

What makes Flash Journalism *stand out is that it contextualizes the Flash technology to journalistic practices. Its six case studies provide readers valuable opportunities to see how pros in the real world use Flash to present news. On top of the case studies, the book's tutorial chapters, in no way a duplication of the existing Flash tutorial books, enable readers to grasp the technology instantly and solidly. Many Action-Scripts in the book could produce elegant effects for journalistic purposes and also save time. This is a must-own book for any mass media learners and practitioners who are interested in the future of news presentation.*
—Dr. Edgar Huang, Associate Professor of Informatics, Indiana University-Purdue University Indianapolis

Flash opens up doors to so many multimedia possibilities—from creating video games to making Web-based applications. It can be difficult to decide what code to spend your time learning for a project, and what code isn't necessary at all for what you are trying to build. Mindy McAdams presents the core information that a storyteller needs. Her step-by-step examples are a guide for those who set out to create multimedia projects of journalistic value.
—Jayson Singe, NeonSky.com

Flash Journalism

How to Create Multimedia News Packages

Mindy McAdams

ELSEVIER

AMSTERDAM • BOSTON • HEIDELBERG • LONDON
NEW YORK • OXFORD • PARIS • SAN DIEGO
SAN FRANCISCO • SINGAPORE • SYDNEY • TOKYO

Focal Press is an imprint of Elsevier

Focal Press is an imprint of Elsevier
30 Corporate Drive, Suite 400, Burlington, MA 01803, USA
Linacre House, Jordan Hill, Oxford OX2 8DP, UK

Recognizing the importance of preserving what has been written, Elsevier prints its books on acid-free paper whenever possible.

Library of Congress Cataloging-in-Publication Data
McAdams, Mindy.
    Flash journalism : how to create multimedia news packages/Mindy McAdams.
        p.   cm.
    Includes bibliographical references and index.
    ISBN 0-240-80697-2 (pbk. : alk. paper)
        1. Online journalsim.   2. Flash (Computer file)   I. Title.
    PN4784.O62M38   2005
    070.4—dc22   2004021185

British Library Cataloguing-in-Publication Data
A catalogue record for this book is available from the British Library.

ISBN: 0-240-80697-2

For information on all Focal Press publications
visit our website at www.books.elsevier.com

04 05 06 07 08 09 10 9 8 7 6 5 4 3 2 1

Printed in the United States of America

To the journalism students at the University of Florida who asked so many questions about Flash

Table of Contents

Part III
Case Studies   297

Case Study 1
washingtonpost.com Sniper Shootings   299

Case Study 2
Star Tribune Slideshow Tool   317

Acknowledgments

This book could not have been written without the advice, support, and ideas of many people in journalism and in journalism education. The online editors and producers, graphic designers, and photojournalists who helped and encouraged this effort number in the dozens, but Andrew DeVigal deserves special mention for building and maintaining Interactive Narratives.org, as does Joe Weiss, not only for teaching all of us with his blog (*http://www.joeweiss.com*) but also for teaching Dave Cone, who in turn taught me so much in 2003. Tom Kennedy, of washingtonpost.com, an alumnus of the University of Florida College of Journalism and Communications, inspired me more than he realized during a dinner conversation in 2002. I also tip my hat to R. Scott Horner and Don Wittekind, both of the South Florida *Sun-Sentinel* and the Society for News Design.

All the Flash journalists whom I interviewed for the case studies in this book did me a great favor by being so generous with their time and sharing so much information. I owe them a hearty thank you and my deepest appreciation for their knowledge.

Fellow educators who spurred me on include Rosental Calmon Alves, of the University of Texas at Austin; David Carlson, my colleague at the University of Florida; Janice Castro, of the Medill School of Journalism at Northwestern University; Paul Grabowitz, of the University of California at Berkeley; Chris Harvey, of the University of Maryland; Janet Kolodzy, of Emerson College, Boston; Thom Lieb of Towson University, Maryland; Mary McGuire, of Carleton University, Ottawa; Larry Pryor, of the USC Annenberg School for Communication; Laura Ruel, of the University of North Carolina, Chapel Hill; and Mike Ward of the University of Central Lancashire. My dean, Terry Hynes, encouraged me to write the book I wanted to write, and my department chair, William McKeen, always remained open-minded about my teaching Flash as part of journalism. David Carlson never failed to listen and offer his expert advice on any ideas I had about online journalism.

Stéphane Richer of Noise Communications, Montréal, helped me learn a great deal about ActionScript in a very short time, especially how to exploit the "_root.onEnterFrame" handler.

Craig Lee, the Web administrator for the College of Journalism and Communications, University of Florida, patiently tested, did troubleshooting, and found answers for me on many occasions. He also drove all the way to Miami once so we could attend a three-day Macromedia seminar (and he showed me where I-95 ends). Kristen Landreville, a graduate student at the University of Florida, assisted me with innumerable details in the final stages of the book.

My editor at Focal Press, Amy Jollymore, proved to be a very patient and supportive force behind the completion of this book. Edgar Huang, of Indiana University–Purdue University Indianapolis, provided an expert technical edit and asked many excellent questions.

The annual conference of the Online News Association has provided a strong connection among practitioners of and educators in online journalism since its founding in 1999. While other organizations concentrate on the business side, ONA always points to the journalism. I owe many of my relationships in this profession to my membership in ONA.

Thanks are also due in large measure to the John S. and James L. Knight Foundation, which endowed the Knight Chair in Journalism at the University of Florida and enabled me to enter the teaching profession and learn from the wonderful students here. The students' willingness to test-drive these lessons and provide feedback enabled me to refine and improve them considerably. The students have earned a heaping helping of credit for everything that is useful in this book.

Mindy McAdams
July 2004

Introduction

Flash is not simple, but you have mastered complex skills before this.

With this book, you should be able to learn how to create online journalism packages using graphical and interactive elements to tell a story. The goal is for you to learn a full repertoire of Flash skills using only this book and the program itself, even if you have never looked at Flash before. This book assumes you are generally comfortable using software, especially some kind of graphics program such as Photoshop; in other words, no time is wasted explaining how to open menus and select tools from a toolbar.

This book does not attempt to tell you everything about Flash. The idea is to tell you what you really *need* to know, in an order that makes sense. Too many Flash books seem to assume you want to know every arcane command available. Why would you? You just need to get the job done. You don't have time to read about sixteen tools when you actually need to use only six. You need to know how Flash handles photos specifically, not just any kind of image. You need to know how to make sound buttons work and not be told that's outside the scope of the book you're reading.

I wrote this book because there was no book like it. A number of online journalists, photojournalists, and journalism educators were talking about using and teaching Flash, a software program produced by Macromedia. They liked what they saw online—certain kinds of moving, visual content that really held their attention and didn't take a ridiculously long time to download—but they had discovered that Flash is not quite as easy to learn as some other programs.

Having had good luck with teaching myself many software programs over the years, I downloaded a free trial version of Flash and went to work. I discovered what others had already learned: Flash is not simple. It seemed especially hard to figure out how to do the journalistic things I wanted to do. Books and online tutorials did not address the problems I needed to solve.

I talked to many professionals who were already using Flash successfully, spent hundreds of hours on the many online forums where generous Flash developers share their knowledge, read at least a dozen books, and completed an online course and a traditional workshop. I used what I had learned to teach Flash to a number of journalism students, and they taught me what various people find difficult about learning Flash—not everyone gets stuck on the same things. That led me to write this book so that journalism students, educators, and professionals could skip a lot of the time-consuming searching and questioning I had to do.

What's in This Book

Whether you are an online editor, a photojournalist, a graphic designer, an educator, or a college student, this book allows you to start your learning journey in whatever way works best for you. If you're a hands-on person, go straight to Part II. If you're more likely to manage the people building Flash projects than to build them yourself, start with Part III. If you want to understand why Flash is a unique tool for journalism, begin with Part I.

In Part I, you'll see why Flash journalism constitutes a new form of storytelling that is distinct from print, broadcast, and much of today's online journalism. Although Flash journalism packages often combine familiar elements from photojournalism, radio journalism, and infographics, the combinations result in something that has not existed before. You'll get an overview of what Flash can do that other Web authoring tools cannot do as well as some caveats about weaknesses of Flash, and you'll learn why Flash has become so widely used online in the past few years.

In Part II, you'll learn how to make things in Flash. Ten self-directed lessons can be completed on your own or as part of a course or workshop. The first five lessons provide the fundamentals needed to create any kind of content in Flash, from drawing and animation to creating buttons that control what happens in the completed Flash presentation on the Web. Lesson 6 introduces a crucial building block of Flash content, the movie clip symbol, which allows you to save time and energy by reusing selected animated sequences. The last four lessons build on the first six to take you beyond the basics to an intermediate level of Flash know-how. Those four lessons are particularly relevant to Flash journalism, because they cover photographs, audio, text elements, and controllable slideshows with sound.

If you work through all ten lessons, you will be able to start building professional-quality Flash journalism packages right away. Remember, your proficiency will increase with each package you create—so start simple, and let your ambitions keep pace with your growing skill set.

To get maximum value from the ten lessons, do everything in the numbered exercises on your own computer, using either Flash MX or Flash MX 2004. If you get stuck (or even if you don't), you can download the relevant FLA files from the book's Web site (*http://flashjournalism.com/book/*) and see exactly how each file is constructed. You can also look at the finished examples there, without downloading them.

The lessons are designed to be used in sequence. Later lessons refer to earlier lessons, in case you have forgotten how to do something that has already been covered. If you feel the urge to jump ahead and work on a lesson out of sequence, don't be surprised if some parts of that lesson are confusing! Use the summary and conclusion at the end of each lesson to make sure you understand all the concepts and practices covered in that lesson. In my experience, students often want to go straight to the final lesson; then they get frustrated because they don't understand how to make things work. I'm advising you not to do that.

Remember, Flash is not simple. You must give yourself time to build your knowledge and skill through using Flash; this will help you avoid frustration.

In Part III, six case studies of professional Flash journalism packages will show you how these techniques are used and expanded upon by experienced designers and developers. The methods used to plan, design, and deliver the finished packages online are explained, as well as how the designers approach and solve problems that are typical in news organizations. Some advanced techniques referred to in these case studies are explained in the Tech Tips that accompany each one.

The case studies will not only help you understand how Flash journalism is done in the real world, but also inspire you to explore more complex techniques beyond those taught in this book's ten lessons. Many other books cover advanced Flash techniques; the designers and developers interviewed for this book agreed that you should expect to continue learning more about Flash, no matter how much you already know.

In the Afterword, you'll see what can be speculated about coming developments in Flash journalism. The multimedia producers and journalists who were interviewed for the case studies are profiled in "About the Flash Journalists," and they offer advice for aspiring Flash experts.

In the Appendices, you'll learn three more advanced Flash authoring techniques: how to create a preloader for larger Flash files, how to build modular Flash packages made up of separate files, and how to put video into Flash.

Formatting Conventions Used

In the lesson instructions, certain words are rendered in **boldface** the first time they are used in any instruction. These include names of panels and tools, the Timeline, and the Stage. The intention is to focus your attention on what you should be doing.

ActionScript is shown in a `monospace serif font`; when you see this, you know you're supposed to type something in the Actions panel (or, in Lesson 10 only, in the external text file).

 Throughout the lesson and the case studies, you'll see an icon in the margin whenever a corresponding file exists on the Web site for this book (*http://flashjournalism.com/book/*). Both the FLA and SWF files are available for you to download and study. You can click any link to a SWF to view it without downloading it.

Some content in the lessons is shown in a box with its own title. These sidebars can be read in any order. Other titled sections flow in line with the exercises and should be read in order.

If the instructions differ for the two versions of Flash covered in this book (MX and MX 2004), the text will say so. If no difference is pointed out, then the instructions work fine in either version.

A Note to Educators

If you are using the lessons in a computer lab, expect each of the first five lessons to take about one hour. Some students will complete them more quickly. The last five lessons will take longer, but most students will be able to complete each of them in about two hours. To reinforce the learning, you should assign additional projects that require the students to use the skills they learned in the lesson(s) for the week. An instructor's manual is available from Focal Press.

I have been able to double up on the early lessons in a three-hour weekly lab, with students completing Lessons 1 and 2 and a small project in the first class, completing Lesson 3 as homework, and then uploading a Flash file to the Web as an out-of-class assignment. They can complete Lessons 4 and 5, and usually part of Lesson 6, during the next class meeting. As homework, they create and upload an animation controlled by scripted buttons.

In the third week, they can complete a photo slideshow with sound. On the Web site (*http://flashjournalism.com/educators/*), you'll find a condensed lesson using a template for a photo slideshow. Use this lesson if you need to fit the entire Flash instruction block into three weeks. Students with a higher interest level should be encouraged to work through Lessons 7–10 in their entirety.

I have also used these lessons in an intensive projects course in which students met twice a week for six weeks, completed all ten lessons during class, produced a written plan for an individual online project, and then used the remainder of the semester to complete the project. This course structure enabled the students to work though all ten lessons in five weeks.

A Note to Professionals

If you're already familiar with Photoshop and/or Dreamweaver, you can expect to complete Lessons 1–5 in five hours or less. Take a break before starting Lesson 6, and spend enough time on it to make sure you really understand how movie clips work; in day-to-day production, movie clips are the building blocks of every Flash movie. Lesson 6 should take between one and two hours to complete.

Lessons 7–10 can be completed in eight hours, depending on your stamina and your aptitude with software. In other words, you should be able to work through all ten lessons in a weekend. This is not the best approach for everyone, of course, but if you're ready to rip into Flash and really wrap your brain around it, you can start as a total beginner on Saturday morning and go back to work Monday morning as an intermediate Flash developer, ready to create engaging online Flash packages for your news organization. Just don't think you can take shortcuts and achieve that result: Use the whole set of ten lessons in order.

A Note to Everyone

One important thing for you to keep in mind: You don't have to do *everything* by yourself.

- If you're not a photojournalist, you will not be producing the great photos that are part of your Flash packages.

- If you're not a graphic artist, you will not be making the information graphics in your Flash packages.

- If you're not skillful with typography, color theory, and page design, you need to get advice on your Flash package designs. A graphic designer can help you clean up your layouts, making the package easier to use and visually appealing.

- If you're going to use sound in your Flash packages (beyond music loops and button clicks), then someone in your organization must be able to capture and edit audio effectively. At a newspaper there may be no one with those skills. Maybe you will decide to add those skills to your own repertoire; maybe you will talk to a radio journalist about partnering with your organization.

- Everyone's writing needs a good copy editor—even if you're a copy editor yourself. Don't shortchange your work by allowing errors in grammar, spelling, or facts to degrade its credibility.

Creating great Flash journalism is a team effort. If you're part of a news organization, you're already part of a team. Make sure you keep your perspective and get other people involved in your Flash packages. They don't need to learn Flash to contribute their photographs, graphics, audio, video, and writing. You can't force other people to give you their time, but you can make them *want* to do it by showing them how well their journalism works in this format.

Part I
Why Flash Journalism?

Chapter 1

A New Form of Storytelling

On January 26, 2001, an earthquake struck the city of Bhuj in northern India. The disaster left most of the buildings in rubble, and tens of thousands died. Half a million people in the state of Gujarat lost their homes. On the other side of the world, news coverage of the devastation seemed both familiar and very remote: a television reporter's voiceover; video of broken concrete, dust, and ruined streets; reports of people who were injured; interviews with other people describing the missing and the dead. Media attention focused on the losses and relief efforts.

The first example of Flash journalism I remember seeing is a slideshow from the Associated Press about the Gujarat earthquake. Tears came to my eyes as I watched it on my computer. The slideshow begins with a low hum of voices and some thumping and crunching, like chunks of concrete dropping onto rock. Photographs of huge collapsed buildings fade in, then fade out. One or two voices become distinct, speaking a language I do not understand; they sound concerned, worried, urgent. Photos show a lifeless hand protruding from a truck, a man wiping his eyes, a row of covered bodies in the street. Car horns blow. People stand in line for food. A child cries out. A man carries a sobbing girl, her ankle wrapped in white bandages.

No voices in English can be heard. No text appears on the screen. There is no motion apart from the fading in and out of each photograph. Somehow the combination of photographic moments and on-site audio put me in the middle of the scene of destruction and pulled me close to the stricken people—in a way video on television never had. Bhuj became nearer to me. Seven months later, on September 11, I remembered those people and that earthquake in India.

The AP slideshow about the Gujarat earthquake is one example of a way to tell a story online, on a computer screen. This type of presentation combines two media forms that have been available for more than a century, still photography and audio recording. The form bears similarities to video—in fact, video images could have been edited to produce a similar presentation—but this form is distinct from video in that it uses only still photos, which capture and freeze a single instant in time. This form differs from a typical TV news segment of the same length in that there is no introduction, no voiceover, no captions. All the sound is natural sound, from the scene, without an interviewer's questions.

SLIDESHOWS WITH PHOTOS AND SOUND

By 2005, most Internet users had seen photo slideshows, some of which play automatically, while others require the user to click a button to change the image. Most of these slideshows include text for caption and credit information. In some cases, the caption is not visible until the user clicks or rolls over a certain element in the window. In other cases, the caption is always visible below or beside the photo.

This slideshow format is specific to digitally delivered media—although photographers have long used slide projectors to show their work to an audience gathered together in one room, and it could also be argued that clicking Next or Back is similar to turning the page in a book or magazine. By itself, then, the slideshow format does not constitute a new form of storytelling. By itself, it is simply a new way to present or deliver photojournalism—a storytelling form that has existed since Roger Fenton went to Balaclava in 1855 to photograph the Crimean War.

TO SEE EXAMPLES OF PHOTO SLIDESHOWS

The (Durham, N.C.) Herald-Sun Gallery:
http://www.herald-sun.com/gallery/

MSNBC.com: "The Week in Pictures"
http://www.msnbc.msn.com/id/3842331/

Star Tribune Slide Shows (Minneapolis):
http://www.startribune.com/stories/319/

washingtonpost.com: "CameraWorks"
http://www.washingtonpost.com/wp-srv/photo/

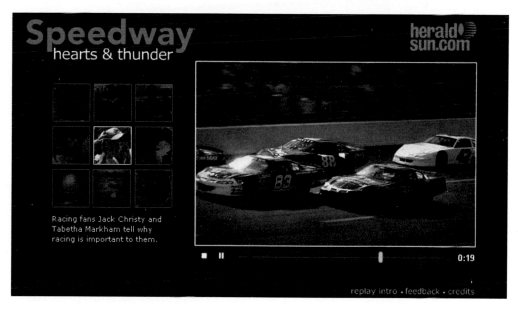

Racing fans Jack Christy and
Tabetha Markham tell why
racing is important to them.

Sound adds a dimension that photos with text captions do not, and cannot, possess (Figure 1.1.01). A photo alone engages only one of the five senses. Sound adds information to the experience of a photo, which can change the story that the viewer experiences:

- If the person in the photo speaks about the moment when the photo was taken, the listener receives one view of the story.

- If the photographer speaks about taking the photo, the listener receives a different view.

- If the audio track contains the natural sound of the scene, the listener receives additional information about the site where the photo was taken.

- If the natural sound was not recorded at the time when the photo was taken, the listener may receive a false impression of the scene.

- If the audio includes music, the listener's emotional response might be manipulated.

The use of audio in these slideshows is not startlingly new; documentary filmmakers have used sound to enhance their visual stories since the 1930s. Recordings of journalistic interviews and natural sound are edited into audio story formats every day for broadcast on public radio stations around the world. In fact, from a radio journalist's point of view, it could be said

Fig. 1.1.01 Combining on location audio with photo-journalism: The Orange County Speedway, a NASCAR racetrack in North Carolina, comes to life in this multimedia feature story from *The* (Durham, N.C.) *Herald-Sun*. Printed by permission of *The Herald-Sun*, Durham, North Carolina. Package produced by Dave Cone.

that *adding photos* to the sound changes the story that the *listener* experiences:

- The scene in the photo might show something that cannot be adequately described with words.

- The photo might show something that differs significantly from the impression given by the speakers in the recorded audio.

- A wide-angle view or an extreme close-up might convey a great deal more than words or natural sound can.

Not all online slideshows include sound; the decision to include it or not depends on the goals for the presentation, as well as professional realities. Sometimes it is just not possible to get relevant sound to accompany photos.

Sound can detract from the quality of the presentation if the audio quality is poor, if the sound editing is badly done, or if the content of the sound is either redundant or irrelevant to the visuals. Done well, however, the addition of sound to photojournalism can exercise tremendous power over the user.

ANIMATED INFOGRAPHICS

In newspaper offices, the word *infographics* (or sometimes just *graphics*) refers to a specific type of illustration that helps tell the story. Usually such a graphic includes one or more blocks of text that help explain what is illustrated. Television newsrooms use the word *graphics* to refer to similar storytelling visuals. Television graphics are usually specified as either OTS (over the shoulder) or full screen; they may be still or motion.

Larger news organizations employ graphic designers to create original news graphics as needed for the daily newscast or print editions. Both large and small news organizations use ready-made graphics provided by subscription services such as the Associated Press, Reuters, and News in Motion (part of Knight Ridder/Tribune Information Services).

After an event such as the destruction of the space shuttle *Columbia* on February 1, 2003, TV viewers expect to see animated graphics that explain what happened. The animation for television might be created with exactly the same software tools as the animation published on a news Web site. If the tools are the same, does that mean the two animations (on TV and on the Web) are likely to be the same?

Not necessarily. While the online graphic designer *could* create an animation that simply plays from beginning to end, exactly like a TV animation, in most cases the online designer will build in some options that enable the user to control parts of the animation. *Control* is the primary difference between an animation on TV and an animation online. The online designer is *not required* to give control to the user, but it is always possible for the designer to do so.

USA Today explained the space shuttle *Columbia* disaster with a package of several animated infographics, including one ("Shuttle Breakup/The Final Hour") that opens with a map showing Africa, Asia, Australia, and the Pacific Ocean. The shuttle appears inside a circle located off the west coast of Australia (Figure 1.1.02). The time is noted: 8:16 a.m. The control in this case affects the pacing of the animation: When the user clicks the Next button, the shuttle moves eastward; the time shown is 8:19 a.m.; the caption text explains that the shuttle began its descent at that time.

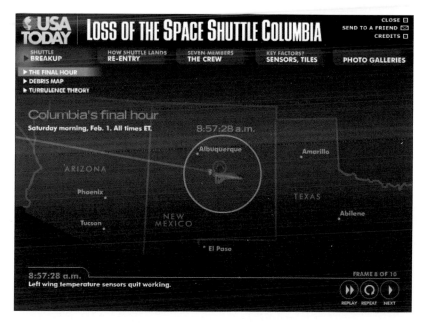

Fig. 1.1.02 *USA Today's* "Loss of the Space Shuttle Columbia" includes an interactive map that illustrates what happened, as well as the location of the shuttle, at what time. Printed by permission of *USA Today.*

USA Today's "Loss of the Space Shuttle Columbia": *http://www. usatoday.com/graphics/shuttle_evolution/gshuttle_disaster12/flash.htm*

Evolution of *USA Today*'s Shuttle Columbia Disaster Graphic: *http://www.usatoday.com/graphics/shuttle_evolution/*

This page illustrates how journalists constructed this breaking news story package online, producing the first version less than one hour after the first reports of a problem with the shuttle, on the morning of February 1, 2003, and continuing with updated versions through April 23.

By clicking multiple times, the user can watch the shuttle cross the Pacific as the map zooms in closer. The time and the caption change with each click. By 8:52:59 a.m., the shuttle is just west of California, and a blinking circle and a warning tone indicate that a sensor in the left wing has gone offline. The use of sound here is especially effective. By 8:59:33 a.m. the map zooms in and the state of Texas almost fills the window. The shuttle is over the city of Dallas. With the last click (Frame 10), the animation of the shuttle fades and is replaced by an inset square showing detail of the debris field.

What distinguishes this example (and other online animations) from those shown on TV? The online user can:

- Absorb the information step by step, at a pace he or she chooses.

- Replay the animation immediately.

- View the animation at a time that is convenient to him or her.

The user's ability to control the pace affects the storytelling significantly. Knowing that users can proceed at their own speed, graphic designers can pack in more detailed information, including text and audio.

In another segment of the *USA Today* shuttle package ("Key Factors/Clues to Columbia's Breakup"), for example, sensors are illustrated in a cutaway view of the shuttle's left wing. Dragging the cursor across a timeline animates the sensors' activity from 8:52 to 8:59 a.m. When the cursor rolls over any of the shuttle's sensors, a text label appears, describing what that particular sensor monitored. The sensor activity tells part of the story of

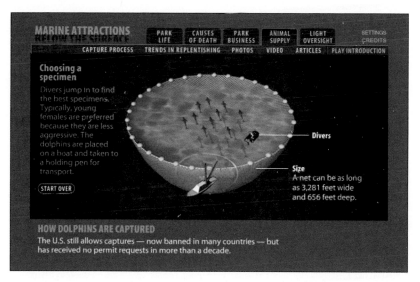

Fig. 1.1.03 The South
Florida *Sun-Sentinel*'s
package "Marine Attrac-
tions: Below the Surface"
includes a four-part
animation that explains
how wild dolphins are
captured for sale to
amusement parks. Printed
by permission of the South
Florida *Sun-Sentinel*.

how systems failed on the shuttle; the user can choose to pursue those
details or not.

The sensor section of the *USA Today* shuttle package obviously required a
great deal of research and fact-checking as part of its production. The visual
approach to this part of the story actually reveals what happened—
although not necessarily *why* it happened—with a clarity that could not
have been achieved in another medium. Journalism, when done right, helps
us understand the world. Sometimes animation provides the best way to
tell a story, to make it easy to understand.

PACKAGES

News organizations discovered years ago that they could bundle numerous
elements and stories together into an online story "package" by creating
links on a Web page. These packages (also called "shells," in some cases) may
include photo slideshows, animated infographics, video, audio, maps, charts,
longer text stories presented as regular Web pages, and links to resources
at other Web sites. Usually, a single Web page serves as an entry into (or
contents page for) the package, and all the package elements are linked to
that page.

Some linked elements may appear in smaller pop-up windows, while others
may be full-size Web pages (which typically link back to the package front
page).

Fig. 1.1.04 Each of the six chapters of "Enrique's Journey," from the *Los Angeles Times*, includes a consistent right-hand rail with links to the photo galleries, maps, and other elements that accompany that chapter. Printed by permission of the *Los Angeles Times*.

Any number or mix of elements can be combined in a package. A package may be a one-time, one-shot story that is launched and never altered. In other cases, a package may be a collection of elements from an ongoing news story that has not yet concluded; this type of package must be designed to accommodate the need for updating.

News organizations typically create an online package page for major ongoing stories such as the war in Iraq or a national election. The headlines of the latest text stories usually are linked automatically, thanks to a script in the Web page code that searches for a keyword. This kind of page is constructed *dynamically*, using information pulled from a database. A one-shot package can be a *static* page, without using any database technology.

"Enrique's Journey," a six-chapter story from the *Los Angeles Times*, follows the quest of a boy from Honduras to find his mother, who left him at age 5 to find work in the United States. Based on three months' reporting work by writer Sonia Nazario and photographer Don Bartletti, the online package includes the text stories and maps that ran in the printed newspaper, as well as a video introduction by Nazario to each chapter of the story, photo slideshows specific to each chapter, charts and statistics in separate pop-up windows, and extensive background notes about Nazario's sources for each event and fact. The elements that accompany each chapter are clearly linked and labeled in a right-hand rail on every Web page in the package (Figure 1.1.04).

The photo slideshows (which do not include audio) mark one of the larger differences between the online and print presentations of Enrique's story: more than a dozen large color photos (100 in all), each with a detailed caption, accompany each of the six chapters. Another difference: the map for each chapter starts with the same large view of Central America but then plays a zoom animation specific to Enrique's location in that chapter.

Some online packages contain few or no examples of Flash journalism. In some cases, a package is simply an archive of past stories about the same topic. In other cases, a package may be a single text story with several elements linked to it, such as a video, a photo slideshow, and a map. The linked elements may have appeared first in another news medium, or they may have been constructed specifically for use online.

EXAMPLES OF PACKAGES

*The Guardian/*Guardian Unlimited: "Special Report: European Union" *http://www.guardian.co.uk/eu/*

Los Angeles Times: "Enrique's Journey" *http://www.latimes.com/news/specials/enrique/*

The New York Times: "Dangerous Business" *http://www.nytimes.com/ref/national/DANGEROUS_BUSINESS.html*

South Florida *Sun-Sentinel:* "Marine Attractions: Below the Surface" *http://www.sun-sentinel.com/news/custom/interactivefeature/sfl-marine-flash.htmlstory*

In other words, not all packages include Flash journalism, and not all examples of Flash journalism are part of packages (although most examples of Flash journalism are linked to a text story).

It is also possible to build a package *entirely* in Flash. Because Flash can incorporate audio, video, animation, photos, and text, and can harmonize all those elements within a single, consistent interface, Flash can be the ideal delivery vehicle for some journalism packages.

INTERACTIVITY

Many digital media products are called *interactive*, but producers and users alike disagree on what "interactivity" means. Before claiming that interactivity makes digital storytelling forms different from other media forms, it will be helpful to take a look at some attempts to define *interactivity*.

Nathan Shedroff, an interaction designer, pointed out that human conversations, playing soccer, and games (online and off) are interactive, whereas Flash, JavaScript, CD-ROMs, and novels are not. (When Shedroff wrote this in 1997, it was far more difficult to include interactivity in Flash.) Shedroff noted that *most* storytelling *is* interactive. He lists six major components of interactivity:

- Feedback
- Control

- Creativity

- Productivity

- Communications

- Adaptivity

A pair of communications researchers, Edward J. Downes and Sally J. McMillan, listed six "dimensions" of interactivity:

- Direction of communication: One-way, as in traditional mass media, or two-way, as in interpersonal communication.

- Time flexibility: Synchronous (real-time, immediate) or asynchronous (stored, accessible at any time).

- Sense of place: Geographical distance, embodiment, presence or tele-presence in virtual places.

- Level of control: Does the sender (author) or the receiver (reader) control the experience?

- Responsiveness: Effort required from the user, customization, extent to which current responses depend on earlier responses or on exchanges between the user and the system.

- Perceived purpose of communication: Persuading, informing, collaborating, etc.

If you compare the two lists, you will find many similarities between them. Shedroff did not mention "direction of communication," but he did list "feedback." Much of journalism is "one-way" in directionality, rather than "two-way," but there are cases in which feedback (from readers, viewers, and advertisers) has had an effect on the work of journalists in both print and broadcast. "Adaptivity" might be the same as "responsiveness"; "productivity" might be close to "perceived purpose."

Another communications researcher, Jens F. Jensen, offered three dimensions of interactivity, each of which functions as a continuum, from least interactive to most interactive:

- Conversational: The degree to which users can create and publish their own content in a two-way media system.

- Selective: The degree to which the users can choose content, either from a fixed set of options or by submitting requests.

- Registrational: The degree to which information about the users is captured and employed to respond and adapt to the users' actions and goals.

Jensen also described a four-dimensional model proposed by another researcher, Lutz Goertz:

- Degree of choices available

- Degree of modifiability

- Number of selections and modifications available

- Degree of linearity or non-linearity

An interesting aspect of Goertz's model: It differentiates between the *areas* in which users can make choices and the *number* of choices possible in each area. Thus, a movie in DVD format would score higher in interactivity than a movie on videotape because the DVD user can select any chapter of the movie from the table of contents and also can select a language for subtitles or soundtrack from a list. If two DVD movies with these two choice areas were compared, the DVD with more chapters and more languages would be rated as more interactive, according to Goertz's model. By merely quantifying levels of interactivity, this model does not determine whether *more* is *better*.

Fig. 1.1.05 P.O.V.'s "Borders," a series on the PBS Web site, includes two "interactive playscapes" created by the Web design firm Futurefarmers. Both look at the environmental implications of the choices we make about what we eat. Printed by permission of P.O.V.'s Borders (*http://www.pbs.org/pov/borders/*). Design by Futurefarmers.

Goertz and Jensen both consider choices or selections available to users, while neither Shedroff nor Downes and McMillan specify that choices contribute to interactivity. All four models or definitions include control, although exactly what can be controlled is not specified. Goertz refers to the *linearity* of the experience, which some researchers explain as a restriction of choices: Must the users follow steps (or parts of the story) in a predetermined order, or can they skip around in any order they like? In a computer game, for example, can the players go anywhere at any time (Figure 1.1.05), or must they complete certain tasks before they can progress to a new level?

So, keeping in mind that more is not always better, and that to be most effective, different kinds of stories require different treatments, here are some questions about interactivity that a journalist or producer might ask *in the planning stages* of an online story project.

Feedback from the Audience

- Can users comment on the story?

- Can they see/hear/read the reactions of other users?

- Can they respond to other users?

- Can the subjects of the story add their point of view?

- Can users ask questions and receive answers?

Adaptivity or Modifiability

- Can the story be updated easily in the future?

- Can corrections be made?

- Can links be added to the story?

- Can new content be added?

Control

- Is the story linear? Is there only one place to start and one place to end?

- Can the users pause something that plays continuously (audio, video, animation, slideshow)?

- Can they mark their place and continue from that point later?

- Can they easily replay or repeat a segment?

- Can they bookmark the presentation? Can they save it on their own computer?

- Can they copy text from the presentation?

- Can they lower or raise the volume of the soundtrack?

- Can they make text larger or smaller, to improve legibility?

- Can they increase the size of images to fit their computer screen?

Choices

- Can the users choose their own path through the story? Is the story constructed in several modular pieces?

- Can they easily skip over parts that do not interest them?

- Can they get more information easily? If they want more detailed information, is it available? If they need a definition or an explanation, can they get it?

- Can they go beyond the site where they are? Can they access original documents, past stories about related issues, and/or external organizations that allow them to become involved and participate?

Communication

- Can users link directly to the story from their own Web pages or Weblogs?

- Can they e-mail a link to their friends?

Responsiveness

- Does the presentation or package "learn" anything about the user? Does it know what the user has already viewed, for example?

- Can the user provide information that enables the presentation to adapt itself to the goals of that individual user?

- Does the user receive an impression of having an effect on the presentation? That is, does anything about the presentation *change* in response to the user's actions?

- Does a script automatically check the user's system and adjust the presentation to provide the best result for that system's configuration?

These questions can be used to determine whether a particular example of Flash journalism is interactive. They are not meant to serve as rules for every Flash presentation. Some stories warrant more interactivity than others—

just as some stories would be improved by audio and others would not. Most examples of online journalism today do not have a high degree of interactivity; this may change in the future as journalists become more accustomed to telling stories with the tools available to them in this medium.

EXAMPLES OF INTERACTIVITY

In MSNBC.com's "Airport Security/Can You Spot the Threats?" you take a 2-minute shift as an airport security person, and find out whether you can spot weapons or explosives hidden inside carry-on baggage.

http://www.msnbc.com/modules/airport_security/screener/

In PBS P.O.V.'s "Borders/Environment/Earth," you can explore a garden, learn about the plants in it, water them, plant new seeds, and leave messages for other visitors to read.

http://www.pbs.org/pov/borders/2004/earth/

"What Is a Print?" from the Museum of Modern Art, New York, lets users try out the techniques used in four types of printmaking: etching, lithography, screenprint, and woodcut.

http://www.moma.org/exhibitions/2001/whatisaprint/print.html

INTERFACE

How do the users know what they can do and what a package contains? The typical Flash journalism package uses the same kind of interface as most Web sites—links. Links may look like buttons, tabs, or perky icons, but when you get right down to what the interface does, it is just a list of links. Click one and you get some new information.

Other possibilities beckon. Maps provide an obvious interface for some journalism stories: the movements of troops in wartime, the events at a crime scene, points on a journey. Timelines (Figure 1.1.06) and calendars work well for retrospectives and biographies.

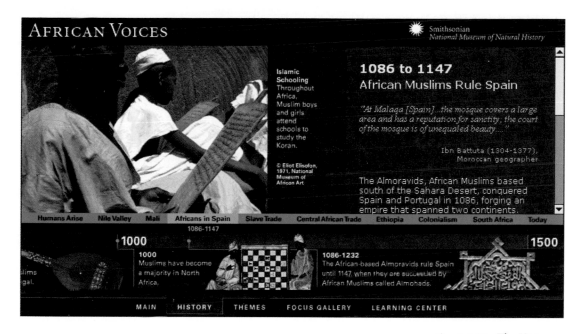

What other methods could be used to help users enjoy and understand a story? A New York–based company named Kuma Reality Games creates military mission simulations based on real current events and makes them available to subscribers to the company's Kuma\War gaming engine (*http://www.kumawar.com*). The company does not market the games as journalism, but a company press release said, "Kuma\War enables consumers to experience actual missions of real soldiers in the war on terror."

While any attempt to associate a video game with journalism would raise numerous ethical issues, a video game interface (without scoring and, say, body counts) could be designed to present a complex story as a puzzle, or possibly as a detective novel. As anyone who has ever played a video game knows, you learn a lot through playing, and the more you know, the better you play. Maybe any attempt at a game with a journalistic mission would turn out more gimmicky than useful, but who knows? It could provide the interface that makes buttons obsolete.

Fig. 1.1.06 The History section of the Smithsonian's online exhibit "African Voices" employs a timeline (at the bottom of the window) that can be dragged left or right. Clicking in the timeline displays a new image in the upper portion of the window. Printed by permission of the African Voices Web site (*http://www.mnh.si.edu/africanvoices/*) in support of the African Voices exhibition at the Smithsonian Institution's National Museum of Natural History.

SUMMARY

If online media enable new forms of journalistic storytelling, it must be possible to identify differences between how stories are told online and how

The CBC's "Anatomy of a Refugee Camp" uses a compass to allow free movement across an illustrated version of a location. Small icons scattered about the camp indicate where the user can click for more information. A more traditional menu is also provided.

http://www.cbc.ca/news/iraq/presentations/refugees/refugee.html

In the *Los Angeles Times*'s "High Stakes Pipeline," a clickable map of Cameroon and Chad serves as an interface to eight videos about the towns affected by an oil pipeline; the story integrates graphics, video, and five photo galleries into a single Flash presentation.

http://www.latimes.com/news/nationworld/world/la-pipelinemain-g,0,6979464.flash

National Geographic used a combination of a map and a timeline to tell the story of the Japanese attack on Pearl Harbor. (Click "Attack Map" to open it.)

http://plasma.nationalgeographic.com/pearlharbor/

The design firm Terra Incognita created the Smithsonian National Museum of Natural History's online exhibit "African Voices" in 2001. Compare the interface with that of a 2004 project (also from Terra Incognita), the Indianapolis Museum of Art's "Cycles." Both sites avoid a typical buttons-only interface.

"African Voices" *http://www.mnh.si.edu/africanvoices/*

"Cycles" *http://www.ima-art.org/cycles/*

360 degrees/Perspectives on the U.S. Criminal Justice System, from the interactive design studio Picture Projects, employs an interface of floating circles to engage the user more actively with the content. The motion of the content orbs tends to hold the user's attention.

Launch page: *http://www.360degrees.org*

Other projects: *http://picture-projects.com*

they are told in broadcast and print news media. Simply showing photographs or video on a computer screen is not very different from showing photographs in a book or newspaper, or video on a TV screen.

This chapter has provided several examples of stories told uniquely online. While elements such as audio and photos are used in other media, the ability to *combine* these forms online marks one—but not the only—signif-icant difference between online and other news media. (The differences between video and still photography must be taken into account as well.)

Both television and print news media use infographics to help tell stories more completely. Printed infographics cannot be animated, but they can include more text than is practical to show on television. Television news graphics can be animated, but they cannot be interactive; they must play in a linear, start-to-finish manner. The addition of depth and viewer control (interactivity) to online infographics makes them different from their coun-terparts in print and broadcast media.

Multiple media may be combined into a single presentation, such as a map that serves as an entry point to videos shot in several locations (Figure 1.1.07). Multiple presentations, or elements, may be linked from a single Web page to create a story package. While television journalists use the word "package" to mean one finished story that airs during a newscast, online journalists use "package" (or sometimes "shell") to mean a compila-tion or set of elements that are all related to one story. An animated map may be one of the elements included; a photo slideshow may be another element in the same package. Some online packages are primarily archives, a set of links to text or video stories that were previously printed or aired.

Interactivity involves more than merely providing several choices to the user—although *choice* is one aspect of interactivity. The ability to provide a real user-controlled experience distinguishes online media from other news media; much more could be done in the future to allow users to get what they want from journalism online and to engage more deeply with the story.

The interface of a multimedia package lays out the options available to the user. Options may be arranged in a simple list, using text or icons, but video games demonstrate that there are many other ways to invite a user to explore and experience an information space. More compelling interfaces might lead to more compelling journalism in the future.

Online media put new ways to tell stories into the hands of journalists. The number of good examples grows every month. As journalists gain an under-standing of the tools needed to produce engaging stories in online media, they are proving again and again that Flash journalism really is something new. Online, journalists can convey ideas to which text, video, photos,

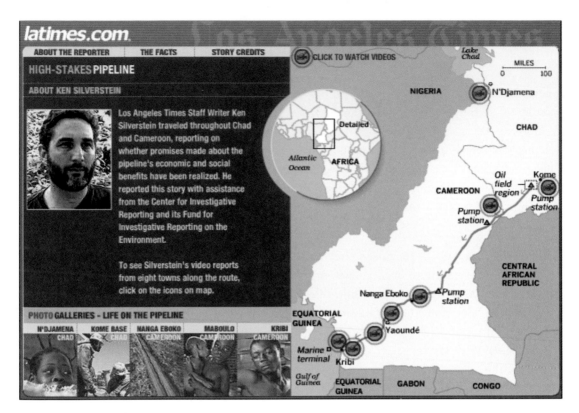

Fig. 1.1.07 "High Stakes Pipeline," from the *Los Angeles Times*, combines Flash video with a map and several photo galleries. Printed by permission of the *Los Angeles Times*.

audio, or graphics alone cannot do justice. Journalists will continue to tell stories via broadcast and print media, of course, but they will also adapt their craft to the new possibilities offered by online media.

REFERENCES

Barnouw, E. (1993). *Documentary: A History of the Non-Fiction Film*, 2nd revised ed. Oxford University Press.

Carlsson, S. E. (n.d.). *History of Film Sound.* http://www.filmsound.org/film-sound-history/

Downes, E. J., & McMillan, S. J. (2000). Defining interactivity: A qualitative identification of key dimensions. *New Media & Society*, 2(2), 157–179.

Faber, J. (1978). *Great News Photos and the Stories Behind Them.* New York: Dover.

Jensen, J. F. (1998, June). Interactivity: Tracking a new concept in media and communication studies. *Nordicom Review*, 19(1), 185–204. http://www.nordicom.gu.se/reviewcontents/ncomreview/ncomreview198/jensen.pdf

Nichols, B. (1995). Documentary and the coming of sound. http://www.filmsound.org/film-sound-history/documentary.htm

Shedroff, N. (1997). Recipe for a successful Website: Interaction design. http://www.nathan.com/thoughts/recipe/inter.html

Stevens, J. E. (2002, August 8). Web shells: An introduction. *Online Journalism Review.* http://www.ojr.org/ojr/business/1030665107.php

Chapter 2

What Flash Brings to Online Media

This book concerns the software package Flash, produced by Macromedia, and its use in journalism. Other popular software packages, such as Adobe's Photoshop or Sony's Sound Forge, are not the subject of books specifically covering their use in journalism. You can find books about the software, and books about photojournalism or radio journalism, for example, but not books about one type of software used in specific journalism applications.

Why is this book specific to the use of one software package? Because at this time, the software and the style of journalism produced with it can hardly be separated. The forms of journalism described in Chapter 1 are produced with Flash in almost all cases; no other software available today can do the job in the same way.

Both as an authoring tool and as a delivery medium, Flash provides benefits not available in Web authoring environments such as Macromedia's Dreamweaver or in standard media players such as QuickTime, Real, and Windows Media Player.

A BRIEF HISTORY OF FLASH

Macromedia acquired a company called FutureWave Software, which had developed a software package called FutureSplash Animator, in December 1996. The following year, Macromedia released Flash as its new online animation package. Macromedia—created in March 1992 from the merger of two California software companies, MacroMind-Paracomp and Authorware—was already well known for Director, software used primarily to develop CD-ROMs.

FutureSplash was originally intended to "dominate the market for graphics software on pen computers," according to its author, Jonathan Gay; it had evolved into an animation program after the market outlook for pen computing darkened in 1995.

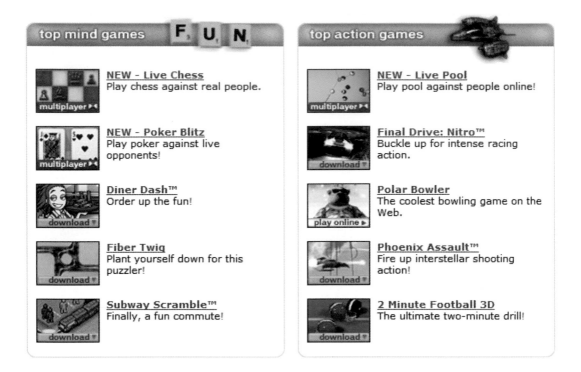

Fig. 1.2.01 Shockwave is still used for games and other online content, which is showcased at Shockwave.com.

FLASH VERSION RELEASE DATES

1997   Flash 1.0
1998   Flash 3
1999   Flash 4
2000   Flash 5
2002   Flash MX (6)
2003   Flash MX 2004 (7)

In the mid-1990s, Web developers had two common choices for animation: They could use animated GIFs (suitable only for very simple, small animations), or they could use Macromedia Director, which has a pretty steep learning curve. Both of these options are still viable today, and Director is still used to create online games and applications that run in the Shockwave player. Flash, however, has distinct advantages over both GIF animations and Shockwave content.

Flash attracted attention immediately for its ability to produce big-screen, complex animations at very small file sizes—which meant you could place a great-looking animated graphic on a Web page, and users would not have to wait too long for it to download. (Shockwave files, by comparison, tend to be much larger, and therefore slower to download.) Using vector graphics instead of bitmaps, and streaming content automatically, Flash was (and is) able to provide instant gratification to impatient Web users.

Flash files can include sound and photos, both at good quality. Animated GIFs cannot handle sound at all, and photos look terrible in the GIF file format.

While Director can do most of what Flash does (and more), Director is better suited for developing content delivered on CDs or DVDs, or through kiosks—even though Shockwave is also used on the Web. Director incorporates real-time 3D animation (Flash does not) and can be used to launch and control other applications (Flash cannot). In other words, Flash, with its features that make it so well suited for use online, comes with some limitations, but none that seriously impede its usefulness in online journalism.

Macromedia has specifically targeted Flash and its capabilities at Web animation and online applications, reserving more demanding and "heavier" capabilities for Director and Shockwave. This does not mean that Flash files are *always* small and lightweight; they can grow to be just as large as Shockwave files if the author is not careful. With the most recent versions of Flash, however, Macromedia has added features that make it even easier to keep the downloads small and the online users happy, such as the ability to load and use externally stored photos, sound, and plain-text files.

DELIVERY MEDIUM: THE FLASH PLAYER

The ability to play video in Flash (starting with Flash player 6), as well as the ability to stream external MP3 audio files and display external JPG images, made the Flash player the most versatile media player available. Loading external files at runtime allows you to keep the Flash file size tiny— as small as 2 KB in some cases—by loading photos, sound, and text from outside the Flash movie. Video in Flash can be wrapped in any kind of interface a designer can imagine, rather than the branded container of a specific media player.

While Director (the application) produces files that play in Shockwave (the player or plug-in), Flash is always called Flash—application, player, plug-in. The *application* is the software someone uses to develop, or author, a Flash file. (More about the application follows.) The *player* is a small, free

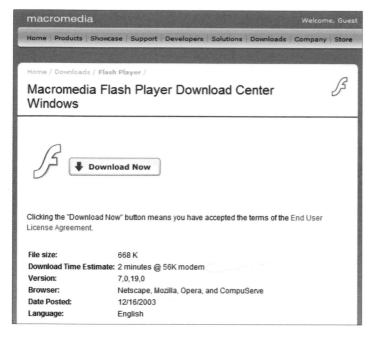

Fig. 1.2.02 The Flash player is free and easy to download and install. Printed by permission of Macromedia.

piece of software that any Mac or Windows user can download (*http:///www.macromedia.com/go/getflashplayer*).

Flash came to be widely used in part because the Flash player is easy to get and easy to install. In most cases, the Flash player can be downloaded and installed in a minute or less on a high-speed connection. The Web browser stays open, and the user does not need to restart the computer. This is a big plus over some other media players that are used online; users generally hate to interrupt their Web browsing and close down or restart anything.

The large installed base for the Flash player provides a reason for the proliferation of Flash content online. In March 2004, according to a study by the NPD Group, the Flash 6 player was installed on more than 93 percent of all Web browsers in use in the United States, Canada, and Europe, and on 88 percent of the Web browsers in Asia. The Flash 7 player (released in mid-2003) had already achieved 52 to 60 percent penetration in those regions by March 2004. That means most Web users do not have to download the Flash player. They already have it. Unlike some other media players, Flash works equally well on Mac and Windows computers. Installing the player does not interfere with other software or put up alarming messages such as "Do you want to reassociate your file types?" (which many users may not understand). The Flash player works in the Netscape, Mozilla, and Opera Web browsers, as well as in Microsoft Internet Explorer.

AUTHORING TOOL: THE FLASH APPLICATION

The number of Web users worldwide who already have the Flash player makes it a good choice for delivering certain kinds of content online. That content must be in the SWF (pronounced "swiff") file format—the format played by the Flash player. (SPL files, which were created by FutureSplash and Flash versions 1 through 3, will also play in the Flash player.) You can use any version of the Flash application (e.g., Flash MX 2004) to make a SWF file, also commonly called "a Flash movie."

When you create and save a file in the Flash application, the format is FLA. The Flash application is the only software that can create and edit FLA files. When you "publish" or export an FLA file from Flash, it becomes a SWF file. You end up with two files, the SWF for uploading to the Web, and the FLA, which can still be edited or revised (and then used to generate a new SWF). This is analogous to working in Photoshop for the Web; typically you work and save files in Photoshop's native PSD format, but you export JPG or GIF files for use on the Web. Similar to the way that a JPG file is much smaller than a PSD file, a SWF is much smaller than an FLA.

Other applications can be used to create SWF files too, but the consensus in the Flash developer community is that you must have Macromedia's Flash if you want a full set of tools for creating interactivity. Applications that create SWF files include Swift 3D (*http://www.swift3d.com*), the SWiSH product line (*http://www.swishzone.com*), and Toon Boom Studio (*http://www. toonboomstudio.com*). These programs do not replace Flash but can be used to author animations and text effects. Adobe used to sell a SWF product called LiveMotion, but it was discontinued in 2004.

Adobe Illustrator will export SWF files, as will Macromedia's own Free-Hand and Fireworks; these SWF files can then be *imported* into the Flash application and incorporated into any movie (any SWF that has not been deliberately "protected" against import can be imported, but with varying degrees of functional usability). For example, a graphic designer accustomed to working in FreeHand or Illustrator might typically create graphics in the familiar drawing program, then *export* SWF files for use in the Flash application, where they could be animated quickly. This can save a lot of time in a news operation; if designers are already working in one of these drawing applications to produce graphics for print or broadcast, they can export a copy of a file in the SWF format for online designers to use in the Flash application.

Support for Flash among broadcast authoring products varies: Avid's Xpress DV and Xpress Pro can encode SWF and Flash's native video format, FLV; Chyron's Lyric application can produce SWF content; Dis-

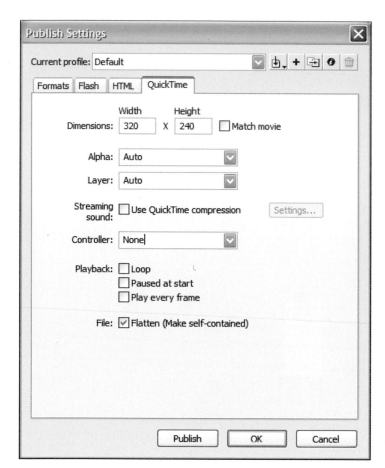

Fig. 1.2.03 Flash movies can be exported in the QuickTime MOV file format.

creet's Combustion 3 includes a Flash Output function. Products such as Quantel's Paintbox and generationQ line can export other formats that can be brought into or used with Flash in various ways. Once you have an AVI or MOV file, though, it's a cinch to run it though Flash's video compression options and integrate it seamlessly into a Flash movie (see Appendix C). Alternatively, you can produce an MOV directly from Flash and export it to tape. A skilled Flash designer might be able to output on-air motion graphics faster than someone using another application.

Software developer Jacek Artymiak sums up why Flash is unique:

"Flash has become popular among Web designers because it is a complete solution: a well-designed authoring application, a robust file format, and a widely distributed player.... [You have] one platform to develop for, no need to worry about the Web-safe color palette, all components can be bundled into a single file, good authoring tools, support for forms, an XML parser, and a powerful programming language.... One of the reasons for Flash's popularity is the fact that it provides what other standards cannot provide: an easy way for the designers to control the final look of the documents they publish on the Web. It is, in a way, the PDF of interactive multimedia. Both formats are so popular because, for the end user, the efforts that go into achieving the desired results are minimal."

The Flash application has changed quite a bit since 1997; the biggest change of all came in late 2003 when Macromedia shipped its MX 2004 suite of software. For the first time, Flash was available in two distinct versions, one called "Professional" and the other not. Depending on what you want to create with the program, or if you're on a tight budget, you may not need to upgrade from Flash MX (version 6) to one of the MX 2004 (version 7) packages. If you do decide to upgrade, or you're buying Flash for the first time, you will need to compare the features of the Professional and non-pro versions. The price difference is about $200. You can download a free trial version from the Macromedia Web site (one trial copy lets you try and compare both versions).

The Professional version includes all the same features as the other version, with additional functionality for creating database-driven applications, delivering high-quality video, and delivering Flash content on devices such as PDAs and cell phones.

WHAT FLASH DOES WELL

Various capabilities of Flash have already been mentioned, but let's take a good look at some things Flash can do well, and then we will consider common problems with Flash content on the Web.

Design Control

Flash movies (SWF files) can be integrated directly into any Web page. The designer can specify the width and height of the Flash movie before exporting it—so Flash content can appear inside a tiny rectangle (e.g., an embedded audio player) or fill the entire page (e.g., a map of the world). The SWF can be positioned exactly, in the same way a JPG or GIF is positioned, anywhere on the page (Figure 1.2.04). It's easy to combine text and other normal HTML elements with a SWF on a Web page. By matching the background color of the Flash movie to the background color of the Web page, the designer can make the movie appear to be part of the page; Flash content need not be surrounded by a player window or frame. Alternatively, Flash movies can be opened in a separate pop-up window. These techniques are explained in Lesson 3: Putting Flash on the Web.

The designer also has precise control over the position of all elements *within* the Flash movie. The user's browser settings and operating system have no effect on the appearance of any object in the Flash movie (unless the author has not embedded the fonts; that is covered in Lesson 9: Working with Text), so long as the user's Flash player version is compatible with all assets included in the SWF.

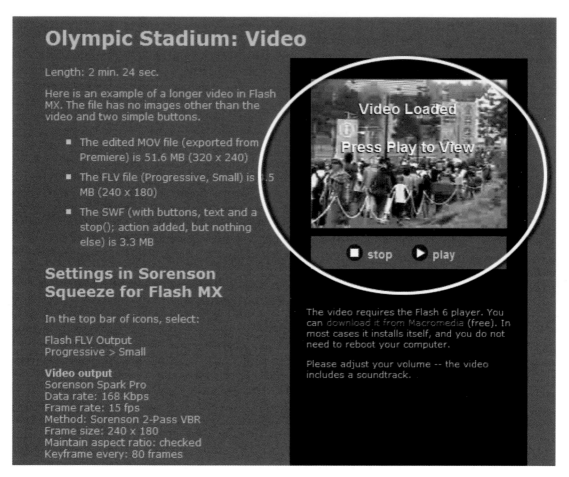

Olympic Stadium: Video

Length: 2 min. 24 sec.

Here is an example of a longer video in Flash MX. The file has no images other than the video and two simple buttons.

- The edited MOV file (exported from Premiere) is 51.6 MB (320 x 240)
- The FLV file (Progressive, Small) is 4.5 MB (240 x 180)
- The SWF (with buttons, text and a stop(); action added, but nothing else) is 3.3 MB

Settings in Sorenson Squeeze for Flash MX

In the top bar of icons, select:

Flash FLV Output
Progressive > Small

Video output
Sorenson Spark Pro
Data rate: 168 Kbps
Frame rate: 15 fps
Method: Sorenson 2-Pass VBR
Frame size: 240 x 180
Maintain aspect ratio: checked
Keyframe every: 80 frames

Video Loaded

Press Play to View

■ stop   ▶ play

The video requires the Flash 6 player. You can download it from Macromedia (free). In most cases it installs itself, and you do not need to reboot your computer.

Please adjust your volume -- the video includes a soundtrack.

Fig. 1.2.04 The circled content is a SWF file embedded in a Web page. The rest of the page is regular HTML.

Integration of Media Types

The designer or author of a Flash movie can incorporate numerous assets of various media types into one package that functions as a single piece. Instead of having separate windows pop up to show video, maps, photo galleries, or text, all these elements can be combined into a single interface, in a single frame (Figure 1.2.05). Flash not only eliminates the need for separate windows; it also eliminates the need for separate players and plug-ins.

Interactivity

Designers can create elaborate (or simple) custom interfaces for Flash movies, with buttons, sliders, and other controls that match the tone and

Fig. 1.2.05 When a video opens in the *Los Angeles Times*'s "High Stakes Pipeline," the map in the background is automatically dimmed. Printed by permission of the *Los Angeles Times*.

style of the content package. Controls can easily be coded for sound so that particular actions by the user produce audible feedback. All manner of images can become responsive to the mouse cursor—one common example is a map that displays text information boxes when the mouse cursor hovers over a hot spot (this is also possible with HTML image maps, but a SWF file will usually be much smaller than the graphic files used for an image map). Icons or other graphics can be made draggable, so a user can position them on a diagram, or operate a lever or dial on a machine. Users can even draw or paint within Flash and save their creations in the application for others to see (*http://www.mrpicassohead.com/create.html*).

Form fields can be used in Flash to allow the user to send information to the SWF (e.g., in a test-yourself quiz application) or to a database via the Internet. An elaborate (non-journalism) example is the iHotelier One-Screen reservation application, which interacts with a database in real-time to show users which rooms and rates are available on which dates (*https://reservations.ihotelier.com/onescreen.cfm*).

Even without forms and databases, ActionScript can be used to store information about the user's choices and direct the Flash movie to react according to what the user has (or has not) done.

Look, Ma—No Scrolling

Elements can be layered in Flash to appear on top of previous elements, or new elements can replace previous elements in the same place, at the same screen coordinates, without going to a new Web page. Flash content can be created without the need for scrolling or paging. Objects can be "closed," "minimized," or dragged to central or marginal positions, if the designer chooses to provide these options. Alternatively, the designer can choose to implement a page metaphor or to use scrolling for contained elements (such as a text box) within the movie.

Modularity

An author with moderate experience can construct sets of Flash movies that communicate with one another, further decreasing file size and sparing users from waiting for content they may not choose to view. Unlimited SWFs can be loaded into one base, or "shell," SWF that calls the others in as needed. The call to "loadMovie" can occur when the user clicks a button, or when the Flash movie progresses to a particular frame in the Timeline (the Timeline will make sense to you after you have completed Lesson 2). Obviously, a dozen or more 50KB files will mean less waiting (for the user) than a single 600KB file. To the user, these loaded SWFs do not appear to be separate in any way from the base movie.

Other external files, such as MP3s and JPGs, can also be called into the Flash movie dynamically. JPGs are loaded with the same ActionScript method ("loadMovie") used for external SWFs. MP3s are loaded with the ActionScript method "loadSound." This capability makes it possible for editors and producers who know nothing about Flash programming to create content that is used in a Flash movie, if they are given instructions about how to name their files. For example, a photo editor can update a "Photo of the Week" feature just by naming the JPG files in a sequence such as photo1.jpg, photo2.jpg, etc., and then dropping them into a folder along with a SWF "shell" that displays each photo in order. The same SWF can display a new set of photos each week, without changing anything other than the JPG files in a particular folder on the Web server and editing a text file containing caption and credit information. This technique is explained in Lesson 10: Building Slideshows with Sound. The "loadSound" method is explained in Lesson 8: Working with Sound.

Motion

The ability to play video debuted in Flash player 6, but Flash was already well known as an efficient tool for delivering animation online. Vector graphics can be moved, scaled, and skewed without any notable increase in file size (vector graphics can be created in Flash itself or in other applications such as Illustrator, FreeHand, and Fireworks, and imported by Flash). By 1999, a number of designers had figured out how to use Flash to pan across a still photo, or focus on a detail and then zoom out, to add drama and engage the users' attention in a feature story. This type of motion—which sometimes is mistaken for video—can be used to produce smaller files with larger, sharper images than are possible using video. These techniques are explained in Lesson 7: Working with Photos.

Using a third-party program such as Swift 3D, graphic artists can create detailed models of objects or places; importing these into Flash as a series of images allows the user to view the model from different angles or seemingly rotate an object. While 3D objects cannot be created within Flash, this technique produces a very similar result at very small file sizes.

Finally, text can be animated in various ways in Flash to produce a "must read" experience for the user. A skilled designer can bring short phrases onscreen (in large, legible fonts) timed to coincide with the appearance of a particular image, a very compelling combination that moves the story forward. Motion text can fade in and out, scroll or slide, shrink or grow—and thanks to vector graphics, the edges of a embedded font will be smooth and clean, no matter how it moves. These techniques are explained in Lesson 9: Working with Text.

Portability

SWF files can be played on any platform that has a Flash player, including many PDAs and cell phones. A Flash movie can also be saved as a "projector" file, which can be played on Windows and Macintosh operating systems without the Flash player. Flash movies can be saved as a QuickTime movie (MOV format) as well; as such, they can be dubbed to tape for broadcast. With a little planning, you can make a content package available on a wider variety of platforms if you use Flash as your final-stage production tool.

Preloading

If the download time for a Flash movie will be rather long for dial-up users, in spite of Flash's native streaming ability (see "Streaming" section that follows), the designer can choose to code a preloader script into the movie. A typical preloader checks how much content has been downloaded and shows the user the percentage; the numeral dynamically increases as more content loads, until it reaches 100 percent—and then the movie begins to play. Users with a high-speed connection see the preloader very briefly, or not at all, while dial-up users can decide whether they want to wait based on the speed at which the percentage is increasing. Preloader scripts can also be used to load future content selectively while the user is involved in the current content. Creating a preloader is covered in Appendix A.

Fig. 1.2.06 The Sonic Memorial Project remembers the victims of September 11 with audio shared by members of the public, presented via a unique interface (*http://www.sonicmemorial.org*). Printed by permission of Sonic Memorial. Produced by Picture Projects and dotsperinch in collaboration with Lost & Found Sound.

Sound

Sound handled by Flash—whether it is part of the SWF file or loaded externally—does not require the users to have any player other than Flash. High-quality music or radio-style journalism can be saved as external MP3 files and played through the SWF, accompanying still photos, animated graphics, or other visual content. Some sites have built tiny stand-alone music players in Flash; the player is embedded in an HTML page or appears in a pop-up window, often with a dynamic text field showing artist, song title, and duration.

Sound effects and music loops can easily be imported into Flash and used to enhance quizzes, games, or interfaces. Audio is covered in Lesson 8: Working with Sound.

Streaming

Flash content automatically streams; that means the Flash movie can begin to play before the entire SWF file has completely downloaded. The download continues while the user begins to enjoy the package. A Flash author who has a thorough understanding of this functionality can build SWFs in ways that require little or no waiting from the user; for example, a brief text introduction can download very rapidly, and the user starts reading it without realizing that other content in the Flash movie is still downloading. A button allowing the user to continue typically appears later, after enough of the upcoming content is available.

Music and video also stream automatically in Flash, if the SWF is constructed to allow it, making the Flash player a highly effective platform for delivering those types of content.

PROBLEMS IN FLASH CONTENT

When Jacek Artymiak called Flash "the PDF of interactive multimedia," his analogy was apt in more than one sense. You can use Adobe's Acrobat application to transform any document or image into a PDF file, but for many online documents, a normal HTML file would be a better choice: HTML is faster to download and more accessible to more online users. With its myriad capabilities, Flash could also be called the Swiss Army Knife of online content—you can use it to do just about anything. But even though my Swiss Army Knife includes two screwdriver heads, I will use a regular screwdriver instead if I can, because the proper tool will always do a better job.

Accessibility

With Flash player 6, Macromedia added support for Microsoft Active Accessibility (MSAA), which allows users of some assistive technologies, such as screen readers for the visually impaired, to receive content from a Flash movie. Content developers who want to comply with the World Wide Web Consortium's Web Content Accessibility Guidelines, or with the U.S. government's Section 508 of the Rehabilitation Act, need to evaluate whether they can use the Flash application to make their content accessible.

Major considerations include whether:

- The user of the Flash package can navigate without using a mouse (that is, can the keyboard alone be used to successfully gain access to all the content?);

- All text in the Flash package is accessible to visually impaired users;

- All audio information is accessible through text alternatives.

Blurred Text

A number of Flash movies on the Web suffer from small text that is too blurry to read; this problem can be corrected by using new features for aliased text built into Flash MX 2004 and later versions, or by using specific techniques with "device fonts" in older versions to avoid the blurriness. These are explained in Lesson 9: Working with Text.

Bookmarking

If a large package with multiple content sections is built entirely in Flash, users will not be able to bookmark a section they want to return to later. They can bookmark only the page that contains the full Flash package. One alternative is to have Flash open a new Web page for each segment of the package, with each new Web page containing the SWF file for that specific section. Another alternative is to script "deep linking" into the Flash movie; programmer Nat Wales accomplished this feat on the Mini Cooper Web site (*http://www.miniusa.com*), but his solution does not work in all Web browsers.

Users often want to copy some text from a news story and e-mail it to a friend, quote it in a report, or save it for future reference. HTML text from a regular Web page can always be copied, but text in Flash can be made not selectable and thus impossible to copy by selecting it in the browser. The Flash author can designate Flash text as selectable to allow users to copy and paste it into e-mail and other applications.

Printing from a Flash presentation can also be impossible. To allow users to print specific text, the Flash author must make some adjustments in the FLA before exporting the file. If the adjustments are not made, no text from the file can be printed.

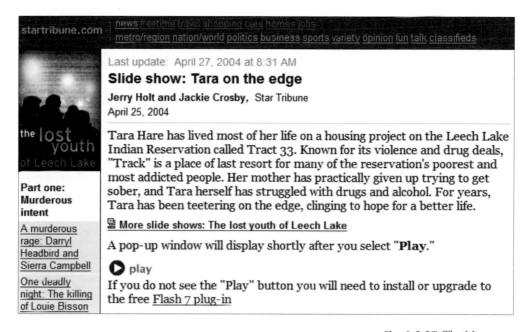

Fig. 1.2.07 The Minneapolis *Star Tribune* provides a regular Web page as a doorway to multimedia content that appears in a pop-up window, making it easy to bookmark the feature. The text on this page can also be read by search engines. Printed by permission of startribune.com.

File Associations

If a Flash movie opens external files, such as JPGs, MP3s, or even other SWFs, and those files become unavailable because they have been moved or deleted, the result will not be as clear as the familiar "File not found" message users see when a regular Web page has moved or disappeared. In most cases, the Flash movie will just stop, or fail to perform, without explanation. It might not be possible for the user to go back; depending on how the Flash movie was constructed, the only option may be to close it and start over from the beginning. Avoiding this problem requires an organization to have, and follow, reliable site management practices.

Linking

It can be difficult to link to a Flash presentation that pops up in a window; many users do not know how to find the URL for content in a pop-up window. If they cannot find the URL, they cannot e-mail it to a friend or blog the Flash presentation—which would bring more visitors to your Web site. Some journalism sites address this by always providing a regular HTML page specific to the Flash presentation, with a link on that page to open the pop-up window (for an example, see *http://www.heraldsun.com/heart/*).

Note that linking out *from* Flash to external Web pages poses no problem at all. Flash buttons can be scripted to open Web pages with complete reliability; Flash text can also link to Web pages. Flash text can open an e-mail link or execute JavaScript, the same as HTML text.

Search Engines

Another advantage to having a permanent URL (see earlier "Linking" section): The page title, meta tag keywords, and text on a regular Web page can help people find your content when they use a search engine. In cases where a Flash movie opens by itself (as the SWF alone) in a pop-up window, these HTML page elements do not exist, and the Flash movie is invisible to many Web search engines. Techniques for displaying Flash in a pop-up window are explained in Lesson 3: Putting Flash on the Web.

Site Navigation

Flash can be used to make a very cool-looking navigation interface for an entire Web site, or for a large journalism package, but this is definitely a case where functionality should take precedence over coolness. If your users cannot see your navigation, they will not be able to get around on your Web site at all; see the "Version or Browser Conflicts" section that follows.

Skip Intro

You have seen these two words; you have probably clicked them, too. Some Flash is nothing more than eye candy, and a lot of eye candy has zero value as information. (Why do you think they call it "candy"?) Evaluate any introductory animation or slideshow for a journalism package and ask yourself whether that intro has any value besides being "Flash-y." If you think users would *want* to skip it, then maybe your site *should* just skip it—and spare the users the trouble.

Some Flash intros are very functional; they can supply necessary information for a first-time user, or point out updates or changes in the package. In other words, an intro does not have to be pointless, even though so many are.

Version or Browser Conflicts

Certain contents of Flash movies built with later versions of the Flash application cannot be displayed in earlier versions of the Flash player. Video, for example, cannot play in versions earlier than Flash player 6. A user with the older player can open the SWF and begin to view or use it, but when the time comes for the video to play, there just won't be any video—no warning, no explanation, just a blank rectangle where that video ought to be.

To avoid this unfortunate result, many Flash developers use a "version detection script" (usually written in JavaScript) on the Web page to check the user's browser automatically and find out which version of the Flash player that user has. (Version detection is discussed further in Lesson 3: Putting Flash on the Web.) If the version is sufficiently recent, the Flash movie starts to play. If not, the user sees a link to Macromedia's Web site and a message that a newer Flash player is needed. This is fine when it actually works—but not all scripts are foolproof. Some news Web sites use faulty scripts that fail to recognize browsers other than Microsoft Internet Explorer, for example; users with the very latest Flash player see a message that they do not have the Flash player, and as a result they cannot view the content unless they use the Microsoft browser. Obviously, some users will refuse to use another browser and simply choose not to view the content.

Some sites avoid detection scripts altogether and instead simply supply a link to the Flash player download page (see Figure 1.2.02). This will not eliminate the problem of partial content display (e.g., no video playing) in older player versions, but at least it does not block users who have the newest version from viewing the Flash content.

SUMMARY

This chapter has explained why Flash is special among Web development tools, and how that pertains to its use in online journalism. Macromedia added Flash to its product list by acquisition just as the importance of the Web was starting to be obvious, and as the market for informational and educational CD-ROMs (the province of Macromedia's Director application) was beginning to shrink.

The Flash player, which is free, works with various Web browsers and computer operating systems and allows a user to see, hear, and interact with

Flash content, which is delivered in the SWF file format. A large majority of Web users already have the Flash player installed. The Flash application is the authoring environment for Flash content; working files are in the FLA file format. The Flash application can produce SWF files; it can also produce QuickTime (MOV), GIF, JPG, and PNG files, as well as stand-alone "projector" files for Windows and Macintosh.

Flash offers a number of advantages for delivering graphical and interactive content online, not least of which are the large installed base for the Flash player and the generally small file sizes for SWF files. Flash's ability to deliver audio, video, legible text, high-quality photographic images, and interactivity set it apart from other Web content applications.

No software is perfect, however. Flash still offers some challenges for Web authors who are committed to accessibility; bookmarking, printing, and search engine placement should also concern careful content developers, especially those working in journalism. Clever designers are always finding new work-arounds for these challenges, and there's always the chance that future versions of Flash will eliminate them altogether.

For its broad user base, versatility, and suitability to the online environment, Flash has no equal today. Its capacity for delivering journalism content in ways that pique and hold the user's interest is unmatched by any other online technology. What's more, you don't need to be a rocket scientist to learn how to use this powerful application—as you will discover in Part II.

REFERENCES

Artymiak, J. (2002, May 21). SWF is not Flash (and other vectored thoughts). http://www.oreillynet.com/pub/a/javascript/2002/05/24/swf_not_flash.html

DiNucci, D. (2003). *Macromedia Flash Interface Design: Twelve Effective Interfaces and Why They Work*. Berkeley, CA: Macromedia/Peachpit Press.

Evangelista, B. (2002, May 5). No Flash in the pan: Macromedia survives a decade by reinventing itself. *San Francisco Chronicle*, p. G3. http://www.sfgate.com/cgi-bin/article.cgi?file=/chronicle/archive/2002/05/05/BU175576.DTL

Feature Comparison (Flash MX 2004 and Flash MX 2004 Professional). http://www.macromedia.com/software/flash/productinfo/features/comparison/

Flash Player Developer Center. http://www.macromedia.com/devnet/flashplayer/

Gay, J. (2001). *The History of Flash*. http://www.macromedia.com/macromedia/events/john_gay/

Introduction to SWF. http://www.openswf.org/spec/SWFfileformat.html

Macromedia Flash MX and Director Comparison. http://www.macromedia.com/software/director/resources/integration/flash/

Macromedia Flash player FAQ. http://www.macromedia.com/software/flashplayer/productinfo/faq/

Macromedia Flash player Version Penetration. http://www.macromedia.com/software/player_census/flashplayer/version_penetration.html

Olsson, K. (1999, July 1). Director vs. Flash. *Webmonkey*. http://hotwired.lycos.com/webmonkey/99/27/index3a.html

U.S. Government. *Section 508: The Road to Accessibility.* http://www.section508.gov/

World Wide Web Consortium. *Web Content Accessibility Guidelines.* http://www.w3.org/TR/WCAG20/

Part II
How to Make Things in Flash

Lesson 1

Drawing Tools

This lesson assumes some familiarity with drawing tools in a graphics program such as Photoshop. The vector-based tools in Flash differ in significant ways, so those differences will be pointed out. You're not expected to be a Photoshop expert. If you don't recognize the names of the tools, roll your mouse cursor over the **Tools** panel (far left side of the Flash window) and pause on each tool. A label will pop up and show you the name of that tool.

If you use Dreamweaver MX, the interface of Flash MX will look familiar to you, with the exception of the **Timeline**. If you have never edited digital video, the Timeline probably will be a new concept for you. If Flash is the first Macromedia application you have used, take some time to open the menus and look around. The Edit, Insert, and Modify menus will probably contain most of the unfamiliar items.

Until you animate an object (in Lesson 2), you will not use the **Timeline**, except to delete your early experiments with the drawing tools. Locate the Timeline now anyway. It's at the top of the Flash application window.

Note: If the center area is empty *and* there's no Timeline (nothing visible but gray), open the File menu and select "New." That gives you a blank white Stage to work on. If the center area is filled with a menu that includes a list titled "Create New," select "Flash Document" there, and you will get a blank white Stage. If you already have a white Stage, use that one.

To the left of the **Timeline** is the **Tools** panel. The sixteen tools at the top are followed by icons that allow you to change the attributes of the selected tool.

Below the Timeline is the **Stage,** a white rectangle on a field of gray. (The gray area is off stage, or out of sight, in the finished Flash movie.) Below

45

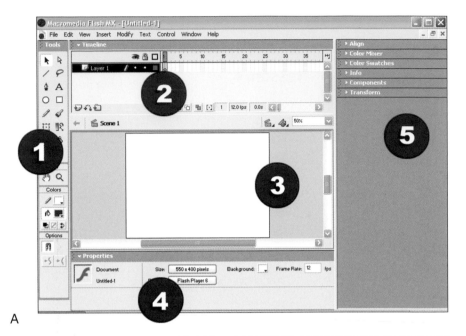

A

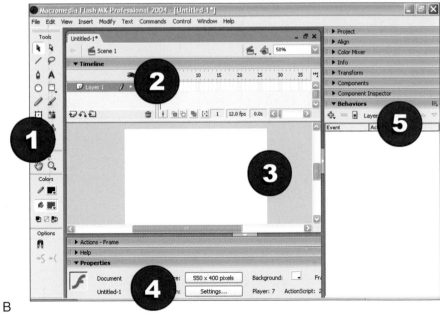

B

Fig. 2.1.01 *A.* The Flash MX interface. *B.* The Flash MX 2004 interface. The interface of Flash MX 2004 changed only slightly from the previous version, Flash MX. The five main areas are the same:

1. The Tools panel allows selection of tools, view, colors, and options.
2. The Timeline controls both motion and timing in the movie.
3. On the Stage, you draw objects or drag them in from the Library.
4. The Properties panel reflects what is selected on the Stage.
5. Panels appear here after they are selected from the Window menu.

the Stage is the **Properties** panel. Take a good look at that, because it's going to *change* every time you select a tool, or an object on the Stage, and that can be confusing at first.

To the right of everything else, you'll see a stack of closed **panels**. Panels in Flash are the equivalent of palettes in Photoshop. They can be opened from the Window menu. If you see the panel name but not the full panel, look for a small triangle widget to the left of the panel name, and click the widget *once* to open the panel (click again to close it). Panels can be undocked and dragged to different places, if you like to work that way. To undock a panel, move the mouse cursor to the left of the small triangle widget. When the cursor becomes a cross with four arrowheads, you can click and drag the panel to undock it, or move it out of the panel stack. You can also dock a floating panel by grabbing it that way.

You will not use the right-side panels in this lesson.

LESSON 1

1 Open Flash and make sure you can see the **Stage** and also the **Tools**, **Timeline**, and **Properties** panels, which are described above. If they are not visible at all, find them on the Window menu. If you see the panel name but the panel is "closed," then open the panel by clicking the small triangle widget to the left of the panel name.

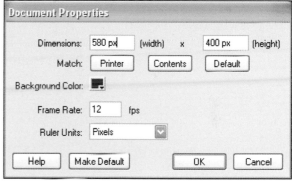

2 In the **Properties** panel, select the size (in pixels) of your Flash movie. Here's how: Click the Size button in the **Properties** panel and a dialog box opens (Figure 2.1.02). In the dialog box, set the *width* and *height* for the final Flash movie (this is the size at which it will appear in a Web browser window, just like a GIF or a JPG). You can also select a *color* for the background of the entire movie. Go ahead, try it.

Of course you're eager to get busy with the drawing tools, but make sure you understand what you're doing here. You can change these settings *at any time;* however, it can be a big pain in the neck to change if you have already built a lot of things specific to *this* width and height.

Also take note of the *frame rate*. If you have not edited video or film, working with *time* as a design element will probably be a little strange at

Fig. 2.1.02 In the Document Properties dialog, notice the settings for:

- Width
- Height
- Background color
- Frame rate (in frames per second)
- Ruler units (in pixels, naturally)

These affect the *entire* Flash movie.

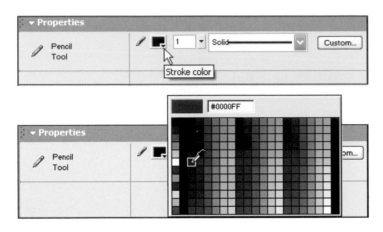

Fig. 2.1.03 To change the stroke color for the Pencil tool, open the palette in the Properties panel *after* you have selected the tool.

first. All you need to know right now is that a frame rate of 12 (the default in Flash) means that 12 frames equals 1 second ("fps" is "frames per second"). If you want a motion sequence to last 2 seconds, at 12 fps it will need to span 24 frames in the **Timeline**. You definitely do *not* want to change the frame rate *after* you have built a lot of things in the movie! It would change the speed of everything in the entire movie.

You will learn a lot more about frames in the Timeline—in Lesson 2.

3   Try out the drawing tools, starting with the **Pencil** tool. Click the tool in the **Tools** panel, then move your mouse cursor to the **Stage.** Click, hold, and drag. If you don't see anything, that probably means your Pencil color is the same as your Stage color. You can change the Pencil color down in the **Properties** panel, which has *changed* to show you the current properties of the Pencil tool (Figure 2.1.03).

Now that you're looking at the **Properties** panel, you'll see that you can also change the "Stroke height" (thickness of the line) and "Stroke style" (for example, make your pencil draw a dotted line). Go ahead, experiment with these properties by changing them and then scribbling with the Pencil tool.

The Pencil tool also has three different *modes* for you to choose, but these are not on the **Properties** panel—they are on the **Tools** panel, near the bottom, under "Options." Click to choose one, and scribble something. Select another mode, and scribble something similar. Compare all three modes to learn how they work.

Fig. 2.1.04 A rounded shape, drawn freehand with the mouse (top), can be straightened with a few clicks (bottom), using the "Straighten" mode in the Tools options.

Now, here's a very specific exercise to try with the **Pencil** tool:

(a) Select a "Stroke height" of 3 (in the **Properties** panel).

(b) Under "Options" on the **Tools** panel, select the "Smooth" mode.

(c) Draw a few hills or humps, all connected (Figure 2.1.04).

(d) Select the **Arrow** tool from the **Tools** panel. (The Arrow tool is used to *select* things on the Stage, and in fact, in Flash MX 2004, it is called the **Selection** tool instead, but it still looks and acts the same way.)

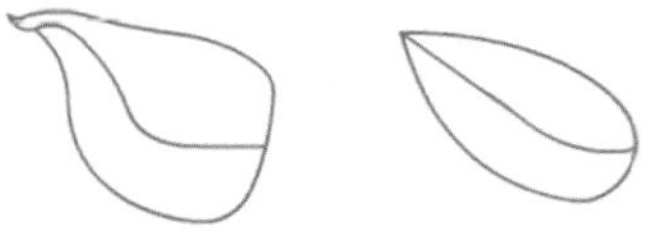

(e) Click on the **Stage** *outside* your humps, hold the mouse button down, and *drag* to select the complete drawing. Notice how an object has a dotted appearance when it is selected.

Fig. 2.1.05 A rather lumpy leaf (left) can be smoothed with several clicks, and then straightened, to achieve a better result (right).

(f) Under "Options" on the **Tools** panel, select the "Straighten" mode. Watch what happens to the humps. Click the Straighten button several times and keep watching.

Note: To select things on the **Stage,** always use the *black* **Arrow/Selection** tool, on the left side of the **Tools** panel, unless otherwise directed. The white arrow-shaped tool is actually the **Subselection** tool, and it works differently from the (black) Arrow tool. In Flash MX 2004, the Arrow tool is called the **Selection** tool instead—but it still looks and acts the same.

---

4   Enough for the **Pencil** tool. You probably have a scribbled mess on the **Stage** that you would like to get rid of. Here is the one time in this lesson that you will use the **Timeline**. You can delete everything in a *frame* if you *select* that frame on the Timeline and then press the Delete key. You can see that there is only one frame (Frame 1, in fact) in your Flash movie, if you look closely at the Timeline (Figure 2.1.06). The black dot and gray background symbolize that the frame has something in it. (If you have clicked the frame, the colors are white dot, black background. Click anywhere else to see the normal state of the frame, which is below the numeral 1, on Layer 1. A vertical red line goes through the frame.)

Fig. 2.1.06 A single frame in the Timeline.

Click that frame (with the black dot) *once*. That *selects* the frame. Press the Delete key on the keyboard. The **Stage** will become empty. The frame will be white, with a white (or empty) dot in it. Even though this is a very small thing, you will soon recognize that the appearance of frames in the **Timeline** is *quite* important.

Remember that the *black dot* means there is something in the frame. The white dot means there's nothing there.

Fig. 2.1.07 The curlicue on the left was drawn free-hand with the mouse, using the Brush tool. Select it with the Arrow/Selection tool, then click the Smooth button (under "Options" in the Tools panel) a few times, and you will get the result on the right.

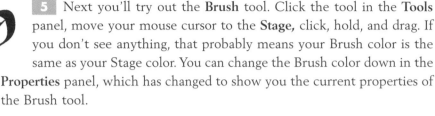

5 Next you'll try out the **Brush** tool. Click the tool in the **Tools** panel, move your mouse cursor to the **Stage,** click, hold, and drag. If you don't see anything, that probably means your Brush color is the same as your Stage color. You can change the Brush color down in the **Properties** panel, which has changed to show you the current properties of the Brush tool.

Unlike the Pencil tool, the **Brush** tool has *size* and *shape* attributes over in the **Tools** panel (even though it may seem that those should appear in the Properties panel). Change the "Brush Size" and make some more brush-strokes on the Stage. Change the "Fill Color" a few times. (Did you think the Brush would be governed by "Stroke Color"? Wrong, but an understandable mistake.) Change the "Brush Shape" and try that out. You can create neat-looking calligraphy with a little patience and the same smoothing effect you used with the Pencil tool above (Figure 2.1.07).

One last trick with the **Brush** tool:

(a) Draw a closed shape, such as an oval.

(b) Change the "Fill Color."

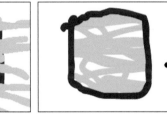

Fig. 2.1.08 Painting outside the lines (left) is no problem with "Paint Inside" mode (right). The small black dot inside the outline is the brush cursor.

(c) Under "Options" in the **Tools** panel, select the Brush mode "Paint Inside."

(d) Click the mouse *inside* your closed shape, keep holding the mouse button, and *drag* back and forth across the shape a few times (Figure 2.1.08). Go outside the lines (the way you *never* did in your childhood coloring books).

(e) When you release the mouse button, you will see the effect of the "Paint Inside" mode.

6 That's sufficient practice with the **Brush** tool. Empty the **Stage** now, just as you did in Step 4 above, by clearing Frame 1 in the **Timeline**.

7 The most commonly used drawing tools in Flash are surely the **Oval, Rectangle,** and **Line** tools. You probably already have some idea of how these tools work individually, but you may not know how the shapes *interact* in Flash. So, make sure you have two *different* colors selected for Stroke and Fill, and then select the **Oval** tool. Click and drag on the **Stage** to draw a big oval. (If you'd rather draw a circle, *hold* the Shift key before you click, and *keep holding it* while you drag your shape.)

With your oval (or circle) complete, click the **Arrow/Selection** tool. You'll remember that you can click and drag with the (black) Arrow tool to select a shape. You can also just click something to select it, and that can be very

useful—as well as somewhat tricky, as you're about to see. So *click once* on the outline of your oval. (After you click, the entire outline, or "stroke color," should appear dotted, rather than solid.)

Now *click*, *hold*, and *drag* the outline. This may surprise you: The entire outline comes away from the solid oval shape (Figure 2.1.09). Let go of the mouse button with the outline *overlapping* the solid fill.

Select the smaller side of your solid oval and drag that. Yes, you have sliced up your shape. While this can seem maddening at first (if you are used to the bitmap drawing tools in Photoshop, for example), it turns out to be a great asset for creating neat-looking shapes if you're not very good at free-hand drawing. In Figure 2.1.09, the almond shape on the right could be rotated 90 degrees to become a human eye (Modify menu > Transform > Rotate 90° CW).

8 If you aren't used to using **Ctrl-Z** (or **Cmd-Z**/Mac) to undo, now is a good time to practice. Imagine that you never wanted to slice up your oval. You want to put it all back together again. Okay! Hold the **Ctrl** (or Cmd/Mac) key and press the letter **Z**. Repeat this until the oval has returned to its original complete state. By default, Flash lets you undo 100 steps. (You can change that to a maximum of 200, but doing so will tie up additional system memory.)

9 If you want to move the entire oval shape, *without* breaking it into pieces, *double-click* the inside part of the shape (the "fill color"). If everything appears dotted (both the fill and the stroke color), you can be sure you have selected everything. The shape can now be dragged as a single unit. If you make a mistake, Ctrl-Z!

This is a good reason to drag with the **Arrow/Selection** tool to select a shape. When you drag a selection box around a shape, you can *see* exactly what you are selecting, and what you're leaving out.

10 Let's switch to the **Rectangle** tool and see how it differs from the **Oval** tool. (Keep your oval on the **Stage**, so you can use it later.) Select the Rectangle tool. Click and drag on the Stage to draw a small rectangle. (If you'd

Fig. 2.1.09 The behavior of the drawing shapes in Flash can be quite useful. Click any part of a shape once to select it. Once selected, it can be dragged away from the rest of the shape.

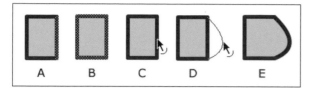

Fig. 2.1.10 What happens when you click on the outline of a shape?

a. A single click selects one side of a rectangle.
b. A double click selects the entire outline (stroke color).
c. Click and hold; look at the cursor.
d. Drag without letting go.
e. The shape can be changed by dragging on a side.

rather draw a square, *hold* the Shift key before you click, and *keep holding it* while you drag your shape.)

Click the **Arrow/Selection** tool to select it. Then *click once* on the outline of your rectangle. It's important to click and *let go* (that *selects* the object), and *then* click, hold, and drag. When you did this for the oval in Step 7, the complete outline (stroke color) pulled away from the inside (fill color)—but for the rectangle, only *one side* of the outline pulls away. You could dismantle the rectangle outline in four parts, if you wanted to do that.

Assuming you might want to move the *entire* outline away from the fill color, use **Ctrl-Z** (or Cmd-Z/Mac) now to restore your rectangle. This time, *double-click* any part of the outline of your rectangle. You should see *all four sides* appear dotted, showing that they are, in fact, selected. Once you see that, you can click and drag the complete outline away from the solid interior.

11 There's one more click-and-drag trick to master. If you click a side of the rectangle but *do not let go* of the mouse button, you can alter the shape by dragging. (You can do the same at a corner of the rectangle, but the result looks different.) Pay close attention to the mouse cursor when you click and hold (Figure 2.1.10), and you will see a clear indication of whether your dragging action will create a *curve* or an *angle*. The little shape that appears to the side of the cursor shows which one it will be.

12 Practice *combining shapes* to see how this capability in Flash makes it easier to create objects that look good, even if you lack real drawing talent. The first step is to make several shapes you want to combine into one. The second step is to drag the shapes into position.

Note: The shape you *select and drag* will be *on top of* the other shape(s). Figure 2.1.11 shows the result of dragging a small rectangle onto a larger circle.

This next step is one of the vector drawing techniques that can be tricky to master—but it's infinitely useful, so it's well worth the effort. While holding down the Shift key, *click once* on each line you want to remove from the final object. By "shift-clicking," you can add a lot of strokes (and fills too) to the *selected* state—that is, the state indicated by a dotted appearance. When you have selected everything you want to remove, press the Delete key once.

13 Let's do one last thing with the **Rectangle** tool, just because it can be useful, and it's so simple. Empty the Stage now, just as you did in Step 4 above, by clearing Frame 1 in the **Timeline**. Select the Rectangle tool. Look at the "Options" section of the **Tools** panel; you'll see that the Rectangle tool has one option called "Round Rectangle Radius." Click it, and you get the opportunity to set *rounded corners* for your rectangle object. The "100" setting produces the most rounding; it's nice to use for oblong button shapes. The "20" setting produces a good-looking frame to enclose text. The "0" setting produces no rounding at all, or in other words, a normal rectangle with squared-off corners. You can change the thickness of the border (stroke color) at any time, even after you have drawn the rectangle—just *double-click* the border and change "Stroke Height" in the **Properties** panel. (The stroke thickness ranges from 0.1 to 10.)

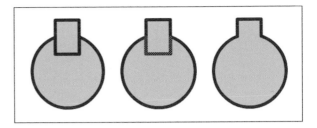

Fig. 2.1.11 By combining shapes, you can produce objects that would be difficult to draw freehand. In the middle illustration above, shift-clicking three times has selected the three straight lines to be deleted. Notice that once a shape is on top of another shape, its outer lines will be broken up by the intersecting lines of the other shape. The illustration at right shows what one press of the Delete key can accomplish

Flash MX 2004 Note

The **Rectangle** tool has two options in MX 2004; the second one is "Snap to Objects," represented by a magnet icon. Click this when you want at least one edge of the rectangle to align perfectly over the edge of another shape on the Stage. (The **Oval** tool has this new option too.) Also, if you *click and hold* the Rectangle tool on the **Tools** panel, you get the option to use the new **PolyStar** tool, which draws a five-sided polygon shape. This is a fun tool, so be sure to try it. Use the Options button on the **Properties** panel *before you draw* to change the number of sides, or to select a star shape *instead of a polygon*. The PolyStar tool does not exist in earlier versions of Flash.

14 You know enough now to experiment with the **Line** tool on your own, but here are a few ideas you may not think of right away. When drawing a triangle, for example, with the Line tool, you do not need to match the end of each line to the end of another. You can cross lines and extend them, then *select* and *delete* the excess part of any line (just as you did in Step 12 above, when you combined shapes). You will also find the Line tool useful for creating a half-circle or a pie with a missing piece (Figure 2.1.12).

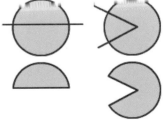

Fig. 2.1.12 Draw straight lines and then drag them into position on top of other shapes to cut away new shapes.

ADDITIONAL TOOLS

Flash provides ten more tools. The **Text** tool will be discussed in detail in Lesson 9. The **Eye Dropper, Lasso, Paint Bucket,** and **Pen** tools are not very different from the equivalent tools in Photoshop and similar software applications. The **Eraser** tool is easy to experiment with—draw something, and then try out the Eraser tool "Options" on the **Tools** panel.

Try out the remaining four tools, which can be very useful:

- **Fill Transform** tool: If you have used a linear or radial *gradient fill* on a shape (see the **Color Mixer** panel), you can use this tool to *move* the point governing the direction of the gradient.

- **Free Transform** tool: Select any shape with this tool, then *scale, skew,* or *rotate* the object by dragging the "handles" on the box. You can open the **Transform** panel (Flash MX: Window menu > Transform; Flash MX 2004: Window menu > Design Panels > Transform) to see numeric measures. Another option: On the Modify menu, go to "Transform" and select actions from the submenu to achieve many of the same effects. In other words, there are two other ways to transform an object, *in addition to* using the tool.

Fig. 2.1.13 Use the Subselection tool to change standard shapes into irregular shapes.

- **Subselection** tool: Select the edge of any object with this tool to get access to *anchor points,* or draggable handles, that allow you to alter the shape of the object (Figure 2.1.13). For example, draw a square, then use the Subselection tool to reshape it into a skinny diamond shape. (This is quite useful in complex animation.) If you cannot get the shape you want with the **Free Transform** tool, then try this one. You can also use this tool to change a *path* you created with the **Pen** tool.

- **Ink Bottle** tool: Use this tool to add an outline (of any color or thickness you choose) to an object *without* an outline. (If the object has an outline already, this tool simply changes the color of that outline.) The outline is called "stroke color" in Flash.

DRAWING AIDS

Snapping

You may have encountered the "snap to" option in another software application, such as QuarkXPress. The option can be turned on or off. In Flash

MX, there are two types of snapping available to you. Flash MX 2004 has additional options for snapping. All are available from the View menu.

Snap to Objects, when enabled, makes a dragged object adhere to the edge of a second object (if you drag it close to the second object). It also works nicely with the **Line** tool in cases where you want a new line to start perfectly at the corner of an object. When you do not want this option to operate, it can be extremely annoying—so learn how to turn it off! You can also enable and disable Snap to Objects from the Options (**Tools** panel) for some tools, such as the **Arrow/Selection** tool—look for the magnet icon.

Snap to Pixels causes a precise pixel grid to appear if you set Magnification (on the View menu) to 400 percent or more. Each time you move an object or draw a new one, it adheres to the pixels (rather than allowing tenths of a pixel).

Aligning

When you need to align objects with one another, you may be used to using guide lines (in Photoshop, for example). Flash provides guide lines (View menu), but the options available on the **Align** panel are far better! By *selecting* any number of objects on the Stage (*shift-click* each one), you can *align* them all by clicking one button on the **Align** panel. The furthest object in the direction you are aligning determines the alignment "edge." For example, if you click "Align right edge" in the Align panel, all the selected objects will align with the right-hand edge of the right-most object selected.

But wait, there's more! You can also *distribute* the selected objects so they are equally spaced. This is especially useful for a row or column of related objects, such as thumbnail photos. Set the first and last objects where you want them, with all the other objects between them. Select all the objects, then click one of the six "Distribute" options.

Grouping

If you draw complex objects made up of several (or many) shapes, you may find it convenient to *group* some of the shapes, either temporarily or permanently. When a shape has been *grouped*, it will not cut other shapes (as described in Step 7 earlier). To *group* shapes that have been selected, press Ctrl-G (or Cmd-G/Mac), or open the Modify menu and select "Group." All the selected shapes are now stuck together.

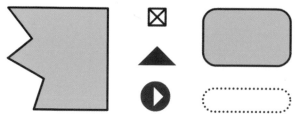

Fig. 2.1.14 You should be able to draw all these shapes in Flash, regardless of your artistic skill (or lack thereof) by using the techniques described in this lesson.

Too much grouping can produce strange effects later when you animate an object, so it's important to know how to *ungroup* also. Once the shapes are ungrouped, they will (again) cut into one another. To *ungroup* shapes that have been selected, press Ctrl-Shift-G (or Cmd-Shift-G/Mac), or open the Modify menu and select "Ungroup." All the selected shapes are now separate again.

DRAWING TOOLS SUMMARY

This should be enough information to set you on the path to working comfortably with the drawing tools in Flash. As with any software, the more time you spend playing with the tools, the better you will become at using them efficiently. As is also true of most software, you can accomplish quite a lot without learning how to use *every* tool. So don't drive yourself crazy trying to use all the tools not discussed here.

There are very good reasons to focus on these six tools initially: **Arrow/Selection, Brush, Line, Oval, Pencil,** and **Rectangle**. If you become comfortable with these, you will be able to accomplish most simple drawing tasks.

Of course, Flash cannot turn you into an artist if you aren't one already. But Flash will make it easy for you to create buttons, frames, pointers, and other simple objects.

If you *are* an artist, and you're used to tools such as Illustrator or FreeHand, you may find Flash frustrating because it lacks features you depend on in those programs. You'll be happy to know you can export Flash-compatible vector graphics from those programs (see Lesson 7).

CONCLUSION

In this lesson, you have learned to:

1. Identify the Tools panel, Timeline, Stage, and Properties panel.

2. Open and close *panels*.

3. Specify the *width* and *height* (in pixels) of the final Flash movie.

4 Select the *background color* for the entire movie.

5 Check or change the *frame rate* for the entire movie.

6 Identify all the items on the Tools panel.

7 Use the Pencil tool, including *stroke color*, *height*, and *style*, and the options *straighten*, *smooth*, and *ink*.

8 Use the Brush tool, including *fill color* and the options *brush mode*, *size*, and *shape*.

9 Draw ovals and circles with the Oval tool.

10 Draw rectangles and squares with the Rectangle tool.

11 Draw straight lines with the Line tool.

12 Use the Arrow/Selection tool to *select* objects (or parts of objects) in four ways: click and drag around the object, single-click, double-click, and shift-click.

13 Use the Arrow/Selection tool to *alter* the shape of an object (click the edge, hold, and drag).

14 Use the Arrow/Selection tool to *move* selected objects (select first; then click, hold, and drag).

15 Position a line, or other shape, in a way that *slices* another line or a solid fill—an easy way to create new shapes that are not ovals or rectangles.

16 *Combine* objects to create new compound shapes.

17 Use Ctrl-Z (or Cmd-Z/Mac) to undo up to 100 actions.

18 Clear a *frame* in the Timeline by selecting it and then erasing everything it contains (Delete key).

19 *Snap* objects to each other, or to a pixel grid.

20 *Align* objects or *distribute* them evenly (Align panel).

21 *Group* and *ungroup* shapes to make it easier to build complex objects.

Lesson 2

Simple Animation

Animating can be done in several ways, whether you're using Flash or old-fashioned acetate cels. In all cases, something moves on the screen. For the approach taken in this lesson, you're not expected to have any artistic skill or talent. You will create two basic shapes and make them travel across the screen independently of each other. This will involve all the fundamental elements of animation in Flash: symbols, the Timeline, frames, keyframes, layers, and tweening.

If you have ever made an animated GIF for the Web, you may have used frame-by-frame animation, which requires the creator to deliberately change the contents of each *frame*. A frame represents an instant in time. In Flash, you can change the duration of that instant. In Lesson 1, you learned how to change the *frame rate*: You can specify how many frames per second a Flash movie has.

For the sake of comparison, motion picture film plays at 24 frames per second, a *frame rate* that produces a pretty good illusion of reality. It was too much work to draw 24 separate frames for each section of an animated cartoon (back when the animators really had to *draw* them), so cartoons often repeated identical frames twice, or even three times. The film still ran at 24 fps, but in reality there were only 8 or 12 unique frames in each second. Those were duplicated to produce 24.

Don't worry about drawing individual frames, though—with Flash, you will draw something one time and use it over and over again.

Rarely is there a need to create an animation sequence frame-by-frame in Flash. That's where *tweening* comes in. Flash can move your object from Point A to Point B if you will just indicate where those two points lie on the Stage (or off the Stage, if you want the object to move out of sight). That part may surprise you with how easy it is—but first, you need to complete some preparatory steps.

LESSON 2

This lesson is divided into two parts. The first exercise deals with the creation of two objects and their conversion to *graphic symbols*. (If the objects have not been converted, they will not animate.) It also introduces the **Library**. The second exercise deals with animating the two symbols.

Exercise 2.1: Creating Graphic Symbols

1 Open Flash and make sure you can see the **Stage** and also the **Tools**, **Timeline**, and **Properties** panels, described in Lesson 1. If the Stage area is empty *and* there's no Timeline (nothing there but gray), open the File menu and select "New." If the Stage area is filled with a menu that includes the option "Create New," select "Flash Document" there.

2 In the **Properties** panel, select the *size* (in pixels) of your Flash movie. Select a *background color*. Select a *frame rate* (some additional details about frame rates appear at the end of this lesson). Keep the frame rate at 12 fps for this lesson. (These choices were explained in Lesson 1, Step 2.)

3 Use the drawing tools to create two separate objects. If you really hate to draw, make one rectangle and one oval, then move on to Step 4. If you're feeling creative, try to make one object that fits inside another. If you want to draw but you can't think of two good objects, try to draw these: an olive and a martini glass (Figure 2.2.01).

4 File menu > Save As. *Name* your file and *save* it. The file extension for your working Flash file (*.fla*) will be appended automatically. Like all filenames on the Web, the name you give to a Flash file should have only lowercase letters, no punctuation, and no spaces.

Fig. 2.2.01 Shapes drawn in Flash: You can draw an olive and a martini glass in Flash even if you are no good at drawing. First, make two separate ovals for the olive, and then select and drag the smaller one into position. Use the Line tool to make the glass. Select "Snap to Objects" from the View menu to make it easy to connect the lines neatly.

Note: On many Windows computers, the file extension has been hidden from you. If you would like to see file extensions when you view files, you can. In any window that displays folders and files, open the (Windows) Tools menu and select "Folder Options." Click the View tab in the Folder Options dialog. Beneath the top folder ("Files and Folders"), find the line "Hide extensions for known file types" and remove the check mark on that line. Click the Apply to All Folders button. Click OK to close the dialog.

5 Now you will make each one of these shapes into reusable symbols. *Select* one of your shapes first.

- Make sure you *select* the entire shape. Check that every part of the shape appears dotted, showing that it has been selected. You can use the (black) **Arrow/Selection** tool to select your shape (*click and drag* a selection box around the entire shape).

- *Do not select both shapes* at the same time, or you would get one symbol instead of two.

6 From the Insert menu (in Flash MX), select "Convert to Symbol." (In Flash MX 2004, it is on the Modify menu instead. You will quickly learn that pressing F8 does the same thing in either version, if your shape is selected.) A dialog box opens. In that dialog box, *select* "Graphic" and *name* your new symbol something obvious (such as "olive"). Click OK.

7 Follow the same procedure for your second shape. When a shape has been converted to a symbol, it will be surrounded by a "bounding box" (a thin blue line). If you don't see the box, select the **Arrow/Selection** tool and click *once* on the symbol.

Warning: If you *double-click* a symbol, you will go into Symbol Editing Mode, which removes you from the normal Timeline. There's no reason to get tangled up with that now, so If you can't get the bounding box to appear, or you discover you can alter the shapes, press Ctrl-E (or Cmd-E/Mac) to return to normal editing and the main Timeline. Be very conscious of how you are clicking the objects on the Stage, because a single click and a double click have *entirely different* results.

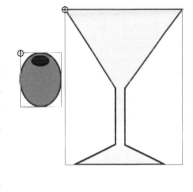

Fig. 2.2.02 After you have converted a shape to a symbol, the new symbol belongs to the Library for this Flash movie. Symbols that are deleted from the Stage remain available in the Library.

8 Now you're about to see the glory of symbols in Flash. Open the **Library** panel (Window menu > Library, or press F11). If you named and converted your two symbols successfully, you will see them in the Library panel with the names you gave them (Figure 2.2.02). Grab one of them in the Library and *drag* it to the **Stage**. Do it several times.

Fig. 2.2.03 Try out the effects you can apply to a symbol with the Color properties. Alpha is especially useful; use it to change the transparency of an instance. Brightness can be used to dim a button, for example.

Fig. 2.2.04 Several instances of the olive symbol were scaled with the Transform panel or changed with the options available in the Properties panel.

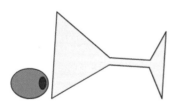

Fig. 2.2.05 The Free Transform tool was used to rotate the glass. To rotate the olive, open the Modify menu, move to Transform, and select Rotate 90° CW.

Note: This may seem like copying and pasting, but it's different: Each *instance* of a symbol in Flash requires almost no storage space in the final Flash movie file. If you had separate *copies* of an image, each copy would carry its full "weight" and increase the file size accordingly.

9 These multiples are called *instances* in Flash. Instances are not the same as copies, but they can be changed independently of one another. Select one of your symbols (click it once) and look at the Properties panel. You can experiment with alpha (transparency) for the selected symbol, or tint, or brightness (Figure 2.2.03). Changes you make to an instance in the Properties panel do not affect the symbol in the Library.

10 Another common thing to do to an *instance* of a symbol is to change its size. You can *scale* it (keeping the proportions the same) or *skew* it (making it look stretched or squashed). To achieve those effects, select the **Free Transform** tool, or open the **Transform** panel (Figure 2.2.04). You can also *rotate* the instance using either the tool or the panel (Figure 2.2.05). Open the Modify menu and check out the Transform options there too.

Can you animate these effects? Of course you can! Just wait until you get to the second exercise in this lesson. (You're almost there.)

11 Finally, delete everything from the frame (as explained in Lesson 1, Step 4). The Stage should be empty. If you have any doubt that your symbols are safe in the Library, you can grab each one and drag it out to the Stage just to make sure.

12 File menu > Save.

Note: Another great benefit to the way symbols work in Flash: As you delete frames and objects in the normal course of editing a Flash movie, all the symbols you created stay intact in the Library. (Libraries can also be imported to other Flash movies, so you can use your best symbols again and again.)

Warning: Make sure you can see the bounding box (Step 7) before you delete a symbol on the Stage. If you do not see the box, you are *inside* the symbol, and you will permanently delete your shapes. If you clicked the symbol and you do not see the box, press Ctrl-E (or Cmd-E/Mac) to *exit* and return to normal editing.

Exercise 2.2: Animating Two Symbols

Now you'll put those two graphic symbols to good use. Begin with an empty **Stage**, and check your *frame rate*. You need to know how many frames 1 second requires, so you can plan your animation. If your frame rate is 12 fps, you will need a sequence of 12 frames to get 1 second of motion.

1 Drag one symbol out onto the **Stage**. You must animate only one symbol at a time.

2 So far, your movie has only one frame in the **Time-line**. Select a "future" frame in the **Timeline**. Since you know the frame rate, you can calculate how many frames you need to make your motion complete in 1 second. Go to the frame in the **Timeline** that is 12

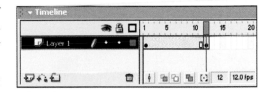

Fig. 2.2.06 Adding a keyframe at Frame 12 extends the **Timeline**.

frames (or whatever your movie's frame rate is) to the right of Frame 1. Click that frame once. The frame will be shaded to show that it is selected.

3 With that later frame (e.g., Frame 12) selected, press F6. This inserts a new *keyframe* (Figure 2.2.06). Inserting a keyframe is a crucial part of animation in Flash! *Notice* how all the frames from Frame 1 (the first black dot) up to the new keyframe (second black dot) have filled in with gray shading. Those frames are no longer empty! (Empty frames are always white.) Every frame in the long gray block contains exactly the same image.

Note: On an iBook (and possibly some other laptops), the function keys (F keys) work as described here *only if* you press and hold Function (another key) *while* you press the F key. However, on most computers you can press the F key alone and get these results.

Note: The difference between a keyframe and all other frames is that a *keyframe* signals *change.* In a keyframe, something can be set as a beginning or an end in a

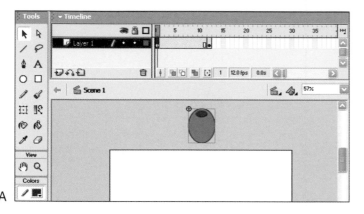

sequence of change. The Flash designer cannot make a change in a frame that is not a keyframe. In the Timeline, a keyframe *always* has a dot inside it. A *black* dot shows that there is at least one object in the keyframe. A *white* dot shows that the keyframe is empty of objects.

4 To see motion between Frame 1 and Frame 12, you must change the position of the object. Right now, it's in the same place in both *keyframes* in your **Timeline**. To make the object move in an animated sequence, you will put it into its starting position in the first keyframe, and into its ending position in the next keyframe. The keyframe containing the object is indicated by a black dot.

First, *select* either keyframe (click *once* directly on the keyframe to select it). Then move the object on the **Stage** by *selecting* it (make sure you have the **Arrow/Selection** tool, and click only *once* to select the symbol) and *dragging* it. Do not double click!

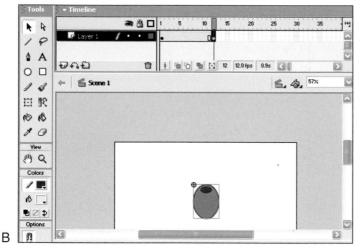

Fig. 2.2.07 *A.* Olive positioned above the Stage, Frame 1. *B.* Olive positioned lower, on the Stage, Frame 12. If you want an olive to drop into the scene from a point off-stage, position the olive above the main Stage area in the first keyframe, and then, in the next keyframe, position the olive where you want it to land.

5 Add a *motion tween*: Click once on any frame *inside* in the long gray block between Frame 1 and Frame 12 in the **Timeline**. (These frames are not keyframes: They do not have a dot.) Then look in the **Properties** panel and find the menu labeled "Tween." Change the menu choice from "None" to "Motion." A *solid line* and an *arrow* pointing to the right appear inside the long block of frames, which is now pale blue instead of gray.

Note: If you ever see a *dotted* line in the sequence, that means the *tween* did not work. The most common reasons: (a) Your object is not a symbol; (b) you have more than one object on the layer; (c) you do not have a keyframe at the end; (d) one of your two keyframes does not contain the symbol you are trying to move.

6 File menu > Save.

7 Test your animation (Method 1): Press Enter/Return. If nothing happens, press it again.

8 Test your animation (Method 2): The *playhead* is a small red rectangle at the top of the **Timeline,** in the bar with the numerals. You can *grab* it and *drag* it left and right to test the motion in your movie; this is called "scrubbing." It will not show you the real speed of the movie, but it can help you diagnose problems in the motion sequence. (You can also move the playhead to any frame and then press Enter/Return to play the movie from that point onward.)

9 Make the motion longer and slower: Click once anywhere inside the *motion tween* block in the **Timeline**. Press F5 several times. Each time you press F5, you *increase* the motion sequence by one frame. (In other words, F5 adds frames—regular frames, *not* keyframes. These are frames with no dot.)

10 Make the motion shorter and faster: Click once anywhere inside the *motion tween* block in the **Timeline**. Press Shift-F5 several times. Each time you press Shift-F5, you *decrease* the motion sequence by one frame. (In other words, Shift-F5 removes frames.)

11 Move the starting point of a sequence: Click *once* on the first keyframe (the frame with a dot in it is the starting frame in a sequence) to *select* it. *Release* the mouse button (this is very necessary). Then *click, hold,* and *drag* to the right (or left) to change the starting frame's position in time. Frames in the sequence will be removed (when you drag to the right) or added (when you move to the left) automatically as you do this. Try this, and test your animation (Steps 7 and 8) to learn how it works.

12 Now it's time to name the **Timeline** layer, because you'll be adding *a second layer* in the next step. Here's how to name (or rename) a layer: On the left side of the Timeline, you'll see one layer (named *Layer 1*). Double-click the *layer name* and type to change it. To make the new name "stick," click anywhere off the layer name, or press Enter/Return. Use a name that makes it easy to remember what's *in* that layer.

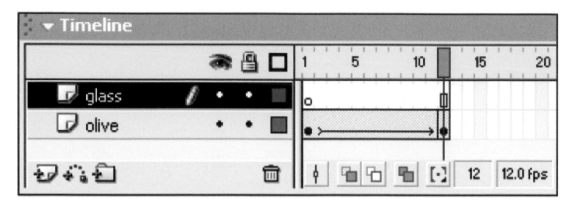

Fig. 2.2.08 When you create a new layer in the Timeline, it is automatically the same length as the existing layer(s). A new layer always has one keyframe, at the beginning. Empty frames are always white.

13 Create a *new* layer: Find the tiny icon (a page with a plus sign) on the left at the bottom of the **Timeline**, under the layer name(s). This icon pops up a label "Insert Layer" when you roll over it. Click that icon once to make a new layer. (The new layer will always be added *above* the selected layer. Layers can be *moved* up or down at any time by dragging them.)

Note: It is essential that you place *each object that will move* in a separate layer by itself. If *any other object* is in the layer, the motion tween will not work.

14 Name the new layer (see Step 12).

15 File menu > Save.

Note: The pencil icon (to the right of the layer name) indicates the *active* layer in the Timeline. When you draw or put something on the Stage, it will be on the layer marked by the pencil icon. Pay attention to which layer you're on *before* you drag any new object to the Stage!

16 Drag your other object from the **Library** to the **Stage.** Make *certain* it has landed in the second layer! Remember: Frames that are white are empty. When frames contain objects, they are a color other than white.

17 Animate your second object by repeating Steps 2 through 5 on the new layer (Figure 2.2.09).

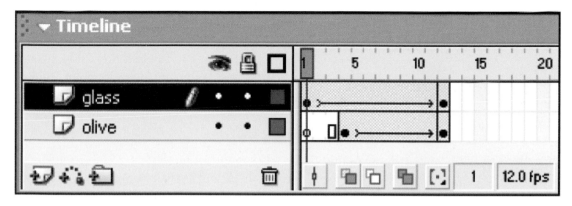

Fig. 2.2.09 The Timeline, with two layers. Each layer contains a motion tween.

18 File menu > Save.

19 Test your movie: Press Ctrl-Enter (Win) or Cmd-Return (Mac). This is *different* from testing the animation by pressing Enter/Return alone, as you will see.

Note: When you test your movie by pressing Ctrl-Enter (Win) or Cmd-Return (Mac), you spawn a second window within the Flash application. If it is "maximized" (full size), it will hide your normal editing window. New Flash users sometimes close the whole application by accident when they try to close the testing window and return to the editing environment. Don't make that mistake.

Note: When you test the movie by pressing Ctrl-Enter (Win) or Cmd-Return (Mac) for the first time, Flash generates a new file, with the file extension *.swf*—this is the file that will be played on the Web. Each time you test the movie again, this file is overwritten with the newest version. You'll learn more about this in Lesson 3.

20 You'll notice that when you test the output Flash file, it loops, or repeats, forever. That is the default for Flash movies. To make the animation *stop*, you must use ActionScript. The standard way to handle Action-Script is to put it *in a layer by itself*; this makes the script easy to find and edit your scripts. So, create a third layer now, and name it "actions" (without the quotes).

21 Within that new layer, click the *last* frame in your movie (Frame 12) and insert a *blank* keyframe there (press F7 once). ActionScript always needs a keyframe.

Fig. 2.2.10 Three frames from a two-layer animation; the frames shown are 1, 4, and 12. Compare with Figure 2.2.09: You should soon be able to "read" a Timeline like this one and visualize what is in each keyframe. In Frame 12, the olive is behind the glass. An object in a lower layer in the Timeline is always "underneath" objects in higher layers.

22 Open the **Actions** panel. (Find it on the Window menu if you don't see it. In Flash MX 2004, it's on the submenu "Development Panels.") If you see the panel name but the panel is closed, then open the panel by clicking the small triangle widget to the left of the panel name.

23 In the **Actions** panel, click in the list on the left side to open "Actions"; then click "Movie Control"; then double-click "stop" (Figure 2.2.11). If nothing happens, check in the **Timeline** and make sure you have that blank *keyframe* selected.

Flash MX 2004 Note

The Actions panel list in Flash MX 2004 has different sections. Instead of "Actions," you'll see "Global Functions." Open that to find "Timeline Control." Inside that section, you will see "stop" (Figure 2.2.12). Adding the script is the same: Just double-click "stop."

Note: You should see a tiny letter "a" (for "ActionScript") on the last keyframe in your "actions" layer. The "a" indicates that Action-Script is written on that frame.

24 File menu > Save.

25 Test your movie: Ctrl-Enter (Win) or Cmd-Return (Mac).

What should happen: The movie plays one time and stops. If it does not stop, you did not write the Action-Script, or you wrote it on the wrong frame, so go back to Step 23 and try again. Don't close the entire Flash application when you close the testing window!

TIPS ABOUT ANIMATION

Frame Rates

How smooth, or how true to life, the motion in your Flash movie appears will depend on the *frame rate* you select. Flash sets a default frame rate of

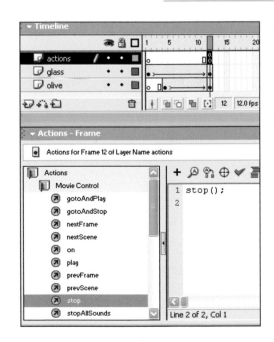

Fig. 2.2.11 Actions panel, Flash MX.

12 fps, as you learned in Lesson 1. If you want the most realistic motion, you might select 24 fps, based on the frame rate of motion picture film. That could increase the size of your Flash file, of course—not the most desirable result.

Macromedia recommends a frame rate of 15 to 18 fps for most Flash movies. However, some Flash developers have noticed that there can be significant differences in the actual playback frame rate on different operating systems. At least one developer recommends 21 fps as a frame rate that will run comparably on both Windows and Mac systems.

This will not matter much in cases where you have not created complex vector animations. If you use a high frame rate in a Flash movie where a lot of bitmaps (for example, photographs) are moving around, the frame rate may be forced down because of the higher demands a moving bitmap makes on the system. *Gradient fills* and *alpha* (transparency) also place a high demand on the user's system when they are moving. The user's computer might freeze up if your Flash movie demands too much processor activity. In other words, certain motion effects might *not* be speeded up by a higher frame rate.

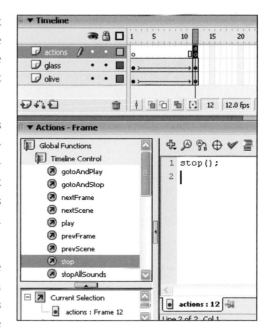

Fig. 2.2.12 Actions panel, Flash MX 2004. Here's what you should see in the **Actions** panel, depending whether you are using Flash MX (Figure 2.2.11) or Flash MX 2004 (Figure 2.2.12). In either case, you have now "written" an ActionScript command telling the movie to stop playing when the playhead reaches Frame 12.

The bottom line: Test your movie on various computers and platforms. For your first animations in Flash, you can't go wrong with a frame rate of 15 fps.

Using Layers

Independent motion takes place on separate layers in Flash. (This is somewhat different from simple layer-based animations you may have learned to do in another program, such as Adobe ImageReady.) Put different animated objects into their own layers, alone. Then adjust each object's movements individually.

It helps a lot to name your layers intelligently, because it prevents mistakes. If you have placed all your non-moving background images on one layer, name that layer "background." When you start working with text, you might find that you prefer to put all non-moving text fields on one layer. Fine! Name that layer "text blocks."

The longer you work with Flash, the more complex your movies will become. Practice good layer management now to make your work easier later.

Masks and Motion Paths

These two advanced techniques will allow you to achieve some effects that would be very time consuming to animate without them.

A *mask* prevents selected areas from being seen. The oddest thing about a mask: You create a solid shape that represents the area you intend to be *seen*, and you position it over the area that will be *visible*. (This temporarily hides the area, but that will change.) The mask shape must be alone on a layer. That layer becomes a *mask layer* when you right-click (Control-click/Mac) on it in the **Timeline** and select "Mask" from the pop-up menu. You can mask more than one layer beneath the same mask layer. You will learn to use a mask in Lesson 7.

A *motion guide layer* allows you to draw a curved or straight line and then "attach" objects on lower layers (as many layers as you like) to make them move along the line. You can make a plane fly along a visible dotted line or a bird follow an erratic invisible trail. For detailed instructions and examples, search for "Tweening motion along a path" in the Flash Help files: Open the Help menu and select "Using Flash," or just press F1.

There and Not There

Objects in the Library that are never used in your movie do not exist in the final exported Flash file (with the file extension *.swf*) and thus they do not add to the file size. That is *not* the case for objects you have dragged out of the Library. If you did not delete them, they are adding to the file size, even if they never show up on the Stage. Objects with an *alpha* of 0 are invisible, but they are still *there*—and so they add to the file size.

This means you must remember to remove objects from the Stage when you've finished with them, or when you have decided not to use them.

SIMPLE ANIMATION SUMMARY

For anyone who has not animated images before, the best approach is to keep it simple. Do not try to make human figures move naturally in your first week with Flash! Work first with simple objects (*instances* of graphic symbols, in the language of Flash). Try to get them to move as you want them to. Experiment with transparency (alpha) and scaling. For example, you can use the **Free Transform** tool to make an object double size in Frame 1, half size in Frame 12, and then apply a *motion tween*. Does the object appear to shrink, or does it appear to move away from you? You can make an object fade to invisibility by starting at an alpha of 100 and ending with an alpha of 0.

If you learn how animation in Flash works by moving rectangles and ovals around, later it will be less complicated for you to move blocks of text, photographs, and objects made up of separate, movable pieces. You might use the drawing tools to trace over a photograph of an object such as a passenger train, and then animate the individual cars of the train during a derailment. (All the cars could be instances of just one symbol.) Remember that each animated object must be alone in its own separate layer. (In Lesson 6, you'll learn how to contain multiple layers for one complex animated object in a single symbol called a movie clip.)

By paying close attention to the **Timeline**, you will learn how to "read" it. Any confusion you have about frames and keyframes will decrease as you practice. Keep your eye on the dots (keyframes) and whether they are black or empty (white). Remember that a keyframe signifies a frame where a *change* begins or ends. Watch the frames and check whether they are gray, blue, or empty (white).

CONCLUSION

In this lesson, you have learned to:

1. Convert a shape to a graphic symbol.

2. Open the Library panel and drag symbols from it to the Stage.

3. Use *alpha*, *brightness*, and *tint* (in the Properties panel) to change an *instance* of a symbol without affecting the symbol as it is stored in the Library.

4 Use the Free Transform tool, Transform panel, and Modify menu > Transform options to *scale, skew,* or *rotate* an instance without affecting the symbol in the Library.

5 Recognize a *keyframe* and distinguish it from a regular frame.

6 Position an object in a starting keyframe and in an ending keyframe.

7 Apply a *motion tween* to cause an object to move.

8 Test an animation.

9 Add frames (F5) and keyframes (F6) to the Timeline.

10 Remove frames and keyframes from the Timeline (Shift-F5).

11 Lengthen or shorten a motion sequence in the Timeline.

12 Change the starting or ending point of a motion sequence by dragging a keyframe.

13 Add and name new *layers* in the Timeline.

14 Rename a layer.

15 Animate multiple objects in separate layers.

16 Test your movie (this generates an *.swf* file).

17 Insert ActionScript on a frame to make the movie stop looping (play only once).

Lesson 3

Putting Flash Online

Before you became interested in Flash, you probably spent at least a little time creating Web pages and putting them online. If you wrote HTML by hand, you probably used an FTP (File Transfer Protocol) program to upload the pages and graphics to a Web server. If you used Dreamweaver, or another Web authoring application, the ability to send files to the server was built into the program.

While you could simply upload the *.swf* file (which, as you learned in Lesson 2, is generated when you press Ctrl-Enter or Cmd-Return to test the movie) and open it in a Web browser directly, that would not afford the best presentation for your Flash movie. It would be enlarged (but not skewed) to fill the browser window. The movie could not have any surrounding content (which you could add if you embedded your movie in a Web page). If you opened the movie in a pop-up window, the window title would be the same as the SWF's filename, rather than a title of your choosing.

This lesson explains how to make your Flash movie appear as you want it to appear to users on the Web.

LESSON 3

There are two standard ways to present a SWF on the Web: As a pop-up window linked from a Web page, or as an object embedded in a Web page (usually with other content on the page). In either case, you should "publish" your movie (File menu > Publish). This *does not* upload your file(s) to a Web server—it generates the files that you will later upload, using other software. *Before* you publish those files, though, you should check—and possibly change—your "Publish Settings" (also selected from the File menu).

This lesson covers:

- The most common Publish Settings.

- What you need to know to create a Web page layout using embedded Flash content.

- How to handle the files and put them online.

- Two ways to create a pop-up window to display your Flash movie.

Exercise 3.1: Publish Settings

1 You can use the movie you saved in Lesson 2 for this exercise. Open the file in Flash, and then select "Publish Settings" from the File menu.

2 The Publish Settings dialog box normally has three tabs: Formats, Flash, and HTML. It can have *more* or *fewer* tabs, depending on the items you select under the Formats tab. Here is a summary of those three option sets.

Formats

Under the first tab, the options for output are listed.

- Normally, only the top two options are checked: "Flash (*.swf*)" and "HTML (*.html*)." In almost all cases, you will keep both of these checked.

- You can uncheck "HTML (*.html*)" if you know you need nothing but the SWF. If you embed the Flash movie in a Web page, you *may* need the OBJECT code Flash generates for HTML, so it never hurts to keep that check mark.

The other format options are less commonly used and will not be covered here. They are described in detail in the Flash Help files (press F1; in Flash MX, go to "Using Flash," then find "Publishing" near the end of the Contents listing; in Flash MX 2004, under "Common Tasks," open "Publish a Flash document").

Flash

Under the second tab, you select settings for the SWF that will be generated.

- You can change the player required to an earlier version to accommodate a larger number of online users (but there is no real reason to go back further than Flash 5*). If you do this, make sure you have not used

* See statistics for Flash Player version penetration at *http://www.macromedia.com/software/player_census/flashplayer/version_penetration.html*.

any functionality that is unavailable to the older player version. For example, Flash MX (6) introduced "components," such as the ScrollBar. If you use the ScrollBar component in your movie, you cannot select a version lower than 6.

- "Load Order" is typically "Bottom up." It determines which layers Flash renders first as the movie loads for the user.

- In Flash MX 2004, you can select the ActionScript version you are using. For all exercises in this book, you can use ActionScript 1.0.

- The "Options" usually checked are "Protect from import" and "Compress Movie." The first prevents other people who download your SWF from importing it to Flash and converting it back to an FLA file. The second is not available in versions before Flash MX (6). Compressing the movie makes the file size smaller; Macromedia says the biggest advantage comes for files with a lot of text or ActionScript. This setting *does not* affect images!

- The "JPEG Quality" setting is discussed in Lesson 7. Changing this setting *does not* affect the quality of imported JPG images! However, it does affect the quality of imported BMP files.

The other settings under the second tab usually stay as they are. More details appear in the Flash Help files.

HTML

Under the third tab, you select settings for the HTML page that will be generated.

- The default template ("Flash Only") will be fine for your first movies, but later you may want to determine whether your users have the appropriate Flash player version to view your movie. If you choose to detect for Flash 6, for example, Flash will generate a Web page that includes many lines of JavaScript; the script tests the user's system for the Flash player version and reacts accordingly. (If you include video in your Flash movie, for example, and you *do not* include this JavaScript, the Flash movie will play for a user who has the Flash 5 player, but the video in the movie will not play at all.)

- In most cases, "Match Movie" (Dimensions) works best. It shows your SWF at the size you set in the **Properties** panel. ("Pixels" requires you to enter the width and height in pixels. "Percent" allows you to set a percentage relative to the size of the user's browser window.)

Developers often change some of the four "Playback" options:

- Leave "Paused At Start" *unchecked*; otherwise, you will need to include a button just to start the movie.

- If you uncheck "Display Menu," it changes what appears on the menu your users get when they right-click (Control-click/Mac) on your movie, but *only* if you embed the movie in a Web page. If "Display Menu" is unchecked *and* the movie is embedded, then the right-click menu shows only two lines: "Settings" and "About Flash Player." In other cases, it lists many options, such as "Zoom In" and "Rewind" (see Figure 2.3.06).

- "Loop" is checked by default. Leave it checked if you want your movie to repeat continuously. Unchecking it will cause your movie to play once and stop, but *only* if the movie is embedded in a Web page—the SWF *will* loop when opened by itself. (To ensure that a movie stops when you want it to stop, use ActionScript as described under "Animating Two Symbols," Lesson 2, Steps 20 through 23.)

- Leave "Device Font" unchecked. (This is explained further in Lesson 9.)

The other settings under the third tab usually stay as they are. More details appear in the Flash Help files.

3 After you have selected the Publish Settings you want, click the Publish button on the dialog box to generate the files. If you click OK, the Publish Settings are saved, but *no files are generated!* (This is a common error for new Flash authors.) If you do not want to save the new settings, click Cancel. If you save the settings (by clicking OK), they will be in effect the next time you select "Publish" from the File menu (in this FLA only).

4 At this point, if you clicked the Publish button, you have a SWF file (the playable Flash movie) and an HTML file. If you find the HTML file and double-click it, it will open in your default Web browser, and your Flash movie will play. In most cases, the position of the movie will be as shown in Figure 2.3.01.

 The browser window will also be its full size (whatever that might be on the user's computer; it varies widely), and not the exact size of your Flash movie.

5 You can also locate and double-click the SWF file that was generated when you clicked the Publish button. It will open and play in the stand-alone Flash player.

Remember that when you "publish" from Flash, you have not uploaded your files to the Web. You must do that separately, from another application such as Dreamweaver.

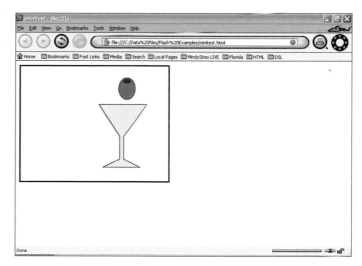

Fig. 2.3.01 By default, the HTML page generated by Flash places the movie alone on the page, in the upper left corner.

WHERE ARE YOUR FILES?

When you publish a Flash movie, Flash puts all the files generated into the same folder with your FLA file. It does not ask where you want to save the new files.

It makes good sense to create a separate project folder for each Flash movie you create so that all the associated files are kept together and remain easy to find and manage. If you have copied an FLA file into a new folder, make sure you open that file in Flash *from* the new folder. Then, whenever you publish, the associated files will go inside the new folder.

Positioning a Flash Movie in the Browser Window

You probably want to have control over your Web page layout. Instead of using the simple HTML page that Flash generates, you will insert the Flash object where you want it to appear within your own layout design. Web developers typically create a page layout with an HTML table, CSS, or a combination of the two.

There are several possibilities for embedding the Flash object in your page. You can:

• Insert the Flash object directly, if your authoring application offers that feature (see the box "Inserting a SWF with Dreamweaver").

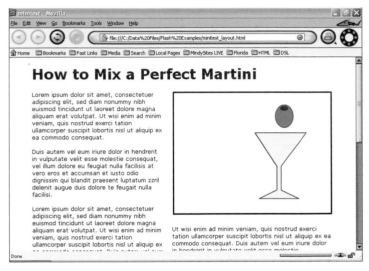

How to Mix a Perfect Martini

Lorem ipsum dolor sit amet, consectetuer adipiscing elit, sed diam nonummy nibh euismod tincidunt ut laoreet dolore magna aliquam erat volutpat. Ut wisi enim ad minim veniam, quis nostrud exerci tation ullamcorper suscipit lobortis nisl ut aliquip ex ea commodo consequat.

Duis autem vel eum iriure dolor in hendrerit in vulputate velit esse molestie consequat, vel illum dolore eu feugiat nulla facilisis at vero eros et accumsan et iusto odio dignissim qui blandit praesent luptatum zzril delenit augue duis dolore te feugait nulla facilisi.

Lorem ipsum dolor sit amet, consectetuer adipiscing elit, sed diam nonummy nibh euismod tincidunt ut laoreet dolore magna aliquam erat volutpat. Ut wisi enim ad minim veniam, quis nostrud exerci tation ullamcorper suscipit lobortis nisl ut aliquip ex

Ut wisi enim ad minim veniam, quis nostrud exerci tation ullamcorper suscipit lobortis nisl ut aliquip ex ea commodo consequat. Duis autem vel eum iriure dolor in hendrerit in vulputate velit esse molestie

Fig. 2.3.02 Open the Flash-generated HTML file in any Web authoring application to impose a page layout. Alternatively, you can create your page layout in the authoring application and add the Flash object afterward.

- Open the HTML page "published" by Flash and edit it as you like in any Web authoring application.

- *Copy* the code from that HTML file and *paste* it into another page that you have created.

If you edit the HTML page, or copy the code, be very careful not to lose any of the code that Flash generated! Flash generates code in one of two standard ways (in most cases), depending on the choices you made in the Publish Settings dialog.

Object and Embed Tags

If you accepted the default setting (in Publish Settings, you kept "Flash Only" as your template under the third tab, as described earlier), you have a chunk of OBJECT code to manage. It begins with this:

```
<OBJECT classid=
```

The opening tag is followed by several parameters and (quite important) an EMBED tag that repeats the same parameters in a different format. *All the code* is necessary to ensure that your Flash movie plays across multiple Web browsers.

The code ends with this:

```
</OBJECT>
```

If you want to position your Flash movie within a table cell (in a layout table in HTML), you must not lose or delete any of the OBJECT code. Sometimes developers go into the code and edit it, but they forget that all the instructions are given twice (once in the OBJECT tag and once in the EMBED tag), so they make errors, and the Flash movie fails to play for some Web users.

JavaScript for Player Version Detection

If you want to test for the Flash player version (in Publish Settings, you chose to *detect* for a specific Flash version, under "Template" on the HTML tab, as described earlier), you have a big clump of JavaScript to manage. It begins with this:

```
<script LANGUAGE=JavaScript1.1>
```

It ends with something similar to this:

```
</SCRIPT><noscript><img SRC="test.gif" WIDTH="550" HEIGHT="400"
usemap="#test" BORDER=0></noscript>
```

If you want to position your Flash movie, for example, within a table cell (in a layout table in HTML), you must not lose or delete any of the JavaScript. Sometimes developers go into the script and edit it, but they forget that all the instructions are given twice (the JavaScript is actually writing the OBJECT tag *and* the EMBED tag), so they make errors, and the Flash movie fails to play for some Web users.

Another common mistake: Failure to include a GIF, as specified at the end of the script. Flash will generate this GIF for you if you select "GIF Image (*.gif*)" under the Formats tab in the "Publish Settings" dialog; the GIF generated by default will show the contents of the *first frame* of your movie. If that's not the frame you want users to see as a stand-in for your movie, create an appropriate GIF, and include it in the same folder with your HTML and SWF files for the movie. You can make Flash generate any frame from your movie as a GIF image; see the Flash Help files.

Basically, you must tell Flash which frame you want to output as a GIF by putting a special *label* on that frame. (Frame labels are explained in Lesson 5.) Then select "GIF" in the Publish Settings dialog, and click the Publish button. Flash will save the labeled keyframe as a GIF.

INSERTING A SWF WITH DREAMWEAVER

If you use Macromedia Dreamweaver for Web page authoring and editing, you can insert any SWF exactly as you insert an image. First, copy the SWF into your site folder.

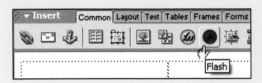

Fig. 2.3.03 Dreamweaver MX includes a button to insert Flash content into a Web page.

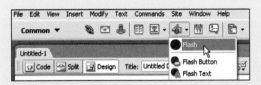

Fig. 2.3.04 In Dreamweaver MX 2004, open the Media submenu to insert Flash content into a Web page.

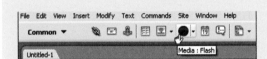

Fig. 2.3.05 After you have opened the Media submenu in Dreamweaver MX 2004, the Insert bar displays a Flash icon.

In Dreamweaver MX, find the Flash icon on the Insert bar (when the Common tab is selected), near the top of the Dreamweaver application window (Figure 2.3.03). Click it, find the SWF file in your site folder, and select the SWF. The Flash content will be inserted into your document at the cursor position.

In Dreamweaver MX 2004, the Flash icon is on a submenu of the Insert bar (when Common is selected). Find the Media icon and click it to open the submenu, then select "Flash" on the submenu (Figure 2.3.04). Find the SWF file in your site folder, and select the SWF. The Flash content will be inserted into your document at the cursor position. Note that after you have done this once, in most cases the Media icon will change to a Flash icon (Figure 2.3.05), which you can click directly next time, without opening the submenu.

In either case, you will not insert any code for *player version detection* (see earlier section "JavaScript for Player Version Detection"). If you want to use that code, you need to copy and paste it directly.

Exercise 3.2: Creating the Page Layout and Uploading the Page

Think of your SWF file as a rectangle, much like a GIF or JPG that you would include on any regular Web page. You can position the SWF anywhere you would normally position a GIF or JPG.

1 Copy the SWF file and the HTML file, and paste both of them into the folder on your hard drive where you keep your other Web site files. This step is crucial!

2 Open the HTML file that Flash generated when you published the movie. You can open it in any Web authoring program, or in a text editor.

3 There are several ways you can handle the layout. In all cases, treat the Flash code (either the OBJECT tag or JavaScript) as you would a GIF or a JPG file. Remember that your movie has a *width* and *height* (see Lesson 1, Step 2), and it will usually look best if it is displayed at that same width and height on the Web page.

- If you have a page layout already designed, open that page also. If you use Dreamweaver, and you are not using a player version detection script, use the method described in the box "Inserting a SWF with Dreamweaver."

- If you use another Web authoring program, or you are using a player version detection script, *select* all the Flash code in the Flash-generated HTML file (as described earlier) and *copy* it. Switch to your page layout file and *paste* the code into the desired position in that page.

- If you want to create a new page layout within the Flash-generated HTML file, add your table and/or CSS code *above* and *below* the Flash code, without altering the Flash code. In other words, keep the block of Flash code intact, either inside a table cell (TD tags) or within DIV tags.

4 Save the page layout file in your Web authoring application, in the folder where you keep your other Web site files.

5 Upload *both* the HTML file and the SWF to your Web server. (The SWF uploads exactly like a GIF or JPG file.)

VERY IMPORTANT NOTE ABOUT FILE LOCATIONS

The code Flash generates (whether it is the raw OBJECT tag or JavaScript for player version detection) assumes that the SWF file is *in the same folder* as the HTML file. If you put the SWF elsewhere, then you must edit the Flash code to provide the correct path to the SWF. You must change the path code *twice*, once in a PARAM attribute and once in the EMBED tag. Flash writes this to show the location of the SWF file:

```
PARAM NAME=movie VALUE="test.swf"
EMBED src="test.swf"
```

If you move your SWF file to a folder named "flash" inside a folder named "mediafiles," you must *rewrite* the code, to include the new path:

```
PARAM NAME=movie VALUE="mediafiles/flash/test.swf"
EMBED src="mediafiles/flash/test.swf"
```

Failure to do this causes the Flash content not to display on the page, because the Web browser cannot locate the SWF file after you have moved it.

Exercise 3.3: Using a Pop-up Window

Making a pop-up window requires a small amount of JavaScript, which is essentially the same for both window options you might use to display a Flash movie. The first case uses the SWF in the window without embedding it in a Web page at all (although the pop-up window is generated by script on a Web page). The second case uses a Web page with the SWF embedded in it, such as the HTML file that Flash can produce for you when you "publish" the movie, as described earlier.

Three advantages make Case No. 2 superior:

• Choices you made regarding Flash's pop-up menu (in the "Publish Settings" dialog) will be in effect, because the SWF is embedded in HTML.

• The pop-up window will have an appropriate title in the title bar.

• You can allow the user to resize the window, but the SWF will *not* resize.

For both cases below, the Flash movie file is named *test.swf*, the width is 300 pixels, and the height is 200 pixels.

Case No. 1: SWF Alone

1 On the page that will generate the pop-up window, create a regular hypertext link, but without a URL:

```
<a href="">Open my Flash movie!</a>
```

2 Insert this *between the quotation marks* in the tag shown in Step 1:

```
javascript:openFlash('test','300','200');
```

3 Insert this script anywhere on the page:

```
<script language="JavaScript" type="text/JavaScript">
var myWindow;
function openFlash(winurl,winwidth,winheight) {
    myWindow = window.open(winurl+".swf",winurl,"width=" ¬
    + winwidth + ",height=" + winheight + ",resizable");
    myWindow.focus();
}
</script>
```

Note: Do not type the symbol ¬, which represents a continuation of the same line of script.

4 Save the HTML file.

5 Upload *both* the HTML file and the SWF to your Web server. (The SWF uploads exactly like a GIF or JPG file.)

This script works in just about any browser and produces no odd behavior. It assumes that your SWF file is in the same folder as the HTML file. The window will not have scrollbars.

Note: If you prefer to use an option in your Web editing software to generate pop-up windows, without writing the JavaScript yourself, follow the instructions in Case No. 2, which follows, to prepare the HTML file with the SWF embedded in it. Then use that file as the URL for the pop-up window.

If you want to prevent users from changing the size of the pop-up window, use this code instead:

```
<script language="JavaScript" type="text/JavaScript">
var myWindow;
function openFlash(winurl,winwidth,winheight) {
    myWindow = window.open(winurl+".swf",winurl,"width=" ¬
    + winwidth + ",height=" + winheight);
    myWindow.focus();
}
</script>
```

Resizing the Flash movie (bigger or smaller) is perfectly okay *as long as there are no bitmaps* in your movie. Basically, a bitmap in Flash is *any imported image* such as a JPG or GIF. If the user changes the size of the SWF by resizing the window, the bitmaps become very ugly because the pixels get stretched. In other words, the bitmap images (including photos) become jagged and lumpy. Flash text and graphics don't do this because they are made up of vectors, not pixels (see Lesson 7 for details).

Case No. 2: SWF and HTML Together

1 Use the HTML file that Flash generated when you published the FLA file, as described in Exercise 3.1. You will make exactly *two* changes to that file.

2 The first change to the file: If you want the Flash movie to appear without any excess space around its edges (and normally, you *do* want that), you must tell all the Web browsers to *reset their default page margins*. There are several ways to do this, depending on whether you use CSS or not.

If you don't use CSS, add these four attributes to the BODY tag of the page in which the SWF is embedded:

```
leftmargin=0 topmargin=0 marginwidth=0 marginheight=0
```

(In Dreamweaver, open Page Properties from the Modify menu and type 0 into the four fields labeled "Left Margin," "Top Margin," "Margin Width," and "Margin Height.")

If you use CSS, this does it:

```
body { margin: 0; }
```

3 The second change to the file: If you want the pop-up window to have a meaningful title in the title bar (and normally, you *do* want that), write one. If you're in the HTML code, find the TITLE tags near the top of the file. In Dreamweaver, open Page Properties from the Modify menu and type your title into the field labeled "Title."

4 Save the file. It is complete.

5 Create (or open) a separate HTML file, which will open as a normal full-sized window, and create the link to your pop-up window as described earlier in Case No. 1. The *single* difference in creating this type is that you are not opening the SWF, so instead of this code:

```
myWindow =
window.open(winurl+".swf",
```

You need the *.html* (or *.htm*) file extension, instead. For example:

```
myWindow =
window.open(winurl+".html",
```

By default, Flash appends the *.html* file extension when it generates an HTML file.

You must also be sure to use the filename of the HTML file that contains the SWF (the file you just saved). If you saved it as *popup.htm*, for example, then this is correct:

```
javascript:openFlash('popup',
'300','200');
```

The width and height should exactly match your Flash movie, as in Case No. 1.

6 Save the second HTML file.

7 Upload *both* HTML files *and* the SWF to your Web server. (The SWF uploads exactly like a GIF or JPG file.)

If you want to allow the user to resize the movie, follow the steps in Case No. 1.

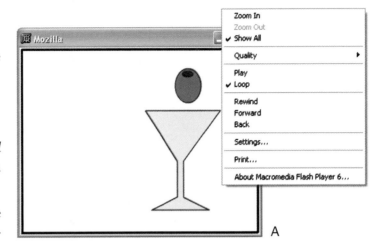

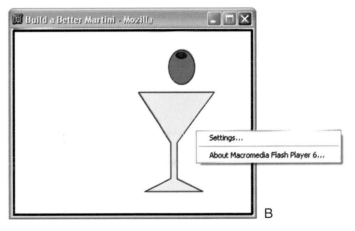

Fig. 2.3.06 The pop-up window in Mozilla (*A* and *B*) and Internet Explorer (*C* and *D*, next page). In Case No. 1 (*A* and *C*), the full Flash menu appears no matter what your Publish Settings were, and the window title is either the browser name or the path. In Case No. 2 (*B* and *D*), the menu will be what you chose in the Publish Settings dialog, and the window title will be what you wrote in the HTML.

If you have followed the steps for Case No. 2, you have *three* files to upload to your Web server: the SWF and two HTML pages.

PUTTING FLASH ONLINE SUMMARY

If you think of the Flash movie *object* as a page element similar to an image, and remember that the SWF file is not so different from a GIF or JPG file, you should have no trouble managing the file and folder issues associated

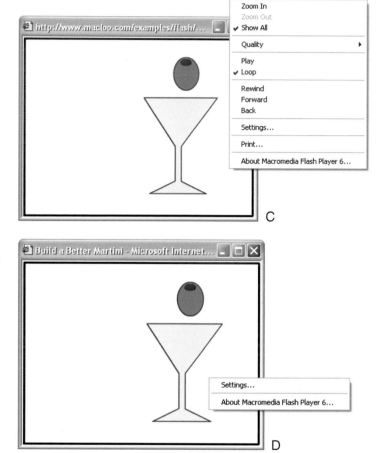

with Flash. They are the same issues that arise with all Web sites and all HTML files. Make sure you use the correct filenames and folder names and put the files where they belong, and everything will go smoothly. Upload your files exactly as you would any other set of files for your Web site.

In the same vein, when you want to put a Flash movie on a page, or in a pop-up window, the object behaves the same way as an image: It takes up a certain amount of space, and it will align inside a table just as an image will, if you give it the code.

As you create more complex Flash movies, you may want to do more with the Publish Settings. At the beginning, you can probably set them up once and then forget about them. Don't make the mistake of rewriting the OBJECT code incompletely, however! If you decide not

Fig. 2.3.06—Cont'd

to publish an HTML file and instead recycle your old code (there's no compelling reason to do this, but some people do), remember that *all* the parameters for the movie appear *two times* in the code block.

CONCLUSION

In this lesson, you have learned to:

1   Select appropriate Publish Settings for your Flash movie.

2   "Publish" both SWF and HTML files from Flash.

3   Anticipate where Flash will put the files it generates.

4   Recognize the code Flash generates for use in an HTML file, depending on your selections in the Publish Settings dialog.

5 Copy that code successfully for use in various page layouts.

6 Position the Flash movie within a page layout that includes text and other elements.

7 Insert a SWF using a Dreamweaver Insert bar button.

8 Edit the Flash-generated code successfully, if you have changed the location of your SWF file.

9 Create a link that opens a separate pop-up window (via JavaScript) containing either the SWF or an HTML page with the SWF embedded in it.

10 Use the Flash-generated SWF alone in a pop-up window.

11 Edit and use the Flash-generated HTML in a pop-up window.

12 Upload your files to your Web server.

Lesson 4

Buttons

Buttons offer the most basic means for making interactive applications in Flash, allowing the user to have some control over the movie. This lesson shows how to create buttons, make them respond to the mouse cursor, and add sound to them. It assumes some familiarity with the drawing tools (Lesson 1) and basic animation techniques (Lesson 2) in Flash. Following the steps in this lesson should also increase your comfort level with those tools and techniques.

Buttons on their own do not do anything; like most buttons in HTML, Flash buttons require at least a little bit of scripting to make them work. Lesson 5 focuses on that aspect of buttons, so you might want to work through Lesson 5 as soon as you finish this one.

Flash includes a library of ready-made buttons for you to use (Flash MX: Window menu > Common Libraries > Buttons; Flash MX 2004: Window menu > Other Panels > Common Libraries > Buttons), but it's likely that you will prefer to create buttons that match the colors and design elements in your Flash movie.

LESSON 4

For your first button, the instructions lead you through the creation of a traditional-looking pushbutton. However, in Flash *anything* can be a button. You can apply these techniques to text, an arrow, a cartoon spaceship, a splash of color, a photograph—there are no limits. Objects on a map can be buttons (e.g., amusements on a map of the state fair). You can even make invisible buttons and position them over the top of something else so that when the mouse rolls over that object, something happens.

Use of the **Text** tool is introduced in Step 4 (even though one entire lesson in this book, Lesson 9, is devoted to the uses of text in Flash), because often you will want to place a text label on a button—or above, below, or beside a button. Flash gives you a lot of control over how your buttons look and how they work. The examples should give you an idea just how versatile buttons can be.

Exercise 4.1: Create a New Button

1 File menu > New (start with a new, empty file).

2 Make sure you can see the **Stage** and also the **Tools**, **Timeline**, and **Properties** panels. As always, check and select the *width, height, frame rate,* and *background color* for the movie, using the **Properties** panel. (Even if you're not going to save this practice session, you should train yourself to consider these settings every time you open a new file in Flash.)

3 Create the shape for your button. Select the **Oval** tool or the **Rectangle** tool (depending on what shape you want the button to have), and select a stroke color and a fill color for the shape in the **Properties** panel. Then use the tool to draw a shape. You can undo (Ctrl-Z/Win or Cmd-Z/Mac) at any time. There is no need to make the shape small—the button can be resized later (with the **Transform** panel), and it's easier to work on a big image.

4 Put text on your button. Select the **Text** tool and then click *once* within the button shape. (Don't worry about the position; you can move the text later.) This causes a text editing box to open (Figures 2.4.01 and 2.4.02). Type one word to appear on the button. Then double-click the word to *select* it. That will allow you to *edit the properties* of the text (in the next step). If the text is *not* selected, you *cannot* change its properties.

5 Use the **Properties** panel to specify the *font family, size,* and *color* for the text. Make sure the *Text Type* is set to "Static" (in the Properties panel)— this is often the best choice for the text type. Make sure the Selectable button (in the Properties panel) is *not* clicked or "pushed in"; it should *always* be "pushed out" (or "off") for button text.

6 Select the **Arrow/Select** tool in the **Tools** panel, then *move* the text to a good position on the button shape. Notice how the text becomes deselected as soon as you click the Arrow tool, but it remains surrounded by a thin line, or bounding box; this indicates that the text object is selected.

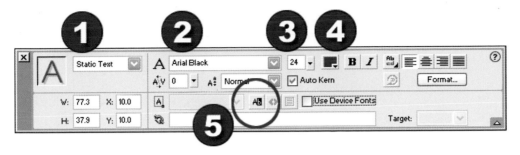

Fig. 2.4.01 Flash MX properties for text.

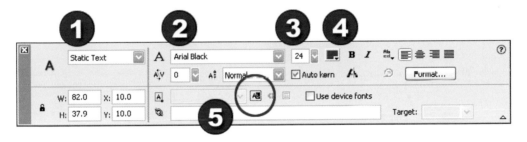

Fig. 2.4.02 Flash MX
2004 properties for text.

Note: You may find it difficult to select the text instead of the fill color of your shape. Practice observing which one is selected when you click. Is there a *blue bounding box* around the text? If so, the text is selected. Is the fill color *dotted* instead of solid? If so, the fill color is selected. It's very useful to learn how to tell what is selected on the Stage.

1. Text type (menu)
2. Font family
3. Font size
4. Color
5. Selectable button (off position)

TIP FOR BUTTON TEXT

On buttons, centered text often looks best. Here's one way to center your text on a button: First position the text so that the box surrounding it touches the *left edge* of the button. Then select the **Text** tool and click *once* on the text, which causes a tiny "handle" to appear at one corner of the box.

Fig. 2.4.03 Drag the text field to cover the entire width of the button.

Grab the handle and drag to the *right* (Figure 2.4.03). If the text box is stretched across the entire width of the button, you can center the text by clicking the Justify/Alignment button on the **Properties** panel (find the Left, Center, Right, and Justify buttons in the *upper right corner* of the panel; they look like the equivalent buttons in text editing programs such as Microsoft Word).

7   When you're satisfied with your button, *save* and *name* your file.

8   Here's how to make the shape become a real button: Select the **Arrow/Selection** tool in the **Tools** panel and drag a box around your *entire* button to select it. Press F8 to "Convert to Symbol." In the dialog box, *name* this symbol and *select* the behavior "Button." Click OK.

Note: You did something very similar in "Creating Graphic Symbols," in Lesson 2, Step 6, when you converted a shape to a *graphic* symbol. A *button* is one of the three types of symbol in Flash.

9   Open the **Library** panel (Window menu > Library) to see that you have a permanent button symbol now, with the name you gave it.

You can use multiple instances of this button, as with any symbol. However, if you want to change the text that appears on this button, you must *duplicate* the symbol (in the **Library**, not on the **Stage**) and make your changes in the new symbol—for example, if you want a Stop button and a Start button, when the text is part of the button, you would use two different symbols. To duplicate a symbol, right-click (Ctrl-click/Mac) the symbol *in the Library panel* and select "Duplicate" from the pop-up menu.

10   Editing the button symbol is a special process, because Flash sets up four frames for you *inside* the button symbol. These frames allow you to easily create a rollover effect and a click effect for your button. Here's how:

(a) **Enter Symbol Editing Mode**: There are several ways to go into this editing mode on a symbol. One way is to *right-click* (Ctrl-click/Mac) the symbol in the **Library** panel and select "Edit" from the pop-up menu. Alternatively, you can *double-click* the image in the Library panel *or* on the **Stage**. In all these cases, the Symbol Editing window *replaces* the normal Stage. In the Symbol Editing window, the **Timeline** is different: It shows *only* the frames for the symbol you are currently editing.

Notice that there are now four frame *names* in the Timeline—Up, Over, Down, and Hit—but only one frame. If you see those four names in the **Timeline**, then you are definitely in the **Symbol Editing** window for a button (Figure 2.4.04).

Fig. 2.4.04 The button Timeline looks like this when you first enter Symbol Editing Mode.

To make the button change when you roll over it (Over) or click it (Down), you will add a frame for each of these *button states* and change the appearance of the button within that frame.

The contents of the *Hit state* frame (the fourth frame) determine the area that responds to the user's mouse cursor.

(b) **Locate the first button frame** (*Up*): Probably the button you drew has the appearance you want when the button is in the normal movie, when the user has not "touched" it yet. That is the *Up state* of the button. It occupies the first frame of the button's **Timeline**—that is the *only* frame you have in a *new* button, before you edit it.

(c) **Add the second frame** (*Over*): To copy the *Up state* into the *Over state*, click once in the *Over* frame, and then press F6 to add a new *keyframe*.

(d) **Edit the second frame** (*Over*): In the Symbol Editing window, change the button image to the appearance you want the button to have *on rollover* (when the mouse moves over the button). For example, change the text color to a brighter color, or make the shape bigger. You can change the colors of the shape and its outline too. You can change the text here, or even add new text above, below, or beside the button.

Fig. 2.4.05 The button Timeline looks like this when you have created four keyframes, one for each button state.

(e) **Add the third frame** (*Down*): To copy the *Over state* into the *Down state*, click once in the *Down* frame, and then press F6 to add a new keyframe.

(f) **Edit the third frame** (*Down*): On the **Stage**, change the image to the appearance you want the button to have *on press* (when the mouse cursor is on the button and the *mouse button* is pressed). For example, change the text color to a darker color. You can change the fill and stroke colors of the shape too.

(g) **Add the fourth frame** (*Hit*): To copy the *Down state* into the *Hit state*, click once in the *Hit* frame, and then press F6 to add a new keyframe.

(h) **Edit the fourth frame** (*Hit*): Often you do not need to change anything in the *Hit* frame in a button symbol **Timeline**. The image in this frame

B

Fig. 2.4.06 *A*. Blue arrow in Flash MX. *B*. Blue arrow in Flash MX 2004. Click the blue arrow to leave Symbol Editing Mode and return to regular editing in the main Timeline. In *A*, Flash MX, the blue arrow is *below* the Timeline panel. In *B*, Flash MX 2004, the blue arrow is *above* the Timeline panel. In either case, you could click "Scene 1" instead to return to regular editing.

determines what area(s) will be treated as "hot" for the button, and in most cases, you want the *entire surface of the button* to be "hot," or clickable. (If the *Hit* frame is empty, the button does not work.) For an oval or rectangular button, you should use the solid oval or rectangular "fill" shape as the *hit area*.

Note: If you use *text alone* as a button, it's best to create a rectangle in the *Hit* frame to cover the entire text area. Otherwise, the button will not work when the mouse cursor is between two letters, or on the empty space in the middle of an O, for example. When the mouse cursor is on the word, the hand cursor symbol (indicating something that is clickable) will flicker on and off repeatedly as the mouse moves over the letters; this can drive users crazy! It also makes the button difficult to click.

(i) **Finish**: *Exit* from **Symbol Editing Mode** and return to editing the main movie. There are three easy ways to do this: (1) Press Ctrl-E (or Cmd-E/Mac); (2) Click the small blue arrow that points left, at the top left corner of the document window, *below* the **Timeline** in Flash MX, or *above* it in MX 2004; (3) Click the text "Scene 1" to the right of the blue arrow.

Note: It can be confusing at first to recognize when you are in Symbol Editing Mode. New Flash authors sometimes exclaim, "What happened to my Timeline?" when they have inadvertently double-clicked a symbol. They are in Symbol Editing Mode and do not realize it. Train yourself to look for that small blue arrow (Figure 2.4.06)—it is the signpost that leads you back to the main Timeline and the normal Stage for editing.

11 File menu > Save.

12 Test your movie: Ctrl-Enter (Win) or Cmd-Return (Mac). You should see the mouseover (or rollover) and click (or press) effects for your button when you move the mouse cursor over it or click on it. Of course, clicking on it does not cause anything else to happen—yet! That is the focus of Lesson 5.

You can use *layers* in a button symbol's **Timeline** to make it easier to construct, and later edit, various parts of a complex button design (Figure

2.4.07). Don't shy away from making original buttons; they can really personalize your Flash movies.

Exercise 4.2: Add Sound to a Button

You can use the button you just made in the previous exercise. Open the FLA file that contains the button if you have closed it, and make sure that one instance of your button appears on the **Stage**. Drag one out of the **Library** if necessary.

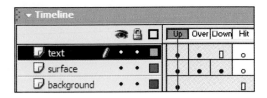

Fig. 2.4.07 In some cases, it may be easier to edit a button that is built with graphic elements on separate layers. The bottom layer visually is also the bottom layer in the Timeline. If you "read" the frames carefully, you can see that the background for this button never changes; it also stands in for the hit area. The surface changes two times, for Over and Down. The text changes once, for Over.

1 Go into **Symbol Editing Mode** for the button: *Double-click* the button on the **Stage**. Note that your changes will affect *all* instances of the symbol.

2 Create a *new layer* for your button in the **Timeline** (see "Animating Two Symbols" Step 13, in Lesson 2 if you need a review). Name the new layer "sound."

3 Add a *blank keyframe* (press F7) for *each* of the four button states in the "sound" layer.

4 Select the *Down* frame in the "sound" layer in the **Timeline**. (Click *once* on that frame to select it.)

5 Open the Common Library of sounds (Flash MX: Window menu > Common Libraries > Sounds) and select a button sound. You can preview any sound by clicking it once in the **Library** panel and then pressing the tiny Play button at the top of the panel, where you will see a waveform representing that sound (Figure 2.4.09).

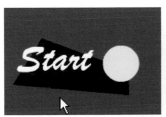  

Fig. 2.4.08 These are the Up (left), Over (center), and Down (right) states of the button whose Timeline appears in Figure 2.4.07.

Fig. 2.4.09 When you click a sound in the Library panel, you'll see its waveform. You can also play it here to see whether you like it.

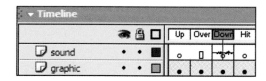

Fig. 2.4.10 After you drop the sound onto the Stage, you will see it represented graphically in the frame you had selected on the Timeline.

Flash MX 2004 Note

Flash MX 2004 does not include the sounds in Common Libraries, but you can download them (free) as an FLA from Macromedia. Once you open the FLA in Flash, you will see instructions on how to install them as a library. Get the FLA here: *http://www.macromedia.com/support/flash/ts/documents/soundlibrary.htm*

6 *Drag* the sound you selected from the **Library** panel to the button on the **Stage**, and drop it onto the button. Make sure you drop the sound onto the button, or the Stage, but *not* onto the frame (Figure 2.4.10).

7 Save and test your movie: Press Ctrl-Enter (Win) or Cmd-Return (Mac). You should hear the sound you selected when you click on your button. Because the sound is on the *Down* frame in the button **Timeline**, you hear it *only* when the button is clicked. (You can go back to Symbol Editing Mode and add a different sound for the *Over* state, too, if you want to.)

If you want more button sounds, go to *http://www.flashkit.com* and download some. There is a wide selection of free sounds at that Web site. Download the sound, and then *import* it to your Flash library (File menu > Import to Library). After you have done that, the new sound works as described earlier. Be careful not to use sounds with overly large file sizes—they will increase the size of your SWF file.

To delete a sound from a button frame, *right-click* (Ctrl-click/Mac) on the frame that contains the sound, and then select "Clear Keyframe" from the pop-up menu. You will need to *insert a new keyframe* afterward. There's another method that also works well: Click once on the frame that contains the sound and look in the **Properties** panel. The name of your sound appears in a menu box labeled "Sound" (Figure 2.4.11). Open the menu and select "None." The sound will disappear from the frame.

BUTTONS SUMMARY

Creating the shapes that look like a button requires you to use the drawing tools, as you learned to do in Lesson 1. You can use text on the button, or

Fig. 2.4.11 This view of the Properties panel appears when you have clicked one frame in the Timeline. All the sounds in your movie's Library are listed in the drop-down menu labeled "Sound." You can also add a sound to a frame by selecting it here.

not, whenever it's appropriate for the function of the button. A button can have any appearance or any shape.

Converting the shape to a button *symbol* is necessary; it provides the four-frame Timeline (within the symbol) that you saw in this lesson. The four-frame **Timeline** makes the button act the way we expect a button to act. However, *three* of the four frames are *empty* until you put something into them. The importance of putting something into the *Hit* frame, in particular, should be clear to you now.

Sound can be overdone, but a soft click to let the user know the button worked can be a nice touch in your Flash movie. If you put sound on a button symbol, it will be the same for *all instances* of that button. You can use the sounds in Flash's Common Libraries, download sounds from the Web, or record your own sounds.

Buttons allow your users to choose what they want to do, so it's advisable for you to become comfortable with making buttons that give a clear indication of their function. By making your own buttons, you customize your Flash movies to match your intentions and provide a good experience for your users. Some Flash authors are quite lazy about making buttons; they always use ready-made buttons from Flash's Common Libraries. This tends to give their work a generic look.

CONCLUSION

In this lesson, you have learned to:

1. Make a button shape.

2. Create and center text on the shape.

3. Convert the shape to a button symbol.

4 Duplicate a symbol (not the same as copying it), so you can edit it without changing the original.

5 Go into Symbol Editing Mode (so that you can edit a symbol, of course).

6 Add keyframes to the button symbol Timeline.

7 Change the four button states: Up, Over, Down, and Hit.

8 Ensure that your button's "hit area" works, even for a text-only button.

9 Exit from Symbol Editing Mode (return to the main Timeline).

10 Test a button.

11 Add layers inside a button's Timeline.

12 Preview a sound in the Library panel.

13 Add sound to a specific button state, such as Down.

14 Delete sound from a button.

15 Import new sound files from outside Flash.

Lesson 5

Making Buttons Do Things

To include interactivity in a Flash movie, you need to allow the users to make choices. If they can't choose what they want, they can only watch or read what's already on the screen. Most Web pages supply choices via hypertext links—click on a link, and something happens (usually you go to a different Web page). You can make hypertext links in Flash too (although in most cases, you wouldn't want your users to leave the Flash movie)—but more often, Flash movies supply choices via buttons.

In Lesson 4 you learned how to make buttons, but not how to make buttons work. That's the subject of this lesson. Making buttons work requires the use of ActionScript, but not very much; often one line of script is enough to make a button do something very useful.

This lesson explains how to place ActionScript on a button so that something actually happens when the user clicks the button. It also demonstrates how to use buttons to take the user to different parts of your Flash movie. Button scripting allows you to pause, fast forward, rewind, and skip around in a Flash movie.

The basic principles of button scripting will be expanded on in Lessons 8 and 10, where you will learn to use buttons to control sound and a photo slideshow.

LESSON 5

In the preliminary part of this lesson, Exercise 5.1, you will build a simple animation so that your buttons have an object to control. You can draw something recognizable using the Flash drawing tools if you have some artistic skills, but if you don't, just draw a rectangle or an oval. The preliminary work is a review of what you learned in Lesson 2. It's important to follow the instructions for moving the object and making two motion tweens in Exercise 5.1, because the buttons you script in Exercise 5.3 will control the *sequence* of the animation. In Exercise 5.2, you will script two buttons; one to stop the action, and the other to restart the action.

Exercise 5.1: Preliminary Work (Build an Animation)

1 Start a new file in Flash, and draw an object on the **Stage**. If you want to exploit the motion theme, draw a vehicle of some kind (the examples show an airplane). A hot air balloon is fairly easy to draw. You could also use a simple rectangle or an oval, although it's more fun with a vehicle.

USING 15 FRAMES PER SECOND

As explained in Lesson 2 ("Frame Rates"), Flash sets a frame rate of 12 frames per second (fps) by default, but Macromedia recommends a frame rate of 15 to 18 fps as ideal. The 15 fps rate works well for video in Flash, in particular. Most digital video is recorded at 29.97 fps, making 15 fps almost perfectly a 2:1 ratio, which allows for a smoother conversion.

If you set the frame rate at 30 fps or higher, in many cases the user's system performance will degrade as the processor struggles to cope with the high speed, and the end result will not be the faster Flash movie you had hoped for. In fact, your movie may stop and start erratically, or "drop frames" (appear to skip).

Starting now, always *change the frame rate* of your Flash projects to 15 fps. You can change the frame rate for the entire movie in the **Properties** panel when it displays the properties of the movie; this was explained in Lesson 1, Step 2.

2 Select the entire object you drew and *convert* it to a graphic symbol (press F8, or open the Insert menu/Flash MX or the Modify menu/MX 2004 and select "Convert to Symbol"). Make sure you select "Graphic" as the behavior. Get in the habit now of always *naming* a symbol when you create it—it will spare you frustration later, when you have multiple items in your Library!

3 Keeping the graphic symbol on the **Stage**, click *once* on Frame 2 in the **Timeline**, and make a new *keyframe* (press F6, or open the Insert menu and select "Keyframe"/Flash MX; in Flash MX 2004, "Keyframe" is on the Timeline submenu). You should now have two gray keyframes, each with a black dot. Right now, each frame contains your graphic symbol in exactly the same position.

4 Click once on Frame 1 to select it. On the **Stage**, click and drag your graphic symbol off the Stage to the *left*. Drop it just to the left of the left-hand edge of the Stage.

5 Click once on Frame 2 to select it. On the **Stage**, click and drag your graphic symbol off the Stage to the *right*. Drop it just to the right of the right-hand edge of the Stage.

6 Click once in Frame 3 and make a new keyframe there (press F6). This makes an exact copy of Frame 2, in which your object is offstage to the right side of the **Stage**. If you would like your object to face toward the left for the return trip, select it in this frame and "flip it." Here's how: With the object selected, open the Modify menu, move the cursor to "Transform," and select "Flip Horizontal" from the submenu.

7 Click once in Frame 4 and make a new keyframe there, too (press F6). This makes an exact copy of Frame 3. On the **Stage**, with Frame 4 still selected, click and drag your graphic symbol off the Stage to the *left*.

You now have four frames, and your symbol should be left (Frame 1), right (Frame 2), right (Frame 3), and left (Frame 4).

8 Click *once* on Frame 3, and add about 15 frames (press F5 repeatedly to add frames).

9 Click *once* on Frame 1, and add about 15 frames (press F5 repeatedly).

You now have a long gray sequence, a single keyframe, another long gray sequence, and another single keyframe. You still have exactly four keyframes (black dots).

10 Select each long gray sequence and add a *motion tween* to each one

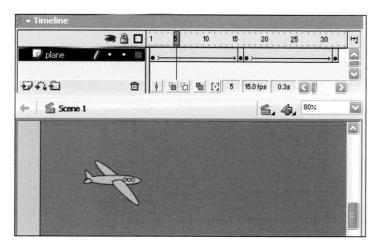

Fig. 2.5.01 The animation has two long sequences, each of which begins and ends with a single keyframe. In the first sequence, the plane flies across the screen toward the right. In the second sequence, the plane crosses the screen toward the left.

(using the **Properties** panel). See "Animating Two Symbols," Lesson 2, Step 5, if you need a review of how to add a motion tween (Figure 2.5.01).

 11 Save and test your movie: Ctrl-Enter (Win) or Cmd-Return (Mac).

What should happen: Your symbol crosses the screen from left to right, from right to left, and repeats without ever stopping. Because you did not add a stop() action to the final frame, the Flash movie loops forever. That's good—that's exactly what you need to continue with the rest of this lesson.

Now you're ready to control this animation with two new buttons.

Exercise 5.2: Stop and Play Buttons

Use the file you just saved and tested in Exercise 5.1.

1 Create a new layer in the **Timeline**, and name the layer "buttons" (without the quotes). See "Animating Two Symbols," Lesson 2, Step 13, if you need a review of how to add a layer.

Note: Remember, any object that is motion tweened must be *alone* on its layer. You must not place the buttons on the same layer with your moving object; if you do, the motion tween will stop working (a broken motion tween is represented on the Timeline by a dotted line).

2 Name your original layer too, just because it's a good habit. You'll make fewer mistakes in Flash if you always name your layers and always pay attention to which layer you're on. In the example, the lower layer is named "plane" because it contains an airplane graphic (Figure 2.5.02).

3 On your "buttons" layer, create a simple button (a plain rectangle or oval is fine) on the **Stage**. Don't forget to "Convert to Symbol." (Review Lesson 4 if necessary.)

4 Open the **Library** (press F11, or open the Window menu and select "Library"), and drag a second *instance* of the same button to the **Stage**. Make sure you're still on the "buttons" layer! You should have two identical buttons side by side. If you prefer, you can use the **Text** tool to put a word on top of each button.

5 The first button you script will make the object stop moving endlessly across the screen, so we'll call it the Stop button. On the **Stage**, select the button that you want to be the Stop button (click it only *once* to select it). Make sure you have selected *only one* button. If both buttons are selected, click once *outside* to deselect them, then click once on the button you want to script.

6 When a button is already selected and you open the **Actions** panel, the Actions panel is set up for script to be applied to that button. Your button is selected, so open the Actions panel (press F9, or open the Window menu and select "Actions"). You used the Actions panel in Lesson 2 to add a stop() action to your movie.

Fig. 2.5.02 Be very careful with your objects and the layers where they reside. If you place a button on a layer that already has a motion tween, that motion tween will "break" and stop working. In the Timeline shown, you can see that the motion tween is still functional because it is a solid line, not a dotted line.

SWITCHING TO "EXPERT MODE" IN FLASH MX

There are two ways to "write" ActionScript in Flash MX. This difference does not exist in Flash MX 2004, where there is only "Expert Mode" (although it's no longer called that).

What Flash MX calls "Normal Mode" is a way to let Flash do some of the work for you, if you're not accustomed to writing script.

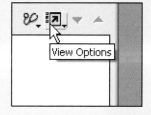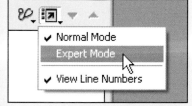

Fig. 2.5.03 On the far right side of the Actions panel in Flash MX, you'll find the button that allows you to switch from "Normal Mode" to "Expert Mode" and back again. The same button exists in Flash MX 2004, but the two modes do not.

This can be great for scripting beginners, because there's less chance for errors. Some people would rather type the script, though, and for those people Flash MX provides "Expert Mode" (Figure 2.5.03).

For this lesson, the instructions will assume you're operating in "Normal Mode," but the script will be shown so you can switch to "Expert Mode" and type it, if you prefer—or if you are using Flash MX 2004.

7 With the **Actions** panel open, you can see a list of commands at the left side of the panel. See "Animating Two Symbols," Lesson 2, Step 23, if you need a review.

Flash MX: Click in the list at left to open "Actions"; then click "Movie Control"; then *double-click* "on" (Figure 2.5.04).

Flash MX 2004: Click in the list at left to open "Global Functions"; then click "Movie Clip Control"; then *double-click* "on" (Figure 2.5.05). A pop-up menu opens. On that menu, *double-click* "release."

The script written so far:

```
on (release) {
}
```

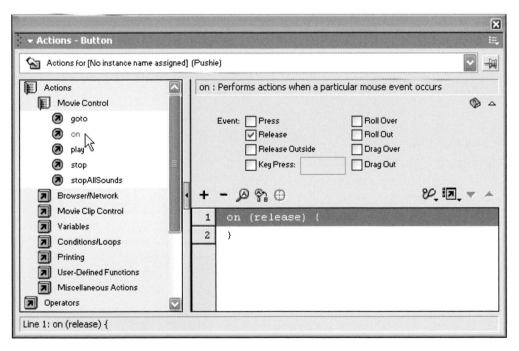

Fig. 2.5.04 Flash MX: The list on the left side of the Actions panel allows you to select chunks of ActionScript without typing it yourself. The script appears in the window on the right side.

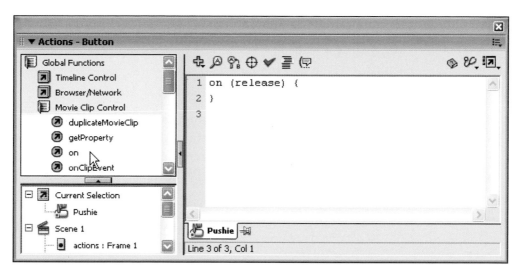

Fig. 2.5.05 Flash MX 2004: The list is slightly different, but it works basically the same way. What you click on the left side will appear as script in the window on the right.

The curly braces { } are waiting for some instructions to be placed in between them. So far, all this script tells Flash is, "When the user clicks and then releases the button, *do something.*"

Note: The usual button instruction is "on (release)" and not "on (press)" because "on (release)" gives users a chance to change their mind; if they press and then drag the mouse away from the button, nothing happens when they release it. With "on (release)," you also allow the users to see the *Down* state of the button (described in "Create a Button," Lesson 4) followed by the *Up* state, which can provide a nice visual effect.

8 You can probably guess what to do next, since this is a Stop button. You need to add the stop() action in between the curly braces.

Flash MX: *Double-click* "stop" in the list at the left side in the **Actions** panel.

Flash MX 2004: Click *once* on "Timeline Control" in the list at the left. Then *double-click* "stop."

The script now:

```
on (release) {
    stop();
}
```

9 Save and test your movie: Ctrl-Enter (Win) or Cmd-Return (Mac).

What should happen: Your animation runs exactly as it did before (see Exercise 5.1). When you click your Stop button, however, the object stops moving. No matter where it was, onscreen or off, it stops there.

10 This makes for a pretty dull animation, so let's provide a way to start the action again after it has been stopped. What you need to do is repeat Steps 5 through 9 for the Play button (the other button you placed on the **Stage**)—but in Step 8, apply the play() action *instead of* the stop() action.

The resulting script on your Play button should look like this:

```
on (release) {
    play();
}
```

11 Save and test your movie: Ctrl-Enter (Win) or Cmd-Return (Mac).

What should happen: Your animation runs exactly as it did before. When you click your Stop button, the object stops moving. However, now when you click your Play button, the object starts moving again, from the same place where it stopped. You can stop and start it again and again. Notice that if you click Stop repeatedly, it has no effect; the animation stays stopped. The same result comes from repeated clicking of your Play button. Each button does only one thing, which is exactly what you scripted it to do.

You now have the skills needed to control a photo slideshow or a video, as well as an animation, by allowing the user to *pause* the action. Stop buttons and Play buttons like these can control the main **Timeline** of any Flash movie, no matter what is happening on the **Timeline**.

The next exercise introduces a finer level of control, which allows the user to view parts of your Flash movie out of order. In other words, it's possible to jump ahead or jump back in the Flash **Timeline**.

 USING BUTTONS TO NAVIGATE ONE FRAME AT A TIME

At times, you may need to create a simple slideshow in a hurry. Flash buttons can make this easy, because ActionScript includes two actions specifically for this purpose: nextFrame() and prevFrame(). These actions work well if you have a series of single keyframes in your **Time-line**, such as a set of photos (not a tweened animation).

Using the techniques you learned in Exercise 5.2, create a Next button and place the following script on it:

```
on (release) {
    nextFrame();
}
```

Create a Back button and place the following script on it:

```
on (release) {
    prevFrame();
}
```

You must put a `stop()` action on Frame 1 of your movie, but you will not need more than that one `stop()` action, no matter how many frames you have. The `nextFrame()` and `prevFrame()` actions stop your movie on each frame by default.

Note that the "on (release)" handler script and the curly braces used here are typical of all the buttons you have made so far.

Exercise 5.3: Buttons That Let You Jump on the Timeline

Use the same file you worked on in Exercise 5.2. Save it with a different filename if you want to preserve it.

In this exercise, you will add two new buttons to the movie. Keep your Stop button as it is, so you can reuse it in Lesson 6. You can keep your Play button also, or delete it from the Stage, if you prefer.

There are two ways to send the *playhead* to a specific place in the **Time-line**: Tell it to go to a frame by number (e.g., go to Frame 10), or tell it to go to a labeled frame. All frames in a movie automatically have numbers, but if you want a frame to have a label, you must give it one. The advantage: If you add or remove frames from a movie, the *frame label* will not change. You can make sure a label stays with the event it is intended to trigger, whereas you can't control the frame numbers. (You encountered the playhead in "Animating Two Symbols," Lesson 2, Step 8. The users never see the playhead, but it is working in your movie nevertheless.)

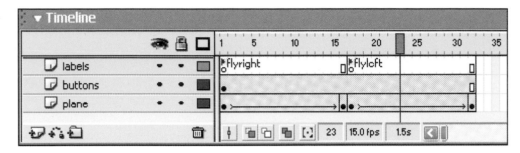

Fig. 2.5.06 After you have created your two labeled frames on the "labels" layer, your Timeline will look similar to this one. A tiny red flag indicates a frame to which a label has been applied.

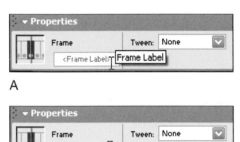

A

B

Fig. 2.5.07 If one frame in the Timeline is selected, the Properties panel shows the properties for that frame. This is where you can create a label for a frame (A). Click inside the Frame field and type a one-word label, with no spaces and no punctuation (B). Tab out of the field when you have finished.

1 The first step is to create two *frame labels* in your movie: One marks the frame where your object begins to move from left to right; the other marks the frame where your object begins to move from right to left. Make *a new layer* in the **Timeline** to hold the labels (it's a good practice to place labels in their own layer, because it keeps the **Timeline** orderly and easy to "read"). Name the new layer "labels" (without the quotes).

2 You already have a *keyframe* as Frame 1 in the "labels" layer. Click *once* on that frame in the **Timeline** to select it.

3 Without clicking anything else, look at the left side of the **Properties** panel. Find the field labeled "Frame" and put your cursor over that field (Figure 2.5.07). Click *once* to be able to type inside the field. Type "flyright" (without the quotes) in the field, and press the Tab key to leave the field. (If you leave the cursor inside the field, the frame label will not "stick.")

4 You're going to make a second labeled frame, and you need to look at the **Timeline** and determine *in which frame* your object begins to move to the left. Find the keyframe that *starts* the second long sequence in your Timeline. It's not the single keyframe, where the object stops for an instant. It's the first keyframe in the second motion sequence. Click that frame *in the "labels" layer* and make a new keyframe there (press F6). Refer to Figure 2.5.06 if necessary.

5 Go into the **Properties** panel and label that frame "flyleft" (without the quotes). Press the Tab key to leave the Frame field.

6 Now it's time to make two new buttons. Select the "buttons" layer in the **Timeline** so the buttons appear on that layer. (It's okay to have lots of buttons in the same layer—buttons don't move.) Drag the same button you used before (for Stop and Play) out of your **Library** and position it on the **Stage**. Do it twice, and you'll have two new *instances* of that button. As before, you can put text above the buttons or not, as you prefer. Of course, the buttons will be easier to understand and use if they have text on (or near) them.

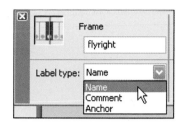

7 You will script the Fly Right button first, so select the button on the **Stage** that will make your object go from left to right. As before, make certain that only the one button is selected, then open the **Actions** panel (press F9).

Fig. 2.5.08 Flash MX 2004 has an extra menu in the **Properties** panel for a selected frame: Label Type. Make sure "Name" is selected in this menu when you are making a frame label that will be used to move the playhead, as in this exercise.

Note: If you added text to a button, you might select the text and *not* the button when you click once, intending to select the button. If that happens, you will see the message "Current selection cannot have actions applied to it" in the **Actions** panel. To correct the problem, make sure you select the button only. You may need to move the text to select the button, and then reposition the text. Or you could put the text in a new layer by itself.

8 With the button selected, and the **Actions** panel open, tell the button what to do. The script will look like this at first:

```
on (release) {
    gotoAndPlay(1);
}
```

You can simply *type* the script, if you prefer.

Flash MX: Click in the list at left to open "Actions", then open "Movie Control"; then *double-click* "goto."

If you have any extra lines in the script, delete them by using the minus button on the **Actions** panel ("Normal Mode" only). You should have *only* the three lines shown above.

Flash MX 2004: Click in the list at left to open "Global Functions." (a) Open "Movie Clip Control"; then *double-click* "on." A pop-up menu opens. On that menu, *double-click* "release." (b) Move your cursor to Line 2 in the **Actions** panel. (c) Open "Timeline Control"; then *double-click* "gotoAndPlay."

9 Here's where the frame labels (Step 3 and Step 5) come in. Inserting a frame label into your script is distinctly different in Flash MX 2004, so be sure to follow the instructions for the version of Flash you are using.

Flash MX: In the **Actions** panel, locate the menu field labeled "Type" ("Normal Mode" only) and *open* the menu. Select "Frame Label" on that menu. Now locate the menu field labeled "Frame" and open that menu (Figure 2.5.09). You should see the two frame labels that you created. (This is a convenient feature of "Normal Mode.") Select the label "flyright."

Flash MX 2004: You need to click into the script and *type* the frame label, with double quotation marks around it. Delete the numeral "1" and make sure you keep the parentheses. Type "flyright" (*with* the quotes) between the parentheses (Figure 2.5.10). Make sure you do not add any spaces or other characters.

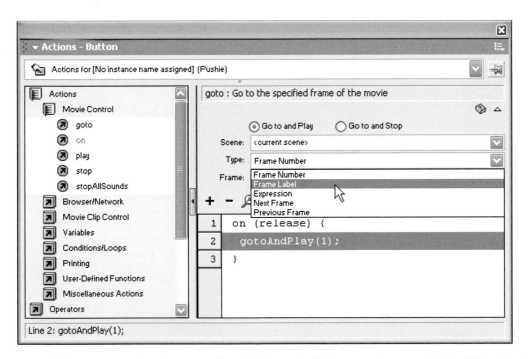

Fig. 2.5.09 In Flash MX's "Normal Mode," to use a frame label instead of a frame number, open the Type field in the Actions panel. Frame labels are more efficient than using frame numbers because if you add or delete frames, the frame number will change.

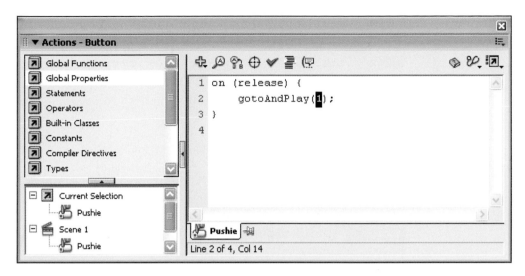

Fig. 2.5.10 In Flash MX 2004, you must delete the numeral and type the frame label directly into the script. Make sure to use quotation marks around the label, inside the parentheses.

Your script now reads:

```
on (release) {
    gotoAndPlay("flyright");
}
```

10 Save and test your movie: Ctrl-Enter (Win) or Cmd-Return (Mac).

What should happen: Whenever you click your Fly Right button, your object briefly disappears and then crosses the screen from left to right. The movie still loops after that, but each time you click the Fly Right button, you trigger the left-to-right sequence, starting at the frame you labeled in Step 3. What's really going on each time you click your Fly Right button: The movie **Timeline's** playhead instantly *jumps* to that labeled frame and plays from that point forward.

11 Select your other new button (your Fly Left button) and repeat Steps 7 through 10. The one difference: In Step 9, you will select or type "flyleft"—because you want your Fly Left button to send the playhead to the frame that you labeled "flyleft" (in Step 5).

When you test your movie, it still loops each time after you have clicked either one of your Fly buttons. You are going to address that in the next step.

12 In the final part of this exercise, you will add two stop() actions to the **Timeline**, so you can see how scripted buttons usually work in a more complex Flash movie. As always, make a new layer in the **Timeline** to hold the ActionScript. Name this layer "actions." It's best if this layer is always at the top of the stack, making it easy to find if you need to go back later and edit the movie.

13 In the "actions" layer of the **Timeline**, create a new keyframe (press F6) above the single keyframe that comes *in between* the two longer motion sequences in your movie. You want the second stop() action to happen at the point *between* the two motion tweens.

14 Select the first *keyframe* in the "actions" layer of the **Timeline** (Frame 1) and open the **Actions** panel (press F9). *Double-click* "stop" in the list at the left side of the panel to apply a stop() action to that frame.

15 Select the second *keyframe* in the "actions" layer of the **Timeline** (the one you made in Step 13). *Double-click* "stop" in the list at the left side of the **Actions** panel to apply a stop() action to that frame also. You should now have a stop() action in each of the two keyframes in the "actions" layer. Refer to Figure 2.5.11 to see how your Timeline should look.

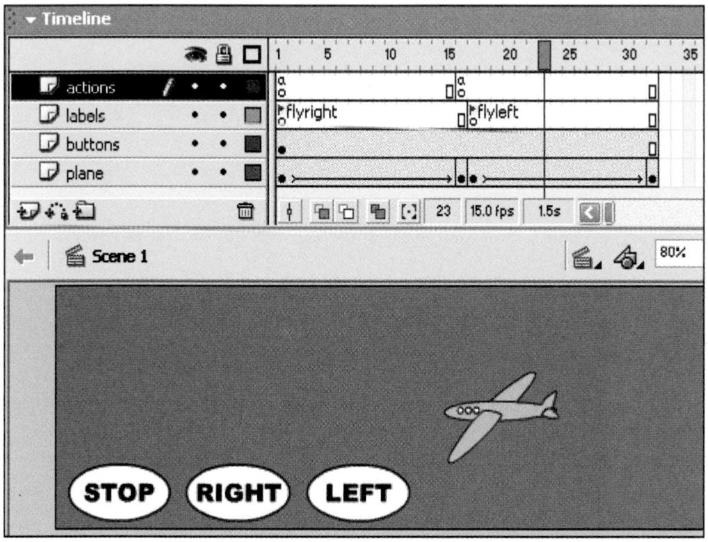

16 Save and test your movie: Ctrl-Enter (Win) or Cmd-Return (Mac).

What should happen: At first, *nothing* happens. You have a stop() action on Frame 1, so the movie does not play automatically. Whenever you click your Fly Right button, your object crosses the screen from left to right. Whenever you click your Fly Left button, your object crosses the screen from right to left. The movie does not loop

Fig. 2.5.11 Each of the two keyframes in the "actions" layer of the Timeline contains a stop() action. The stop() on Frame 1 means there is no motion until the user clicks a button. The stop() on Frame 16 means that after the plane flies from left to right, the motion stops. When the plane flies from right to left (Frames 17 to 32), the movie will automatically loop to Frame 1, where it will stop. Think about where you might want to put a stop() action *instead of* on Frame 1.

 now. The buttons control all the motion in the movie.

Note: Save this file so you can use it again in Lesson 6.

You should be dissatisfied with the way your Fly Right button works. Try to troubleshoot the problem. What's making the button not work, then work properly, then not work? (Hint: After the first time, you have to click your button *twice* to make your object move left to right.) Look at your **Timeline** and notice where the "flyright" frame label is—in Frame 1, where there is also a stop() action. Aha!

There are two ways to solve this problem: Either move the frame label "flyright" to Frame 2 and keep the stop() action on Frame 1, or delete the stop() action from Frame 1 and put it on the *final* frame of the **Timeline** instead. Then the left-to-right motion would occur once, without a button being clicked, when the movie is first opened, and you would no longer need to click the Fly Right button twice to get it going.

You now have the skills needed to control a more complex Flash movie made up of *many* sequences (not just two!) that can be viewed in any order. The combination of *frame labels* and buttons scripted with gotoAndPlay()—or gotoAndStop()—allows you to send the playhead to any part of the **Timeline**, at any point in the movie. This is an essential building block in interactive Flash movies.

Imagine how you can use this technique to give users what they want most—allowing them to select, for example, the inside view, outside view, or bird's-eye view, of a new sports stadium. All three views can exist on the same **Timeline**. Buttons send the users to the view they select. A bird's-eye view of *any* scene can have Flash buttons laid over it, so that when the mouse rolls over the scene, text pops up to tell the users what they will see if they click; when they click, they go to another position in the Timeline.

USING A FLASH BUTTON TO OPEN A WEB PAGE

If you need to open a Web page from within a Flash movie, you can use script on a button to do it.

```
on (release) {
    getURL("http://flashjournalism.com/");
}
```

Note that the "on (release)" handler script and the curly braces are typical of all the buttons you have made so far.

You can use either an absolute URL (beginning with *http://*) or a relative URL in the script. To ensure that the page opens in a new Web browser window, you can add an optional *target* after the URL:

```
getURL("http://flashjournalism.com/", "_blank");
```

Without the target, the new page will open in the current window, replacing your Flash movie. This could look pretty bad if you created a small pop-up window with no browser buttons on it to contain your Flash movie.

MAKING BUTTONS DO THINGS SUMMARY

The techniques demonstrated in this lesson are used in almost every Flash movie. Very few Flash journalism packages are simple animations that do nothing but play straight through from the first frame to the last frame. Users can stop and replay animated graphics and photo slideshows, or choose different options from a menu, or click on a map location and zoom in for a closer view. All these effects happen because a button has been scripted to respond when the user clicks it.

With ActionScript, you can make a Flash button control almost anything in your movie. The logical first steps are making the movie stop or resume playing. By creating frame labels that mark where a new action or activity begins in the **Timeline**, you can also script buttons to jump to any part of the movie, in any order.

The next time you click on something in a Flash movie and zoom in close, or a new animation begins, think about how that happens in the **Timeline**. The movie was probably stopped before you clicked. When you clicked, a script told Flash what to do. If the scene zoomed in, the script probably moved to a new frame inside a movie clip (the subject of Lesson 6). If an animation started, the playhead may have moved to a frame later—or *earlier*—in the main movie.

Consider this: A button doesn't need to look like a button. Some buttons in Flash are pictures of things, such as buildings, rooms, dots on a map, airplanes, or tanks. Some buttons in Flash are even invisible; that is, they lie over top of an image, with no graphics on the "Up" state frame, but the script on that invisible button works just as well as the script on a regular button that you can see.

Using buttons in your Flash movies allows you to add interaction and offer more choices to the users. Scripted buttons are essential to multimedia storytelling, so don't be afraid to use them.

CONCLUSION

In this lesson, you have learned to:

1 Use a frame rate of 15 fps for most Flash movies.

2 Create a separate layer in the Timeline to hold all your buttons.

3 Use multiple instances of the same button symbol.

4 Place ActionScript on a button using the Actions panel.

5 Switch between "Normal Mode" and "Expert Mode" in the Actions panel (Flash MX and earlier).

6 Use on (release) instead of on (press) for most button actions, because it gives the user a chance to back out.

7 Stop the Timeline with a button click by using the stop() action on a button.

8 Start the Timeline playing with a button click, by using the play() action on a button.

9 Use nextFrame() and prevFrame() to let users navigate through the Timeline one frame at a time.

10 Create a separate layer in the Timeline for frame labels.

11 Create a frame label on a keyframe, using the Properties panel.

12 Use frame labels instead of frame numbers.

13 Send the playhead to a specific labeled frame in the Timeline by using the gotoAndPlay() action on a button.

14 Add a stop() action to *more than one* keyframe in the Timeline, so that separate segments of the movie can be played independently.

15 Use a button to open a Web page outside the Flash movie.

Lesson 6

Movie Clips

The first time someone builds a complex Flash project, the Timeline stretches out forever and becomes very difficult to work with. At some point in the authoring process, the designer may discover Scenes and try using those to manage the huge, unwieldy sequence of frames. However, scenes don't make the Timeline more compact; they only break it up, the way a book is broken up into chapters. What works much better is to use movie clips for any motion or action that must be repeated or that must remain available to the user.

Movie clips are a type of symbol in Flash (the three types are graphic, button, and movie clip). They act like mini-movies inside the main movie, so they can play parallel to (or simultaneously with) other parts of the movie. With movie clips, a Flash movie that had 100 or more frames could be pared down to as little as one frame!

In this lesson, you'll create a movie clip in an otherwise empty Flash movie and learn to go into and out of Symbol Editing Mode, where you build the Timeline for the movie clip. Next, you'll add a new movie clip to the FLA file you created in Lesson 5 and learn how a movie clip interacts with the main movie's Timeline. Finally, you will create a movie clip controlled by a button that allows an object to slide into and out of the main movie at any time.

LESSON 6

There are three separate movie clip exercises below. While that may seem like overkill, movie clips offer incredible versatility to a Flash designer, and yet it takes some practice before working with them begins to feel comfortable. After you figure out how useful they are, you will begin to realize that almost every cool thing you've ever seen in a Flash movie was done with movie clips. They really are worth the effort.

Fig. 2.6.01 In Lesson 1, Step 11, you learned a technique using the Arrow/Selection tool to drag a line into a curved shape. Put two of these together, and you'll have the outline of an eye.

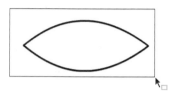

Fig. 2.6.02 Select a shape by dragging with the Arrow/Selection tool.

Fig. 2.6.03 When a grouped shape is selected, you see the blue bounding box around it. If you don't see the blue bounding box, you have not selected the shape.

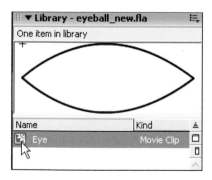

Fig. 2.6.04 Open the Library panel and *double-click* the movie clip there to go into Symbol Editing Mode.

Exercise 6.1: A Moving Eyeball

Start with a new Flash document and change your *frame rate* to 15 fps. See Lesson 1, Step 2 to review how to change the frame rate.

Don't be intimidated by all the steps in this exercise. Almost everything here should already be familiar to you, now that you are an intermediate Flash student. That's right—if you've gotten this far, you're not a beginner anymore. Congratulations!

1 Make an eye shape on the **Stage** (just the outline of an eye), as shown in Figure 2.6.01.

2 *Select* the entire shape by dragging a box around it with the **Arrow/Selection** tool (Figure 2.6.02). Then *group* the shape (Modify menu > Group). This prevents it being broken up inadvertently.

3 With the shape *still selected* (make sure you see the blue bounding box, as shown in Figure 2.6.03), Convert to Symbol (press F8). In the dialog box, choose "Movie clip," and give the symbol a sensible name, such as "eye" (without the quotes).

4 Double-click the symbol to enter **Symbol Editing Mode**. When you are in Symbol Editing Mode, you'll see a *blue arrow* on the left, just below the layers list in the **Timeline** in Flash MX (Figure 2.6.05A), or above the layers list in Flash MX 2004 (Figure 2.6.05B). To the *right* of the blue arrow, you'll see "Scene 1," and to the *right* of that, you'll see the name you gave to your movie clip. This was explained in detail in "Create a New Button," Lesson 4, Step 10, where you had button states on the Timeline; in a movie clip symbol, you do not have the four button states.

Warning: Make certain that your mouse cursor is *on the outline* when you double-click the eye shape. The cursor must be on a stroke or fill color within the symbol. If the cursor is on empty space (even if it is inside your outline), you *will not* enter **Symbol Editing Mode**. If your eye outline has no fill color, it can be very tricky to select it by double-clicking, so be sure you get it right. If it's just too difficult, open the **Library** panel (press F11), find the movie clip, and *double-click* it in the list there. That will put you into Symbol Editing Mode.

When you're in **Symbol Editing Mode**, you're working in an independent Timeline that operates *separately* from the main Timeline of the Flash movie. To return to the regular editing environment, *click the blue arrow.* (Alternatively, you can press Ctrl-E/Win or Cmd-E/Mac.) To enter Symbol Editing Mode for a movie clip (or a button), double-click the object. You can double-click it either on the **Stage** or in the **Library**.

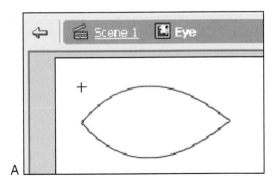

A

5 In **Symbol Editing Mode**, you have one layer in this movie clip's **Timeline**, and it's holding the eye shape you made. Rename that layer to "eye outline."

B

6 Make a *new layer* and name it "eyeball." See "Animating Two Symbols," Lesson 2, Step 13, if you need a review of how to add and name a layer.

Fig. 2.6.05 The little blue arrow (seen in Flash MX, A; seen in Flash MX 2004, B) is your ticket back to the main movie Timeline. When you see the blue arrow, you know you're in Symbol Editing Mode, where you have the movie clip's Timeline *instead of* the main movie Timeline. You can return to the main movie Timeline by clicking the blue arrow or by clicking "Scene 1."

7 Click Frame 1 in the new "eyeball" layer and draw an eyeball on the **Stage**. It's quite important that you're in a different layer, because the eyeball is going to move while the eye outline (below it) stays in place.

8 *Select* the entire eyeball shape and Convert to Symbol (press F8). In the dialog box, choose "Graphic," and give the symbol a name, such as "eyeball." You must make it a symbol, because you're going to use a motion tween on it. (The eye outline will not move, so it's okay just to group it on its layer as you have done.)

9 Select and drag the eyeball to a position *inside* the eye outline, on the left side in the outline. (Of course, the eyeball and the outline are still on separate layers, but it should look as if the eyeball is inside the outline.)

10 Click in Frame 2 of the "eyeball" layer on the **Timeline**, and add a new keyframe (press F6).

11 Click in Frame 3 of the "eyeball" layer on the **Timeline**, and add a new keyframe there, too (press F6). You now have three keyframes with the eyeball in the same position.

12 Click in Frame 2 of the "eyeball" layer and then move the eyeball on the **Stage** to the *right* side of the eye outline (still inside the outline).

WHAT IS A SCENE?

Flash allows you to divide a movie into pieces, the way a book is divided into chapters, by adding scenes to your movie. Scenes play automatically in the order in which they are listed in the **Scene** panel (Flash MX: Window menu > Scene; Flash MX 2004: Window menu > Design Panels > Scene). Flash automatically names your scenes in order (Scene 1, Scene 2, etc.), but you can rename any scene by double-clicking it in the panel. You can rearrange your movie by changing the order of the scenes; simply drag them into a new order in the Scenes panel. The panel also allows you to add, duplicate, or delete scenes.

It's important to understand that scenes are *nothing like a movie clip*; a scene remains part of the main movie **Timeline**. Only one scene can play at a time. Scenes cannot be dragged onto the **Stage**, because scenes are not symbols. A movie clip is a symbol, so it can be positioned and resized, appear in multiple instances, and be manipulated with ActionScript in ways that a scene cannot. A movie clip appears in the **Library**. A scene appears only in the Scenes panel.

Flash automatically creates "Scene 1" for you when you start a new file. If you do nothing to change it, the movie continues in Scene 1 forever. You may never need to use any additional scenes at all.

Do not make any new scenes as part of this exercise, because you may find it confusing.

Frame 1   Frame 2   Frame 3

Fig. 2.6.06 After you complete Step 13, the three frames in your movie clip Timeline should look like this.

13 Click in Frame 1 of the "eye outline" layer and add two regular frames (press F5 twice). This extends the **Timeline** on the lower layer and makes the outline of the eye visible under all the frames in the upper layer (Figure 2.6.06).

14 File menu > Save.

15 Click Frame 1 in the "eyeball" layer and add five frames (press F5 five times).

16 Click the next keyframe (it should be Frame 7 now) and add five frames there, too (press F5 five times).

17 Click any frame in the first gray block of frames on the "eyeball" layer and apply a motion tween. Refer to Lesson 2 ("Animating Two Symbols," Step 5) if you need a review of how to add a motion tween.

18 Click any frame in the second gray block of frames on the "eyeball" layer and apply a motion tween there, too.

19 Now the eyeball is moving left to right and right to left, but the "eye outline" layer must be extended again (it is still only three frames long). To do that easily, click in the "eye outline" layer under the *last keyframe* in the "eyeball" layer (that should be Frame 13), and press F5 *once* (Figure 2.6.07). Frames are automatically added to fill out the layer from Frame 1 up to the frame position you clicked. This is a very useful technique to know!

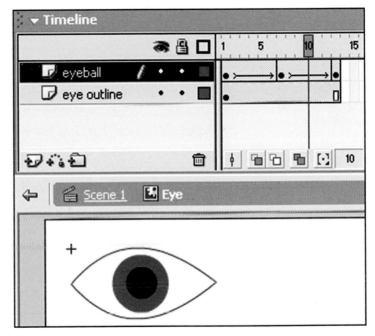

20 Exit from **Symbol Editing Mode** by clicking the blue arrow pointed out in Step 4.

21 Save and test your movie: Ctrl-Enter (Win) or Cmd-Return (Mac).

Fig. 2.6.07 After you finish Step 19, your completed movie clip Timeline should look like this, with two layers and two motion tweens.

What should happen. The single eye is looking endlessly left, right, left, right.

22 Just for fun (and really, to demonstrate how movie clips actually work), open the **Library** (press F11) and *drag several instances* of your "eye" movie clip onto the **Stage**. You have only one layer and one frame on your main movie **Timeline**, but that's okay. Put all the "eye" instances there together. The more, the merrier.

23 Save and test your movie: Ctrl-Enter (Win) or Cmd-Return (Mac). Kind of creepy, isn't it? But think about what is happening, and how useful it could be in various situations in Flash animations.

24 One last trick: Back on the **Stage**, select one of the instances of the "eye" movie clip and "flip it." Here's how: With the object selected, open the Modify menu, move the cursor to "Transform," and select "Flip Horizontal" from the submenu.

25 Save and test your movie: Ctrl-Enter (Win) or Cmd-Return (Mac). Compare the movement of the "flipped" eye with the others.

You may not be able to think of a good use for a roving eye, but now you should understand one of the important ways in which a movie clip can be used. Whenever a Flash designer needs a repeated motion in a movie, the best way to meet that need is to take the repeated motion off the main movie Timeline and put it *inside* a movie clip symbol.

Imagine you have a map showing the locations of key events at a crime scene. Each location is marked by a dot that pulses bright and dark, bright and dark. What is that dot? It's a movie clip. Every dot on the map is an instance of the same movie clip (and one that's pretty simple to make). Maybe you think that dot should be a button, so the user can click it and read about the crime scene, one location at a time. Okay. Make a movie clip of a dot that pulses, and then put that movie clip into the "Up" frame inside a button symbol. Or, alternatively, build the movie clip *inside* that "Up" frame. Are you starting to get some new ideas?

Exercise 6.2: A Moving Background

For this exercise, use the final file you made in Lesson 5 ("Buttons That Let You Jump on the Timeline"). If you're concerned about possibly ruining it, save the FLA file with a new filename and use the new file here. The reason to use that file, which you have already built and tested, is that it will effectively demonstrate how the movie clip plays independently of your main movie Timeline. Alternatively, you can download a copy of the FLA from the Web site for this book.

1 Make a new layer in the **Timeline**, above the "buttons" layer and below "labels." Name the new layer "movie clip." (See "Animating Two Symbols," Lesson 2, Step 13, to review how to add a layer.)

2 Click Frame 1 on the new "movie clip" layer and draw a cloud on the **Stage**. It's important that you're in an empty layer to do this. (An easy way to draw a cloud: Select the **Oval** tool, select *white* for the fill color, and select *no color* for the stroke color. The "no color" symbol is at the top right corner of the color palette. Then draw about six different white ovals over-lapping one another for an instant puffy cloud.)

Note: Make sure your cloud has a *fill color*. If you draw the cloud with the pencil tool, the inside of the shape will be *empty* until you fill it (using the Paint Bucket tool, for example).

---

3 *Select* the entire cloud shape (Figure 2.6.08) and Convert to Symbol (press F8). In the dialog box, choose "Movie Clip" and give the symbol a name, such as "clouds" (eventually, there will be more than one cloud).

4 Double-click the shape to enter **Symbol Editing Mode**. Symbol Editing Mode is explained in Exercise 6.1, Step 4.

Make sure you see the blue arrow!

5 Inside the movie clip, the cloud is still just a shape. You are going to tween the cloud, so you must make it a *graphic symbol* here, inside the movie clip. The entire cloud shape should still be selected. (If it isn't, select it.) Convert to Symbol (press F8), choose "Graphic," and give the symbol a name, such as "cloud." (It's okay with Flash if you have a movie clip symbol named "clouds" and a graphic symbol named "cloud," but Flash will not let you give *both* objects exactly the same name. You can give layers any name, but symbols are more particular.)

Fig. 2.6.08 Selecting a shape can be tricky if it has no fill, or if you click the stroke color (outline) only. The cloud on the left has only its stroke color selected. The cloud on the right is selected in its entirety. If you Convert to Symbol and the entire symbol is not selected, the symbol will contain *only* the selected parts. So make sure you really have selected *everything* before you Convert to Symbol!

6 You have one layer in your movie clip **Timeline**. Rename that layer to "cloud 1."

7 Add two *new layers* to the movie clip **Timeline**. Name one "cloud 2" and the other "cloud 3." You must have *three layers*, because you are going to move *three clouds* by applying a motion tween to each one (Figure 2.6.09). Remember that any object that is motion tweened must be *alone* on its layer.

8 Click in Frame 1 of the "cloud 2" layer to select it.

9 Open the **Library** (press F11). You should see both your "clouds" movie clip and your "cloud" graphic listed there. Make sure you can see

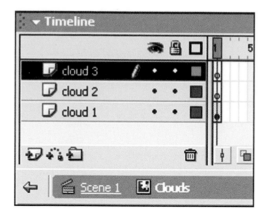

Fig. 2.6.09 You will have three layers inside the movie clip, with one moving cloud on each layer.

which one is the movie clip and which one is the graphic. Grab the *graphic* and drag it to the **Stage**, close to the other cloud that's already there.

10 The new cloud on the **Stage** should be selected (if it's selected, it has a blue bounding box around it). If it's not, click it *once* to select it.

11 Change the look of your second cloud: Select the **Free Transform** tool from the **Tools** panel and *drag* the tiny square "handles" that appear around the cloud. You can squish it, stretch it, rotate it, change its size—or all four.

Note: The separate clouds dragged out from the **Library** are *instances* of the same graphic symbol—just as the multiple eyes in the previous exercise were all *instances* of one movie clip symbol (Figure 2.6.10). In Flash, you can transform an *instance* (with the **Free Transform** tool or the **Transform** panel) without affecting the *symbol*. This technique is far superior to making a new cloud symbol, because the Flash file size *does not increase* if you use three (or 300) *instances* of the same graphic symbol. If you created a new cloud symbol (even if you duplicated this one) the Flash file size *would* increase.

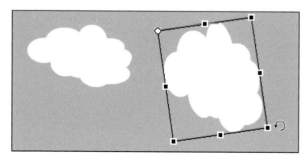

Fig. 2.6.10 The cloud on the left is the original, as dragged out of the Library. The cloud on the right is another instance of the same symbol in the midst of its transformation with the Free Transform tool.

12 File menu > Save.

13 Click in Frame 1 of the "cloud 3" layer to select it, and then repeat Steps 9 through 12 to create a third cloud that looks different from the other two clouds. Each cloud is in its own layer inside this movie clip (remember, you are still in **Symbol Editing Mode**), so you will be able to make each cloud move with a motion tween.

14 Think for a moment about the *frame rate* of your movie and how quickly you want to see the three clouds move across the screen. For example, if the frame rate of the Flash movie is 12 fps, and you want the clouds to take 2 seconds to cross the screen, then select Frame 24 in the **Timeline**. If your frame rate is 15 fps, then 2 seconds requires 30 frames.

Select the *same single frame* in all three layers by *shift-clicking* down the column—that is, shift-click once on Frame 24 in the "cloud 3" layer, then shift-click once on Frame 24 in the "cloud 2" layer, then shift-click once on Frame 24 in the "cloud 1" layer. With all three frames selected, press F6 *once* to extend the Timeline out to Frame 24 on all three layers (Figure 2.6.11). Notice that you also

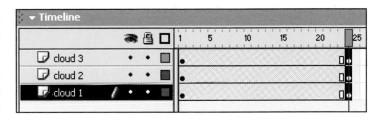

Fig. 2.6.11 Each of the layers ends with a keyframe, because you will be adding a motion tween on each layer.

created a new keyframe at the end of each layer (because you pressed F6, and not F5).

15 Without touching the **Timeline** at all (leave the playhead where it is, on Frame 24), *select* a cloud (click it just once) and drag it off the **Stage** and far to the *right*, into the gray area that is off-screen in the final Flash movie. Repeat for each of the clouds. In the final animation, the clouds will float off the Stage to the right.

16 You can apply a motion tween to all three layers if you *shift-click* in the middle of the top layer and then *shift-click* below that frame in each of the other layers. With three frames selected (one in each layer), open the "Tween" menu in the **Properties** panel and select "Motion." Each layer gets its own separate motion tween (Figure 2.6.12).

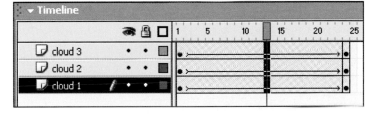

Fig. 2.6.12 You can apply a motion tween to three layers all at once if you shift-click each of the layers.

Another way to add a motion tween: Right-click (or Control-click/Mac) on the frame to get a pop-up menu; select "Create Motion Tween" from that menu.

17 Save and test your movie: Ctrl-Enter (Win) or Cmd-Return (Mac). You should see the clouds start in the middle of the screen, then move off-screen to the right, then pop up in the middle of the screen again, and repeat. This is *not what you want* to see in your final movie, but we did it this way to demonstrate something about movie clips: The *frame* where you begin the movie clip (Frame 1 inside the movie clip) and the *position* of everything in that frame are very important!

18 You do not have to redo any work—just reposition *the entire movie clip*. First, make sure you are *not* in Symbol Editing Mode anymore. If you see the blue arrow, click it to *return to the main Timeline*. (Because you just

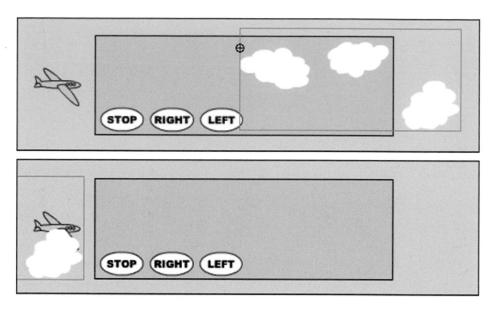

Fig. 2.6.13 Top: The "clouds" movie clip in its original position, which is too far to the right. The clouds need to begin offstage to the left instead. (You can see the registration point of the movie clip; it is seen here as a crosshair in a circle. Your movie clip may have its registration point in another place.) Bottom: The "clouds" movie clip in its proper location after it was dragged to the left. After you reposition the movie clip, you will probably need to add frames in the middle of all three motion tweens in the Timeline. You may also need to change the position of each cloud in the final keyframe.

tested your movie, the arrow should be grayed out, not blue. If the arrow is gray, then you are already in the main Timeline.)

19 Reposition the "clouds" movie clip by grabbing and dragging it off the **Stage** to the far left side (Figure 2.6.13). To grab the movie clip that contains the clouds, click *once* on any cloud (not on the space between the clouds). When you do that, you should see the blue bounding box *surrounding all three clouds.* You may need to drag the movie clip in two steps (drag, let go; then drag again) to get it where you want it to be, because it's probably very wide.

Note: Make certain you reposition the *movie clip instance* first, rather than changing the position of objects *inside* the movie clip. If the blue bounding box surrounds all the clouds, then you know you have selected the whole movie clip.

WHAT IS A REGISTRATION POINT?

A movie clip may become difficult to work with if you move objects away from the original *registration point* of the movie clip symbol. On the **Stage**, when a symbol is selected, a tiny crosshair indicates the symbol's registration point.

Fig. 2.6.14 The registration point for a symbol is set when you Convert to Symbol. The black square determines its location in a three-by-three grid, relative to the symbol's bounding box.

The registration point of any symbol can be set when you first create the symbol: A three-by-three grid in the Convert to Symbol dialog box provides nine options for the location of the *registration point* (Figure 2.6.14). Click any square in the grid to set the registration point for the new symbol.

For most symbols, you will want the registration point to be either in the *center* or in the *upper left corner*. Putting it in the upper left corner, for example, makes it easy to position a symbol relative to the upper left corner of the Stage.

The role of the registration point will be covered in more detail in the next exercise and in Lesson 7.

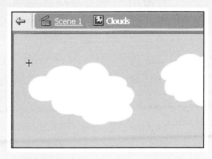

Fig. 2.6.15 Inside the movie clip, the registration point appears as a tiny crosshair (upper left).

20 Save and test your movie: Ctrl-Enter (Win) or Cmd-Return (Mac).

What should happen: The clouds appear on the left side, float across the screen to the right, disappear offscreen, reappear on the left, and repeat. The buttons you made in Lesson 5 still work the same way; notice that they do not control the clouds at all. This is a key point: Try all three of your buttons; they have *no effect* on the flying clouds.

Timing in the movie clip: If the clouds move too quickly or too slowly for your taste, edit the motion tween sequence inside the movie clip. To do that, *double-click* any cloud to go back into **Symbol Editing Mode**, where you will see the clouds' three-layer Timeline again, and you can add or delete frames in any layer there. You should be starting to get the hang of this; can you recognize your "clouds" movie clip as an independent movie inside your main movie?

Final frame position in the movie clip: You can also change the position of the clouds in the last frame. If they do not drift offscreen on the right side, you may need to change their position in the final frame of each layer by dragging them farther to the right. Remember, you can change the position of an object only in a *keyframe* (where you see the black dot). Even though your clouds are in a movie clip, they are moving in a very simple way—left to right, from offstage at left to offstage at right.

It usually takes some time to get the motion in a full-screen movie clip to be just the way you want it, especially when you're new at this. The more you work with movie clips, the easier it becomes. It's usually best to work with the movie clip in place on the **Stage**, where you can see the other objects on the Stage in a dimmed view, because it helps you get the position right for objects in the movie clip. If you open a movie clip symbol from the **Library** instead, you cannot see how it looks in relation to the rest of the movie, and it may be harder to edit.

Movie clip position in the layer stack: Another thing you may want to change: If you followed the instructions in Step 1, the clouds may cover your buttons as they cross the screen, cover your moving object when you click a button to make it appear, or both. To put the clouds *behind* everything else in the movie, *grab* the *"movie clip" layer* in the main **Timeline** and *drag* it down to the position *below* all the other layers. If you want it to be behind the buttons but in front of the other object, drag the "movie clip" layer to the position between the "buttons" layer and the bottom layer.

Think of the layers in the Timeline as a stack of things, with things in the upper layers covering things in the lower layers. You can rearrange your layers at any time.

Button control of movie clips: The SWF you completed here demonstrates an important fact about movie clips: The Stop button you made in Lesson 5 has no effect on the movie clip. Test it and see. Notice that the button still works on the original object that's on the main Timeline, but it does not stop the clouds. That's because the Timeline of a movie clip really is *independent* of the main Timeline. It is not controlled by the ActionScript that controls the main Timeline.

You *can* use a button on the main Timeline to control a movie clip, but you must add another bit of ActionScript to the button to make it "talk to" the movie clip directly. You'll learn how to do that in the next exercise.

Exercise 6.3: A Sliding Panel

Many Flash journalism packages use a sliding panel to show the production credits for the package or to let the users see additional information about the material onscreen. The panel itself is inside a movie clip. The buttons that control the panel may be inside or outside the movie clip; in this exercise you will put the button *outside* the movie clip (on the main Timeline) so you can learn how to control a movie clip from the main Timeline.

For this exercise, start a new file in Flash.

1 Make a rectangular shape that is about one-third the size of the **Stage**. It can be horizontal or vertical. Put text or a shape on it so that it's not blank.

2 Select the entire shape and Convert to Symbol (press F8). Choose "Graphic" and give the symbol a name, such as "panel." By enclosing the rectangle *and everything on it* in a single symbol, you make it something that can be moved as a single object. If you didn't do this, you would have to move the rectangle and the text (or shape) on separate layers, which would be awkward at best.

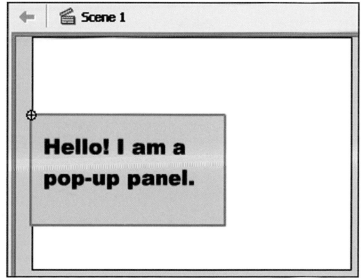

3 Imagine how you want the panel to look in relation to the **Stage** when the panel is visible or "up." Drag it into that exact position (Figure 2.6.16).

Fig. 2.6.16 This panel will slide out from the left edge of the Stage. It is shown here in the visible or "up" position.

4 With the symbol still *selected* (you will see the blue bounding box around the symbol), put it into a movie clip: Convert to Symbol (press F8), choose "Movie Clip," and give the movie clip symbol a name, such as

Fig. 2.6.17 Select a registration point for the movie clip by clicking any block in the three-by-three grid. In this case, the point will be the upper left corner of the movie clip symbol.

"Sliding Panel." In this case, it is useful to choose a specific *registration point* for the symbol while you are in the Convert to Symbol dialog box (Figure 2.6.17). The *upper left corner* will work best for this sliding panel.

5 *Double-click* the panel to go into **Symbol Editing Mode** for the movie clip. Be careful that you did not click deeper and get into editing mode for the graphic symbol! Look for the blue arrow, "Scene 1," and the name of the movie clip ("Sliding Panel"). If you see the name of the graphic symbol to the right of that, then you went too deep. If you're too deep, click the blue arrow *once* to go up one level, where you'll see *only* the name of the movie clip symbol.

6 In the movie clip, you will position your panel in each of three *keyframes*, make two motion tweens (slide in and slide out), and apply two frame labels and two stop() actions. (This is very much like what you did in the main Timeline in "Preliminary Work," Lesson 5.) If you pause now and think about it, maybe you can visualize the Timeline that will result. Try it and see. You need to get used to planning how to build objects like this one; whenever something moves independently of the main Timeline, you will plan how it will operate on its own movie clip Timeline.

First, you will need three layers. Name the first layer in your movie clip Timeline "panel" (without the quotes), and add two new layers. Name the top layer "actions" and the middle layer "labels." (You know what will go in each of these layers, right?)

7 Create a new *keyframe* in the "panel" layer: Click Frame 2 in that layer and press F6. This copies the contents of Frame 1 into Frame 2.

8 Click Frame 1 in the "panel" layer and drag the panel to the place where it should be when it is invisible or "down." You may want to leave a bit of the edge visible, or you may want to hide it completely (Figure 2.6.18).

9 To ensure smooth sliding action: Look at the **Properties** panel and find the two fields labeled "X" and "Y" on the left side. If you are sliding your panel horizontally, the "Y" value should be the same numeral in both keyframes (to keep the vertical position the same throughout). If you are sliding the panel vertically, the "X" value should be the same numeral in both keyframes (to keep the horizontal position the same throughout).

Note: Select the symbol (click it once) to see its "X" and "Y" fields in the **Properties** panel. If the symbol is not selected, or if more than one object is selected, you will not see the "X" and "Y" fields. "Y" refers to the vertical position of the selected object, and "X" refers to the horizontal position of the selected object.

Fig. 2.6.18 In Frame 1 in the movie clip Timeline, the panel is in its offscreen position. A small part of the right-hand edge will be visible when the panel is offscreen or "out." That is the portion that overlaps the white area of the Stage.

10 You need to have your panel in exactly the same position when it starts to slide *out* and when it completes the slide *in*. An easy way to do that is to *copy the frame* you just worked in (Frame 1) and paste it into the Frame 3 position (in the same layer, of course). To do that, *right-click* (Ctrl-click/Mac) on Frame 1. On the menu that pops up, select "Copy Frames." Then *right-click* (Ctrl-click/Mac) on Frame 3 in the "panel" layer of the **Timeline** (there's nothing there yet). On the menu that pops up, select "Paste Frames." This will paste an exact copy of everything in Frame 1 into Frame 3—a very handy function to know (Figure 2.6.19)!

11 To create the sliding action, add several frames (press F5) to the first keyframe (Frame 1) and also to the second keyframe. Apply a motion tween to each of the two frame sequences you made. You have done this in previous lessons; for a review, see Lesson 2.

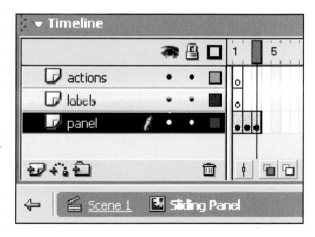

Fig. 2.6.19 The movie clip Timeline after Step 10.

12 You can test the motion and timing of this movie clip alone by pressing Enter/Return. If it's too fast, add frames to each motion tween. If it's too slow, delete frames. The sliding action is just a simple animation. If the panel seems to jump around, go back to Step 9 and check your "X" and "Y" properties in each *keyframe*.

13 File menu > Save.

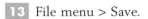

14 In the "actions" layer, you need two stop() actions: The first one must be on Frame 1, because the panel must stay out of sight until the user clicks a button. The other stop() action must be on the frame where the panel is fully extended or visible onscreen. Remember to make a *keyframe* (press F6) for each stop() action (Frame 1 is already a keyframe).

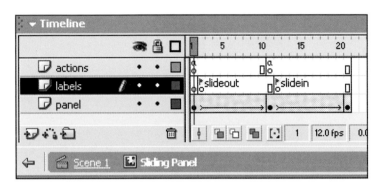

15 In the "labels" layer, you need two labels: The first one will be "slideout" and the second will be "slidein." The "slideout" label should be in Frame 2 (*after* the first stop() action frame). The "slidein" label should be in the frame *after* the second stop() action frame (Figure 2.6.20). (In case you're wondering: Yes, some people do put frame labels in the same layer with actions, but it can become messy.) For a review of how to put a label on a frame, see "Buttons That Let You Jump on the Timeline," Lesson 5, Steps 2 and 3.

Fig. 2.6.20 The movie clip Timeline after Step 15.

Note: It's considered most professional to extend all layers to the same final frame in the Timeline. If the last frame in the "panel" layer is Frame 21, for example, then both the "actions" layer and the "labels" layer should also have 21 frames. The Timeline looks neater this way, and it's also easier to "read."

---

16 File menu > Save.

If you test the movie now (Ctrl-Enter/Win or Cmd-Return/Mac), you'll see that the sliding panel never slides. Well, you put a stop() action on Frame 1, didn't you? That panel won't go anywhere until you write some ActionScript to control it! You could put a button on the movie clip Timeline, but instead you will put a button on the main Timeline in this exercise, so you can learn how to control a movie clip *from* the main Timeline.

17 Exit **Symbol Editing Mode** (click the blue arrow) and check to make sure you are back on the main **Timeline** now. There is only *one frame* there (Figure 2.6.21).

18 Before you can control the movie clip, you must give the *instance* on the **Stage** a name. If you filled the Stage with eyeballs in Exercise 6.1, Step

21, you can appreciate the fact that the movie clip *symbol* name by itself cannot tell us *which* instance on the Stage to control. If you need to control a movie clip instance with ActionScript, you must give the *individual instance* a unique name after you have placed it on the Stage.

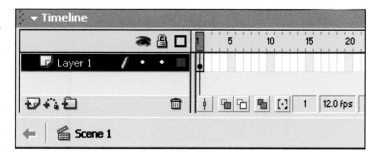

Fig. 2.6.21 The main Timeline of the entire movie, after the movie clip is complete and the two buttons have been dragged onto the Stage. The main Timeline has only one frame and one layer. The single frame contains the movie clip instance and also two buttons. None of these objects move on this Timeline, so they do not need to be on separate layers.

This is very similar to putting a label on a frame: Select the *movie clip instance* on the **Stage** (click it only *once*; you will see the blue bounding box if the movie clip is selected), then look at the left side of the **Properties** panel for the "Instance Name" field. Click into the field and type a name, such as "slider_mc" (without the quotes). Tab out of the field to make sure the name sticks (Figure 2.6.22).

Note: Macromedia suggests that we add a suffix to an *instance name* so that the **Actions** panel can give us pop-up code hints (in Flash MX, these are available only in "Expert Mode"). The suffix for a movie clip instance is *_mc*; the suffix for a button is *_btn*. A graphic symbol cannot have an instance name. The other suffixes are listed in the Flash Help files. In Flash MX, look under Writing Scripts with ActionScript > "Using code hints." In Flash MX 2004, open ActionScript Reference Guide > Writing and Debugging Scripts > Using the ActionScript editor > "Writing code that triggers code hints." Using the suffix can be very helpful.

---

19 You will create *two* buttons (View and Hide) on the **Stage** to control the movie clip. You can open Flash's Common Libraries > Buttons (find it on the Window menu; in Flash MX 2004 it's hiding under "Other Panels") and drag two ready-made buttons onto the Stage. (The buttons in the Ovals folder are nice; you could use green for View and red for Hide.)

20 First you will script your View button. Select the button on the **Stage** and open the **Actions** panel (press F9). In "Stop and Play Buttons," Lesson 5, Step 7, you learned to script a button to *do something* "on (release)." That's the first step for this button too, so see if you can do it from memory. If not, check back in Lesson 5. Your script should look like this:

```
on (release) {
}
```

Note: In Flash MX 2004, put your mouse cursor *before* the closing curly brace so the rest of the script is written at the right place (between the curly braces).

---

21 Now you'll need to venture into a new section of the list on the left side of the **Actions** panel. The steps depend on which version of Flash you are using, so be sure you're following the directions for your version.

Flash MX: Go down the list to Objects > Movie > MovieClip > Methods. Under "Methods," *double-click* "gotoAndPlay." Your script now reads:

```
on (release) {
    <not set yet>.gotoAndPlay();
}
```

In "Normal Mode" (Flash MX only), you now have fields in the **Actions** panel where you can type the name of the movie clip *instance* (in "Object") and the *frame label* (in "Parameters") you created in Step 15 (Figure 2.6.23). Remember that you're scripting the View button, so you want the movie clip to play the motion tween sequence you labeled "slideout." When you type the name of your movie clip instance, do not use quotation marks. When you type the frame label, however, you must enclose it in quotes (Figure 2.6.24).

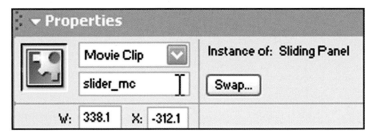

Fig. 2.6.22 The Instance Name field is visible in the Properties panel if a movie clip instance has been selected on the Stage. Click into the field and give the instance a unique name.

Your final script on your View button will look like this:

```
on (release) {
    slider_mc.gotoAndPlay("slideout");
}
```

You can simply type this script if you switch to "Expert Mode," as explained in Lesson 5.

Fig. 2.6.23 Flash MX: After you double-click "gotoAndPlay" in this part of the Actions list, you'll see how it differs from the other version of this action, which you first used in Lesson 5.

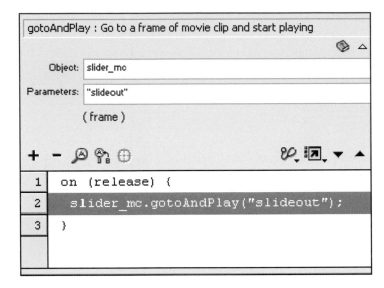

Fig. 2.6.24 Flash MX: You need to know the *instance name* you gave to your movie clip in Step 18 and also the name of the frame label you put on Frame 1 of the movie clip in Step 15. The movie clip is the Object, and the frame label is the Parameter. The Object is not enclosed in quotation marks. The Parameter requires quotation marks.

Flash MX 2004: In the **Actions** panel, start by opening the Insert Target Path dialog (Figure 2.6.25). In that dialog, find and *double-click* the movie clip *instance name* you wrote in Step 18. This inserts the path to the movie clip you want to control with this button.

Now you need to type *immediately after* the path text (do not insert any spaces): Type just a period. A menu should pop up as soon as you type the dot; the menu shows you the possible commands that can follow this target. (You may have heard of "dot syntax." Well, this is the "dot.") On the menu, find and *double-click* "gotoAndPlay" (Figure 2.6.26). Your script now reads:

```
on (release) {
    this.slider_mc.gotoAndPlay(
}
```

After that open parenthesis, the script must tell Flash where to go and what to play *inside your movie clip Timeline*. That means you want to get the frame label you wrote on Frame 2, Step 15. What *was* that frame label? It would

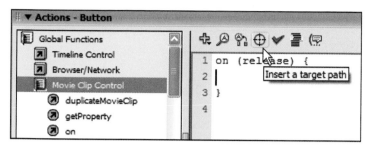

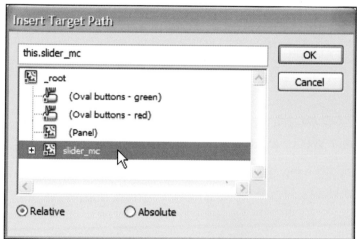

Fig. 2.6.25 Flash MX 2004: Open the Insert Target Path dialog from the Actions panel. In the dialog box, double-click the instance name of your movie clip (here the name is "slider_mc").

be nice if Flash allowed you to look it up, but no such luck (Figure 2.6.27). If you happen to remember that it is "slideout," you can type it now. Be sure to *include the double quotation marks* around the word.

There is one nice feature that will save a little time and effort; it's called "pinning" the script in the **Actions** panel. Before you leave the button script to go and look for your frame label down inside some movie clip on the **Stage**, you can "pin" the button script you're working on by clicking once on the "Pin active script" icon in the

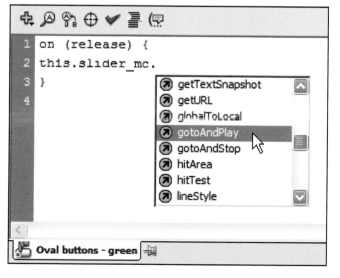

Fig. 2.6.26 Double-click "gotoAndPlay" on the pop-up menu.

bottom of the Actions panel (Figure 2.6.28). Don't forget to "unpin" the script when you're finished with it.

Your final script on your View button will look like this:

```
on (release) {
    this.slider_mc.gotoAndPlay("slideout");
}
```

You can simply type this script, if you prefer.

Note: Sometimes ActionScript requires the use of the keyword "this" inside an event handler. It is not *required* in this case, but Flash MX 2004 writes "this" (followed by a dot) whenever it might be needed, when you select script from the list in the Actions panel. Older versions of Flash do not add "this" when the script works without it. So while the two versions of Flash write this script differently, it works the same way.

---

22 Okay, the button has been scripted! Save the file and test your movie (Ctrl-Enter/Win or Cmd-Return/Mac).

What should happen: Each time you click your View button, the panel slides into view. Your Hide button does not work yet.

23 The last thing to do is script your Hide button to make the panel slide back in. Remember that you labeled that motion tween sequence "slidein" (Step 15). Repeat Steps 20 through 22 for the Hide button, then save and test your movie.

What should happen: Each time you click your View button, the panel slides into view. Each time you click your Hide button, the panel slides away and out of sight. There's a problem, though. Click your View button two or three times in a row to see what it is. Uh-oh. Now click your Hide button two or three times. Same problem.

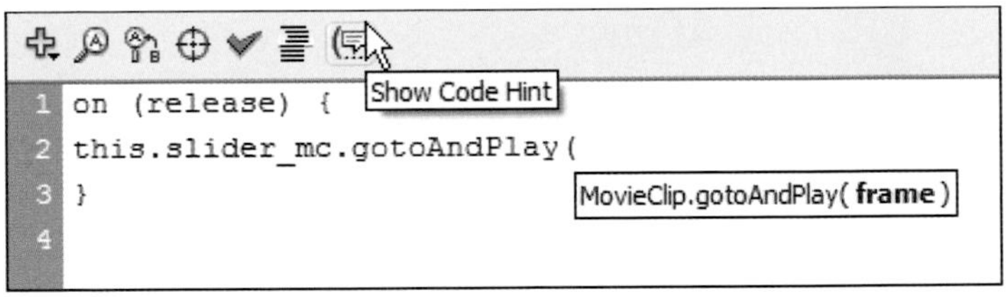

Fig. 2.6.27 You can view a "code hint" to help you figure out what to type next, but unfortunately, you cannot look up the frame label you made in Step 15. You have to remember it or go back into your movie clip Timeline and copy it there.

There is a quick way to fix this problem, and it requires four lines of Action-Script inside your movie clip **Timeline**. To make this extra simple, just type the code.

24 Go into **Symbol Editing Mode** for your sliding panel, and make sure you see the movie clip **Timeline**, which has two *keyframes* in the "actions" layer.

USING QUOTES IN ACTIONSCRIPT

Beginning Flash authors may be confused about when to use quotes around a word in ActionScript and when to put a name before "gotoAndPlay." If you compare the script in Exercise 6.3 to the one in Exercise 5.3, you'll see that the structure there is parallel to this one, and the frame label there is enclosed in quotes, as it is here. However, there is no movie clip instance name in Lesson 5, because the button there was on the *same Timeline* as the frame label. Here, however, the frame label is inside a movie clip, so it is the Timeline of the *movie clip instance* you're "talking" to (or scripting to).

It's all about Timelines. If `gotoAndPlay("something")` refers to the Timeline where a button is, then the action stands alone. If it refers to another Timeline, then the script must supply a path to that Timeline *before* "gotoAndPlay." So consider the Timeline you're on and whether the script you're writing needs to look for *another* Timeline.

The reference to another Timeline is *not* enclosed in quotation marks, and it *must* be followed by a dot. The only things allowed inside the parentheses after "gotoAndPlay" are a frame label (in quotes) *or* a frame number (no quotes).

25 Select the first keyframe in the "actions" layer. Open the **Actions** panel (press F9). Below the `stop()` action, type these two lines:

```
_parent.hide_btn._visible = false;
_parent.view_btn._visible = true;
```

26 Select the other keyframe in the "actions" layer. In the **Actions** panel, below the `stop()` action, type these two lines:

```
_parent.view_btn._visible = false;
_parent.hide_btn._visible = true;
```

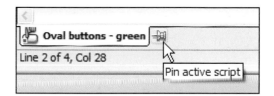

Fig. 2.6.28 The pin icon at the bottom of the Actions panel lets you hold a script in the window while you look at other parts of the movie.

27 You have probably figured out that this script will make your buttons visible or not visible when the movie clip playhead reaches that frame. Have you also realized that a button that is *not visible* cannot be clicked? Aha! But there's something else you must do, or this won't work. Think about that script. Is anything in your movie *named* "view_btn" or "hide_btn"? No. You need to *name your button instances* if you want this script to work. Naming a button instance is exactly like naming a movie clip instance, though, so you already know how to do it. (If you forgot, look at Figure 2.6.22.) So, go on—name each of your buttons to match what your script calls them.

28 Save and test your movie: Ctrl-Enter (Win) or Cmd-Return (Mac).

What should happen: When you first play your movie, you see only the View button. After you click that, and the panel slides into view, the View button disappears and the Hide button becomes visible. After you click the Hide button, and the panel slides in, the Hide button disappears and the View button becomes visible.

Note: When ActionScript uses the special term "_parent," the script looks at the next Timeline "up" in the movie's nested structure of Timelines. In this exercise, the main Timeline is the "_parent" of the "slider_mc" movie clip Timeline.

At this point, you may be wondering how to put the button on the sliding panel itself, inside the movie clip. This lesson is long enough already, so you won't see how to do that here. If you're curious, though, you will find alternative versions of this same movie on the book's Web site. Download the FLAs and look at the script on the buttons, and you will quickly figure out how it's done.

If you put the button into the movie clip, with the sliding panel, keep in mind what you read about Timelines in "Using Quotes in ActionScript" in this lesson. Also consider that if you make a new *keyframe* in a button layer, you can completely *change the script* for the button on that new keyframe. (Don't place a button on the same layer as the sliding panel itself, though, or you will break the motion tween!)

Peek at Lesson 8 to see examples of a single button that toggles its functionality (a Pause/Play button and a Mute/Unmute button).

MOVIE CLIPS SUMMARY

Movie clips are one of three types of *symbol* in Flash. (The other two types: graphic and button.) A movie clip has its own Timeline that plays independently of the movie's main Timeline. A movie clip's Timeline can be stopped on its Frame 1 and controlled by ActionScript outside the movie clip—this functionality is key to many effects seen in professional Flash projects.

Movie clips can also be used for simple visual effects that repeat (or loop), such as a pulsating dot on a map, a moving eyeball, or a scrolling background. In such cases, no ActionScript is needed. The movie clip will be visible for as long as it is on the main Timeline. (If you make a new keyframe and delete the movie clip there, the movie clip will disappear.) Any movie clip will loop unless a `stop()` action exists on its Timeline, or ActionScript outside the movie clip tells it to stop, using its *instance name*. A movie clip on the **Stage** can be controlled *only* if it has an instance name.

A movie clip can contain many layers and many objects. Its Timeline can be longer (or shorter) than the movie's main Timeline. However, the *frame rate* of a movie clip is always the same as the frame rate of the main movie. You can't change that. The background color of a movie clip is also dependent on the main movie.

A movie clip can be placed on the Stage in the same layer with other movie clips and/or buttons, unless a motion tween will be applied to the movie clip instance itself. That is, if you move an entire movie clip on the main Timeline, then the movie clip must be alone on a layer, the same as any object in a motion tween.

CONCLUSION

In this lesson, you have learned to:

1 Convert three different kinds of shapes or objects on the Stage to a movie clip: a grouped shape (Exercise 6.1), an ungrouped shape (Exercise 6.2), and a graphic symbol (Exercise 6.3). Think about it and you'll realize that none of these was actually "converted"; each one was simply *put into* a movie clip. The shape or object remained what it was *inside* the movie clip.

2 Group a shape, so it does not get cut apart by other shapes.

3 Recognize the blue bounding box, which shows you that a grouped shape or a symbol is selected on the Stage.

4 Enter Symbol Editing Mode (by double-clicking a movie clip on the Stage).

5 Exit Symbol Editing Mode (by clicking the blue arrow or the Scene name).

6 Add a new layer in a movie clip Timeline.

7 Create a new graphic symbol inside a movie clip.

8 Add frames and keyframes in a movie clip Timeline.

9 Add a motion tween in a movie clip Timeline.

10 Place multiple instances of a movie clip on the Stage at one time, all in the same layer.

11 Transform a movie clip instance on the Stage.

12 Place a movie clip in a layer that extends to the end of the main movie Timeline, so that the movie clip is always present (the "clouds" clip).

13 Drag the layer containing a movie clip up or down in the Timeline to position the movie clip in front of or behind other objects on other layers.

14 Reposition a movie clip instance on the Stage to coordinate objects and movement inside the movie clip with objects in the main Timeline.

15 Set the registration point for a symbol.

16 Position an object on the Stage using the X and Y coordinates in the Properties panel.

17 Use the X and Y coordinates to ensure a smooth sliding motion for an object.

18 Copy a keyframe and paste its contents into a new frame.

19 Assign an instance name to a movie clip instance on the Stage.

20 Assign instance names to buttons on the Stage.

21 Script a button on the main Timeline to play a labeled sequence in a movie clip.

22 Use script on a frame to make a button not visible and not functional.

23 Create a stationary object with a continuously moving element (the "eye" movie clip).

24 Create a continuously scrolling background scene (the "clouds" movie clip).

25 Create a sliding panel that the user can control.

Lesson 7

Working with Photos

Flash allows you to *import* various types of images, and it distinguishes between two types: vector and bitmap. Photographs are always bitmaps. An image you create *within* Flash is always a vector image, whether it is a simple rectangle or a complex diagram. Both bitmaps and vectors can be imported from outside Flash.

- A *vector* image can be scaled (made larger or smaller) with absolutely no difference in quality: The lines remain smooth and the colors remain solid. The SWF file size does not increase significantly if you use gigantic vector images instead of small ones.

- When a *bitmap* image is scaled larger, the quality decreases: The edges become jagged, and the individual pixels become larger, making the entire image appear blocky and unnatural. Bitmaps with large file sizes can increase the final SWF file size significantly.

The file types JPG, GIF, and PNG are all bitmaps when imported into Flash, as well as the file types BMP, EPS, and PDF. You may be familiar with these file types from previous Web or photo work you have done. Bitmaps are always created and edited in programs outside Flash. For a complete list of the file formats that can be imported into Flash, see the Flash Help files.

You can import vector images to Flash from some other programs that create vector images; these include Macromedia's Fireworks and FreeHand and Adobe's Illustrator. You can export SWF files from these programs, which can then be imported to Flash.

Now that you know the basic terminology, just remember that Flash uses the term "bitmap" very broadly—and the term includes *more* than photos. Photos are *always* bitmaps in Flash, no matter what file format they are in when you import them. Photojournalists typically save their photo files in the JPG format, but photos can be saved in other formats, too.

ABOUT THIS LESSON

This lesson explains tasks that require you to use some features and properties of Flash that novice users don't necessarily need or know much about. These are tasks of particular interest to photographers and photojournalists. After you have worked through all the exercises, you should be able to do just about anything you envision doing with photos in Flash.

This lesson includes several exercises and informational sidebars. You may not want to work through each one of the exercises at this time, but note that the first two exercises, about importing and optimizing photo files, contain information that can make *a very significant difference* in the final file size and download time of your Flash movies. You may want to simply *read* those two exercises rather than work through them, but it's important not to skip them.

Depending on your reasons for using a photo in Flash, you may be concerned about having the highest possible image quality. For example, a background image with text over top of it will not need to be sharp and perfect—so you could select a lower *Quality setting* and save a lot of kilobytes in file size. Whether you want your photos to look perfect or not, this lesson will show you how to get the results you want in the final SWF.

LESSON 7

Before you begin this lesson, make sure you have at least *two versions* of the *same* photo file. Edit the photo in Photoshop or a similar program. Crop or resize the photo to a *width* of between 500 and 600 pixels and a *height* of between 300 and 400 pixels. (If the photo is vertical rather than horizontal, make sure the height is *no more than* 400 pixels.)

For the first version, save the photo in the JPG file format with a quality of medium or high; this is the *compressed* version of the file. For the second version, save the same photo as a BMP; this is the *uncompressed* version of the file.

PHOTO EDITING TIPS

1. Decide on the screen size (width and height) of your Flash movie *before* you edit your photos. (See Lesson 1, Step 2, if you need instructions.) That way, you'll know the maximum width and height for your photos.

2. Because almost 40 percent of Internet users still use a screen resolution of 800 × 600 pixels (http://www.thecounter.com/stats/2004/May/res.php), the best practice is to set the width and height of your Flash movie to accommodate that resolution. The largest dimensions considered acceptable: 700 pixels (width) by 400 pixels (height). This size allows the SWF to be displayed in the browser window without requiring the user to scroll. (The buttons at the top of the browser window take up a lot of space, which is why 400 pixels is the maximum height for the Flash movie.) If you're using a pop-up window without browser buttons, menu bar, scrollbars, or status bar, you can go up to 750 × 450.

3. You cannot efficiently edit a photo in Flash, although you can launch an external program and edit a photo after it has been imported to Flash. You should make sure the photo looks as you want it to look *before* you import it. That includes the *exact width and height* you want the photo to be within the Flash movie.

4. If you save your photos at a larger width and height than necessary in the Flash movie, you are unnecessarily increasing the SWF file size and the user's waiting time during the download. This is not a good practice!

5. Decide whether you will put text or other elements (such as buttons) *above*, *below*, or *beside* your photos. For example, if your Flash movie is 400 pixels high and your photos are also 400 pixels high, there will be no space left for anything above or below the photo. Also consider whether some text will be longer than one line. How much space will you need for the longest text?

6. Flash will not display progressive JPGs. ("Progressive" is an option you can select when you save an image as a JPG file in Photoshop and similar programs.) If you want to use a progressive JPG in Flash, you must first *resave it* in another program (e.g., Photoshop) as a non-progressive JPG.

Exercise 7.1: Importing and Optimizing Compressed Photo Files

Start with a new, empty file in Flash.

1 Change the size of the Flash movie to 600 pixels (width) by 400 pixels (height). Change the frame rate to 15 fps. Change the background color, if you want it to be a color other than white. See Lesson 1, Step 2, if you need instructions for how to do this.

2 Open the File menu and select "Import to Library." (In Flash MX 2004, it's on the Import submenu.) A dialog box opens, allowing you to find the photo file on your computer that you want to import to Flash. Find the *compressed* (JPG) photo file you prepared, select it, and click Open.

Note: If you want to import *more than one* photo, you can Ctrl-click (Win) or Cmd-click (Mac) each photo filename to select several files and import them all at one time. You can shift-click to select a contiguous set of files.

Flash MX 2004 Note

The File menu now has a submenu under "Import"; on the submenu you'll find "Import to Stage," "Import to Library," and "Open External Library."

3 Open the **Library** (press F11). You will see the imported photo file there. Click *once* on the photo filename to see a thumbnail image of your photo in the window at the top of the Library panel.

4 To place the photo on the **Stage**, *drag it* from the **Library** to the Stage.

Note: You can import a photo directly to the **Stage** by selecting "Import" instead of "Import to Library" from the File menu (or "Import to Stage" in Flash MX 2004). Alternatively, you can copy a photo outside Flash and *paste* it on the Stage. In professional practice, however, you are more likely to import a set of photos to the **Library** at one time and place them on the Stage afterward. No matter which method you use to import photos to Flash, all photos will appear in the Library.

5 To center the photo easily on the **Stage**, open the Align panel from the Window menu. Make sure the photo is *selected* (click it once). In the

Align panel, first click the Align/Distribute to Stage button (labeled "To Stage"). Then click the second button in the top row of the panel (Align horizontal center). Then click the fifth button in the top row of the panel (Align vertical center). These two buttons allow you to position the photo in the exact center of the Stage (Figure 2.7.01).

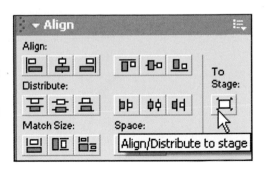

6 Save your movie as "phototest1.fla" and test it: Ctrl-Enter (Win) or Cmd-Return (Mac). Your photo should look good!

7 You don't want your final Flash file to be so huge that users refuse to wait for it to download—and that is a very real concern when you put photos into your movie. One solution is to keep all your photos *outside* the SWF and load them externally. You will learn how to do that in Lesson 10. Here, we need to look at how to optimize photo files that are *inside* the Flash movie, because sometimes you have good reasons for the photos to be internal.

In this case, you have a *compressed* (JPG) file in your movie. Take a look at the original file outside Flash and see how large the file is (in kilobytes, or KB). For example:

Fig. 2.7.01 The Align panel provides one-click options for aligning objects. If you want to align objects in relation to the entire Stage, click the button as shown. If you want to align objects relative to one another, unclick that button first. When the button appears "pushed in," all the alignments made will be relative to the entire Stage.

Table 2.7.01

Filename	Width × Height (pixels)	File Size (outside Flash)	JPG Quality (Photoshop)
deliverybike.jpg	500 × 365	64.6 KB	High (60)

Then look at the file size of the SWF file you just tested in Step 6. For the file containing the photo *deliverybike.jpg*, the SWF file size is 64.7 KB. Because there is nothing in the FLA except the photo (in one frame), you can infer the direct relationship between the file size of the photo and the file size of the SWF.

8 One way to reduce the file size of the SWF, of course, is to make the photo file size smaller *before* you import it to Flash. Alternatively, you can change the amount of compression that Flash applies to the photo. It is *very important* to understand that the methods for doing this are different for *compressed* and *uncompressed* files, so keep in mind that you are working with a *compressed* file (JPG) in this exercise! (Later in this lesson you will learn the procedure for an uncompressed file and compare the results.)

In the same file you saved above, *right-click* (Ctrl-click/Mac) the photo file in the **Library**. Select "Properties" from the pop-up menu. The Bitmap Properties dialog box opens (Figure 2.7.02). *Uncheck* the box labeled "Use imported JPEG data." Doing that allows you to change the Quality setting for this photo. Type "50" (without the quotes) in the Quality field, then click OK (Figure 2.7.03).

Note: If you check "Allow smoothing," Flash will use anti-aliasing to smooth the edges of objects in the bitmap. In most photos, this has no effect on file size, either checked or unchecked. Checked, it will reduce pixelation but may make your photo appear blurry.

9 Save your movie with a *new* filename, such as "phototest2.fla," and test it: Ctrl-Enter (Win) or Cmd-Return (Mac). Your photo will not look as good as the first version of this file; it will be blurrier, more pixelated, or both. You can open the two SWFs side by side to compare the quality of your photo in each version. (The difference between the two photos may be subtle if the original was not of good quality.)

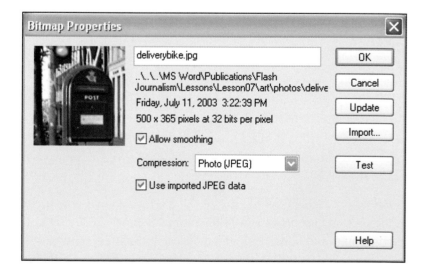

Fig. 2.7.02 The default setting for JPG file compression in Flash. This keeps both the quality and the file size of the imported photo (in JPG format) the same as it was outside Flash.

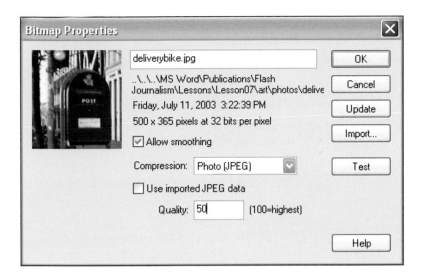

Fig. 2.7.03 Change the amount of compression applied to this single JPG image. A higher number means better quality and a larger file size. A lower number means worse quality and a smaller file size. Click the Test button to see the new file size.

Look at the file size of the second SWF. For the file containing the photo *deliverybike.jpg*, the file size of the second SWF is 29.9 KB, compared with 64.7 KB for the first SWF (the file with no additional compression applied by Flash). You can see that reducing the quality to 50 percent in the Bitmap Properties dialog makes a significant difference.

Table 2.7.02

Filename	JPG File Size (outside Flash)	SWF File Size (default Bitmap Properties)	SWF File Size (Bitmap Properties Quality = 50%)
deliverybike.jpg	64.6 KB	64.7 KB	29.9 KB

In many cases, you will not want to sacrifice so much image quality. However, just changing the Quality setting to 90 percent in the Bitmap Properties dialog for each imported JPG can greatly reduce the SWF file size for a file containing *several* photos!

Obviously, there's a tradeoff to consider. You would like to make the file size of the SWF as small as possible so that it downloads quickly. However, in most cases you would not want to publish blurry or pixilated photos.

If you want to prove it, conduct a test similar to the one above: With one JPG image on the Stage in a one-frame movie, save an FLA two ways: (1) use the default JPEG Quality setting in the Publish Settings dialog, and

(2) use a much smaller number in the JPEG Quality setting in the Publish Settings dialog. This number has no effect on *either* the quality of the imported JPGs *or* on the file size of a SWF that contains only *compressed* imported images.

Note: The *only way* to change the quality of imported JPGs *within Flash* is to change the Quality setting in the Bitmap Properties dialog for each *individual* JPG file in the **Library** of the FLA file—as you have just done. A common misconception is that you can change the quality of imported JPGs in the Publish Settings dialog (explained in Lesson 3 and in the following exercise), but that is not true. You can use the Publish Settings dialog to change the quality and compression of *uncompressed* image files, such as BMP files, but *not* JPG files.

Exercise 7.2: Importing and Optimizing Uncompressed Photo Files

In this exercise, you will do almost exactly the same thing you did above, but you will use an *uncompressed* file (a BMP) instead of a *compressed* file (JPG).

There is a very good reason for this exercise: You may find that you can control the *quality* of imported photos better if you import *uncompressed* files and adjust the compression settings within Flash. This will be quite important to photojournalists, although it may seem less important to other people.

1 Open your file named "phototest1.fla" from the exercise above and immediately save it as "phototest3.fla" (to allow for comparison later).

2 Open the File menu and select "Import to Library." A dialog box opens, allowing you to find the photo file you want to import to Flash. Find the *uncompressed* (BMP) photo file, select it, and click Open.

3 Open the **Library** (press F11). You will see *both* photo files there—your JPG from the previous exercise *and* your freshly imported uncompressed file.

4 Select the photo on the **Stage**. (That image should still be the JPG from the previous exercise.) As always, *click only once* to select an object on the Stage.

5 With the photo selected on the **Stage**, look in the **Properties** panel and find the Swap button. Click it. In the Swap Bitmap dialog box, you can *select the other file* in your **Library**—the one you just imported (Figure 2.7.04). This feature is very convenient, because it places the new image in exactly the same position as the one it replaces. No need to center the new one as long as the two photos are the same width and height.

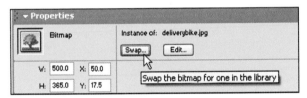

Fig. 2.7.04 Open the Swap Bitmap dialog, which allows you to replace one image with another.

6 You can change the compression and quality of this uncompressed image in exactly the same way you did in the previous exercise, and *in another way* as well. Before you try it, check the file size of the uncompressed file outside Flash and see how large it is (in kilobytes, or KB). For example:

Table 2.7.03

Filename	Width × Height (pixels)	File Size (outside Flash)	Depth (Photoshop)
deliverybike.bmp	500 × 365	534 KB	24 bit

This is typical—an uncompressed photo file will always be *much* larger than the compressed (JPG) file.

You might expect the resulting SWF file to be just as large as this image file, because that is what you saw in the previous exercise. To see whether that's how Flash really works, follow the instructions in the next two steps.

7 In the **Library**, right-click (Ctrl-click/Mac) the filename of the *uncompressed* photo. Select "Properties" from the pop-up menu. The Bitmap Properties dialog box opens. Make sure the box labeled "Use imported JPEG data" is *checked*. Then click OK. (You *could* change the settings here, but you're about to see a different method for changing image compression and quality.)

8 Open the File menu and select "Publish Settings." In the Publish Settings dialog, click the tab labeled "Flash" (Figure 2.7.05). In the box labeled "JPEG Quality," type "80" (without the quotes). Click OK.

9 Save and test your movie: Ctrl-Enter (Win) or Cmd-Return (Mac). Then check the file size. For example:

Table 2.7.04

Filename	BMP File Size (outside Flash)	SWF File Size (JPEG Quality = 80%)
deliverybike.bmp	534 KB	53 KB

If you open "phototest1.swf" and "phototest3.swf" side by side and compare the two, you may decide that the photo quality in "phototest3.swf" is just as good as, or even slightly better than, the photo quality in "phototest1.swf"—and yet the file size of "phototest3.swf" is likely to be smaller (your results may vary, depending on your photo).

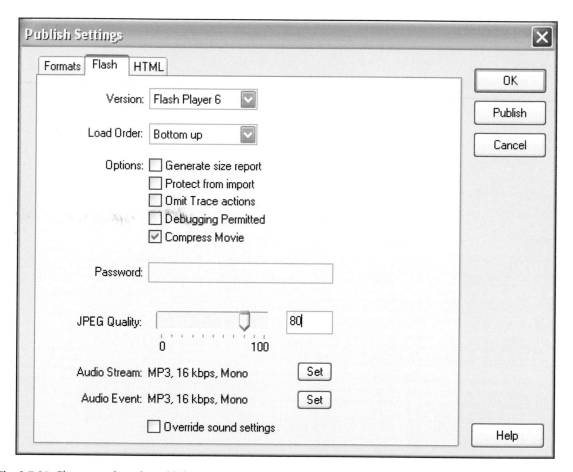

Fig. 2.7.05 Changes made in the Publish Settings dialog affect all uncompressed images in the FLA file, unless the individual Bitmap Properties for an image have been changed through the Library. Changes made in the Publish Settings dialog do not affect compressed images (JPGs).

Table 2.7.05

File Type	Change Quality for One	Change Quality for All
JPG (compressed)	Right-click filename in Library. Select "Properties." In Bitmap Properties, uncheck "Use imported JPEG data." Change number in Quality field.	Cannot be done.
BMP (uncompressed)	Same steps as above. In Bitmap Properties, uncheck "Use document default quality." Change number in Quality field.	File menu > Publish Settings. Select the Flash tab. JPEG Quality: Change number in this field, or use the slider. Note: If Bitmap Properties were changed (see left), those settings override these for just that one image.

At a glance: Changing the quality settings for imported images.

Note that if you import only *uncompressed* images (no JPGs) to your FLA file, you will change the quality of *all* the imported images in the movie when you change the JPEG Quality setting in the Publish Settings dialog (as you just did in Step 8). That can be rather convenient when you have a lot of imported images in your Flash movie!

You can override the JPEG Quality setting in the Publish Settings dialog for any single uncompressed image by opening the Bitmap Properties dialog (right-click/Windows or Ctrl-click/Mac on the image filename in the **Library**).

BITMAP PROPERTIES: PHOTO VS. LOSSLESS

In the Bitmap Properties dialog, you can choose either "Photo (JPEG)" or "Lossless (PNG/GIF)" for compression type. The logic behind your selection should follow the standard practice in Web page design: Any image with complex tones or shading should be saved as a JPG (all photos; any complex illustrations with realistic detail); images with mostly flat color should be saved as a GIF (cartoons, simple line drawings with no shading, most text and buttons).

When in doubt, save the original *uncompressed* file twice (using Photoshop and its "Save for Web" option, for example)—once as a JPG and once as a GIF—and compare the image quality *and* the file size of each one.

The PNG format is not widely supported by today's Web browsers, so it is rarely used on Web pages. Flash *does* support PNG files, so you might also experiment with the results of saving as a PNG, which is an option in Photoshop's "Save for Web." Some photojournalists have been quite happy with the results they get when saving photos in the PNG-24 format and importing them to Flash.

Exercise 7.3: Moving Photos in Flash

Now that you've learned how to get photos into Flash, you can animate them easily. This widely used technique can be mistaken for video. The next time you see a moving photographic image on a Web site, think about whether you could achieve the same effect with one or more still photos. The answer is often yes!

For this exercise, you can use the same file you saved in the previous exercise ("phototest3.fla"). One imported bitmap image is enough to complete this exercise. The photo you use in this exercise should be at least 400 pixels wide or high.

1 Begin with a one-frame **Timeline** and one photo centered on the **Stage**, as in the previous exercise. (The imported photo should be an uncompressed BMP.) Set the *frame rate* to 15 fps to make it easy to follow the instructions in this exercise.

2 Select the photo on the **Stage** (click it once) and *convert it to a graphic symbol* (press F8). This step is absolutely crucial, because any object you move in Flash *must* be a symbol. While you have the Convert to Symbol dialog open, make sure the *registration point* for this object is in the *upper left corner*. (The reason for this will become clear very soon!) If you need to change the registration point, you must do it now: Click the box in the *upper left corner* of the three-by-three matrix, as shown in Figure 2.7.07.

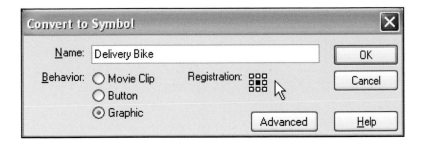

Fig. 2.7.06 The registration point will be in the center of the object if you do not change it here. The black square shows the location of the registration point relative to the entire area of the symbol.

Fig. 2.7.07 By clicking the box in the upper left corner of the three-by-three matrix, you set the registration point to be at the upper left corner of the object.

3 Add 4 seconds' worth of frames to the **Timeline** (your frame rate should be 15 fps, so click Frame 60 in the Timeline, then press F5 once to add 59 frames).

4 Add a keyframe at Frames 15, 30, 45, and 60: Select a frame and press F6; repeat for each of those frames. (If you have a frame rate other than 15 fps, create keyframes at 1-second intervals equal to *your* frame rate instead.)

5 Change the *width* of your movie to *half* the width of your photo, and change the *height* of the movie to *half* the height of your photo. For example, if your photo is 400 pixels wide and 300 pixels high, your new movie size should be 200 pixels wide by 150 pixels high. (See Lesson 1, Step 2, if you need instructions for how to change the size of the Flash movie.)

6 Save your file with a new name (such as "phototest_motion.fla").

Note: The **Properties** panel normally shows the X and Y coordinates for the registration point of the selected symbol (Figure 2.7.08), which in this case is in the upper

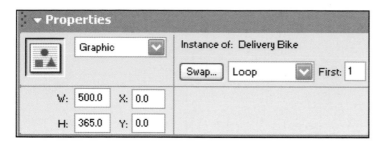

Fig. 2.7.08 Find the X and Y coordinates for a selected object on the Stage by looking in the Properties panel. After changing the X or Y value, press the Tab key to make the new value stick.

left corner. If the registration point were in a different location, you could see (and change) the X and Y coordinates for the symbol's upper left corner (instead of the registration point) by *selecting* that corner in the **Info** panel.

7 You already know how to move an object by dragging it to a new position on the **Stage**, so you will use a different technique in this exercise. You will position the photo by changing its X and Y coordinates. Flash makes this very simple, because when you have *selected* an object on the Stage (click it *once* to select it), you will see the X and Y coordinates for that object on the left side of the **Properties** panel.

Changing an object's position this way is useful, because it ensures smooth motion and smooth transitions.

So, first click on Frame 1 in the **Timeline**. Then select the photo on the **Stage** (click it *once* to select it). In the **Properties** panel, *double-click* inside the field labeled "X" and type "0" (the numeral zero, without the quotes). Press the Tab key.

Now the cursor should be inside the field labeled "Y," and all the characters in that field should be selected. Type "0" again (the numeral zero, without the quotes) and press the Tab key (Figure 2.7.09).

Note: Pressing the Tab key to leave the field is *necessary* because the new value does not always "stick." Sometimes Flash adds seemingly random tenths to the value, but pressing Tab ensures that you get round numbers.

You should be able to see that the *upper left* corner of your photo is now exactly aligned with the upper left corner of the **Stage**. (You can't see the Stage anymore, because your photo is covering it completely.)

Note: If you did not set the registration point for this symbol to the *upper left corner* of the symbol (see Step 2), this may not work properly. The registration point of the symbol will be at the X and Y coordinates shown in the **Properties** panel.

Fig. 2.7.09 Frame 1. X: 0, Y: 0. Frame 60 is the same as this one.

Fig. 2.7.10 Frame 15. X: 0, Y: −181.0. This photo is 365 pixels high.

Fig. 2.7.11 Frame 30. X: −249.0, Y: −181.0. This photo is 500 pixels wide.

Fig. 2.7.12 Frame 45. X: −249.0, Y: 0. The four images show what will be visible in the final Flash movie—the photo will slide up, then left, then down, then right.

8 Click in Frame 15 in the **Timeline**. Now you will reposition the photo to align the *lower left* corner of the photo with the lower left corner of the Stage. (After you apply the motion tween, the photo will appear to slide straight down.) The X coordinate stays the same, because X is the horizontal position of the object, and you are not moving it horizontally yet (Figure 2.7.10).

The Y coordinate must be the *negative* of half the *height* of your photo, plus 1. If your photo is 300 pixels high, for example, change the Y value to −149. Y represents the top-edge position of this object, because the *registration point* is at the top edge. You are moving the object upward from 0, and that is why Y is a negative number. When an object's registration point is below 0, the Y coordinate is a positive number.

Zoom in (use the Zoom tool) on the bottom edge of the photo and check to make sure you have covered the Stage.

Fig. 2.7.13 When you test your movie, the default view may be full screen. This is not the real size of your SWF.

Fig. 2.7.14 In "Test Movie" mode, if you restore the screen (the opposite of maximize), you will see the true size of your SWF (the window on the right).

9 Apply a motion tween to the first sequence in this movie. That is, click once in the **Timeline** anywhere between Frames 1 and 15 and select "Motion" from the **Properties** panel. (See "Animating Two Symbols," Lesson 2, Step 5, if you need a review.)

10 Save and test your movie: Ctrl-Enter (Win) or Cmd-Return (Mac).

Note: If your Flash application window is maximized (full screen), the test will not look very impressive. You'll see the *entire* photo moving in that case (Figure 2.7.13)—but remember, your **Stage** is actually *smaller* than the photo. If you restore (the opposite of maximize) the *Flash test window* (Figure 2.7.14), you'll get an accurate impression of how the motion works, because you'll see the movie at its actual size. (In Windows, the restore button is the middle one in the upper right corner of the window. In the Mac OS, it's the middle button in the upper left corner of the window.)

11 Time to move on to Frame 30, the third keyframe in your **Timeline**. Here, you will reposition the photo to align the *lower right* corner of the photo with the lower right corner of the Stage. (After you apply the motion tween, the photo will appear to slide leftward.) The Y coordinate must match the one in Frame 15, because Y is the top-edge position of the object, and that should not change in this frame. In other words, the vertical position remains the same, and so Y must be the same.

The easiest way to set this up is to click on Frame 15 in the Timeline, click once on the photo, double-click in the Y field, and copy the numeral there. Then click Frame 30 in the Timeline, click once on the photo, double-click in the Y field, and paste.

The X coordinate in Frame 30 must be the *negative* of half the *width* of your photo, plus 1. If your photo is 400 pixels wide, for example, change the X value to −199. X represents the left-edge position of the object, because the *registration point* is at the left edge. You are moving the object left from 0 (or backward), and that is why X is a negative number. When an object's registration point is to the right of zero (or forward), the X coordinate is a positive number.

Zoom in (use the Zoom tool) on the right edge of the photo and check to make sure you have covered the Stage.

12 Apply a motion tween to the second sequence in this movie. That is, click once in the **Timeline** anywhere between Frames 15 and 30 and select "Motion" from the **Properties** panel. *As an alternative*, you can right-click (Ctrl-click/Mac) in the Timeline and select "Create Motion Tween" from the pop-up menu. You may find this to be a more convenient way to apply a motion tween.

Table 2.7.06

Axis	Direction	Coordinate Represents	Negative	Positive
X	Horizontal	Horizontal position of object's registration point relative to the Stage	Registration point to left of zero point	Registration point to right of zero point
Y	Vertical	Vertical position of object's registration point relative to the Stage	Registration point above zero point	Registration point below zero point

13 Save and test your movie: Ctrl-Enter (Win) or Cmd-Return (Mac). Remember the size concern described in Step 10.

It's okay that this movie is looping. There is no need to change that.

14 Frame 45 is the last place where you need to change the coordinates, and in fact you need to change only the X coordinate. You will reposition the photo to align the *top right* corner of the photo with the top right corner of the Stage.

Now that you understand that the Y coordinate refers to the top edge of this object, you know that Y is 0 if the top of the photo matches the top of the Stage.

So what will the X coordinate be? Is the left edge of the photo in the same position as a previous frame? Yes—the photo is sliding straight up from its position in Frame 30. So the value of X for the photo in Frame 45 is the same as the value of X for the photo in Frame 30.

Click on Frame 30 in the Timeline, click once on the photo, double-click in the X field, and copy the numeral there. Then click Frame 45 in the Timeline, click once on the photo, double-click in the X field, and paste.

15 Apply a motion tween to the third sequence in this movie.

16 Save and test your movie: Ctrl-Enter (Win) or Cmd-Return (Mac).

17 In Frame 60, both the X and Y coordinates of the photo must be 0. Change them now. This allows you to complete a continuous loop by simply adding a motion tween in the fourth sequence of this movie.

18 Right-click (Ctrl-click/Mac) in the **Timeline** between Frame 45 and Frame 60 and select "Create Motion Tween" from the pop-up menu.

19 Save and test your movie: Ctrl-Enter (Win) or Cmd-Return (Mac).

20 You should notice a momentary *hesitation* in your loop. This occurs when the loop goes from Frame 60 back to Frame 1—because the two frames are *identical*. While it may seem trivial, this hesitation can appear awkward in some movies, depending on the frame rate and the size of the photo being tweened.

Fixing this is very simple: Click on the frame immediately *before* the final keyframe (in this case, Frame 59) and create a *new keyframe* there (press F6). Then right-click (Ctrl-click/Mac) once on Frame 60 and select

MOTION TWEENS, BITMAPS, AND SYMBOLS

If you place a photo on the **Stage** and then apply a motion tween—*without* converting it to a symbol first—Flash creates a graphic symbol for you. Although this may seem convenient, actually it is bad: It will increase the file size of the final SWF if you move the same photo more than once.

Each time you apply a motion tween to that "unconverted" photo, an *additional* graphic symbol is created. Flash will name these "Tween 1," "Tween 2," "Tween 3," etc. If you see symbols with those names in your **Library**, you have made this error!

Instead of allowing this to happen, you should convert the photo (or any bitmap) to a symbol (press F8) *immediately* when you first place it on the **Stage**. Afterward, be sure to use the symbol (and *not* the original photo file) *each time you use the image* in your movie. An exception can be made *only if*: (a) the photo never moves, and (b) the photo is used *only once* in the movie. If both of those conditions are true, you don't need a symbol; however, in all other cases, you do.

A good practice is to stash your bitmaps in their own folder, separate from all of your symbols, in the **Library** (Figure 2.7.15). This helps to prevent mistakes because it hides the bitmaps from you, so you are more likely to use the symbol (as you should). Figure 2.7.15 shows how to create a folder inside the Library.

Note: Files imported to the **Library** but not used in the movie are not exported in the SWF. With numerous photos in the Library but not on the **Stage** in any part of the movie, the SWF file size is only 1 KB.

"Remove Frames" from the pop-up menu. This deletes Frame 60, the duplicate of Frame 1.

21 Save and test your movie: Ctrl-Enter (Win) or Cmd-Return (Mac). Voilà! The hesitation is gone, because now *only one frame* in the loop places the photo at the coordinates 0, 0.

You already know what to do *if the motion is too fast*: Add an equal number of frames to *each* of the four motion sequences (click inside a sequence in the **Timeline** and press F5 several times).

If the motion *is too slow*, remove an equal number of frames from *each* of the four motion sequences (click inside a sequence in the **Timeline** and press Shift-F5 several times).

You can figure out how to apply this technique to many different kinds of photos—especially outdoor scenes. Just *don't zoom in* on a photo that is already at 100 percent of its actual size; that is the subject of the next exercise.

A note about file size: The example file was 41 KB before any frames or motion tweens were added. Remember that the photo was converted to a symbol immediately before any frames were added. The final SWF file is 43 KB.

Exercise 7.4: Zooming In on a Photo

For this exercise, you need only one photo. Ideally the photo will have a detail worth zooming in to see close-up.

As you probably figured out when reading about bitmaps at the beginning of this lesson, if you have a photo at 100 percent of its real width and height in Flash and then you zoom in, things will get ugly. Instead of increased detail, you will see bigger pixels.

To avoid that result, you must start with a photo that is already at the *maximum* size it will be *after* zooming in. So, you need to think about the numbers. If you

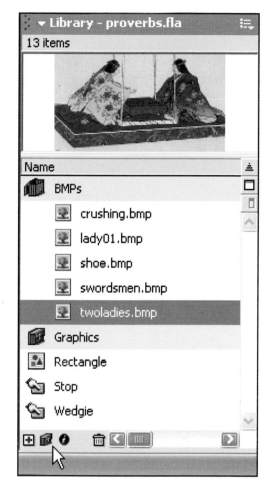

Fig. 2.7.15 Two folders have been created to organize the Library for this FLA file. The bitmaps are inside one folder, while the graphic symbols are in another folder. The cursor points to the folder icon on the bottom edge of the Library panel. Click the folder icon to create a new folder. In this case, the bitmaps are art prints rather than photos. They were converted to symbol because they are motion tweened.

visualize the full-view photo in the Flash movie at 400 pixels wide and 300 pixels high, and you want to zoom in 4× (or 400 percent), you must import a photo that is 1600 pixels by 1200 pixels. That will be a rather large file and maybe not very practical. You can try it, but check the size of the resulting file. Try putting the Quality setting at 30 percent for an imported BMP file (Exercise 7.2) if you need to zoom a large photo.

Taken from the opposite perspective, you can divide both the width and height of your photo by 4 and use those dimensions as the maximum display size. For example:

Table 2.7.07

Filename	Width × Height (pixels)	Width/4	Height/4
deliverybike.bmp	500 × 365	125 pixels	91.25

That example would result in a very small image. Do your math and decide whether the photo you used before is large enough to use in this exercise. If not, prepare another photo (saved in BMP format) and use it instead.

Start with a new, empty file in Flash. Set the *frame rate* to 15 fps.

1 Import an *uncompressed* photo file. See Exercise 7.2, Step 2.

2 Drag the photo from the **Library** panel to the **Stage**.

3 Select the photo and Convert to Symbol (press F8): Name the symbol, select "Graphic," and set the *registration point* to the upper left corner (see Exercise 7.3, Step 2). Zooming will require a motion tween, so this photo *must* be a symbol. Make sure you Convert to Symbol *before* adding any frames to the Timeline to avoid the problem described in "Motion Tweens, Bitmaps, and Symbols" in this lesson.

4 Save and name your file.

5 Before you add any frames to the **Timeline**, you will change the position of the *transformation point* of the symbol. The transformation point is visible when the **Free Transform** tool is selected (Figure 2.7.16), and its

position determines the focus of the zooming motion. So select your symbol on the **Stage** (click it *once*) and then select the Free Transform tool in the Tools panel.

6 The transformation point is represented by a white dot, which is probably at the center of your symbol. In Flash MX, it might be at the upper left corner. No matter where it is, you can move it when the **Free Transform** tool is selected (Figure 2.7.17). Click, hold, and drag the white dot to the object in your photo where you want the zoom action to center. When the animation is complete, you'll see the effect.

Fig. 2.7.16 The transformation point is represented by a white dot, seen here at the center of the symbol, to the left of the cursor.

Now you'll shrink your photo to its starting size, and afterward you will position it on the Stage.

7 Open the **Transform** panel. If you can't find it, use the Window menu (in Flash MX 2004, it's on the Design Panels submenu). The *width* and *height* fields in the panel should each read "100.0%"; make sure there is a check mark in the Constrain box (Figure 2.7.18). This ensures that the photo width and height stay in proportion to each other.

8 *Double-click* into the Width field (the one on the left) to select all its contents. Type "25" (without the quotes). Press the Tab key; the Width field will say 25.0 percent (or 25 percent in Flash MX 2004) after you tab out of the field. The Height field should also say 25.0 percent (or 25 percent) after you press Tab. (If the numbers don't match, the Constrain box is not checked. Checkmark that box.) If 25 percent is smaller or larger than you want for your photo, use a number that works better for you.

Fig. 2.7.17 Grab and drag the transformation point to change its position. This will be the focal point of the zooming action. Here the white dot has been moved to the face of the man in the background.

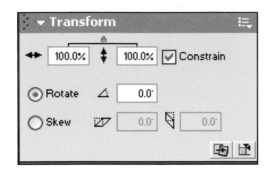

Fig. 2.7.18 The Transform panel shows the scale of the currently selected object.

Press the Enter/Return key to leave the Height field and apply the transformation. In Flash MX 2004, nothing happens unless you press Enter/Return. (The Tab key has no effect.)

9 Set the X and Y coordinates of the photo to 0 (zero). See Exercise 7.3, Step 7. This aligns the upper left corner of the photo with the upper left corner of the **Stage**.

10 Change the Alpha of the symbol to 99 percent. Alpha is an option on the Color menu in the **Properties** panel. This can prevent an unpleasant shifting effect during the movement of a photo.

11 Extend the **Timeline** to 2 seconds by adding sufficient frames to Layer 1.

12 Make the final frame a *new keyframe* (click that frame and press F6).

13 Now you'll make the symbol its full size in the final frame. Select that frame (click it once). Use the **Transform** panel to change the proportions to 100 percent (as in Step 8).

14 Add a motion tween to the frame sequence in the **Timeline**. See "Animating Two Symbols," Lesson 2, Step 5, if you need a review.

15 Save and test your movie: Ctrl-Enter (Win) or Cmd-Return (Mac). What happens is not pretty (yet), but the basic zoom effect is finished.

You must do two more things to make this look good. First, add a *mask* on a layer above the photo. Second, position the photo in the final frame so that the *close-up detail* is where it should be in the zoomed-in photo.

16 You will begin with the mask, which will hide the outer edges of the full-size photo. Add a new layer to the **Timeline** and name it "mask" (it can have any name; it's just convenient to name it "mask"). Name the lower layer "photo," so you remember to maintain good work habits in Flash (always name all your layers when you have more than one).

17 Click Frame 1 in the "mask" layer. To create the mask, you must *draw a shape* to exactly cover the small version (Frame 1) of your photo. Initially, this shape *hides* the object you want to be seen, but in the end, the mask shape becomes a window to *reveal* the object.

Select the **Rectangle** tool from the **Tools** panel and draw a rectangle. The color and size are unimportant at this time. Delete the "stroke" outline from the rectangle (double-click precisely on the outline to select the entire outline, then press the Delete key)—a mask shape needs only a single fill color.

18 With the rectangle shape selected, change its *width* and *height* in the **Properties** panel to exactly match the width and height of your *reduced-size* photo (the symbol size in Frame 1). After you type the width into the field labeled "W" (on the far left side of the **Properties** panel), press the Tab key to make it stick (Figure 2.7.19). Do the same after you type the height into the field labeled "H." (If you don't press Tab, Flash is likely to add some random tenths to your numbers.)

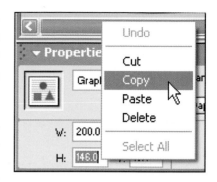

Fig. 2.7.19 Properties for the photo symbol in Frame 1: Double-click into the W or H field to select the value. Then right-click (Ctrl-click/Mac) to get the pop-up menu (alternatively, you could press Ctrl-C or Cmd-C) and *copy* the value.

What is the width and height of your *reduced-size* photo? Click it and look at the **Properties** panel to find out. With the photo in Frame 1 selected, you can copy the W value from the **Properties** panel, then select the rectangle shape, and paste the value into the W field in the **Properties** panel (Figure 2.7.20). Try it and see—this may seem annoying, but a Flash designer will do this often. It becomes simple if you practice it.

19 Position the rectangle precisely over your photo in Frame 1. You can use the X and Y coordinates to do this.

Note: If you have "Snap to Objects" enabled (in the View menu), you can grab the rectangle at its upper left corner and drag it to "snap" to the registration point of the photo.

Fig. 2.7.20 Properties for the rectangle shape in the "mask" layer: After selecting the object you want to resize, double-click in the W or H field. Right-click (Ctrl-click/Mac) to get the pop-up menu (or use Ctrl-V or Cmd-V) to *paste* the value. Press the Tab key to make the value "stick."

20 Here's how you make the mask effect happen: Right-click (Ctrl-click/Mac) on the "mask" layer in the **Timeline**. Select "Mask" from the pop-up menu.

Your **Timeline** now should look similar to the one shown in Figure 2.7.21.

Notice that the masked layer (labeled "photo") is indented beneath the mask layer (labeled "mask"). This indicates that the mask affects that indented layer and will work correctly. Notice also that both the "mask" layer and the "photo" layer are *locked*. The lock icon to the right of the layer name shows this. While the two layers are locked, the rectangle shape is

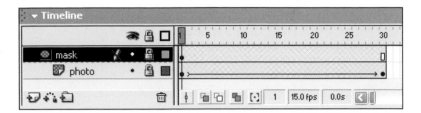

Fig. 2.7.21 Both the "mask" layer and the "photo" layer are locked. In this state, any shape within the mask layer is invisible, and it hides everything outside its edges in the masked layer below it.

invisible, and the mask is in effect while you are editing the movie. You can test the motion now by simply pressing Enter (Win) or Return (Mac).

While the layers are *locked*, you cannot make changes in those layers. You can *unlock* a layer by clicking the *lock icon* to the right of the layer name. To *lock* it again, click the *black dot* that replaced the lock icon.

21 Add a new layer, name it "actions," and make a keyframe in the final frame (press F6). Place a stop() action in that final frame. See "Animating Two Symbols," Lesson 2, Step 23, if you need a review.

22 To see the effect of the mask, save and test your movie: Ctrl-Enter (Win) or Cmd-Return (Mac).

23 The last step is to position the photo in the final frame, if necessary, so that the *close-up detail* is where it should be in the zoomed-in photo. Moving the transformation point (Steps 5 and 6) may have made this unnecessary, but you might want to move the photo to reposition the focal point.

First you must unlock the "photo" layer so you can change it. To *unlock* the layer, click the *lock icon* to the right of the layer name.

As soon as you *unlock* the "photo" layer, the rectangle shape (on the "mask" layer) becomes visible again. To *hide it* in editing mode, click the *black dot* to the right of the layer name ("mask") below the *eye icon* in the **Timeline** (Figure 2.7.22). That replaces the black dot with an X, and it makes the layer invisible. (You can do this on any layer, not only on Mask layers.)

Note: Hiding a layer in editing mode has *no effect* on the final SWF file.

24 Now you can reposition the photo in the final frame of your movie. To see whether you have it right: (a) click the X in the "mask" layer and (b) click the *black dot* under the *lock icon* in the "photo" layer to restore the mask effect. If you need to reposition the photo again: (a) click the *black dot* under the *eye icon* in the "mask" layer and (b) the *lock icon* in the "photo" layer to make that layer editable again.

 When you're satisfied with your zoom, save and test your movie: Ctrl-Enter (Win) or Cmd-Return (Mac). If the zoom seems too fast or to slow, add or remove frames to alter the speed.

Warning: If your photo does a lot of rippling or warping as it zooms, double-check to make sure you used an *uncompressed* image file, *not* a JPG. You might also see this unpleasant effect on a computer with a slower processor.

Fig. 2.7.22 The "mask" layer is still locked, but the rectangle is not visible on the Stage. Its invisibility is indicated by the red "X" beneath the eye icon. Without that "X", you would see the rectangle shape covering your photo on the Stage. The "photo" layer is unlocked, as indicated by the dot beneath the lock icon.

Exercise 7.5: Fading Photos into Each Other

This exercise explains how to accomplish a cross-fade between photos. To follow the instructions, you should have three related photos saved as *uncompressed* files (BMP). Crop each photo to the same width and height, using a program such as Photoshop. Each photo shown here is the same size: 320 pixels wide and 240 pixels high. This way, the pictures can be

Fig. 2.7.23 Here is the result of a photo at 33 percent of its original size (left) zoomed in to 100 percent (right). The final frame has been repositioned so that the person walking is central.

Fig. 2.7.24 Photo 1 (top), Photo 2 (middle), and Photo 3 (bottom). Each of these photos is a BMP (uncompressed), 226 KB, and 320 × 240. With JPEG Quality at 90 percent in the Publish Settings dialog, the final SWF file using these three photos is 88 KB.

positioned precisely on top of each other, each in a separate layer in the Timeline. The movie size is 360 × 280, allowing a 20-pixel margin all around the photos.

Note: Photos of different sizes don't look great in cross-fades. If you want to use a fade transition on photos of varying width and height, use a movie clip to fade each photo in from (and out to) the background color. This is explained in Lesson 10.

Start with a new, empty file in Flash. Set the *frame rate* to 15 fps. Set the background color to a neutral shade such as black, and set the width and height to provide a margin around your photos.

1 Import your three photos to the **Library**.

2 Create two *new layers* in the **Timeline**. Name the bottom layer "Photo 1," the middle layer "Photo 2," and the top layer "Photo 3." You will stack the photos in reverse order, because Photo 2 will cover Photo 1, and then Photo 3 will cover Photo 2 (Figure 2.7.25).

3 Select Frame 1 in the layer "Photo 1," and drag your first photo onto the Stage.

4 Select the photo and convert it to a graphic symbol (press F8). Make sure the *registration point* for this object is in the *upper left corner* (see Exercise 7.3, Step 2). Give the symbol a descriptive name (this makes it easier to manage the **Library**). One method is to give the symbol the same name as the imported photo file, e.g. "Delivery Bike" is the graphic symbol containing *deliverybike.bmp*.

5 With the photo selected, in the **Properties** panel, change the X and Y coordinates to position this photo exactly as all the photos will be positioned. For example, if you have a 20-pixel margin all the way around the photos, both your X and your Y will be 20.

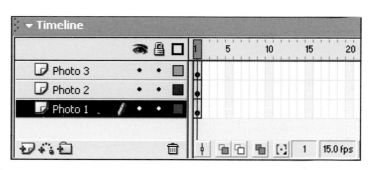

6 Repeat Steps 3, 4, and 5 for the other two layers, placing the appropriate photo in each layer. Make sure to *convert each photo* to a graphic symbol!

Fig. 2.7.25 Photos that fade over each other must be in separate layers on the Timeline.

7 Save your file. No need to test it yet, but it's always a good idea to save after you have spent some time positioning objects.

8 Now you need to make the photos fade in and out. Begin by extending the **Timeline**. To do that, select Frame 45 in all three layers (shift-click) and press F5 once. You'll handle the fade effect the same way on each layer, and afterward you'll set up the sequence to show Photo 1, then Photo 2, then Photo 3. In other words, the three layers will be identical until later in the exercise.

9 Create new keyframes in *each layer* at Frames 15, 30, and 45.

10 Click in Frame 1 in the "Photo 3" layer, then click once on the photo to *select* it. Look at the far right side the **Properties** panel and find the menu labeled "Color." Open the menu and select "Alpha." Then click into the Alpha Amount field and type "0" (zero, without the quotes). Tab out of the field to make the value stick (Figure 2.7.26).

When an object has an alpha of zero, the object is completely transparent. (You can think of *alpha* as transparency.) Each of the photos will start out transparent, just like this one; it will be simplest if you work on only one layer at a time.

11 Click in Frame 45 in the "Photo 3" layer, then click once on the photo. In the **Properties** panel, open the menu labeled "Color" and select "Alpha."

Fig. 2.7.26 Setting the alpha to zero is the first step to fading in.

Because the last time you changed alpha, you changed it to 0 (zero), it should automatically be 0 now. (If it's not, just type 0 again.)

12 Click in Frame 15 in the "Photo 3" layer, then click once on the photo. In the **Properties** panel, open the menu labeled "Color" and select "Alpha." Here you need the photo to be fully visible, or *not transparent*. Normally that would mean "100 percent" in the Alpha Amount field—but not when you are fading bitmaps in Flash. If you use "100%" you will see an ugly shifting effect on certain computers in the final movie (in any browser), so standard professional practice is to use "99%" instead. Type "99" (without the quotes) into the field and tab out of it.

13 Finally, click in Frame 30 in the "Photo 3" layer, then click once on the photo. In the **Properties** panel, open the menu labeled "Color" and select "Alpha." Because the last time you changed the alpha to 99, it should automatically be 99 now. (If it's not, just type 99 again.)

14 Save the file just to be cautious.

15 Repeat the procedures in Steps 10 through 14 for the other two layers. It will work best if you *lock* the "Photo 3" layer to work on "Photo 2," and then *lock* both "Photo 3" and "Photo 2" to work on "Photo 1" (Figure 2.7.27).

To *lock* a layer, click once on the *black dot* under the *lock icon* to the right of the layer name. The black dot will be replaced by an identical lock icon. To *unlock* a layer, click the *lock icon* to the right of the layer name. When a layer is *locked*, you cannot edit it. It's very useful to lock a layer when you need to work on a layer below it—it can prevent mistakes!

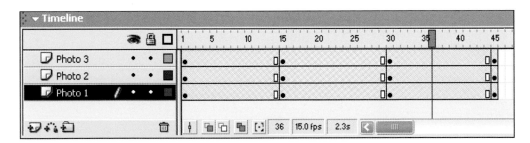

Fig. 2.7.27 Your Timeline should look like this after you complete Step 15. All layers have been *unlocked*. In Frames 1 and 45 in each layer, the *alpha* for the photo should be 0. In Frames 15 and 30 in each layer, the *alpha* for the photo should be 99. This Timeline is ready for you to apply the motion tweens.

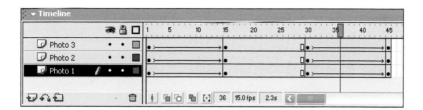

Fig. 2.7.28 After Step 17, your Timeline should look like this. It is ready for you to set up a staggered timing sequence for the three photos.

16 Next, add a motion tween between Frames 1 and 15 on *each* layer. This will cause the photos to fade in from 0 alpha to 99 alpha. That may not seem like "motion," but it definitely requires a motion tween.

17 Add a motion tween between Frames 30 and 45 on *each* layer. This will cause the photos to fade out from 99 alpha to 0 alpha (Figure 2.7.28).

18 Save the file. If you want to test it, go ahead—but it won't be pretty. All three photos will fade in and then out *at the same time*.

19 Now you need to *stagger the layers* so the photos fade in one at a time, not all at once. Because the layer "Photo 1" contains the first photo, it does not change. Start with the layer "Photo 2": *Select* the entire layer by clicking once on the *layer name*.

20 With the entire layer *selected* (it will be black, to show that it is selected), *click and hold* on Frame 1. That is, position the mouse cursor over Frame 1, press the button, and don't let go! While holding the button down, *slide toward the right*, being careful to stay inside the same layer. (Don't move up or down in the Timeline—just drag steadily to the right.) When the first frame is at about the Frame 30 position, *release* the mouse button.

This is a useful technique to master, because it's a lot easier to slide the whole layer right (or left) than to press F5 again and again.

What you should see now is a blank, empty, white sequence of about 15 frames at the beginning of the "Photo 2" layer (Figure 2.7.29). If the first frame of *the first motion tween* in that layer is *not* at Frame 30, add or remove frames *in the white sequence* to fix that. You will maintain 15-frame intervals for everything in this movie so that all the timing is equal.

21 Now you must do the same thing with the layer "Photo 3": *Select* the entire layer by clicking on the *layer name*. Follow the instructions in Step 20, but with one difference—*drag this sequence* all the way to Frame 60.

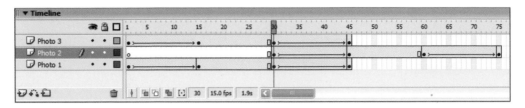

Fig. 2.7.29 The Timeline looks like this after you have moved all the frames in the "Photo 2" layer, according to the instructions in Step 20.

It should be clear to you from looking at the **Timeline** now that the image in the layer "Photo 1" will begin to fade in immediately. When it begins to fade out (Frame 30), the image in the layer "Photo 2" will begin to fade in. When the image in the layer "Photo 2" begins to fade out (Frame 60), the image in the layer "Photo 3" will begin to fade in.

22 Save and test your movie: Ctrl-Enter (Win) or Cmd-Return (Mac).

23 You need to add a keyframe with a `stop()` action in a new layer above the final frame, Frame 105, because the loop does not look very good—after two nice cross-fades, the final photo fades away completely. Only when it is gone does the first photo fade in again. It's pretty fast, and you may not notice it too much—but in a looping movie, it looks like a mistake.

What if you do want to *loop* these fading photos and maintain the same fade effect (smoothly) when the loop returns to the beginning? That's what you will do next.

Exercise 7.6: Looping a Fade Effect

Start with the file from the last exercise, completed through Step 22 (without a `stop()` action).

1 Add *a new layer* above the three layers you already have and name the new layer "actions." That new, empty layer should automatically fill 105 frames (the length of your movie). If you added this layer in Exercise 7.5, Step 23, just delete the final frame, in which you added the `stop()` action.

2 In the "Photo 2" layer, click Frame 76 and add a *blank keyframe* (press F7). Then click Frame 105 in the same layer and fill that space with empty frames (press F5 once). This *extends the layer* to match the two above it; this is considered good practice by professional Flash designers. It helps you understand your **Timeline** more clearly when all the layers are the same length.

3 The "Photo 1" layer is now the only short layer. We're going to insert blank frames up to Frame 90, but *not after* Frame 90. So, add a *blank keyframe* at Frame 46 (click that frame, and press F7), and then *extend* the blank frames to Frame 89 (click that frame, and press F5).

4 Save the file.

5 In the "Photo 1" layer, *double-click* in the first motion sequence (between Frames 1 and 15 in that

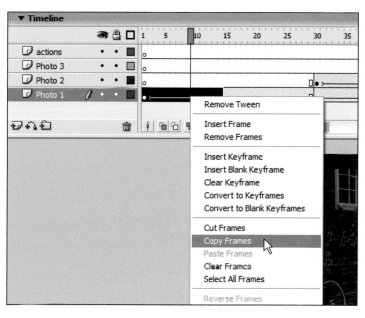

Fig. 2.7.30 If you double-click inside a frame sequence on the Timeline, it is selected. Right-click (Control-click/Mac) *once* to open the pop-up menu and copy those frames.

layer). That sequence of 14 frames will turn black to show that it is selected. Without moving the mouse, *right-click* (Ctrl-click/Mac) *once* to get a pop-up menu (Figure 2.7.30). From the menu, *select* "Copy Frames." This is a fantastically useful operation to know!

6 Click in Frame 90 in the "Photo 1" layer (really, there is no frame there yet, but that's all right). *Right-click* (Ctrl-click/Mac) *once* to open the pop-up menu, and then select "Paste Frames." A regular paste will not work the same way, so be sure to use the menu.

7 You get a broken motion tween (you know it's broken because the line is dotted, not solid), but that's easy enough to fix. Right-click (Ctrl-click/Mac) once on Frame 15 in your "Photo 1" layer and select "Copy Frames" from the menu. Then right-click (Ctrl-click/Mac) *after* the last frame in that layer (that should be Frame 104) and select "Paste Frames." The motion tween is no longer broken.

What you just did was to copy the *fade-in sequence* for your first photo and duplicate it directly under the *fade-out sequence* for your third photo. This should be starting to make sense now—the first photo will be fading in while the last one is fading out. Great! But what will happen when the movie loops back to Frame 1? The same photo will fade in again! That would look awful (you can test it and see for yourself)—so you are about to prevent it from happening.

8 Where you really want the playhead to go after Frame 105 is the place near the beginning of the movie *where the first photo is already fully visible*: Frame 15. To make it go there, you will *label* that frame, in the "actions" layer. (You can be lazy this time and not create a new layer for labels; there's only one label in this movie.) You'll also write one line of ActionScript on the final frame (in the "actions" layer) so the movie knows where to go.

So click once on Frame 15 in the "actions" layer and make a *new keyframe* (press F6). Then click into the Frame Label field in the **Properties** panel and type "restart" (without the quotes). Press Tab to leave the field and make the frame label stick. If you need a review of frame labels, see "Buttons That Let You Jump on the Timeline," Lesson 5, Step 3.

9 All that remains is to tell the movie to go to the frame labeled "restart" when it loops, instead of to Frame 1. Click Frame 105 in your "actions" layer and make a keyframe there (press F6). Open the **Actions** panel (press F9).

Flash MX: In the list on the left side of the panel, open the sections "Actions" and then "Movie Control" by clicking each one once. Under "Movie Control," find "gotoAndPlay" and *double-click* it. Assuming that you are in "Normal Mode," change "Type" to "Frame Label." Open the "Frame" menu and *select* "restart."

Flash MX 2004: In the list on the left side of the panel, open the sections "Global Functions" and then "Timeline Control" by clicking each one once. Under "Timeline Control," find "gotoAndPlay" and *double-click* it. Now click once in between the parentheses and type "restart" (including the quotation marks). Remember, frame labels always appear in quotes in ActionScript.

Your ActionScript should look like this in either version:

```
gotoAndPlay("restart");
```

If you need a review of this procedure, see "Buttons That Let You Jump on the Timeline," Lesson 5, Steps 8 and 9. This case is slightly different, because you have written the ActionScript on a *frame* instead of on a *button*. That means the action will be executed as soon as the movie reaches that frame.

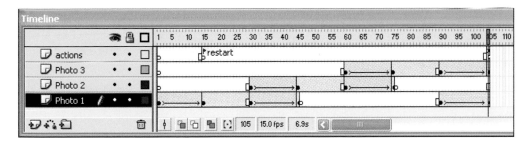

Fig. 2.7.31 The Timeline for the finished movie, including a frame label in Frame 15 and ActionScript in Frame 105. This Timeline looks complex, but only because the photo layers have been staggered. Each sequence lasts 1 second (15 frames).

10 Save and test your movie: Ctrl-Enter (Win) or Cmd-Return (Mac). You should have a perfect loop with identical cross-fades every time. Your **Timeline** should look like the one shown in Figure 2.7.31.

As you become more experienced with Flash, you will discover that writing a line or two of ActionScript on the *final frame* of a Timeline is frequently useful. You can direct all sorts of things to happen this way—not just stopping the movie!

Note: Notice the empty white frames on the bottom layer (Frames 46 to 89). Your movie plays better, and may be smaller, when you remove objects from the Timeline that are not seen. Although that photo had an alpha of 0 in Frame 45 and in Frame 90, it's better that it's completely gone from the Timeline. This way, it's not adding any extra weight to the movie.

DOING IT ALL WITH MOVIE CLIPS INSTEAD

Now that you understand the staggered timing of the cross-fades used in the previous exercise, consider how much easier it might be to do this with movie clips instead. Don't panic—it *really could be* easier.

First, imagine each photo as a separate, individual movie clip, like the ones you built in Lesson 6. Each photo would have its own separate **Timeline** in that case.

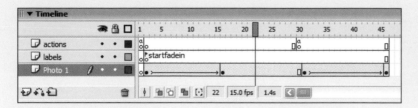

Fig. 2.7.32 Each photo can be contained in a separate movie clip, which means you build the Timeline only once.

The Timeline for *each photo's movie clip* would look exactly the same (Figure 2.7.32).

In Figure 2.7.32, the ActionScript in Frame 1 is a simple `stop()` action, nothing more.

The frame label in Frame 2 is just like the frame labels you used in Exercise 7.6, Step 8. Notice that Frame 1 in the "Photo 1" layer is an *empty* keyframe in this Timeline.

The big difference—and the newest idea for you, probably—is that the three separate movie clips would *communicate* with each other. At the point in the clip where you want the next photo to fade in (always in Frame 30, if all clips have the same Timeline), you would add a new keyframe (in the "actions" layer, of course) and write one line of ActionScript in that keyframe:

```
_parent.photo2_mc.gotoAndPlay("startfadein");
```

When a movie clip plays and reaches the end of its Timeline, it loops back to Frame 1. In this case, you wrote a `stop()` action on Frame 1, and so it will stop there and wait—until this Timeline is set into action again by *another* movie clip!

You have previously encountered all the concepts in that line of ActionScript:

1. "_parent" refers to the Timeline that *contains* this movie clip. Flash must look *outside* this movie clip to find the other movie clips (the ones holding the other photos). This word "_parent" is what tells Flash where to look. Whenever ActionScript refers to an object *outside* a movie clip, it must refer to it in a way that shows the position of the outside object *relative to* the movie clip where the ActionScript is written.

2. "photo2_mc" is the *instance name* given to another movie clip that is outside this one. You learned about giving an instance name to a movie clip in the exercise "Sliding Panel," Lesson 6, Step 18.

3. "startfadein" is the frame label in that *other* movie clip with the instance name "photo2_mc"—don't forget that you will have all the movie clips constructed the same way, so the label on Frame 2 will be the same word in each movie clip.

This concept is somewhat complex, so to save space in print, no more will be said about it here. On the Web site for this book, go to the Lesson 7 page and download the FLA file under "Fading Photos into Each Other, Version 3" (fades_with_movie_clips.fla) to see exactly how these movie clips are used. You'll see that the main movie Timeline is only two frames. The first frame contains a basic preloader script so that the photo movie clips all have time to load.

By *duplicating* the movie clip, you spare yourself having to construct the Timeline more than once.

While the example uses only three photos, it would be just as easy to use more (although you would need to consider the increase in file size). This file (86 KB with three movie clips) is actually 2 KB smaller than the one with the same three photos (88 KB) used in the previous exercise.

There are more sophisticated ways to handle the movie clips, and if you have a knack for scripting, you will probably figure them out quickly. For example, you could use ActionScript to create new instances of your movie clip on the Stage and feed the name of each photo symbol into the clip from an array. Assuming that most readers are brand-new to scripting, that's outside the scope of this book.

Exercise 7.7: Using a Photo as the Background

If you would like to use a photo as a *full background* for an entire Flash movie, the main things to consider are the *size* (width and height) of the Flash movie, the *size* of the photo (both file size and dimensions) and the *position* of the photo.

1 Determine the size of your Flash movie. Say it is 700 pixels wide and 400 pixels high. In that case, you need to have a photo that is 700 × 400. (Alternatively, you may match the size of the Flash movie to the size of

the photo.) Do not use a photo that is bigger than the movie—those are excess kilobytes!

2 Import a photo file to the **Library** (File menu > Import to Library; in Flash MX 2004, this is on the "Import" submenu).

3 If there are already other layers in your movie, create a *new layer* in the **Timeline** and drag it to the *bottom* of the stack of layers. Name it "background" (without the quotes), for example.

4 Click once on Frame 1 in the new layer, and drag the photo from the **Library** to the **Stage**. If this photo never moves, there is no need to Convert to Symbol. This layer has only one keyframe (Frame 1) and extends the full length of the Timeline, so the photo is visible throughout the entire movie.

5 Position the photo at X: 0, Y: 0, so that it aligns with the edges of the **Stage**.

 6 If you add more frames to layers above the "background" layer, make sure also to add frames to *extend* the "background" layer out to the same place in the Timeline. Otherwise, the background photo will disappear partway through your movie.

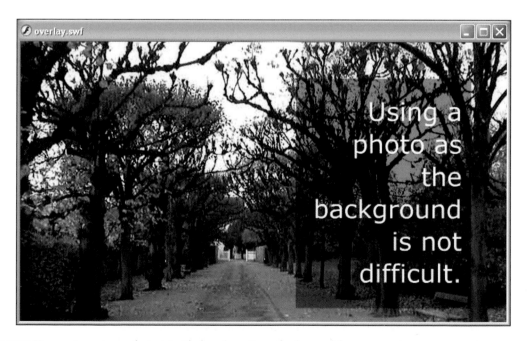

Fig. 2.7.33 You can import any photo into Flash and use it as a background for your movie.

On the Web site for this book, go to the Lesson 7 page and download the FLA file under "Using a Photo as the Background" to see exactly how to use a photo as a background image for multiple frames in a Flash movie. View the SWF to see how semi-transparent color overlays can be used to tint the background photo or to make text easier to read. Reducing the quality of the bitmap (the photo) as explained in Exercise 7.2 will make a big difference in the file size. In most cases, a quality setting of 30 percent will be fine for a background photo.

IMPORTING A SEQUENCE OF IMAGES

Flash will do a lot of work for you, if you give it a little help. If you have an image sequence (for example, 12 photos that illustrate how to pitch a baseball):

1. Name the files sequentially, e.g., *pitch1.jpg*, *pitch2.jpg* ... *pitch12.jpg*.

2. Click once on the one (empty) frame in the **Timeline** where you want the sequence to begin.

3. Begin the usual import steps but pay attention to Step 4. It may not be what you expect.

Flash MX: File menu > Import (*not* "Import to Library" in this case).

Flash MX 2004: File menu > Import > Import to Stage.

4. In the dialog box, select only the *first* image file, and then click Open.

5. Flash will ask you if you want to import the sequence. Click Yes.

Flash will automatically put each image in a new keyframe, in order, in the same layer. This can save you a lot of time. If you use uncompressed image files instead of JPGs, you can compress them all with one step (see Exercise 7.2, Step 8).

Flash does not ask you where you want the images to be; it simply centers them. To get them to go automatically where you want them, resize your movie (using the Properties panel) *before* you import the files. Do the math to figure out what size will place them where you want them, working from the knowledge that Flash will center them relative to the width and height of the full Stage. You could reposition the images one by one after importing, of course, but that would take more time. If you resize first, you can then change the movie size back to what it was, and your images are all positioned for you.

If you then add a *new layer* with two buttons, and apply the Action-Script `prevFrame()` to one button and `nextFrame()` to the other, you will have an instant slideshow. These buttons were explained in "Using Buttons to Navigate One Frame at a Time," Lesson 5.

WORKING WITH PHOTOS SUMMARY

Using photos online always demands that the producer balance the *quality* and the *screen size* of the images with the *technical capabilities* and *attention span* of the intended viewers of the photographs. Even if you are delivering the photos via Flash on a CD or DVD, you must consider the width and height (in pixels, not inches) of the users' screens. You can always scale a photo down (to a smaller width and height than actual size) in Flash, but if you scale it up, it will not look good anymore (because it is a bitmap, not a vector image).

You can now move, zoom, and fade photos smoothly and professionally, using little or no ActionScript. Any time you're going to move or transform a photo image, the first step is Convert to Symbol. Like any symbol, a photo that moves must be *alone* on its layer.

You can adjust the image quality of a photo to a precise degree and make your own decisions about the unavoidable tradeoffs between image quality and file size, which affects the user's download time. You have learned that the best results usually come from importing an *uncompressed* photo file and allowing Flash to perform the compression on it.

You have encountered several new aspects of the Flash production environment, such as the X and Y coordinate fields, the width and height fields in the **Properties** panel, the registration point and the transformation point of a symbol, masks, and alpha (transparency). All these features and properties give you the ability to control the movement of photographs in Flash. The "lock/unlock layers" and "show/hide layers" options in the **Timeline** enable you to work competently with layers and build more sophisticated Flash movies.

At a minimum, you should be able to bring photos into Flash and make certain they look as good as you want them to look, and yet not require even one more kilobyte of memory than absolutely necessary.

CONCLUSION

In this lesson, you have learned to:

1. Differentiate between a bitmap and a vector image.

2. Plan the width and height of your Flash movie relative to the width and height of your photos.

3. Import photos (or other images) to the Library.

4. Align an image relative to the Stage using the Align panel.

5. Open the Bitmap Properties dialog from the Library.

6. Change the Quality setting for an individual bitmap image (in the Bitmap Properties dialog).

7. Swap one symbol for another (Properties panel).

8. Change the JPEG Quality setting (in the Publish Settings dialog) for all uncompressed bitmaps.

9. In the Bitmap Properties dialog, determine whether to choose "Photo (JPEG)" or "Lossless (PNG/GIF)" for compression type.

10. Convert a photo to a graphic symbol.

11. Change the registration point for a symbol.

12. Change the transformation point for a symbol.

13. Move a symbol by changing its X and Y coordinates to ensure straight, steady movement.

14. Correct for hesitation in a looping animation by removing one frame.

15 Avoid having extra symbols (Tween 1, Tween 2, etc.) created when you move a photo.

16 Create folders in the Library to organize your assets.

17 Plan for zooming in on a photo.

18 Using the Transform panel to zoom in or out.

19 Create a mask effect to hide part of an image.

20 Lock and unlock individual layers in the Timeline.

21 Show and hide individual layers in the Timeline.

22 Work with the alpha (transparency) property of a symbol.

23 Use 99 percent alpha instead of 100 percent when fading photos.

24 Move all the frames on one layer.

25 Stagger layers to allow a smooth fade effect between photos.

26 Copy and paste entire frames or sequences of frames.

27 Create a smooth, continuous loop of photos that fade into each other.

28 Use a large photo as a background image in a Flash movie.

29 Place a complete sequence of images on the Timeline in one step.

Lesson 8

Working with Sound

Flash offers several choices for putting sound into a movie. You saw one option in Lesson 4, when you added sound to a button: *Select* a keyframe (not a blank frame, but definitely a keyframe) where you want the sound to begin, and then *drag* the sound from the Library to the Stage. Simple!

Sound can be added to any part of the Timeline (not only to buttons) in the same way. Some Flash authors always handle sound this way—putting it directly on the Timeline. If you do add sound that way, always be sure to place it *in its own layer*, separate from all other objects.

However, putting sound directly onto the Timeline provides the least control. If you want to use buttons to control your sound and give your users the ability to pause or mute the audio, you should be using Action-Script. It's not that big a deal, so don't get worried about it. You can easily load external MP3 files at runtime, or you can import audio files into your FLA and save it all as a single file.

In this lesson, you will use short bits of ActionScript to bring sound into the movie, start and stop the sound, and control other aspects of the sound. With these techniques, you can cause actions to happen automatically when a sound finishes playing, or even synchronize events in the Timeline to particular moments in your soundtrack. You will also see how to add script to buttons that will allow the user to stop, restart, pause, and mute the sound.

At the end of the lesson, you'll find details about sound formats allowed in Flash, sound file compression, and the difference between an "event" sound and a "streaming" sound.

LESSON 8

Sound files can add a lot to Flash journalism: Music sets the mood; spoken voice conveys information; natural sound provides a sense of place. It's outside the scope of this book to say much about gathering sound and editing it on your computer, but a few points are too important to ignore.

- You do not need any digital equipment to transfer sound into a computer. Buy a very inexpensive "male to male" mini cable at any electronics store; plug one end into the *headphone* jack of a cassette recorder (or any other playback device) and the other end into the *microphone* jack of a computer; press the Play button on the playback device.

- Both Windows and Mac platforms include basic sound recording software. A free sound editing program that works on the Windows, Mac, and Linux platforms is Audacity (*http://sourceforge.net/projects/audacity/*). There are many other sound editing programs available. While you're *playing* the sound from the playback device, you must be *recording* with the sound recording software.

- The quality of your microphone has a greater effect on sound quality than the quality of your recording device. If you want to record people speaking and natural sound, invest in a better microphone.

- Plenty of music files, especially loops, are available free online. Start at *Flashkit.com*; go to the "Sound Loops" section of the site. For commercial use, use a pay service such as *Sounddogs.com*.

- U.S. copyright law protects recorded music. If you copy a song from a music CD into your Flash movie, you are breaking the law. Even a short segment that you transform into a loop is protected by law. There is no "30-second rule" in U.S. law, although many people think there is. Another common misconception holds that students and teachers may copy recorded music legally "for educational purposes"—but if you put your Flash movie on the Web, you have gone outside the classroom environment, and the education exception no longer applies.

Note: The U.S. Copyright Office says, "Under the *fair use* doctrine of the U.S. copyright statute, it is permissible to use limited portions of a work including quotes, for purposes such as commentary, criticism, news reporting, and scholarly reports. There are no legal rules permitting the use of a specific number of words, a certain number of musical notes, or percentage of a work." Source: *http://www.copyright.gov/help/faq/faq-fairuse.html*

What You Need to Begin This Lesson

All the sounds supplied in Flash's "Common Libraries" (explained under "Add Sound to a Button," Lesson 4, Step 5) are better suited to *button events* than to continuous play—so, to work through this lesson, you will need to download (or create) a longer sound file such as a spoken-voice narration, an interview, or a music loop. You may want to download several sound files; it would be best to have at least one *uncompressed*—WAV (Windows) or AIFF (Mac)—file and at least one MP3 file. They need not contain the same sound. Music would work, but if you will be putting the SWF online keep in mind the warning about copyright law on the previous page.

If you have a recording in either WAV or AIFF format, most sound editing programs will allow you to resave that file in the MP3 format.

Consider both the *length* and *file size* of the files you choose to work with. Your uncompressed file (WAY or AIFF) should be less than 1 megabyte (less than 1,000 KB) for ease of use *in this lesson.* Your MP3 file should be even smaller. As for length, 15 to 30 seconds will be easy to work with, although you could use a longer file. Music loops can be as short as 10 seconds, or even less.

A word about "loops": If you want continuous music playing in your Flash movie, it's best to select a file that has been deliberately edited to loop *cleanly.* That means your ear cannot detect the moment when the loop ends and then begins again. Many of the loops available online are not edited very well, and the transition is quite obvious (and therefore, not good). You may be able to edit the file to improve it—or you could just download a different file.

Working with ActionScript

This lesson concerns what Flash calls the *Sound object.* If you prefer to look for ActionScript in the list on the left side of the **Actions** panel (instead of typing it), it's useful to remember that *Sound* is an *object* and a *class*—and so its *methods, properties,* and *events* can be found under Objects > Movie > Sound in Flash MX; in Flash MX 2004, find them under Built-in Classes > Media > Sound. You will not have to memorize all those terms! It can be helpful to know that there is a place in the Actions panel where you can find *everything* related to the Sound object.

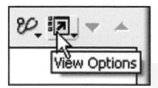

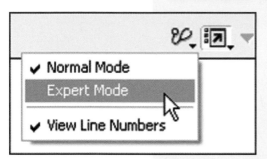

Once you have the "Sound" section open in the Actions panel, you have access to all the ActionScript that affects or controls sound in Flash.

BEHAVIORS IN FLASH MX 2004

Behaviors, which are new to Flash MX 2004, are intended to make it easy for Flash authors to attach actions or functions to objects on the Stage or frames in the Timeline. You might consider Behaviors as the replacement for "Normal Mode," which existed in Flash MX but vanished in Flash MX 2004. (Switching out of Normal Mode is explained in Figure 2.8.01.) However, a limited number of Behaviors are available. Much of the functionality discussed in this lesson cannot be accomplished using Behaviors.

Fig. 2.8.01 On the far right side of the Actions panel in Flash MX, you'll find the button that allows you to switch from "Normal Mode" to "Expert Mode" and back again. When you're in Expert Mode, you can simply type the script given in this lesson. Flash MX 2004 does not have these two modes, so you can always type the script directly.

If you use the **Actions** panel to view the ActionScript written automatically by a Behavior you selected, in many cases you'll see that the script is exactly what you would have written by following instructions in this book. In some cases, though, you'll see a huge clump of script that neither this book, nor any other, would ask you to write. To load or attach a sound, for example, the Behavior writes ten or more lines of script on your keyframe. In this lesson, you will learn how to do it with three lines of script instead.

To apply a Behavior, *select* either a movie clip instance on the Stage or a keyframe in the Timeline, and then select the Behavior you want from the Behaviors panel. If you don't see the panel, open it from the Window menu > Development Panels > Behaviors.

There's nothing wrong with using Behaviors in Flash MX 2004, but they are supposed to be self-explanatory, so we'll give no more space to them here. There's a very good tutorial at the Ultrashock site: *http://www.ultrashock.com/tutorials/flashmx2004/effects-01.php*

The lesson will supply the ActionScript necessary to make everything happen. If you are in "Normal Mode" in the Actions panel in Flash MX, you cannot type the script; rather, you *must* select it from the list on the left side of the panel. This can become tedious. If you switch to "Expert Mode" (Fig. 2.8.01), you can type the script directly. You can use either option. Try both ways to see which one you prefer.

In Flash MX 2004, you're always in Expert Mode.

Two Ways to Handle the Sound File

Two *methods* allow you to work with a specified sound file: `attachSound()` and `loadSound()`. Each one works differently, so you'll always want to consider which method is best suited to a particular sound in your movie. (You can use *both* methods in one movie, but you would not use both on the *same sound file* in the same movie.) The two biggest differences between the two methods are the resulting *file size* of the SWF and the *availability* of the sound.

- When you use `attachSound()`, the sound file is *inside* your movie, and the SWF file will be somewhat *larger* as a result. However, you do not need to upload the sound file separately to your Web server, and Flash can compress the sound a lot. If you're using several sound files, or one very large file, this method can make your SWF unreasonably large (and slow to download). In many cases, you should consider adding a pre-loader; see Appendix A. Use `attachSound()` any time you want a sound to loop repeatedly, and also use it for short sounds you will use multiple times in the movie.

- When you use `loadSound()`, the sound file is *outside* your movie, and Flash can even stream it for your user (if you give the command). Alternatively, you can load it in a non-streaming form, but then it must load in its entirety before it can start to play. The biggest drawback to loading external sound files: They will begin playing sooner or later, depending on the user's Internet connection speed, and you may need a preloader script to check to make sure they have loaded, or started to load, before you try to use them in the movie.

The considerations, then, are the SWF file size (bigger or smaller); the ability to repeat the sound without waiting; the amount of time the user will need to wait, either for the entire Flash file, or for the MP3. You will use `attachSound()` first, and then work with `loadSound()` in the second exercise.

Fig. 2.8.02 After you open the pop-up menu for a sound in the Library, select "Linkage" to specify how ActionScript can use this file.

Exercise 8.1: Sound Inside the Flash File

A short music file intended to loop (or repeat) will work well in this exercise.

Start with a new, empty file in Flash.

1 When you use `attachSound()` to bring the sound file into the Flash movie (as you will in this exercise), you must first *import* the sound file to the **Library**. It's best to import an *uncompressed* sound file (WAV or AIFF) and allow Flash to perform its own MP3 compression when you save the SWF file. (If you import an MP3 file, which is already compressed, the sound quality in your final Flash movie may not be as good, because Flash will compress it even more.)

To import a sound file in Flash MX: File menu > Import to Library.

To import a sound file in Flash MX 2004: File menu > Import > Import to Library.

Find the file on your hard drive, select it, and click Open.

2 Now open the **Library** panel (press F11). You should see the name of the sound file you just imported, with a speaker icon to the left of the filename. *Right-click* (Ctrl-click/Mac) that icon to open a menu. On that menu, select "Linkage" (Figure 2.8.02).

3 In the Linkage Properties dialog box, select "Export for ActionScript." Leave the check mark on "Export in first frame." Then give this file an ID by *typing* one word in the field labeled "Identifier" (Fig. 2.8.03). *Do not* use any spaces or punctuation. You will use this ID only once afterward, but it's quite necessary! Click OK when you've finished.

Fig. 2.8.03 Give the file an ID and check "Export for ActionScript."

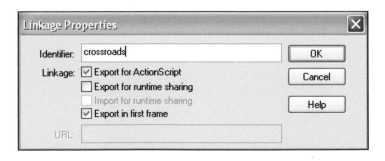

Note: If you look closely at Figure 2.8.02, you'll see that the filename for this sound file is "xroadsnew.wav"; in the Linkage Properties box, the identifier (or ID) "crossroads" *stands in* for that filename.

---

4 Now you're ready to write the first piece of ActionScript. Make a new layer in the **Timeline** and name it "actions" (without the quotes). Click on Frame 1 in that layer and open the **Actions** panel (press F9). If you're using Flash MX and you want to switch to Expert Mode, see Figure 2.8.01.

5 Because Sound is an *object* in Flash, you must create a *variable*, name it, and essentially set up that variable as a Sound object. Here's how (this is the first line of the script):

```
x = new Sound();
```

The variable is named "x"—you can name it "mySound" or "audio1" or any number of names instead, but of course the *variable name* should be short, and it must not include any spaces or punctuation. Make sure you assign a variable name *only once* in a movie—no other value can be assigned to "x," unless you want to replace this Sound object. You may remember variables from algebra class, where a variable is a symbol (usually a letter) that represents a number. The value of a variable can be changed after it is set the first time. In scripting, a variable can also hold values that are not numeric.

6 Now you get to *attach* the sound file you prepared in the previous steps. What are you "attaching" it to? In this case, you're attaching it to the "_root," or the main **Timeline**. This is the one time you use the ID you gave the sound file in the Linkage Properties dialog box (see Step 3).

```
x.attachSound("crossroads");
```

Notice that you must use the *variable name* ("x" in this case) again, followed by a dot. You are applying the action to that variable (the specific Sound object held in "x"). The quotation marks around the ID are required! (You will use different IDs for different files, so of course *you* might never use "crossroads" in your own work. The ID is just a nickname or alias for the sound file.)

7 The sound file is in your movie now (as you would see in the file size, if you saved and tested it), but it will not start playing until you tell it to start. Again, you will use the variable name ("x" in this case) to refer to your sound file:

```
x.start(0, 5);
```

The two *parameters* in parentheses are required. The first parameter is the number of seconds "offset," or how far into the sound file the sound will start to play. Usually this parameter is 0 (zero), as shown above, because you want the sound to start at the beginning. The second parameter is the number of times the sound will loop, or repeat. The numeral 5 here means this sound will play five times in total. If you do not want the sound to loop at all, use 0 (zero). If you want the sound to loop forever, use a large number; 100 is usually sufficient!

 8 Save and test your movie: Ctrl-Enter (Win) or Cmd-Return (Mac). The sound should play perfectly, five times.

Script on Frame 1:

```
x = new Sound();
x.attachSound("crossroads");
x.start(0, 5);
```

Note: If you put these three lines of script in Frame 1 on a longer Timeline with animation, the sound will play for *the same length of time* as it plays in a one-frame movie. It will even *continue* playing when the movie comes to the last frame and stops—if you write a `stop()` action on the last frame of the Timeline, it will stop the playhead, but *it will not stop the sound!* Something far worse happens if you do not have a `stop()` action in the Timeline, and your movie is longer than one frame: The movie will loop, and the sound may play multiple times, overlapping itself. Make sure your Timeline has a `stop()` action on the final frame, unless it is a one-frame movie. A single-frame movie does not need a `stop()` action.

9 Add about 3 seconds worth of frames to the Timeline. Do not add or change any ActionScript in your movie.

10 Save and test your movie: Ctrl-Enter (Win) or Cmd-Return (Mac). You should experience a cacophony of overlapping sound.

11 Make a keyframe on the final frame of the Timeline and add a `stop()` action there.

12 Save and test your movie: Ctrl-Enter (Win) or Cmd-Return (Mac). You should not hear the cacophony now. But your sound is playing for more than 3 seconds, in spite of the `stop()` action.

13 To ensure that the sound will *stop playing* on a particular frame, click on that frame in the **Timeline**, make it a keyframe (press F6), open the **Actions** panel (press F9), and add the following line of script there:

`x.stop();`

This will work on *any* keyframe (not only on the final frame of the movie). The variable name ("x" in this case) determines *which sound* will stop playing. There are no parameters for this action, but the parentheses must be used anyway.

Notice the difference between the script that stops the main **Timeline** and the script that stops the sound. The variable name ("x" in this case), followed by a dot, specifies an object to which the script *after the dot* will be applied.

Note: You cannot write ActionScript on a frame *unless* it is a keyframe.

Script on final frame:
```
stop();
x.stop();
```

14 You can write the same `start()` and `stop()` actions onto buttons, instead of frames, to give users the option of stopping and restarting the sound. To do so, create a button on the **Stage** (see Lesson 4 if you need a review). Select the button on the Stage (click it *once*), open the **Actions** panel (press F9), and write:

```
on (release) {
    x.stop();
}
```

Note: If the button is on the main Timeline ("_root") and the **x.attachSound()** method was *also* used on the main Timeline, the sound *will stop* when the user clicks this button. However, if either the sound ("x" in this case) or the button is on a *different* Timeline (that is, inside a movie clip symbol), additional script is required to provide the *path* to the variable named "x." Using paths was discussed briefly under "A Sliding Panel" in Lesson 6, where you had to use the *instance name* of your movie clip to control it with a button. This probably will not affect you now, at this point in your Flash learning curve, but as your Flash skills improve, you will use movie clips more often. Whenever you put sound or buttons inside movie clips, you must include *explicit paths* in your ActionScript to account for the location of both the *script* and the *objects* to which the script refers.

15 Now that you have a working Stop button, there is no way for the user to restart the sound after clicking that button. To provide one, place a *second* button on the **Stage** to act as your Play button. Select it, open the **Actions** panel (press F9), and write:

```
on (release) {
    x.start(0, 100);
}
```

You must use the two *parameters* (the numerals in parentheses) again, as shown. These were explained in Step 7.

16 Save and test your movie: Ctrl-Enter (Win) or Cmd-Return (Mac).

There's a problem with this script. Here's how to experience it: Stop the sound by pressing the Stop button you made. Then restart the sound by pressing the Play button you made. So far, so good, right? Now press your Play button *a second time*. And a third time. And, if you can stand it, a fourth time.

17 Here's how to fix that problem: Select your Play button on the **Stage**, open the **Actions** panel (press F9), and add just one line:

```
on (release) {
    x.stop();
    x.start(0, 100);
}
```

This may seem odd, but if you always *stop* a sound *before* you start it, you will never suffer from overlapping copies of the same track playing at the same time. Thank goodness. You can do this on a frame as well as on a button.

18 Save and test your movie: Ctrl-Enter (Win) or Cmd-Return (Mac). No more overlapping sound.

Note: To avoid any possibility of unwanted overlapping sound, use the `stop()` action immediately before any `start()` action for a Sound object—even on Frame 1. There's no effect if the sound is not playing (it will just start normally); if the sound *is* playing, it will stop and then restart immediately.

In general, you'll find that `attachSound()` works best with music loops and sound effects, although you can also use it for narration. Now let's look at how to load MP3s dynamically.

STOPPING ALL SOUNDS AT ONCE

You can add multiple sounds to an FLA, using a unique variable name (such as "x," "y," and "z") for each one, and controlling each one with its own button. To ensure that only one sound plays, add this single line of ActionScript *before* the `start()` action on the button:

```
stopAllSounds();
```

This way, you do not need to stop each and every sound that *might* be playing. Only the sounds that are currently playing will stop when this action executes. A sound on the Timeline, however, will start playing again as soon as the playhead moves forward; this is one reason why putting sound on the Timeline can be trickier than using attached or loaded sounds.

Exercise 8.2: Sound Outside the Flash File

When you use `loadSound()` to play a sound file from a Flash movie (as you will in this exercise), the sound file never becomes part of the SWF file. It is a separate file that must be uploaded separately to your Web server.

This method works *only* with files in the MP3 format. The sound will download to the user's computer when the `loadSound()` script in the SWF

Fig. 2.8.04 If your sound file is in the same folder with the SWF (top), use the filename alone. But if your sound file is inside a folder (bottom), add the folder name to the path in your ActionScript.

executes. If the file size is very large, the user's connection is slow, or there's a lot going on in the movie, it may take a while before the sound starts to play. So even though the sound file is not part of the user's *initial* Flash download, you should consider carefully before you load any file larger than a megabyte!

Select your sound file carefully, check the file size, and then also *decide where that file will be* on your Web server relative to the SWF file. You must give Flash a *path* to the sound file as part of the loadSound() method, so if you move the sound file later (relative to the SWF), you will also need to change the ActionScript (Figure 2.8.04). The path can be absolute (for example, "http://www.myserver.com/sounds/lala.mp3") or relative (for example, "sounds/lala.mp3").

A non-looping music file or a spoken-voice file will work well in this exercise.

Start with a new, empty file in Flash.

1 Make a new layer in the Timeline and name it "actions" (without the quotes). Click on Frame 1 in that layer and open the Actions panel (press F9). If you're using Flash MX and you want to switch to Expert Mode, see Figure 2.8.01.

2 Exactly as with the other method for handling a sound file (see Exercise 8.1), with this method you must create a *variable*, name it, and essentially set up that variable as a Sound object. Here's how (this is the first line of the script):

```
x = new Sound();
```

This is exactly the same as the first line of script in Exercise 8.1.

Note: You must not use "x" as your variable name if you have *already* used "x" for another variable in the *same* FLA file. If you repeat a variable name, the previous contents of that variable are *replaced* by the new contents. (If you *intend* to replace the contents of "x," you may use it again.)

---

3 In the next line of ActionScript, knowing the location of your sound file (relative to the FLA and SWF files) is essential:

```
x.loadSound("mp3s/rainforest.mp3", true);
```

Whatever the path is to that sound file, enclose it in quotation marks. Make sure you include the file extension (*.mp3*) at the end of the filename too.

What about that second parameter, "true"? When you write "true," the sound file will *stream*. When you write "false," the sound file will *not stream*. In some situations, you may want streaming, or not. This is explained in more detail at the end of this lesson. In this exercise, we will assume you have a longer file and you *do* want it to stream. In that case, the sound file begins to play automatically as soon as possible—it does not make the user wait until the entire file has finished downloading.

Note: When you stream a sound file, you leave it to Flash to decide when the user starts to hear something. Flash will begin to play the audio when it determines that enough of the file has downloaded. The timing will vary depending on the user's Internet connection. So while normally the sound would begin playing very soon after it was loaded, there is no guarantee. If you require the sound to start on cue, you will want to check to see that it has loaded completely *before* it's needed; for an example, see the Lesson 8 files on the Web site for this book (filename: sound12.fla).

Script on Frame 1:

```
x = new Sound();
x.loadSound("mp3s/rainforest.mp3", true);
```

4 So you're already able to save and test your movie: Ctrl-Enter (Win) or Cmd-Return (Mac). What a pleasure! So why didn't we do this instead of the first exercise, in the first place?

There are reasons why you may not want to use this method for every sound.

- You cannot loop the sound gracefully with the loadSound() method. A streaming file is not saved in memory, so it needs to be loaded again each time it plays.

- Depending on the speed of the user's connection, or network traffic levels, the streamed sound may take a long while to start playing. In contrast, a sound included in the SWF with the attachSound() method can always start immediately.

So it's really true that you should consider *which Sound method* is best suited to a particular use of sound in your movie.

5 Stopping this sound is exactly the same as shown in Exercise 8.1, Step 13. You can also create a button on the **Stage** and script it to stop the sound, as shown in Exercise 8.1, Step 14. Take a moment to think about this: Stopping the sound is *no different* regardless of which method you used to handle the sound.

6 If you want to provide a button that starts the streaming sound *again*, after it has been stopped, the script on the button can reload the sound file:

```
on (release) {
    x.loadSound("mp3s/rainforest.mp3", true);
}
```

Or you can use the start() action instead, since you already loaded this file:

```
on (release) {
    x.start(0, 0);
}
```

One excellent use for the loadSound() method: If you have a lot of separate sound files, and the user may choose to listen to a few of them, but probably not all of them, this method allows the user to download only the files of interest. A music jukebox application would use this method.

Exercise 8.3: Detecting When a Sound Has Played to the End

Imagine that you want the image on screen to change as soon as a sound file has finished playing. (You could also start a new sound; we'll get to that next.) You'll need to determine when the sound ends and then initiate some other action.

This *event detection* works whether you have used attachSound() or load-Sound(). In either case, let's assume you named your sound object variable "x," as shown earlier. That's important, because it must be clear *which sound* you are waiting for.

For this exercise, you can use one of the files you saved previously in this lesson.

1 Click on Frame 1 in the "actions" layer and open the **Actions** panel (press F9). Below the other script there, type this:

```
x.onSoundComplete = function() {
}
```

It may look odd, but you're leaving a space for the instructions about what to do when the sound completes. The curly braces { } will contain those instructions. Notice where your variable name ("x" in this case) appears, followed by a dot.

2 As you learned in Lesson 5, it's easy to send the playhead to any part of the **Timeline** (and thus to any part of the movie) if you use frame labels. If you don't have any frame labels in your movie, make one now. Put a stop() action on Frame 1, and position your labeled keyframe farther to the right in your Timeline (say, around Frame 10). Put a shape or some image in that keyframe too, so you can see that your test movie really works.

In the Timeline shown in Figure 2.8.05, the **Stage** holds one thing until Frame 10. In Frame 10, a new image is on the Stage. There is a stop() action on Frame 1 and another stop() action on Frame 10. The label (on Frame 10) is "jumphere."

3 To send the playhead to Frame 10, using a keyframe with the label "jumphere," the ActionScript would read:

```
gotoAndStop("jumphere");
```

4 Since that's all you need to complete this action, that's all the script you must add to the onSoundComplete event (between the curly braces):

```
x.onSoundComplete = function() {
    gotoAndStop("jumphere");
}
```

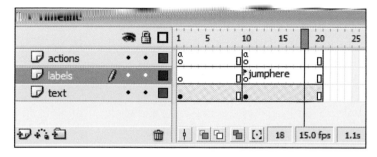

Fig. 2.8.05 This Timeline illustrates how to set up this exercise by creating a frame label on a frame containing an image. The playhead will stay on Frame 1 until the sound loaded there finishes playing. Then the script shown in Step 4 will send the playhead to the labeled frame.

Note: You could place *any instructions you like* between the curly braces. You may not want to send the playhead to a new frame in the **Timeline**; perhaps you want to start a movie clip animation instead, or start a new sound, as explained in Exercise 8.4.

---

5 Save and test your movie: Ctrl-Enter (Win) or Cmd-Return (Mac).

What should happen: (a) The sound plays in its entirety as the Stage remains empty. (b) As soon as the sound ends, the image in the labeled frame appears. This mirrors what is shown in the Timeline in Figure 2.8.05.

Exercise 8.4: Playing Two Tracks at the Same Time

In this example, you will use the loadSound() method, but you can do the same thing with the attachSound() method. The only way this can be done with the loadSound() method is by assigning each sound to a movie clip instance. You'll do it that way here because it is more versatile, even though at first you may think it's more work. (You would not need the movie clips with the attachSound() method, but you would still need to use a different *variable name* for each sound file.)

Start with a new, empty file in Flash.

1 Create an empty movie clip and drag an *instance* of it from the **Library** to the **Stage**. Name the instance "clip01_mc" (without the quotes), and be sure to tab out of the Instance Name field. Drag another instance of the *same* movie clip to the Stage, and name this one "clip02_mc" (you can position these clips on the Stage, or off to one side, since they do not contain any images; they are just containers for the sound). Giving an *instance name* to a movie clip was explained in "A Sliding Panel," Lesson 6, Step 18.

How to create an empty movie clip: With *nothing* selected on the **Stage,** open the Insert menu and select "New Symbol." Select "Movie clip," name the symbol (a good name is "Empty Clip"), and click OK. *Exit* from Symbol Editing Mode by pressing Ctrl-E (or Cmd-E/Mac).

2 Make a new layer in the **Timeline** and name it "actions" (without the quotes). Click on Frame 1 in that layer and open the **Actions** panel (press F9). Type:

```
x = new Sound("clip01_mc");
x.loadSound("mp3s/rainforest.mp3", true);
y = new Sound("clip02_mc");
y.loadSound("mp3s/voicetest.mp3", true);
```

This is all the script you need to load the two files at the same time. Notice how you are using the instance names you gave to the two movie clips in Step 1. Of course, you must use the filenames and paths of your own sound files. Note that the *variable name* for the second sound object ("y" in this case) must be *different* from the first one ("x" in this case).

The two loaded MP3 files are essentially streaming into their respective movie clips.

3 Save and test your movie: Ctrl-Enter (Win) or Cmd-Return (Mac).

What should happen: Both sound files begin to play at roughly the same time. If the files are very large, there may be a delay.

4 Now try the same idea, but play the second sound *after the first one has finished*. To do it, change the script you typed in Step 2. (Alternatively, start a new file.) Write this script on Frame 1:

```
x = new Sound("clip01_mc");
y = new Sound("clip02_mc");
x.loadSound("rainforest.mp3", true);
x.onSoundComplete = function() {
    y.loadSound("voicetest.mp3", true);
}
```

Compare this script with the script in Exercise 8.3, Step 4. You should be able to understand how the onSoundComplete event works in both examples. This event can be quite useful to you, because it makes it easy to force changes in your movie to wait for the end of a specific audio file—even an *external* MP3 file.

5 Save and test your movie: Ctrl-Enter (Win) or Cmd-Return (Mac).

What should happen: The "x" sound file plays to completion, and then the "y" sound file begins and plays to completion.

Exercise 8.5: Scripting a Pause Button

This script works with either the attachSound() method or the loadSound() method. If you remember that the start() action has two parameters in parentheses (Exercise 8.1, Step 7), you may also remember that the first parameter is the number of seconds "offset," or *how far into* the sound file the sound will start to play. Now you'll see how that can be useful, because you will need to be able to restart the sound at the place where it was paused.

You can use the "offset" parameter with a loaded sound (an external MP3 file).

There are two *properties* of the Sound object: *duration* and *position*. You can use *duration* to find out how long a sound file is, in milliseconds; we will not use that property here, but it can be useful in other cases. For example, this stores in "d" the length of the sound file "x":

```
d = x.duration;
```

You can use *position* to see how long the sound file has already played, in milliseconds. For example, this stores in "p" the position (amount of time played so far) of the sound file "x":

```
p = x.position;
```

Keep in mind that the "seconds offset" parameter requires *whole* seconds—not milliseconds! This may seem a bit too mathematical for your liking, but stick with it if you want to be able to control the sound files in your Flash movies. Buttons that control sound require a longer chunk of ActionScript, but it's worth the effort.

Start with a new, empty file in Flash.

1 Make a new layer in the **Timeline** and name it "actions" (without the quotes). Click on Frame 1 in that layer and open the **Actions** panel (press F9). Type:

```
x = new Sound();
x.attachSound("jazzy");
x.start(0, 0);
```

Import a sound file to the **Library**. Use a file that is longer (maybe 1 minute). Because you are using the `attachSound()` method, the file format should be either WAV (Windows) or AIFF (Mac). Of course, your ID does not need to be "jazzy"—it will be whatever ID you type when you use "Linkage" on the sound file imported to your Library (this was all covered under Exercise 8.1, Step 3).

2 Create a button on the **Stage**. This will be your Pause button. Select the button (click it *once*) and open the **Actions** panel (press F9). Type this script for the button:

```
on (release) {
    if (musicplay == true) {
        p = Math.floor(x.position / 1000);
        x.stop();
        musicplay = false;
    } else {
        x.start(p, 0);
        musicplay = true;
    }
}
```

That script may look complex to you, so here is what it does, line by line:

Table 2.8.01

`on (release) {`	Begin the button handler.
`if (musicplay == true) {`	Test for a condition: If a variable named "musicplay" is true, then do what is inside the curly braces. The double equals sign means "is equivalent to."
`p = Math.floor(x.position / 1000);`	Assign a value to the variable named "p": The value is determined by the expression following the equals sign. "x.position" is how long the sound file ("x") has already played, in milliseconds. Divide it by 1,000 to get whole seconds. Apply the "Math.floor" method to that to eliminate all the decimal places; in other words, make it an integer.
`x.stop();`	Now that we have the position of "x" (saved in "p") we can stop it.
`musicplay = false;`	We want to continue using the variable named "musicplay," so now we set it to "false" (because the sound is not playing). Note that to reset the value, we use a normal (single) equals sign.
`} else {`	If the first condition was not found (if "musicplay" was *not* true), do this instead.

Table 2.8.01 Continued

`x.start(p, 0);`	Start the sound file playing at the number held in the value of "p."
`musicplay = true;`	We want to continue using the variable named "musicplay," so now we set it to "true" (because the sound is playing). To reset the value, we use a normal (single) equals sign.
`}`	End the if-else conditional statements.
`}`	End the button handler.

3 There's one more step to make the button work properly. Click on Frame 1 in the "actions" layer and open the **Actions** panel (F9). Add this line *after* the three lines that are already there (see Step 1):

```
musicplay = true;
```

That line is setting the value of the variable named "musicplay" *for the first time*. Since the line above it is `x.start(0, 0)` it's safe to assume that the sound *is* playing.

 4 Save and test your movie: Ctrl-Enter (Win) or Cmd-Return (Mac).

What should happen: The *first* time you click on the button you made, the "x" sound file stops playing. The *second* time you click on the button, the "x" sound file begins playing at the point where you first clicked. Each subsequent click will be off, on, off, on, and the button will always "capture" the position of the sound file—because of *this* script:

```
p = Math.floor(x.position / 1000);
```

It's most important that you understand that the *current position* of the sound file is read and saved *each time* the button is clicked. That's what makes this script work.

Note: The *method* "Math.floor" works better than "Math.round" in this case, because the floor is the closest integer that is *less than or equal to* the number following in parentheses. If you used "Math.round," the restarted sound might be a little ahead of where it stopped.

If you'd like to try this with a loaded MP3 (an external file), the only script changes are on Frame 1 (the script on your Pause button does not change at all):

```
x = new Sound();
x.loadSound("mp3s/cabrobro.mp3", false);
x.onLoad = function(success) {
    x.start(0, 0);
    musicplay = true;
}
```

Here the value *false* tells the file not to stream. If you want to stream it, use *true* instead.

Exercise 8.6: Scripting a Mute Button

This script works with either the `attachSound()` method or the `loadSound()` method. Rather than pause the sound, you allow it to continue playing at a volume of zero, or inaudible. You would use this technique when the sound must stay in sync with other things in the movie.

Start with a new, empty file in Flash. Use a longer sound file (30 seconds or more) for this exercise.

1 Make a new layer in the **Timeline** and name it "actions" (without the quotes). Click on Frame 1 in that layer and open the **Actions** panel (press F9). Write the script on Frame 1 for the Sound object method you want to use, as shown in Exercise 8.1 and Exercise 8.2.

2 Create a button on the **Stage** (Frame 1). Select the button, and open the **Actions** panel (press F9). Type this script for the button:

```
on (release) {
    if (x.getVolume() > 0) {
        x.setVolume(0);
    } else {
        x.setVolume(100);
    }
}
```

Here's what that script does, line by line:

Table 2.8.02

`on (release) {`	Begin the button handler.
`if (x.getVolume() > 0) {`	Test for a condition: If the `getVolume` *method* returns a value greater than 0 (zero), then do what is inside the curly braces.
`x.setVolume(0);`	Use the `setVolume` *method* to change the volume to 0 (zero), or inaudible, while the sound file continues to play (silently).
`} else {`	If the first condition was not found (if the volume was not greater than 0), do this instead.
`x.setVolume(100);`	Use the `setVolume` *method* to change the volume to 100, the maximum level (this is the default volume in Flash).
`}`	End the if-else conditional statements.
`}`	End the button handler.

3 Save and test your movie: Ctrl-Enter (Win) or Cmd-Return (Mac).

What should happen: The *first* time you click on the button you made, the "x" sound file seems to stop playing (but actually, it is still playing at volume 0). The *second* time you click on the button, the volume returns to normal (100), but you have missed some of the sound (because it continued to play while you were not hearing it). Each subsequent click will be off, on, off, on.

Note: A mute button is very useful when you have timed photographs to play synchronously with a soundtrack in a Flash movie. In that case, a Pause button for the sound alone is no good. You do not want the sound to stop and then pick up exactly where it was stopped, after three or four additional photographs have been displayed—because then the presentation would be out of sync.

Exercise 8.7: Synchronizing Images to Loaded Audio

This last sound exercise addresses something that many journalists want to do: Combine a radio documentary–style sound file and a photo story, with each photo appearing reliably when a particular thing is heard in the audio.

For this exercise, you will need an MP3 file of about 20 to 30 seconds and about five or six images. You don't have to use photos to learn how to do this. You can draw stick figures if you must; just make sure they all look different so you can see that they are changing in sync with the audio file. You will also need a Play button and a Replay button (or use the Play button twice).

Start with a new, empty file in Flash. Set your *frame rate* to 15 fps.

Fig. 2.8.06 The Windows Sound Recorder shows the position of a WAV file in hundredths of a second.

1   Open your MP3 file in any sound editing program that allows you to determine *in seconds* (preferably in tenths of a second) where you want each image to appear, in relation to the sound as it plays (Figures 2.8.06 and 2.8.07). For example, if a voice says "tiger cubs," you will want a photo of baby tigers to appear then, and when the voice says "polar bears," change the image to a photo of bears. Make *a precise list* of each timing point when you want the image to change. In a zoo slideshow with five photos, for example, your audio list might read: Giraffe 0; Tigers 3.5; Bears 5.9; Elephant 9.5; Walrus 13.7; End 20. (This list represents a 20-second audio file.) These numbers will be used in the example below, so note that 5.9 here means 5 seconds and 9/10 of a second. In the script below, this number will be represented by a whole number, 59, because the script works with tenths of a second (59/10 equals 5.9).

That's all you need the sound editing software for. You don't need to resave your MP3 file unless you changed it.

2   Place your photos on the **Timeline** in single keyframes, all in the same layer. They do not need to be converted to symbols, because they do not move. Each photo requires only one frame. You'll see why in a moment!

Table 2.8.03

Photo	Subject	Timing in audio file (in seconds)	× 10	"Position" property (1000 = 1 second)
1	Giraffe	0	0	0
2	Tigers	3.5	35	3500
3	Bears	5.9	59	5900
4	Elephant	9.5	95	9500
5	Walrus	13.7	137	13700

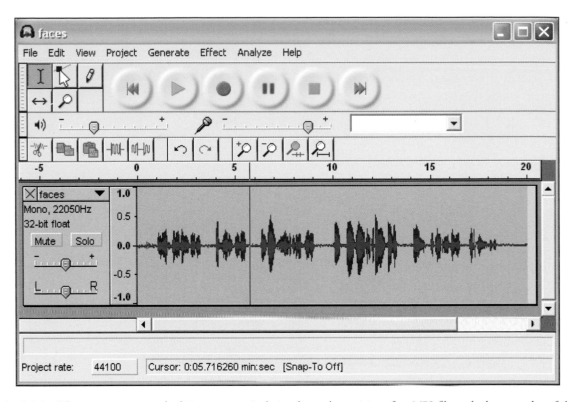

Fig. 2.8.07 The open source sound editing program Audacity shows the position of an MP3 file at the bottom edge of the application window as the "cursor position."

3 Add one new *keyframe* at the beginning and another new *keyframe* at the end of the layer holding all your photos. If you have five photos, you will now have seven frames in total. The script will work no matter how many frames you have.

4 Put your Play button on the **Stage** in Frame 1 and your Replay button on the Stage in the last frame.

5 Name the layer "photos," and then add a new layer above it, named "actions."

6 Click on Frame 1 in your "actions" layer and open the **Actions** panel (press F9). Write this script on Frame 1 (it will be explained later):

```
stop();
x = new Sound();
a = new Array(1,35,59,95,137,198);
```

```
n = 0;
function checkAudio() {
    p = Math.floor(x.position / 100); // yes 100, not 1000
    if (p > a[n]) {
        n++;
        nextFrame();
    }
}
```

You'll need to *change all the numbers* in the third line to match your own audio list, which you made in Step 1. Notice that the decimals are gone (compare the numbers here to those given as an example in Step 1). It will be easier to work with integers, so multiply each number in your audio list by 10, and compensate by dividing your sound position by 100 instead of the usual 1000 (as shown in the sixth line of the script). The *position* equal to 5900 would mean 5.9 seconds. By dividing by 100 instead of 1000, the script allows you to eliminate the decimals in your array. You need one less number in the array than your total number of frames. If you have seven frames total, for example, you need six numbers in your array. Make the first number 1, no matter what. Be careful to use a comma after each number, except the last.

7 Select the Play button in Frame 1 (click *once* to select it) and write this script on the button:

```
on (release) {
    x.stop();
    x.loadSound("mp3s/faces.mp3", true);
    _root.onEnterFrame = checkAudio;
}
```

Make sure to replace the *path* to the audio file with your own correct path instead!

8 Click on the final frame (make sure it is a *keyframe*) in your "actions" layer and write this script on the frame:

```
stop();
delete _root.onEnterFrame;
```

9 Finally, select the Replay button in your final frame (click *once* to select it) and write this script on the button:

```
on (release) {
    gotoAndStop(1);
}
```

10 Save and test your movie: Ctrl-Enter (Win) or Cmd-Return (Mac).

What should happen: Nothing happens until you click your Play button. Then the audio plays and the images on your Timeline should show themselves one by one, in sync with the audio file. The show stops on the final frame. If you click Replay, it returns to Frame 1 and stops there.

How this works is a bit technical, but you have used most of the script before (mostly in this lesson). You understand a `stop()` action, `on (release)`, and `gotoAndStop(1)`. So all you need to think about are the Array object and the nifty `_root.onEnterFrame` event handler, which provides a way to check something over and over again until a desired condition is true.

What's Happening in Step 6

The Array object exists in most scripting and programming languages. It provides a way to store a lot of values in one big group and, as in this case, to cycle through them one at a time as needed. Each value in an array is considered equal to a kind of sequenced variable. For example, with an array named "fruit" that contained ("banana", "apple", "lemon"), you could use the individual members of the array by calling them "fruit[0]" or "fruit[1]."

```
fruit[0] = "banana"
fruit[1] = "apple"
fruit[2] = "lemon"
```

In this script, the array is named "a":

```
a[0] = 1
a[1] = 35
a[2] = 59
```

So, first you set the value of a variable named "n" to equal 0. Then you used that variable ("n") to *stand in for* the number (following "a" in square brackets) that stands for a particular member of your array. You checked to see whether "p" was *greater than* the value of the current member of your array (starting with "a[0]," the first member):

```
if (p > a[n])
```

And if it was, the script *incremented* "n"—meaning it added 1 to "n"—and so it will check the *next* member of the array the *next* time it runs:

```
n++;
```

If the condition was true, the script also moved the playhead to the next frame in the Timeline, meaning the next image is shown:

```
nextFrame();
```

If you can understand that the flexibility of the Array object is what makes it possible for this script to work on a Timeline containing five images or 500 images—without changing anything but the sound file and the numbers contained in the array—you are on your way to advanced ActionScripting!

What's Happening in Step 7

You already know everything the script on the Play button is doing, except this:

```
_root.onEnterFrame = checkAudio;
```

It means that every time the "_root" (the main Timeline) enters a frame, the function named "checkAudio" will execute. That means if your frame rate is 15 fps, the function will run 15 times every second. And where is the function "checkAudio"? It's on Frame 1, where you wrote it. (We cannot write regular functions on buttons, only on frames.)

What does "checkAudio" do? It looks at the position of your streaming audio file (see Exercise 8.5), gets the value, divides it by 100, and rounds it down to the closest integer. Then it compares that integer ("p") to the value of the current member of the array (a value taken from the array and contained in "a[n]"). In other words, it asks, "Are we there yet?" If the answer is yes, it changes the image for you by advancing to the next frame in your Timeline.

What's Happening in Step 8

On the final frame of your Timeline, the movie stops, and this action is executed:

```
delete _root.onEnterFrame;
```

This removes, or cancels, the repeated execution of the function "checkAudio," which is what the _root.onEnterFrame event handler was doing, 15 times every second, throughout your whole movie. And now you don't need it anymore.

What's Happening in Step 9

You already know that clicking the Replay button sends you back to Frame 1 of your movie:

```
gotoAndStop(1);
```

That's all you need to do to play this movie again, because everything starts again when you click the Play button there. Just keep in mind that if you change the script or add more script elsewhere in your movie, some things shown here may not work the same way.

STREAMING AND EVENT SOUNDS

Streaming Sounds

A streaming sound begins playing as soon as possible, even before the entire sound file has loaded (the timing depends on the speed of the user's connection). A streaming sound that is on the Timeline is synchronized to the Timeline, meaning that Flash will *drop frames* in an animation (that is, frames will be skipped) if the program cannot draw them quickly enough to keep up with the sound. Not necessarily a good thing!

A streaming sounds stops when the movie stops, but *only* if that streaming sound is on the main Timeline. If a sound has been either attached or loaded (the two methods explained in this lesson), it will go on playing until it ends, or is deliberately stopped with ActionScript, even if the movie stops.

A SPECIAL CASE: ATTACHSOUND AND PRELOADERS

When you learned how to use the attachSound() method in Steps 2–3, Exercise 8.1, the instructions were to leave the check mark on "Export in first frame." There is one case where you must take a different approach: When you have a preloader on the movie (preloaders are explained in Appendix A).

If you allow "Export in first frame," the user will not see your preloader until the *entire sound file* has loaded into memory. This largely defeats the purpose of the preloader, because the user would be staring at a blank Flash window for a long time, instead of seeing how much longer the wait will be. However, if you simply remove the check mark, your sound will not load at all—not good.

The solution is to *both* (a) remove the check mark in the Linkage Properties dialog, *and* (b) place the sound on the Timeline using the **Properties** panel. Here's how: Create a new keyframe a short distance into the **Timeline** (such as Frame 7 or 8). Then, with that frame selected, *select* your linked sound file from the Sound menu on the right side of the **Properties** panel. You must also choose "Stop" from the Sync menu there, as shown in Figure 2.8.08. This allows your preloader to function normally, and the attached sound will begin to preload less than 1 second after the movie begins.

If you're *not* using a preloader (because your SWF is small), you can safely allow "Export in first frame."

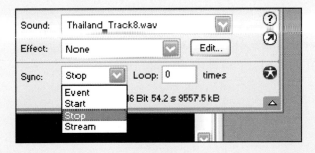

Fig. 2.8.08 By placing the linked sound on the Timeline after Frame 1, you enable a preloader to behave as it should.

Use streaming sound for narration, interviews, readings, and most music. It should never be used for music loops or for short sounds such as button sound effects (because there is likely to be a delay).

Event Sounds

An event sound downloads completely before it can begin playing. If it was loaded (not placed on the Timeline), it requires the start() action to begin. Event sounds always play until they are complete, even if the movie stops, *unless* the stop() action is used on the sound itself.

Use event sounds for button feedback and other sound effects. Make sure the sound is loaded *before* it becomes necessary to play it.

FILE FORMATS AND SETTINGS

Acceptable Sound Formats

Three file formats for sound can be imported into Flash: WAV (Windows only), AIFF (Mac only), and MP3 (both Windows and Mac). The WAV and AIFF formats are uncompressed; Flash will perform compression on these when you export your SWF (when you either test the movie or select "Publish" from the File menu; see below for details). MP3 files will also be compressed on export, so it's usually best not to import MP3 files to Flash with attachSound(). The other sound method, loadSound(), supports *only* MP3 files, as explained in Exercise 8.2.

If QuickTime (version 4 or later) is installed on your computer, you can import several additional file formats for sound. On Windows, you can import AIFF, sound-only QuickTime Movies (MOV), and Sun AU, as well as WAV. On the Mac OS, you can import Sound Designer II, sound-only QuickTime Movies (MOV), Sun AU, System 7 sounds, and WAV, as well as AIFF.

Settings for Sound Editing

According to Macromedia, when you use WAV or AIFF files (uncompressed sound files), ideally you should use these settings: 16-bit, 22 kHz, mono.

Flash can import either 8- or 16-bit sounds at three sampling rates: 11 kHz, 22 kHz, or 44 kHz (actually 11.025 kHz, 22.05 kHz, or 44.1 kHz). The higher the sampling rate, the better the quality and the larger the file size, generally. If your sound has been recorded at any other sampling rate, it will be resampled when you import it into Flash, and some degradation may result. An 8-bit sound file has considerably less quality than a 16-bit sound file, but 8-bit may be adequate for some simple sound effects. Stereo uses *twice* as much data as mono—so unless the file absolutely *must* be stereo, use mono!

Settings for Publishing the SWF

To change compression settings for an individual sound file within Flash, right-click (or Ctrl-click/Mac) that sound in the **Library** and select "Export Settings" from the pop-up menu. The Sound Settings dialog box provides a menu with several options. When sound quality is really important, you should experiment with these to find out which produces the best result. For most Flash work, however, the "Default" option is perfectly all right. Leaving the "Default" option here means the file uses the global compression settings in the Publish Settings dialog.

To change global compression settings for event sounds or stream sounds, open the File menu and select "Publish Settings." In the dialog box, under the tab labeled "Flash," you'll see two buttons that allow you to change "Audio Stream" and "Audio Event." The default setting for each of these is MP3, 16 Kbps, mono. If you have not changed the compression settings for any individual sound file in the Library, then these global settings will apply to all event sounds and all streaming sounds in the Flash movie.

Note: Flash exports *all* streaming sounds in a movie to the SWF as one streaming file; the *highest* setting selected is applied to all streaming sounds. If you have changed the settings for any one streaming sound in the movie to higher quality, that will affect all streaming sounds in that movie.

For more information about sound compression settings, look in the Flash Help files.

WORKING WITH SOUND SUMMARY

If you're going to use Flash to tell stories, you will need to learn to use sound files skillfully. Let the people in your photographs speak to the audience. Help users experience a place by letting them *hear* that place. The sound of water lapping at the edge of a lake, or an airplane roaring into the sky, can put the users' imagination at the scene.

Adding a sound effect to a button or to a frame in the Timeline is quite easy, and so is adding a music loop that simply plays again and again. Adding real journalistic sound requires a bit more effort, because the users should be able to pause or turn off the sound if they want to—and that means you need to use some ActionScript. This lesson has shown that using Action-Script to control sound in Flash is largely a matter of thinking about how the sound will be used in the Flash movie and adding buttons to give users some control over the sound. You must also test the sound functionality under various conditions, especially if you are using loaded, streaming MP3 files.

The final size of the Flash SWF file must always be considered, and if you think carefully about how sounds will be used in the Flash movie, you can make wise decisions about whether to include them in the file with `attachSound()`—resulting in a larger SWF—or load them as needed with `loadSound()`—resulting in a smaller SWF. With either method, you can tie the beginning of a longer sound file to a specific frame in the Flash movie, or synchronize an event in the movie to the conclusion of a sound file.

CONCLUSION

In this lesson, you have learned to:

1 Find methods and properties of the *Sound object* in the Actions panel.

2 Use two ActionScript *methods* of the Sound object: `attachSound()` and `loadSound()`.

3 Import a sound file to the Library.

4 Set the Linkage Properties to export an attached sound file for use with ActionScript, including the assignment of a unique ID name ("identifier") to the sound file.

5 Use a variable name (such as "x") to work with the Sound object.

6 Start an attached sound (make it begin to play), including the starting point within the sound file ("offset"), and the number of times the sound will loop or repeat.

7 Stop an attached sound (make it stop playing).

8 Script a Stop button and a Play button to control a specific sound file.

9 Stop a sound on the final frame of your movie.

10 Prevent a sound from overlapping itself (for example, when a movie loops).

11 Stop all sounds that are currently playing.

12 Load an MP3 file "on demand" from a file outside the Flash movie.

13 Control whether the loaded sound streams or does not stream.

14 Stop a loaded sound (make it stop playing).

15 Restart a loaded sound (by loading it again).

16 Use the `onSoundComplete` event to make something happen when a sound finishes playing.

17 Play two loaded MP3 files at the same time.

18 Set up a second loaded MP3 file to play only *after* a first loaded MP3 file has ended.

19 Script a Pause/Play button (one that toggles pause and play) for a specific sound file, using the "position" *property* of the Sound object.

20 Script a Mute/Unmute button (one that toggles zero volume and full volume) for a specific sound file, using the ActionScript *methods* `getVolume()` and `setVolume()`.

21 Make a list of audio timing points to use with ActionScript to sync images to a loaded streaming sound file.

22 Store a set of values in an Array object and use them individually.

23 Use the `_root.onEnterFrame` event handler to repeatedly execute a checking function.

24 Remove the `_root.onEnterFrame` event handler when you don't need it anymore.

25 Fix a preloader bug that occurs when using the `attachSound()` method.

Lesson 9

Working with Text

Text can seem like a no-brainer in Flash. What's the big deal? You grab the text tool, you type some words, it works. At least, it seems to work—until one day, when you are looking over someone's shoulder as she opens your Flash movie on the Web, and you see some strange, ugly typography that you never put there. What happened? You didn't embed your font.

If you understand how Flash handles text, and why the program has three different types of text field to choose from, you can avoid unfortunate mistakes and design flaws. You can spare your users from illegible, blurred text; you can easily make scrolling text boxes in seconds; you can even invite users to type in information and get results. Unlike standard HTML Web pages, Flash allows you to have excellent control over typography. But to enjoy that control, you must first learn about what Flash does (or doesn't do) with each of the three types of text field it can create.

LESSON 9

Creating text elements in Flash involves, primarily, the **Text** tool and the **Properties** panel. You used both in Lesson 4 to put text on a button, and you'll find a diagram there that identifies five key elements in the Properties panel for text.

Any time you want to create text in Flash, start by selecting the **Text** tool. Next, you must select the *type* of text (Figures 2.9.01 and 2.9.02). The three types available are listed in the Text Type menu on the **Properties** panel: Static, Dynamic, and Input. As you'll see, each of these has different properties and different results in your final SWF.

You will work with each type of text in different exercises below, but you can use all three in any Flash movie. You can even use *all three types* in a single frame on a single layer. Each *instance* of the TextField object, however,

Fig. 2.9.01 To choose the type of text, open the Text Type menu in the Properties panel. The panel shown is from Flash MX.

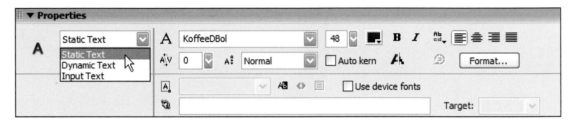

Fig. 2.9.02 The Properties panel for text in Flash MX 2004 is almost identical to the one in Flash MX. Individual differences will be explained in this lesson.

has only one type as a *property* of that object. (Don't confuse "type" with "font family": Again, the three types are Static, Dynamic, and Input.)

You will probably use Static text most of the time, unless you are reading from a database or an external text file. Even animated text in Flash is created with Static text.

Exercise 9.1: Static Text, a Tour of What You Can Do

Start a new file in Flash.

1 Select the **Text** tool in the **Tools** panel.

2 Open the Text Type menu in the **Properties** panel and select "Static" for this exercise. Most of the time, in normal uses, you will use Static text in your Flash movies.

3 Click once on the **Stage** and type a few words.

4 Select all the text you typed by clicking and dragging over it (Figure 2.9.03). Alternatively, you can right-click (or Ctrl-click/Mac) and choose "Select All" from the pop-up menu.

Fig. 2.9.03 At left, the text in the text field is not selected. In the illustration at right, all the text in the text field is selected.

Fig. 2.9.04 Two steps are necessary to make text that reads sideways: First use the Text Direction button.

Fig. 2.9.05 Second, use the Rotation button.

5 With the text selected, you can change the font, font size, "text (fill) color," and justification/alignment (left, center, right, full) by using the **Properties** panel. You have probably worked with those properties of text in other applications such as Microsoft Word. Go ahead and try each of these to make sure you can locate them in the Properties panel.

6 Now let's look at a few more unusual properties of the text field. First, you can easily change the *direction of the text* from horizontal to vertical by using the Text Direction button on the right side of the **Properties** panel (Figure 2.9.04). Then, *after* you have done that, you can change the *rotation* of the text, using the button just below the Text Direction button (Figure 2.9.05).

Flash MX 2004 Note

If you have previously changed the orientation of a Static text field from horizontal to vertical, the next time you select the Text tool, it will create a text field with the vertical orientation. You can change this before you use the tool by clicking the Text Direction button on the Properties panel.

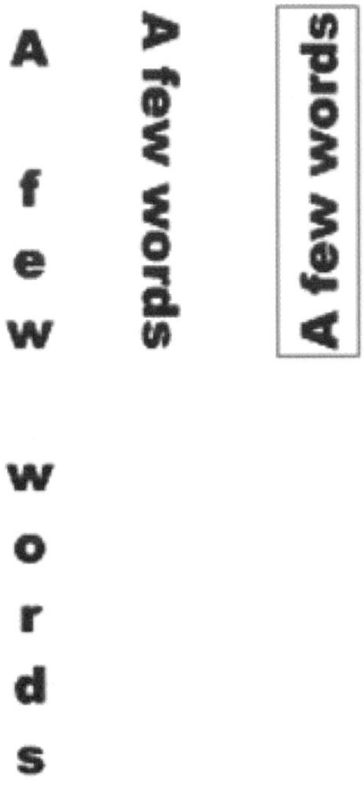

A

f

e

w

w

o

r

d

s

A few words

A few words

Fig. 2.9.06 Using the Text Direction button on the Properties panel, you can reorient a single line of text (left). Afterward, you can change the rotation of that text (center) using the Rotation options, also on the Properties panel. Finally, you can use the Transform options (on the Modify menu) to change the starting point for the vertical line of text (right). With the text field selected, open the Modify menu, go to "Transform," and then select "Flip Horizontal." Next, select "Flip Vertical."

7 Continuing the tour of the **Properties** panel for Static text, you can increase or decrease the *space between letters*, using the Character Spacing field. You can type a number into the field (then tab out of it so the number sticks), or open and use the slider to the right of the field, which lets you see the effect dynamically (Figure 2.9.07).

8 Next comes a basic skill to master—you will use this frequently! Whenever you select the **Text** tool (Static text) and begin typing, you are in "single-line mode." That is, the text will not wrap to the next line automatically. While you *could* press Enter/Return to force the text to go to the next line, that would make a lot of extra work for you if you decided later to change the width or the font. It's also very awkward to paste a longer block of text into the text field when you are in single-line mode. So you should know how to *change* to "multi-line mode" when you are using Static text.

Figure 2.9.09 shows how to change the Static text field to multiline and set the width you want.

9 Now that you have dragged the text field to the width you want, you can *copy* a block of text from a text editor program, such as MS Word, and *paste* it into the text field in Flash. To *change the width* after you have pasted the text, grab and drag the square "handle" in the upper right corner of the text field box. If you do not see the handle, select the Text tool and click *once* on the text *inside* the box. The text will become active, and the handle will be visible.

10 Let's do some serious formatting work with this text field. Change the *font*, *font size*, and *color* of the text to be small but still legible. The next step will work best if you have 100 words or more in the text field: Click the Format button on the far right side of the **Properties** panel. Use the Format Options dialog to change the paragraph indent, line spacing, and left and right margins for this text field (Figure 2.9.10). Click the Done/OK button when you have finished.

Warning: After you have changed the Format Options, the next new text field you create will have *the same options* already set for it. To return to the defaults, you will need to open the Format Options dialog again, with the new text field

Fig. 2.9.07 The slider can be used to change character spacing.

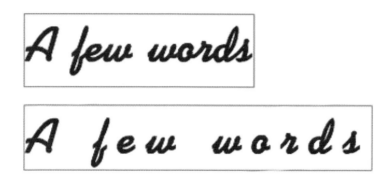

Fig. 2.9.08 The default character spacing (*top*) is zero. When character spacing is increased, the letters are farther apart (*bottom*).

Step 1   Step 2   Step 3   Step 4

Fig. 2.9.09 Changing from single-line to multiline with Static text in Flash requires you to grab the tiny "handle" in the upper right corner of the text field box on the Stage.

Step 1: Select the Text tool and click once on the Stage.

Step 2: Position your cursor above the "handle" until the cursor becomes a two-headed arrow, as shown.

Step 3: Click, hold, and drag the box to the right, to the width you want for this text block.

Step 4: Let go, and the text field box will now retain the width you selected. Text will wrap to the next line automatically. The "handle" has changed to square (it had been round). To change the width later (even after text has been entered), grab the square "handle" again and drag it right or left.

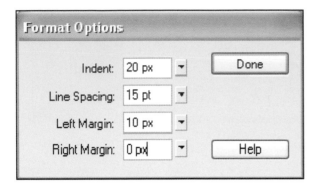

Fig. 2.9.10 The Format Options dialog allows you to set some properties that affect an entire block of text, for the currently selected text field.

selected, and change the options back. If you start a new Flash file without quitting from Flash, the changed options will still be in effect. Only when you exit completely will the options automatically be reset to the defaults.

11 Another useful feature of Static text is that you can easily make any word, or string of words, in a text field *act as a link* to open a Web page. To do this, first *select* only the word or words you want to act as a link (click, hold, and drag to select them). Then *click into* the URL Link field in the **Properties** panel and either *type* or *paste* the complete URL of the Web page (Figure 2.9.11).

12 Tab out of the URL Link field. That puts your cursor into the Target field in the **Properties** panel, which is exactly where you want to be. The reason: You will now select *the way you want the Web page to open* when the user clicks your link text (Figure 2.9.12). Do you want the new Web page to *replace* the Web page that contains your Flash movie in the same window? If so, then "_top" is a good choice from the Target menu. Do you want the Web page to open in a new, separate browser window? If so, then "_blank" is a good choice from the Target menu.

Fig. 2.9.11 Type a URL into the URL Link field to make Flash text act as a link.

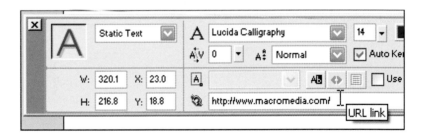

Fig. 2.9.12 Select an appropriate target from the Target menu. This determines how the new Web page will open in the user's Web browser.

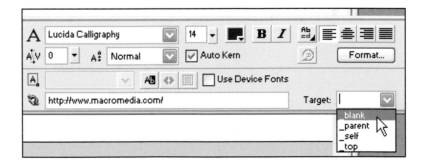

Note: The target in this case is part of HTML, not part of Flash. It creates an attribute in the link code that is read by the Web browser only. A good source for additional information, if you need it, is Miko O'Sullivan's HTML Code Tutorial: *http://www.htmlcodetutorial.com/linking/_A_TARGET.html*

13 A question arises: How does the user *know* there is a link in your Flash text? Unlike HTML, Flash does not make the link text a different color from the rest of the text, and Flash does not underline text at all. Well, Flash doesn't—but you can. You can select the word or phrase and change the color in the **Properties** panel. Then you can use the **Line** tool to add an underline in the same color. This is a tedious solution, but otherwise, you have a problem.

A more efficient solution is to create a simple rectangle symbol, with the same height as your text. The fill color should create a nice contrast to your text color, to maintain legibility. Place the rectangle *under* any linked word or phrase (Modify menu > Arrange > Send to Back) and use the **Free Transform** tool to make it the same width as the word or phrase. Use an instance of this graphic symbol under any linked text you have. (Note: A button symbol *will not work* underneath URL link text.)

14 There are just three more things you really should know about setting up your Static text in Flash. The first concerns *kerning*. Most fonts on your computer contain information about kerning that is specific to the font. Kerning adjusts the space *between* characters based on which two characters are side by side. Narrow letters such as the lowercase *i* and *t* are kerned differently from wider letters such as *M*, for example. To tell Flash to *use the automatic kerning* built into the font, put a check in the Auto Kern box

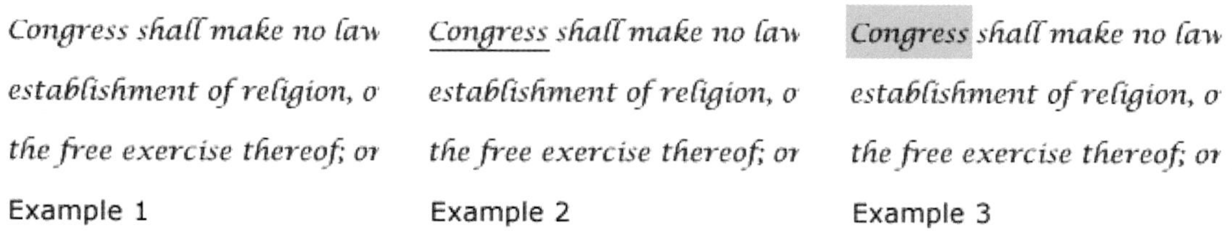

Congress shall make no law
establishment of religion, or
the free exercise thereof; or
Example 1

Congress shall make no law
establishment of religion, or
the free exercise thereof; or
Example 2

Congress shall make no law
establishment of religion, or
the free exercise thereof; or
Example 3

Fig. 2.9.13 Three ways to handle URL Link text in Flash: In the first example, the word "Congress" is linked, but how would the user know? In the second example, the Flash author has changed the color of the word and added an underline. In the third example, the Flash author has added a graphic symbol underneath the word.

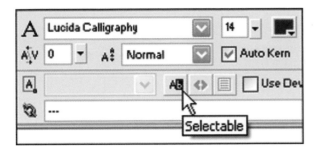

Fig. 2.9.14 Here the Selectable button is not clicked. The user will not be able to copy and paste text from this text field in Flash. If you want the text to be selectable, click this button so it appears to be pushed in.

in the **Properties** panel. This is almost always a good thing. (You should remove the check mark, however, if you change the character spacing, as explained in Step 7.)

15 The next thing concerns the Selectable button in the **Properties** panel (Figure 2.9.14). Using this button, you can choose whether to make the text in any text field in Flash *selectable* by the user, which means the user could copy it and then paste it outside Flash.

16 Last but not least, *never* use the Width and Height fields in the **Properties** panel to adjust the size of the text field; it will *skew the shape* of the text. In other words, the text will be *distorted* if you change these properties. If you need to adjust the *width* of a Static text field, follow the instructions in Step 9. The *height* of a Static text field will change automatically when you add or delete text. To make it taller, just type more into it.

The final important items on the **Properties** panel for Static text are the Use Device Fonts check box and (in MX 2004 only) the Alias Text button. See "Legible Text: Avoiding the Blurry Text Syndrome" to learn how to use both of those to best advantage.

Keep in mind that most text needs in Flash are served well by using Static text, and the differences between Static text and the other two types are specifically addressed in the following exercises. To get text to look the way you want it to look, use the techniques covered in this exercise.

LEGIBLE TEXT: AVOIDING THE BLURRY TEXT SYNDROME

Before we discuss Dynamic text, it's important to address one of the biggest problems in Flash: Small text that is too blurry to read. If you have looked at a lot of Flash journalism packages, you have probably noticed this more than once. It happens only when the font size is small; sometimes the text becomes blurred at 14 pixels, sometimes at 12 pixels; it really depends on the font family used. The same font family will look perfect when it is just a few pixels larger.

It happens because Flash MX (and all earlier versions of Flash) does not permit "anti-aliasing" to be disabled. Fonts in Flash MX are normally anti-aliased to ensure smooth edges, but at the smaller font sizes, anti-aliasing produces a smudged effect. (Larger text, however, looks jagged when not anti-aliased.) It may look okay to you on your screen while you are authoring, but on someone else's screen (especially a 1280 × 1024 LCD monitor), your 12-pixel text becomes unreadable.

One solution might be to make sure to use only large-enough font sizes, but that's not really practical. In any Flash journalism package, there are likely to be some text elements (such as button labels or a copyright notice) that need to be small.

The good news is, there are ways to ensure that a smaller font size remains readable (or at least, not blurry—text could still be just *too tiny*) for all readers:

- Use what Flash calls Device Fonts.

- Use what developers call "pixel fonts" (see "Pixel Fonts: Sharp, Tiny Text").

- In Flash MX 2004 and later versions of Flash, use the Alias Text button, but *only if* you are saving your SWF for Flash Player 7 or later.

With Static text, there are *two steps* to using Device Fonts:

1 With the text field *selected* on the **Stage** (you will see the *blue bounding box* around the text field if it is selected), check the Device Fonts box in the **Properties** panel.

2 From the Font menu in the **Properties** panel, select one of Flash's three "device fonts." These are *_sans, _serif,* and *_typewriter.* All three are at the *top* of the Font menu.

Figure 2.9.16 shows the difference between using and not using Device Fonts in this way.

If you check the Device Fonts box *and* use one of the three Flash device fonts from the menu, you do not know *exactly* what the type

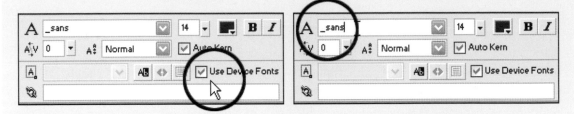

Fig. 2.9.15 If you want smaller text to be sharp and clear, there are two steps when using Static text.

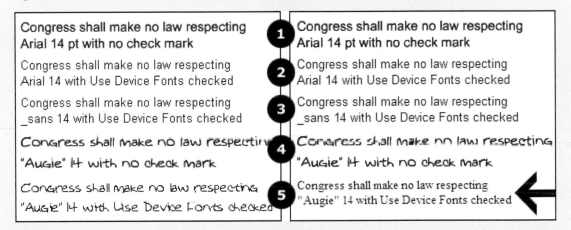

Fig. 2.9.16 The two blocks of text show the same SWF file, opened on two different computers, both running the Windows XP operating system.

1. Left and right are identical; Device Fonts were not used. The font is embedded in the SWF and will look the same on all computers.

2. Left and right are identical in this case, but see No. 5: If one of the computers did not have the font Arial installed, the text would look different. Also, at size 14, you can see a slight difference between this version of the font and the one in No. 1. The anti-aliased version looks slightly bolder.

3. This is what you should use if the text must be small: a Flash device font (such as _sans_) with Device Fonts checked. Compare the appearance of the type here with No. 2 above it: Both computers in this case use Arial as the Device Font _sans_, but that will not necessarily be so for every computer. If a computer uses another font as the default, Nos. 2 and 3 would look different from each other. The important thing is not the exact font displayed, but rather that this text will not be blurry!

4. Left and right are identical; Device Fonts were not used. The user sees the TrueType font named Augie even if that font is not installed on the user's computer. This is the same use of type as No. 1, but compare it with No. 5 below it, on both left and right.

5. Left, the computer has the font named Augie installed, but its appearance is jagged now (compared with No. 4). Right, the computer does not have Augie, so the computer substituted whatever font seemed appropriate—to the computer. Note that the substitution looks nothing like the intended font. This result (on the right) is to be avoided at all costs.

will look like on anyone's computer (although they are likely to be Arial, Times or Times New Roman, and Courier or Courier New). You are selecting only a general typography classification. You *do know* that the effect will not be as radically different as the one in No. 5 in Figure 2.9.16, and you can make the font size small (11 or 12) and still have clear, legible text.

With Static text that is *large enough* not to appear blurry (e.g., font size about 14 and larger for most font families), do not check the Device Fonts box, and do not select one of the three Flash device fonts. There is no need to use Device Fonts with Static text when the font size is large enough to be crisp and clear.

By selecting Static text and *not checking* the Device Fonts box, you ensure that the text on the user's computer appears exactly the way it appeared on your computer when you designed it. You can select a fancy font family and be confident that the user will see it.

Flash MX 2004 Note

The Alias Text button is new in MX 2004; it turns off anti-aliasing for any font and allows you to embed it (Figure 2.9.17). The effect works for all three types of text (Static, Dynamic, and Input) if the SWF is saved for and viewed in the Flash Player 7 or later. In earlier versions of the player, it works only for Static text.

Note: Some font families cannot be exported by Flash. To make sure your font will be all right, open the View menu and select "Antialias Text"; you can work with this option selected at all times, and most people do. With this option selected, you will see *jagged edges* for any font that Flash is unable to export. In such cases, you should use a different font family instead.

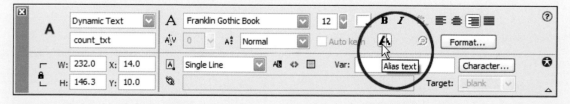

Fig. 2.9.17 The Alias Text button (new in MX 2004) allows you to control whether small text is anti-aliased. To disable anti-aliasing and sharpen small text, click the button when the text field is selected.

Fig. 2.9.18 Here the font Verdana is shown at size 10 in an SWF. The circle shows the size 10 text magnified three times. The text was created in Flash MX 2004 with the Alias Text button "on."

The Alia[s] [butt]on is new in MX 2004; it turns off anti-[aliasing tex]t and allows you to embed it. The effect [works for all] types of text (Static, Dynamic, and [... it] is saved for and viewed in the Flash [... player.] In earlier versions of the player, it works [... static] text.

Fig. 2.9.19 Here is the same text as that shown in Figure 2.9.18. The only difference is that this version was created in Flash MX 2004 with the Alias Text button "off."

The Alias Te[xt butto]n is new in MX 2004; it turns off anti-[aliasing tex]t and allows you to embed it. The effect [works for all] types of text (Static, Dynamic, and [... it is] saved for and viewed in the Flash Player [... earli]er versions of the player, it works only for [static text.]

aliasing for works for

Exercise 9.2: Dynamic Text, a Tour of What You Can Do

Earlier you learned that you will use Static text *most of the time* in your Flash movies. You will use Dynamic text in cases where you want to load text from outside the Flash movie (e.g., from a plain text file, an XML file, or a database). You will use Dynamic text if you want text to change dynamically (e.g., when a visible timer counts down from 100 seconds to 0). You will also use Dynamic text if you want to make a scrolling text box with the Flash ScrollBar component. In most other cases, you can use Static text.

Start a new file in Flash.

1 Select the **Text** tool in the **Tools** panel.

2 Open the Text Type menu in the **Properties** panel and select "Dynamic" for this exercise.

3 Click once on the **Stage** and type a few words.

4 Look at the **Properties** panel. You'll see that the properties of Dynamic text are similar to those of Static text, but there are some key differences. We will focus on the differences here.

5 The rest of this exercise is a demonstration of something you can do with Dynamic text that *cannot be done* with Static text. *Select* all the text in your Dynamic text field and *replace* it with the phrase "20 times" (without the quotes).

6 Click the Right/Bottom Justify button (called Align Right in MX 2004) on the right side of the **Properties** panel to *right-align* the text in this field (you'll see why soon).

7 *Resize* the width of the text field by dragging the "handle" left or right so the text fits on a single line. If you do not see the handle, *double-click* on the text inside the field. The handle on a Dynamic text field is always in the lower right corner.

Fig. 2.9.20 Properties of Dynamic text.

Fig. 2.9.21 The differences between the properties of Dynamic text (Figure 2.9.20) and Static text (Figure 2.9.21) should determine which is the better one to use in a given situation. You cannot change the direction of Dynamic text to make it read vertically, for example. You cannot Auto Kern text that is Dynamic, and you cannot change the Character Spacing. You can set the font, font size, color, and justification/alignment for Dynamic text, just as you can for Static text. You can make either type of text "selectable."

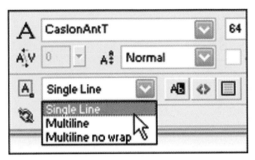

Fig. 2.9.22 Select the Line Type in the Properties panel for Dynamic text. This cannot be done for Static text.

Fig. 2.9.23 Enter an instance name for this text field. This cannot be done for Static text.

8 In the **Properties** panel, open the Line Type menu and *select* "Single Line." (Static text does not have this property.)

9 Save your file, just for safety's sake.

10 Click into the Instance Name field and type "count_txt" (without the quotes), then tab out of the field (Figure 2.9.23). You are giving an *instance name* to an instance of the TextField object, as far as Flash is concerned. The reason you do this: It allows you to use ActionScript to control this text field. You have given an instance name to a movie clip (Lesson 8) in the same way.

11 Create a button on the **Stage**, or find one in the Common Libraries (there are some nice ones in the folder named "Arcade buttons"). You will script this button to interact with the text field—specifically, the button will *change* the text.

12 Open the **Actions** panel (press F9) and switch to "Expert Mode," if you are using Flash MX (see "Working with ActionScript" in Lesson 8). *Select* the button on the **Stage** (click it *once*) and write the following script:

```
on (release) {
    n++;
    if (n > 20) {
        count_txt.text = "End game";
    } else {
        count_txt.text = n + " times";
    }
}
```

The script tells Flash that: (a) Each time the button is pressed and released, the *variable* "n" should be incremented by 1; it means the same thing as n = n + 1. (b) Then, if the *value* of "n" is greater than 20, Flash should write the text "End game" into your text field with the *instance name* "count_txt." (c) However ("else"), if "n" is not greater than 20, Flash should write the value of "n," and a space, and the word "times" into your text field.

The script depends on your having named the text field instance in Step 10.

Fig. 2.9.24 A Dynamic text field and a button can interact with each other.

13 Save and test your movie: Ctrl-Enter (Win) or Cmd-Return (Mac). Make sure you click the button more than 20 times. It's dynamic, isn't it?

Note: Notice how the word "times" does not move at all; that is because you right-justified the text in Step 6. If you had left-justified it, that word would shift left or right with each click, depending on the width of each numeral to the left of it. That would not look as professional; you don't want to see the text sliding back and forth without reason.

14 Two more steps will clean up this file and show you other important characteristics of Dynamic text. First, on the **Stage,** delete the text inside your Dynamic text field. Be careful not to delete the text field itself! Just delete the text, and leave the empty field as is. When the empty field is selected, you will see its blue bounding box. When the field is not selected, you will see a *dotted outline* of the field.

15 Save and test your movie.

What should happen: Nothing is visible except the button. The text appears for the first time when you click the button for the first time.

16 Now you need to guarantee that users will see the text as you intended it to look. To do this, you will *embed the font* (or part of the font) deliberately. The important difference here (compared with Static text) is that if you fail to embed the font for a Dynamic text field, *it is not embedded automatically.* A substitution is likely to occur on any user's computer, and the result could be ugly—*very* ugly, in some cases.

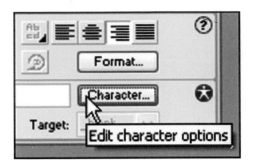

Fig. 2.9.25 Edit the Character Options for the text field: This is not available for Static text.

To embed the font, *select* the text field (click it *once*). In the **Properties** panel, on the far right side, click the Character button. The Character Options dialog will open (Figure 2.9.25).

17 In the Character Options dialog, the *most efficient* selections in this case would be very specific, because you know exactly what characters will be used in this text field.

Flash MX: Select "Only" as shown in Figure 2.9.26. Then check "Numerals (0–9)" because you will need all of those. Finally, in the field at the bottom, type only the letters that will be used in this movie. You do not need to type the *m* and the *e* in *game* because those two letters already appear in *time*. Click Done to finish.

Flash MX 2004: Select "Specify Ranges" as shown in Figure 2.9.27. Then select "Numerals (0–9)" because you will need all of those. Finally, in the field at the bottom, type only the letters that will be used in this movie. You do not need to type the *m* and the *e* in *game* because those two letters already appear in *time*. Click OK to finish.

18 Save and test your movie: Ctrl-Enter (Win) or Cmd-Return (Mac). It should work as it did before. The difference is that now it will work on other people's computers, too.

19 Finally, conduct a small test to see why embedding only *part* of a font is important. Check and record the *file size* of your SWF now. (The SWF used in the examples here is 11 KB.) After doing that, open the Character Options dialog again and, in Flash MX, select "All Characters" *instead of* "Only." In MX 2004, select the top four options in the scrolling box (shift-click each one).

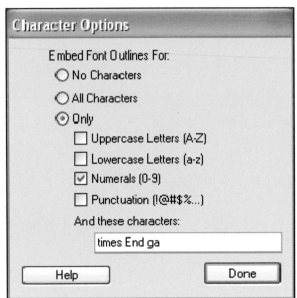

Fig. 2.9.26 You can specify exactly which characters will be embedded for any Dynamic text field by using the Character Options dialog. If you don't know what text might appear in the text field (for example, some longer articles or captions will be loaded into the field), you should select "All Characters." In this exercise, however, you know exactly which characters will be used, so you should limit the embedded characters to those that will be needed. (Flash MX dialog shown here.)

Save and test your movie again. It should look and act exactly the same—but *recheck the file size.* (The SWF used in the examples here became 47 KB after all characters were embedded, instead of the original limited set explained in Step 17.)

The difference in file size can be *even more extreme* with other font families, so it's worth it to test this. Often a font family includes a large number of characters you don't know about; embedding all of those can add a lot of weight to your SWFs.

Before moving on, take a moment to think about other uses for Dynamic text. As seen in this exercise, various user-initiated actions can be triggers for new text being written. In addition, ActionScript *on a frame* can change what appears in a text field. A script can write new text into a text field based on a timer (also written in Action-Script) or based on another event, such as the end of a sound file. You'll see more of this in Lesson 10, when photo captions and credits are written dynamically whenever the photo changes.

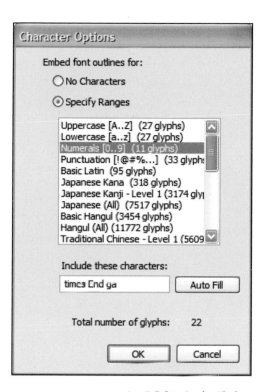

Fig. 2.9.27 In the Flash MX 2004 version of the Character Options dialog, you have a long list of choices if you select "Specify Ranges." You also have a handy Auto Fill button, which will add the current contents of the text field, if there are any.

The SWF you created here required only one frame in the Timeline, but imagine how a beginning Flash author might think it required twenty (or more) frames.

Exercise 9.3: Scrolling Text with the ScrollBar Component

Although it is possible to create a scrolling text box from scratch (by writing ActionScript to control the scrolling motion of a text field), you will probably prefer using the ScrollBar component because it's less work and will save time. So, this exercise shows you how to create a scrolling text box with the ScrollBar component.

With Flash MX, Macromedia introduced what are called *components.* A component is a finished piece of Flash script, which may also include graphics, that is intended to be dragged and dropped into your movie and then work automatically. Independent Flash developers can create components on their own and share them with other developers.

Flash MX and later versions come with a set of ready-to-use components. To see them, open the **Components** panel (use the Window menu to open the panel if you cannot find it; or Window menu > Development Panels in Flash MX 2004). Both MX and MX 2004 come with a set called "UI Components."

THE SCROLLBAR AND FLASH MX 2004

Oddly enough, the set of UI Components originally included with Flash MX 2004 does not include the fantastically useful ScrollBar component—the focus of this exercise. But don't worry, you can download it free from the Macromedia Flash Exchange. Make sure you get the set named "Flash MX Components for Flash MX 2004." You can find it by searching for "scrollbar" in the Flash Exchange. After you download the set, you must *install* it.

Download extensions and components here:
http://www.macromedia.com/cfusion/exchange/

New components must be installed with the Macromedia Extension Manager, which you can open from the Flash Help menu > Manage Extensions. To perform the installation, open the File menu in the Extension Manager and select "Install Extension"; then find the downloaded extension in the folder where you saved it.

But wait, there's more: Obviously Macromedia was listening to hundreds, possibly thousands, of Flash developers whining, "Sometimes we just want a simple scrollbar!" So when the company released a free update to Flash MX 2004 (Version 7.2), it included a brand-new UIScrollBar component. However, it is not exactly the same as the component in the set "Flash MX Components for Flash MX 2004," which can be modified in the same ways as the old ScrollBar from the older version of Flash (e.g., you can change the color of the ScrollBar with ActionScript). This is because components changed a lot between MX and MX 2004, and the new UIScrollBar conforms to the new component architecture.

If you have Flash MX 2004 Version 7.2 or higher, you will already have the new UIScrollBar in the component set named "UI Components." Try it and see whether you like it. If you don't, you can still download the other set from the Flash Exchange and use the older ScrollBar instead.

To use the ScrollBar component, you must have either a Dynamic text field or an Input text field. The Scroll-Bar component does not work with Static text fields, because they cannot be given an instance name.

Start a new file in Flash.

1 Select the **Text** tool in the **Tools** panel.

2 Open the Text Type menu on the **Properties** panel and select "Dynamic" for this exercise.

3 In the **Properties** panel, open the Line Type menu and select "Multiline."

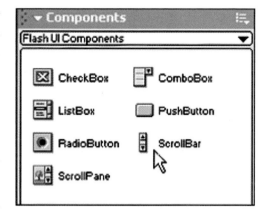

Fig. 2.9.28 This set of components is included in Flash MX. Note that the ScrollBar is different from the ScrollPane. All the components are described and explained in the Flash MX Help files > "Using Components."

4 Change the font, font size, and color of the text to be small but still legible. Use the device font *_sans* to ensure legibility; sans-serif fonts are generally easier to read on a screen than serif fonts. Alternatively, if you choose a named font instead, be sure to *embed* it, as explained in Exercise 9.2, Steps 16–17.

5 Click *once* on the **Stage,** then grab the square "handle" in the lower right corner of the text field and *drag* it out to the size you want for your scrolling text box. (This illustrates another difference between Dynamic text and Static text: You cannot set the height of a Static text field.)

6 Give the text field an *instance name* now, if you need one. The ScrollBar component requires an instance name, so it will assign one to your text field if there is none. It will use an existing name if one exists. Do not change the instance name for a scrolling text field after the ScrollBar component has been attached.

7 Type just a few words into the text field. You *should not* fill it up with text (yet).

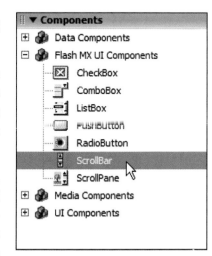

Fig. 2.9.29 Some components are included in Flash MX 2004, but the ScrollBar must be downloaded as part of the set "Flash MX Components for Flash MX 2004."

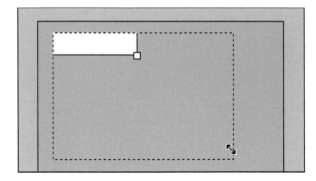

Fig. 2.9.30 After you have set the properties for your text field, click on the Stage and then drag out the Dynamic text field to the size you need. When you let go of the mouse button, the text field will be the same size as the dotted outline.

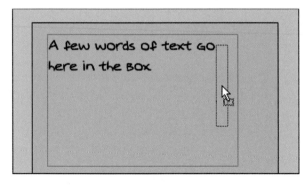

Fig. 2.9.31 Drag the ScrollBar component into the text field.

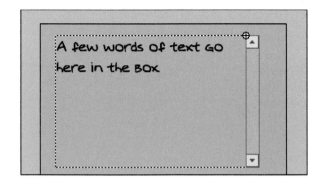

Fig. 2.9.32 After you release the mouse button, the ScrollBar attaches itself and sizes itself automatically to match the height of the text field.

8 The ScrollBar component will attach itself only when "Snap to Objects" is selected. Open the View menu and make sure "Snap to Objects" is selected. (In Flash MX 2004, it is on the Snapping submenu.) If "Snap to Objects" shows a check mark, that means it is already selected. If there is no check mark, then click once to select it.

9 In the **Components** panel, grab the Scroll-Bar and *drag* it to the inside edge of your text field (Figure 2.9.31). You do not have to position it exactly, but make sure it is closer to the *side* than to the *bottom* (because the ScrollBar can be either vertical or horizontal). Let go of the mouse button, and the ScrollBar "snaps" into place.

10 Save and test your movie: Ctrl-Enter (Win) or Cmd-Return (Mac). You'll see your new scrollbar in place, but because the text is shorter than the height of the text field, it will not scroll (yet).

11 Back on the **Stage,** add some more text inside the text field. You can copy some text outside Flash and paste it into the field. Use the cursor keys to move to the bottom of the text field, or to the top—the ScrollBar *does not function* while you are editing the FLA file. To test your ScrollBar component, you need to have several lines of text that exceed the height of the text field, and you need to go into Test Movie mode.

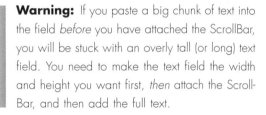

Warning: If you paste a big chunk of text into the field *before* you have attached the ScrollBar, you will be stuck with an overly tall (or long) text field. You need to make the text field the width and height you want first, *then* attach the Scroll-Bar, and then add the full text.

Note: If you must *change the size* of the text field after you have added the ScrollBar component, first *select* and *delete* the ScrollBar component. Then resize the text field by first clicking into the text field, and then dragging the handle. Finally, add the Scroll-Bar component (drag it out of your **Library** this time) to snap onto the newly resized text field. *Never* change the size of a text field by using the W and H fields in the **Properties** panel; if you do, the text will become distorted.

12 Save and test your movie again. If you entered enough text into the text field, you should be able to use the scrollbar normally.

Note: If you would like to change the colors of the ScrollBar component, go to the Web site for this book, Tips section, Tip No. 3. It requires seven lines of ActionScript, which you can copy and paste from the Tip page.

13 If you want to have a color behind the text in the scrolling box, it's easy to create a new layer in the **Timeline** and place the new layer below the text field layer. Lock the text field layer first, so it does not move. On the new layer, use the **Rectangle** tool to create a box in the color you prefer, with or without a stroke (outline) color. Align the top left corner of the rectangle with the top left corner of the text field. Then use the **Free Transform** tool to size the rectangle (Figure 2.9.33).

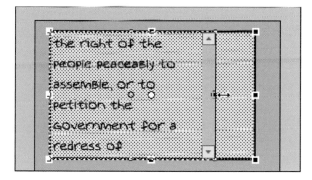

Fig. 2.9.33 On a new layer below the text field layer, make a rectangle, and then transform it to fit as you like.

14 Save and test your movie again. If you're happy with how this scrolling text box looks, you might want to use it in another movie. You could copy the frames into a movie clip symbol; then, by opening this FLA file as a Library (Flash MX: File menu > Open as Library; Flash MX 2004: File menu > Import > Open External Library), you could drag the movie clip onto the Stage in another FLA file and reuse it there.

Note: Using the ScrollBar component adds about 6 KB to the final file size of your SWF. Certain font families may add 10 KB or more to the SWF, when the full font is embedded using the Character Options dialog.

MOVING AND TRANSFORMING TEXT

New users of Flash often want to make text move—a lot. Moving text, or flying text, can look cool, but it can also be annoying. It can even be boring, if there is too much of it, or if it moves too slowly. Or it may move too quickly for users to read. So don't go crazy with moving text, at the risk of alienating users and driving them away.

That said, of course you will want to make some moving text. To start, you must *convert* a text field into a *symbol*. This is the same as converting a shape to a symbol: You select the text field (click it *once*) and then Convert to Symbol (press F8). If you need to edit the text later, you must *double-click* it to go into Symbol Editing Mode.

Once you have the text inside a symbol, you animate it just as you would any other symbol (see Lesson 2). It can fly across the Stage from left to right, from right to left, from top to bottom. It can scroll up slowly from bottom to top. It can fade in and fade out.

One thing you may have trouble with: How do you make the text expand or shrink? Don't forget that it is a symbol now, and to transform a symbol, you use the **Free Transform** tool from the **Tools** panel, or use the **Transform** panel. Of course, text can zoom in and out. It can change size and shape while it is moving, or while it stands still. Just use motion tweens; you already know how (see Lesson 2). Text can even change color, or alpha (transparency). A symbol that contains text can do everything that any other symbol can do.

If you want the text to move across a photo, just place the text into a layer above the photo in the Timeline.

Certain fancy effects with skewed or twisted test are achieved only by using shape tweens, which this book has not addressed. Shape tweens with text usually add significantly to the file size of the final SWF, so for the sake of usability, motion tweens do a better job.

One last piece of advice about animating text: Use a mask if you want text to appear letter by letter, or when you want a sliding-in effect. Moving a rectangle shape in a mask layer can be more efficient than breaking apart the text and animating the letters frame by frame, although you can do it that way if you have a lot of spare time on your hands. (How to add a mask layer was explained under "Zooming In on a Photo," Lesson 7, Steps 16–20.)

Exercise 9.4: Input Text, a Tour of What You Can Do

The difference between Input text and the other two text types in Flash is that the user can write or edit the text inside an Input text field. Select the Input text type in the **Properties** panel only if you need to allow users to type into a field. This is most common when you are building a database application, but you might also build a locally run application with Action-Script, such as a tax or mortgage calculator that asks for a ZIP or postal code.

Start a new file in Flash.

1   Select the **Text** tool on the **Tools** panel.

2   Open the Text Type menu on the **Properties** panel and select "Input" for this exercise.

3   Click *once* on the **Stage** and type "Click here and type your name" (without the quotes).

Fig. 2.9.34 Properties of Input text.

Fig. 2.9.35 There are few differences between the properties of Input text (Figure 2.9.34) and Dynamic text (Figure 2.9.35). However, the two types of fields behave very differently.

4 Change the font, font size, color, and justification/alignment of your text, if necessary.

5 Create a second, separate text field below the first one. Use the **Properties** panel to make this *second* text field Dynamic. (You'll see why in a moment.) You can use a different font and color in the Dynamic text field, but keep the *font size* close to the same as what you have in the Input text field.

6 Give each of the two text fields a *different instance name* (illustrated in Figure 2.9.23). Name the Input text field "entername_txt" (without the quotes), and be sure to tab out of the Instance Name field. Name the Dynamic text field "namehere_txt" (without the quotes). Use these exact names, because they will appear in a line of ActionScript below.

7 *Select* your Input text field (click it *once*) and set the maximum characters allowed, by *typing* a number in the lower right corner of the Properties panel (Figure 2.9.36). To determine what number to type, experiment to see how many characters will fit in your Dynamic text field. Yes, that's right—you want *the text typed by the user* to show up in your Dynamic text field, so you need to check the capacity of *that* text field. However, the typing will happen inside the Input text field, so that is where you set the maximum characters allowed.

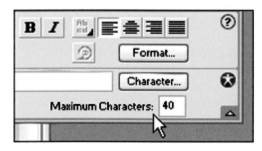

Fig. 2.9.36 By setting the maximum number of characters allowed in an Input text field, you limit what the user can type into the field. This is usually preferred. Only Input text has this property.

8 Create *two new layers* in the **Timeline.** *Drag* one layer below your layer that contains the two text fields. Name the top layer "actions," the middle layer "text," and the bottom layer "frames."

9 Click into Frame 1 of your "frames" layer, and then *draw* two rectangles. Each rectangle will go *underneath* a text field, to provide a box for the text. Make sure each rectangle is slightly larger than the text field associated with it. The rectangles must have a lighter "fill" color than the text color, or else the text will be hard to read. These rectangles are merely visual aids; you can skip them if you want to, but it does make the functionality easier to understand when someone looks at the final Flash movie—the rectangle shows them where to type.

10 If either one of your fields is going to do anything, you'll need to write some ActionScript. So, select Frame 1 in the "actions" layer. Open the **Actions** panel and type (in "Expert Mode," if you are using Flash MX):

```
function copytext() {
    namehere_txt.text = entername txt.text;
}
_root.onEnterFrame = copytext;
```

With this script, you have done two things: (a) In the first three lines, you created a new function called "copytext." (b) In the final line, you told Flash to execute that function at the frame rate of the main movie ("_root")—for example, 15 times per second. You were introduced to _root.onEnterFrame in Lesson 8.

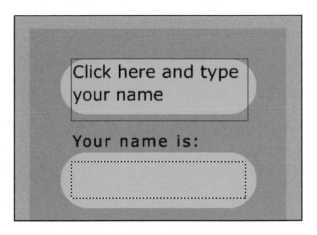

Fig. 2.9.37 The top field is an Input text field with some text in it. The bottom field is a Dynamic text field that is empty. The two rectangles (with rounded corners) are on a separate layer below the text fields.

The "copytext" function shown here copies whatever is typed in the Input text field ("entername_txt") to the Dynamic text field ("namehere_txt"). It happens instantly *as the text is being typed* because the function is being executed 15 times a second, thanks to the _root.onEnterFrame event handler.

11 Save and test your movie: Ctrl-Enter (Win) or Cmd-Return (Mac).

What should happen: You can *select* and *delete* the text in your Input text field. When you *type* anything into that field, whatever you type appears immediately in the Dynamic text field below it. If you *delete* something in the top field, it disappears in the lower field.

Because of the code shown earlier, when you first launch the SWF, *both of your fields* say "Click here and type your name." That would probably confuse users! To prevent that, you can add to your script an *if* statement that tests whether the phrase "Click here and type your name" is in the Input text field, and if so, leaves the Dynamic text field blank. Here is the alternative script:

```
function copytext() {
    if (entername_txt.text == "Click here and type your name") {
        namehere_txt.text = "";
    } else {
        namehere_txt.text = entername_txt.text;
    }
}
_root.onEnterFrame = copytext;
```

Take note of the *double equals sign* (==) in the first line of the *if statement*: It is necessary when you are testing a condition; the *if statement* will not work if you use a regular, single equals sign (if you did, it would simply *change* the contents of the field).

12 Save and test your movie again.

What should happen: Now when you begin, the top text field should say "Click here and type your name," as before, but the bottom field should be empty—*until you begin typing* into the top field.

Input text typically is used to send information to a database, or to another part of a Flash movie. For example, you could ask the user to enter a password in an Input text field, and then use ActionScript to go to a part of the Timeline that only special users are permitted to view. All users who did not type the correct password would go to a part of the Timeline that said, "Sorry, you didn't know the password." To accomplish this, you would use an *if statement* similar to the one shown earlier:

```
var password = "donut";
function checkpw() {
    if (enterpw_txt.text == password) {
        gotoAndPlay("enterSecretArea");
    } else {
        gotoAndStop("sorryNoEntry");
    }
}
```

The script does this: *If* the password typed *is equivalent to* (double equals sign) the correct password, then go to a certain frame in the Timeline, labeled "enterSecretArea." Otherwise (*else*), go to the "sorryNoEntry" frame in the Timeline.

You could script a button to execute the function called "checkpw":

```
on (release) {
    checkpw();
}
```

 The user would click the button after entering text into the password field.

PIXEL FONTS: SHARP, TINY TEXT

A "pixel font" is a font family that has been designed to map exactly to the pixels on the computer screen, with no anti-aliasing (smoothed edges). This ensures that the letters appear sharp and distinct even at a very small size. Although Flash MX 2004 allows you to turn off anti-aliasing (see "Legible Text: Avoiding the Blurry Text Syndrome," in this lesson) to get sharp text at a small size, that option does not always yield the best results; many fonts look downright ugly without anti-aliasing. Also, that option is not available if you are saving the SWF for the Flash player 6 or earlier. So, many Flash designers choose to use pixel fonts when they need small text.

There are several places online to get pixel fonts. One popular site is Fonts For Flash, which always offers a few free fonts for download-ing, so you can try them out. Make sure you follow the *instructions* given on the site so that the fonts appear sharp and not blurred:

1. Go to *http://www.fontsforflash.com/*

2. Choose "FAQs" from the menu on the left side.

3. Scroll to find "How to Use FFF Fonts."

Some of the considerations are to make sure that the character spacing and kerning are both 0 (zero) and that line spacing (in the Format Options dialog) is an integer. These properties were discussed in Exercise 9.1. Scrolling can cause these fonts to blur if your scrolling script allows the line to stop on a tenth of a pixel instead of a whole integer.

Like all other fonts, pixel fonts will be embedded in your Flash movie automatically if you specify Static text. If you specify Dynamic or Input text, you must deliberately embed the font to ensure that the users see it as you intended (see Exercise 9.2, Steps 16–19).

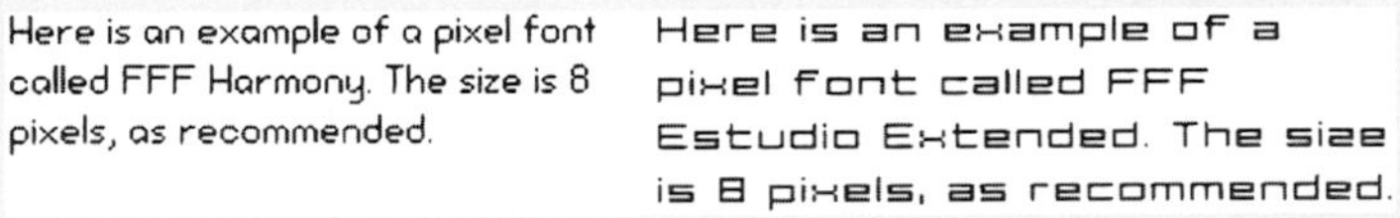

Here is an example of a pixel font called FFF Harmony. The size is 8 pixels, as recommended.	Here is an example of a pixel font called FFF Estudio Extended. The size is 8 pixels, as recommended.

Fig. 2.9.38 Two different examples of pixel fonts available from Fonts For Flash.

Most pixel fonts are optimized for a height of 8 pixels, which may be too small for some users' eyesight. If you need to include a lot of text in a Flash package, a better choice might be to use Device Fonts (explained in "Legible Text" in this lesson).

Download or Buy Pixel Fonts

Atomic Media   *http://www.atomicmedia.net/*

Fonts for Flash   *http://www.fontsforflash.com/*

Mini Fonts   *http://www.minifonts.com/*

Miniml   *http://miniml.com/fonts/*

More Information About Pixel Fonts

http://www.minifonts.com/info.html

WORKING WITH TEXT SUMMARY

Skillful use of text in Flash can decrease your SWF file sizes, guarantee legibility, and ensure that the fonts you choose are the fonts your users will actually see. In general, beginning Flash authors can use Static text for everything, unless they have a specific reason not to.

Flash journalism packages often include a fair amount of text that would normally be specified at 11 to 14 pixels in height. Make certain that this text will not be too small or too blurry—or both—on any user's monitor. The most sensible choice for larger chunks of text at this size is usually Device Fonts (*_sans*), but bear in mind that users might see different-looking text from what you see on your monitor, whether you select *_sans*, *_serif*, or *_typewriter*. The difference may affect the amount of space needed to display the text (the width and actual height of various 12-pixel *_sans* fonts will vary). Using the ScrollBar component can be very practical, because a scrolling text field can adjust itself to accommodate whatever font family appears there, and none of the text will be cut off.

When you are using Static text and you select *_sans*, *_serif*, or *_typewriter*, you must also check the Device Fonts box in the Properties panel for that text field. If you select one of those three device fonts when using Dynamic or Input text, do not embed your fonts.

If you use Dynamic or Input text, always be sure to embed your fonts whenever you *do not* select *_sans, _serif,* or *_typewriter.* When you embed the font (using the Character button on the Properties panel), your users will see exactly what you see. However, you may be increasing your SWF file size significantly by embedding a font, so keep an eye on that too. Always consider embedding less than the complete font, if you are sure you can foresee all possible characters that will be needed; this usually makes a serious difference in the file size.

If you need some tiny text for photo credits, navigation buttons, map labels, or anything else, look into pixel fonts as an alternative to Device Fonts, but remember that they have special rules.

Finally, keep in mind that moving text is so easy to create in Flash, some designers forget that users may get tired of it—fast. If there's a good reason to zoom, slide, or fade the text, make sure you give the users enough time to read it, and possibly even an option to pause it.

CONCLUSION

In this lesson, you have learned to:

1 Use three different types of text field in Flash: Static, Dynamic, and Input.

2 Create a text field on the Stage using the Text tool.

3 Select a type for that text field using the Properties panel.

4 Change the font, font size, color, and justification/alignment (left, center, right, full), using the Properties panel.

5 Change the direction of the text from horizontal to vertical (Static text only).

6 Change the spacing between letters.

7 Change a Static text field from "single line" to "multiline" mode, which also sets the width for that text field and forces lines to wrap automatically.

8 Use the Format Options dialog to set the paragraph indent, line spacing, and left and right margins for a text field.

9 Create HTML links for selected text within a text field.

10 Specify a window target for an HTML link.

11 Allow users to copy and paste text, or not, from your Flash movie.

12 Avoid skewing or distorting your text as a result of resizing a text field.

13 Eliminate blurry text by using Device Fonts, or the Alias Text button in Flash MX 2004.

14 Change a Dynamic text field from "single line" to "multiline" mode.

15 Use an *instance name* with a Dynamic text field so you can use Action-Script to write text to that field on the fly.

16 Embed entire fonts, or just selected characters, using the Character Options dialog, to ensure that users see the fonts as you intended.

17 Use script on a button to write text into a Dynamic text field.

18 Create a scrolling text field using Macromedia's ScrollBar component.

19 Animate text with motion tweens: Text can slide, jump, fade, grow, shrink, or skew.

20 Create a text field into which users can type (Input text).

21 Set the maximum number of characters an Input text field will allow.

22 Use a Dynamic text field to instantly "play back" what a user types into an Input text field.

23 Use an Input text field to allow the user to enter a password.

24 Use "pixel fonts" to create very sharp, legible text at tiny font sizes.

Lesson 10

Building Slideshows with Sound

A photo slideshow with sound can be a very simplistic Flash movie, and you may have already built one (or several) using the skills you picked up from the previous lessons in this book. A slideshow can also be a complex package with a wide range of functionality provided by movie clips and user input.

This lesson will introduce two new capabilities: Loading individual photos dynamically from outside the Flash file, and loading captions, credits, and other text information from a plain text file. The use of audio will revisit techniques explained in Lesson 8. This lesson is more than a cookbook for making slideshows, though. It brings together various techniques covered earlier and incorporates them into the process of building a multimedia journalism package for online delivery. Even though the examples here use photographs, the images could just as well be illustrations or diagrams saved as separate SWFs. So think of this lesson as instructions for combining images, text, and sound to tell a story in a way that gives the user some control over how the content is received.

The final result is a Flash slideshow "shell" that can easily be loaded with any set of photos, captions, and credits without editing the FLA. You can edit the appearance of the shell to your liking and still maintain the functionality it includes.

If you are one of those impatient readers who has turned to this lesson first, without working through the previous lessons, you should not expect to understand what's going on here. References are made to earlier lessons, and you could try to catch up by looking at the referenced sections quickly—but unless you have previous experience with Flash and with scripting, it's likely that you will feel frustrated if you attempt to work through this lesson without the benefit of what has gone before.

LESSON 10

You can use the techniques in Lesson 7 to bring photos *into* Flash, but when a slideshow includes a lot of photos, the file size of the final SWF would be too large to be practical. Different online packages may call for different treatments, so first consider what you want to achieve, and then decide whether you want to load the photos (as in this lesson) or import them (as in Lesson 7).

Since the photos used in this lesson are outside the Flash movie, each one should be edited to its *true final size* (i.e., 700 pixels *or less* in width and 400 pixels *or less* in height, as explained in Lesson 7) and saved as JPGs. Keep a close watch on the file size of each JPG as you edit your photos. On a dial-up connection, the user may have to wait a few seconds to see even a 30-KB photo. Don't forget that Flash does not display JPGs saved as "progressive" (see Lesson 7).

If you want to understand how the slideshows function, you should work through each exercise here, in order. By the end of this lesson, you should be able to build any slideshow functionality you need. There's quite a bit of ActionScript involved, but you should be able to comprehend all of it if you take your time and read the explanations. Scripting is the key to a well-functioning slideshow—there's no way around that.

PLANNING THE PACKAGE LAYOUT

Before you begin building a Flash journalism package, give some thought to how everything will look, where the various elements will appear within the movie, and what functionality you will need. Some Flash authors sketch a project out on paper or on a whiteboard; others build a mockup or prototype in Photoshop, Illustrator, or FreeHand. Think about the rectangle that contains all the elements. What needs to show inside the rectangle? Are the same items always visible?

Space is one of the key considerations: How wide and how tall will each element be? How will your widest photo fit on the Stage with your longest block of text? Will any text elements be visible continuously through the movie (e.g., the title of the package or the copyright notice)? Don't forget that margins count, too, so a 400-

pixel-high photo needs a movie height of *more than* 400 pixels to provide a little space above and below the image.

Positioning each element is also important. If there are slide-out panels, where will they slide from? Will photos be centered within a given space, or will the top and left edges always be at the same place? Where will the buttons be? If navigation options appear and hide, what do they cover when they are visible? How will the user find them when they are hidden?

Thinking (and sketching) before you begin working in Flash usually pays off in reducing the time you spend redoing things that turn out badly.

Exercise 10.1: Simple Slideshow Using a Level

In this first exercise, you will script Next and Previous buttons to load photos from outside the Flash movie. This introduces you to the simplest way to load external files.

1 Prepare several photos for use in your slideshow (six or seven will be enough). You can use this same set of photos in all the exercises. Save each one as a JPG, and make sure both the width and height will fit nicely inside your Flash movie. Remember to leave some room on the **Stage** for captions, a credit line, and buttons.

2 Name your JPG files *sequentially* (in these exercises, we will use the filenames "photo1.jpg," "photo2.jpg" . . . "photo7.jpg"). This will make it easy for you to *reuse* the ActionScript you write—and in fact, you can reuse the entire slideshow—just by moving it into a folder with another set of photos that use the *same filename system*.

Note: Do not use a naming format with a leading zero (e.g., "photo_01.jpg"), because the ActionScript used will rely on simple addition (n + 1) to move through your photo files, and a zero would interfere.

3 In Flash, start a new file. Save the new file immediately into the *same folder* as the photos you named in Step 1. (The ActionScript shown in this

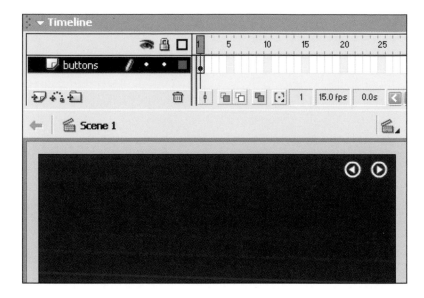

Fig. 2.10.01 The buttons are in place. The slideshow is almost ready at this point.

exercise depends on the SWF and the photos being together in the same folder.)

4 Create two different buttons: One to move to the next photo, and the other to move to the previous photo. You can use buttons from Flash's Common Libraries (Window menu > Common Libraries > Buttons, or in Flash MX 2004, Window menu > Other Panels > Common Libraries > Buttons). The folder "Circle Buttons" has nice Next and Previous buttons.

5 *Drag* your two buttons onto the **Stage** and position them near the *upper right* corner (Figure 2.10.01).

6 First, you will script *each button* to load a different photo. This simple script should help make it clear how more complex script works in later exercises in this lesson. Later you will change the script you write here, so just consider this a test case—but an important one.

Click *once* on your Next button to *select* it. Then open the **Actions** panel. (If you need a review of how to script a button, refer to "Stop and Play Buttons," Lesson 5, Step 7.) The ActionScript you must write on this button is:

```
on (release) {
    loadMovieNum("photo1.jpg", 10);
}
```

The filename in quotation marks is the "URL" (the file to be loaded), and the numeral 10 is the "level." Levels are explained below.

You can switch to "Expert Mode" and just type the script, as shown, if you are using Flash MX. If you prefer to use the **Actions** panel list, in Flash MX you should select the `loadMovie()` action, under "Browser/Network." In Flash MX 2004, the `loadMovieNum()` action is listed separately, so you can select that one directly. (Flash MX's "Expert Mode" was explained Lesson 5. Flash MX 2004 does not have any other mode for scripting, so you're always in "Expert Mode.")

7 Now click *once* on your other button (the Previous button) to *select* it. Repeat the same steps you took for the Next button, with one exception: Use the filename of a *different* photo (such as *photo7.jpg*) instead.

8 Save and test your movie: Ctrl-Enter (Win) or Cmd-Return (Mac). Try out both of your buttons. Wow, instant photo slideshow! (Okay, it has only two photos, but it was pretty quick, wasn't it?) When you click either button, you are loading a JPG into your movie on the fly, without having imported it to the FLA.

Make sure you look at your movie at its *actual size* ("restore" the test window instead of looking at it "maximized," as illustrated in Lesson 7, Figure 2.7.14). You must do this to see a problem with the position of your photos: Each one is jammed into the upper left corner of the Flash window—not exactly the perfect position (Figure 2.10.02). You'll fix that in the next exercise.

But first, a quick explanation of what you just did. When you use `loadMovieNum()`, you must tell Flash a *level* onto which to load the photo. Because you used the *same* number for the *level* on both buttons (10), the second photo always replaces the first photo, and vice versa. If you had used two *different* numbers instead, you would have seen one of your photos on top of the other. If the two photos are exactly the same width and height, that would not be a big problem—but otherwise, you would see some unsightly overlaps.

It's important to know that by using the *same* level number, you always *replace* whatever had been in that level. This can be a handy way to load external files into your movie, but it's not ideal for photos, since you can't control the margins.

Fig. 2.10.02 The photo loads from outside the Flash file, but it appears tightly wedged into the upper left corner.

Note: You can load separate SWF files into the movie in exactly this way. Just replace the filename of the photo in the button script with the filename of a SWF. Many multi-part Flash presentations are constructed this way, with the main movie providing just a shell to hold multiple external SWF files. See Appendix B for further information about this.

The "_root" or bottom level of the main movie is always Level 0. Whatever the movie in Level 0 is, it sets the *frame rate*, *background color*, and *maximum frame size* for all other loaded movies. If you use the number 0 (zero) with loadMovieNum() you will replace *everything* with the new file you are loading. In this case, if you loaded a photo into Level 0, you would lose the two buttons, and then you couldn't move through the photos.

There's no way to get the loaded JPGs out of the top left corner when you use loadMovieNum() and so you'll learn a different method in the next exercise.

Exercise 10.2: Simple Slideshow Using a Movie Clip

In this exercise, you will script Next and Previous buttons to load photos from outside the Flash movie and put them into an *empty movie clip*. Doing so allows you to position the photos wherever you like on the **Stage**, unlike the technique used in previous exercise.

Start with the same FLA file you created in the previous exercise. Save it with a new filename if you want to preserve that first version (always a good practice to follow).

1 The first step is to create an *empty movie clip* and place it on the **Stage**. This empty movie clip will serve as a target (or container) for the loaded photos. It will allow you to move your photos out of the corner and control their position.

Creating an empty movie clip was explained in "Playing Two Tracks at the Same Time," Lesson 8, Step 1. Basically, you must make sure that *nothing* is selected on the **Stage**, and then open the Insert menu and select "New Symbol." Select "Movie Clip" and name the new symbol (a good name is "Empty Clip"). You will automatically be in Symbol Editing Mode as soon as you click OK. *Exit* from Symbol Editing Mode by pressing Ctrl-E (or Cmd-E/Mac).

Drag an *instance* of the new symbol out of the **Library** and onto the **Stage**.

The *empty movie clip* is represented on the **Stage** by a very small white dot with a crosshair in it—when the movie clip is selected. The dot represents both the symbol's registration point and its transformation point. Since you just dragged it to the Stage, you should see the white dot and the crosshair. If you clicked something else, the crosshair will disappear, but the white dot will still be there.

2 Do not underestimate the tiny white dot. Select it (click it *once*) and give it an *instance name* down in the **Properties** panel (a good name is "loader_mc"). Make sure to tab out of the Instance Name field so that the name sticks. (You gave an instance name to your sliding panel in Lesson 6.) The clip needs an instance name so you can address it with ActionScript (Figure 2.10.03).

3 One last step with the *empty movie clip* (the tiny white dot): Set its X and Y coordinates to provide a margin around your photos. Do that in

Fig. 2.10.03 If you're having trouble naming the movie clip instance, pay attention to what the Properties panel tells you. When the movie clip is selected, you will see its name after the words "Instance of" on the panel.

the **Properties** panel (if necessary, review "Moving Photos in Flash," Lesson 7).

For example, if you want the *upper left corner* of each photo to be 20 pixels to the right of the leftmost edge and 20 pixels down from the top edge of the Flash movie, set *both* the X and the Y of your "loader_mc" movie clip to 20. Make sure the movie clip is *selected* on the Stage when you try to do this: Do you see the *crosshair* in the white dot?

With loaded files, whether they are JPGs or SWFs, and whether they load into a level or into an empty movie clip, the *upper left corner* of the loaded file always matches the *upper left corner* of what it's loaded into. An empty movie clip has no pixels inside it, so the location of the tiny white dot *is* the upper left corner of the clip.

Now that your empty movie clip instance ("loader_mc") has a name and a position, it is set up to receive the photos that you want to load.

4 You need to change the ActionScript on *each* button to get this working properly. Click *once* on your Next button to *select* it. Open the **Actions** panel. The ActionScript you want now is this (instead of what you used in the previous exercise):

```
on (release) {
    loader_mc.loadMovie("photo1.jpg");
}
```

In Flash MX, you could dig around in the **Actions** list to find this script (Objects > Movie > Movie Clip > Methods > loadMovie), but it will be much easier to switch to "Expert Mode" and simply *type it*. ("Expert Mode" and how to switch were explained in Lesson 5.)

The script tells Flash: "When the user clicks and releases this button, the *movie clip instance* named 'loader_mc' must load a *file* named 'photo1.jpg.' "

Compare this script to the script in Exercise 10.1, Step 6. The differences are minor, but crucial, and show how to load to a movie clip vs. how to load to a level.

5 Change the script on your Previous button to this (use a valid file-name for one of your own photos):

Fig. 2.10.04 The photos still load from outside the Flash file, but now they have margins on the left and top. The position of the upper left corner of the photo is the same as the position of your empty movie clip on the Stage.

```
on (release) {
    loader_mc.loadMovie("photo7.jpg");
}
```

6 Save and test your movie: Ctrl-Enter (Win) or Cmd-Return (Mac). Try out both of your buttons. They show two photos as they did in Exercise 10.1, but now the photos have a margin on the top and left sides (Figure 2.10.04).

If you look at your movie at its *actual size* ("restore" the test window instead of looking at it "maximized," as illustrated in Lesson 7, Figure 2.7.14), you'll see that you have *fixed the problem* from the previous exercise.

Note: Not only can you position the empty movie clip on the Stage (by dragging it, or by changing its X and Y in the Properties panel); you can also *reposition* it using ActionScript to dynamically change its X and Y. For an example, see the Web site for this book.

Next, we want to load *more than two* photos—with ActionScript—without adding any frames to the movie.

Exercise 10.3: Automating the Photos

In this exercise, you will add some new script on Frame 1 in the Timeline to allow your two buttons to load an *unlimited* number of photos from outside the Flash movie. You will also change the script on the Next and Previous buttons to do the work. A detailed explanation is included *after* the exercise to help you understand what the script is doing.

The good news is that you are writing reusable script: That means the ActionScript you write here can stay *as is* for future slideshows you produce. Once you have a well-functioning slideshow SWF, you can simply drop any set of photographs and captions into it.

1 Start with the same FLA file you used in the previous exercise. Save it with a new filename if you want to preserve that earlier file.

2 Create a *new layer* in the **Timeline** and name it "actions" (without the quotes). Did you name your original layer earlier? If not, name it "mc and buttons" (without the quotes) now. Click *once* on Frame 1 in the "actions" layer to *select* the frame.

3 Open the **Actions** panel and go into "Expert Mode" if you are using Flash MX. From this point onward, it will be much more efficient for you to type script directly instead of using "Normal Mode" (which does not exist in Flash MX 2004). Type these lines exactly as shown:

```
total_photos = 7;
function get_photo(newnumber) {
    current_photo = "photo" + newnumber + ".jpg";
    loader_mc.loadMovie(current_photo);
}
```

If you have more than seven photos, or fewer, use the number you have (instead of "7") in the first line of the script.

This script assumes that your photo files are named sequentially ("photo1.jpg," "photo2.jpg" . . . "photo7.jpg"). If they are not, the script will not work.

Script is *very unforgiving* of typos, so pay close attention to every mark of punctuation to get it right. Capitalization also counts, so do not change the case shown.

4 Now click *once* on your Next button to *select* it. In the **Actions** panel, replace all the existing script on the Next button with this:

```
on (release) {
    if (n < total_photos) {
        n++;
    } else {
        n = 1;
    }
    get_photo(n);
}
```

Note: Indenting lines in a script is a convention that programmers use to make it easier to read their script and understand it. It helps you keep track of your curly braces too.

---

5 Finally, click *once* on your Previous button to *select* it. In the **Actions** panel, replace all the existing script on the Previous button with this:

```
on (release) {
    if (n > 1) {
        n--;
    } else {
        n = total_photos;
    }
    get_photo(n);
}
```

6 Save and test your movie. Try out both of your buttons.

What should happen: You cycle through all the photos in your folder, in sequence, either forward (while pressing your Next button) or backward (while pressing your Previous button).

If it doesn't work, the problem probably is (a) a typo in your script, (b) a typo in a photo filename, or (c) a missing photo file in the sequence.

What the Script Is Doing in Exercise 10.3

Table 10.01 Script on Frame 1

`total_photos = 7;`	"total_photos" is a *variable name*, which will be used later in the script to represent a specific value. The *value* assigned in this case is 7. The value can be changed, and should be if you have fewer or more than seven photos.
`function get_photo(newnumber) {`	You can create a function and name it whatever you like (apart from some terms that Flash reserves for special uses). A function is a *set of instructions* that you can call (cause to run) at any time. The word "function" in this line creates a new function; it is named "get_photo." Later, the script on your buttons will *call the function* and, at that time, the function will be *executed*. The *parameter* named "newnumber" will be filled in with a *value* at that time. The open curly brace at the end of the line signals the start of the definition of the function.
`current_photo = "photo" +` `newnumber + ".jpg";`	A new *variable* named "current_photo" is created here. Whenever the function runs, the *value* of this variable becomes "photoX.jpg"—where the "X" is filled in by the current value of "newnumber."
`loader_mc.loadMovie(current_photo);`	This line is almost the same as the one that you placed on your buttons in Exercise 10.2, except that now the filename of the photo is supplied by the *value* of the *variable* named "current_photo" (see the line just above this one). You are moving the loading action from the buttons and into this function instead.
`}`	The closing curly brace signals the end of the definition of the function named "get_photo."

Table 10.02 Script on the Next button

`on (release) {`	The "on (release)" handler tells Flash what to do when this button is pressed and released. The open curly brace at the end of the line signals the start of the instructions.
`if (n < total_photos) {`	An "if" statement starts here. The condition depends on the *value* of the *variable* "total_photos," which in this case is 7 (see script on Frame 1). If "n" is less than (<) that, then the thing in the next line of script will happen. The open curly brace at the end of the line marks the beginning of the "if" statement instructions.
`n++;`	The *value* of "n" is *incremented*; that is, the value of the *variable* "n" now equals n + 1.
`} else {`	If the condition given above is not true (that is, if "n" is not less than the *value* of the *variable* "total_photos"), then the next thing will happen.
`n = 1;`	The *value* of "n" becomes 1.
`}`	The closing curly brace marks the end of the "if" statement.
`get_photo(n);`	The function defined on Frame 1 is *called* here, and the value of "n" is *passed* to it. For example, if "n" equals 2, then "newnumber" in the function "get_photo" will equal 2.
`}`	The closing curly brace signals the end of the "on (release)" instructions.

Table 10.03 Script on the Previous button

`on (release) {`	The "on (release)" handler tells Flash what to do when this button is pressed and released. The open curly brace at the end of the line signals the start of the instructions.
`if (n > 1) {`	The condition here: If "n" is greater than (>) 1, then the thing in the next line of script will happen. The open curly brace at the end of the line marks the beginning of the "if" statement.
`n--;`	The *value* of "n" is *decremented*; that is, the value of the *variable* "n" now equals n − 1.
`} else {`	If the condition given above is not true (that is, if "n" is not greater than 1), then the next thing will happen.
`n = total_photos;`	The *value* of "n" becomes the same as the *value* of the variable "total_photos," which in this case is 7 (see script on Frame 1).
`}`	The closing curly brace marks the end of the "if" statement.
`get_photo(n);`	The function defined on Frame 1 is *called* here, and the value of "n" is *passed* to it. For example, if "n" equals 2, then "newnumber" in the function "get_photo" will equal 2.
`}`	The closing curly brace signals the end of the "on (release)" instructions.

Fig. 2.10.05 Sometimes you discover a design error after you test your slideshow. This photo is too wide for the Flash movie design (look at the buttons in the upper right corner). To prevent this, someone should have told the photo editor a maximum width for the photos. If this happens to you, either crop the photo or change the size of the Flash movie.

Exercise 10.4: Add Automated Captions

In this exercise, you will use ActionScript to *bring in captions* from outside the Flash file. This allows you, or someone else, to supply caption and credit information for the entire slideshow by simply typing text into a plain text editor, such as Windows Notepad, or Mac TextEdit or SimpleText—instead of opening and changing the FLA file. This convenience is made possible by matching a number in the *variable name* for the caption and the credit to the number in the *filename* for the photo, as you will see.

This process enables you to copy and reuse the same SWF for any photo slideshow you create in the future. All you need to do is type the caption and credit info for the new photos into a separate plain text file, following the style explained below.

1 Start with the same FLA file you used in the previous exercise. Save it with a new filename if you want to preserve the earlier file.

2 Create a *new layer* below your "actions" layer, and name it "text" (without the quotes). Click *once* on Frame 1 in that layer to *select* the frame.

3 Create a *Dynamic text field* to hold your captions on the right side of the **Stage** (Lesson 9 explains how to set the type of text field). Format your new text field this way:

(a) Select "Multiline" in the Line Type field in the **Properties** panel.

(b) Click on the Stage and drag the field to make it large enough to hold each of your captions.

(c) Make sure you select a contrasting color for the text to make it readable against the color of the Stage.

(d) Select the device font "*_sans.*"

(e) Select a font size of 12.

(f) Select "Left/Top Justify" (MX)/"Align Left" (MX 2004).

(g) Make sure "Selectable" is off, or disabled.

(h) In the Character Options dialog, make sure "No Characters" is selected.

(i) Give the text field the *instance name* "caption_txt" (without the quotes).

All these selections are explained in Lesson 9.

4 Create a second, smaller Dynamic text field for your photo credit information and position it below the first one (so that the credit appears near the lower edge of the screen). Format it the same way, but *with one exception*: Give this text field the *instance name* "credit_txt" (without the quotes). By giving each text field a unique instance name, you can control the contents of the fields independently with ActionScript.

Fig. 2.10.06 Check all your settings for the text field named "caption_txt" carefully.

Leave both of the text fields *empty*—do not type text into them.

5 Open your plain text editor program (such as Windows Notepad, or Mac TextEdit or SimpleText) and type (or paste) the caption and credit information for each one of your photos. Type the caption for photo1.jpg on a single line, and then, *on the next line*, type the credit information for photo1.jpg. On the third line, type the caption for photo2.jpg. On the fourth line, type the credit for photo2.jpg, etc. Do not leave empty lines *between* entries, and do not use hard returns *within* entries.

Enable "Word Wrap" in your text editor so you don't need to scroll sideways.

Save the plain text file with the name "captions.txt" (without the quotes). Make sure you save it into the *same folder* with the FLA file and your photos.

6 In the plain text file, before each *caption*, add this text (changing the *number* each time to match the number of the photo file to which the caption refers; start with 1):

```
&caption5=
```

This associates this caption with photo5.jpg. Do not add any space after the equals sign. (The ampersand lets Flash know this is a new variable. It is required.)

7 In the plain-text file, before each *credit*, add this text (changing the number each time to match the number of the photo file to which the credit refers; start with 1):

```
&credit5=
```

This would go before the credit text for the file named "photo5.jpg" in the folder with all your photos.

Note: The *variable names* in an external plain text file are your own creations, like other variable names. Flash does not understand what "caption" or "credit" means. You could add other variables to a text file, if you needed them; for example, "location" or "date." Just make sure to start each one with the ampersand.

8 All right—now you're ready to add *exactly four lines* of ActionScript to make this work. In the "actions" layer of your **Timeline**, click *once* on

```
1 &caption1=Chepstow Castle, Wales. The upper bailey (
. photo) was added in the first half of the 13th centu
. eastern wall surmounts a very steep slope (much stee
. appears in this photo). 27 December 2002.
2 &credit1=Photo by Mindy McAdams
3 &caption2=The keep hall, or Great Tower, perches on
. Wye River. Chepstow Castle, Wales. 27 December 2002.
4 &credit2=Photo by Melinda J. McAdams
5 &caption3=A window on the river side overlooks a cou
. of this area where Wales and England meet. Chepstow
. December 2002.
6 &credit3=Photo by Mindy McAdams
7 &caption4=Construction on this castle began in 1067
```

Fig. 2.10.07 In a plain text editor, the caption and credit information looks like this.

Frame 1 to *select* it. Open the **Actions** panel and place your cursor at the start of Line 2 in the script. Press Enter/Return to make a blank line. Add these *two new lines* there:

```
myCaptions = new LoadVars();
myCaptions.load("captions.txt");
```

Of course, you recognize the filename of your brand-new plain text file. These two lines enable the Flash movie to *find* and *read from* that text file. Flash will expect to find it in the same folder with this SWF.

9 Now (still in the **Actions** panel and still on Frame 1) place your cursor at the start of Line 7 and press Enter/Return to make a blank line there, just *above* the final curly brace. Add these *two new lines* there:

```
caption_txt.text = eval("myCaptions.caption" + newnumber);
credit_txt.text = eval("myCaptions.credit" + newnumber);
```

These two lines *display the text* from your plain text file in the two Dynamic text fields you created in Step 3 and Step 4 in this exercise. The syntax is very specific, so you must make sure this ActionScript matches the *instance names* you gave to the two dynamic text fields, plus ".text" tacked onto the end (because Flash is looking at the *"text" property* of the field, rather than "color" or some other property).

These lines use *the same parameter*, "newnumber," from the function "get_photo" that tells Flash which photo file to load into the movie clip. That's why you must coordinate the numbers so that "caption5" and "credit5" match "photo5.jpg"—everything using the number 5 refers to the same thing. The two new lines are inside that function (between the curly braces), so they can use the same value for "newnumber."

If this book is your first introduction to scripting, you are probably just starting to understand that script can be made more efficient when you work within the limitations of computer logic. By numbering things in sequence and matching the numbers for related items, you create a system that's very compatible with the way computers do things.

10 Save and test your movie: Ctrl-Enter (Win) or Cmd-Return (Mac).

What should happen: Your captions and credits show up with the appropriate photos. If they don't: (a) Check your script carefully. (b) Check the filename of your plain text file. (c) Make sure your text file is in the same folder with your photos and your FLA file.

What you have right now is a very simple slideshow that can accommodate dozens or even hundreds of photos, each with its own caption and credit. It's not elegant, but it's highly functional.

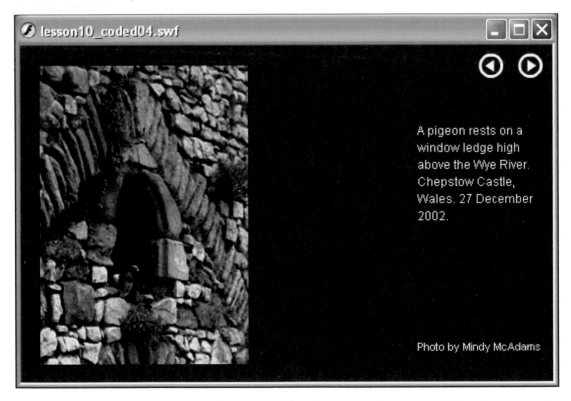

Fig. 2.10.08 In this slideshow, each photo and its caption and credit appear at the same X and Y coordinates, regardless of the width of the photo.

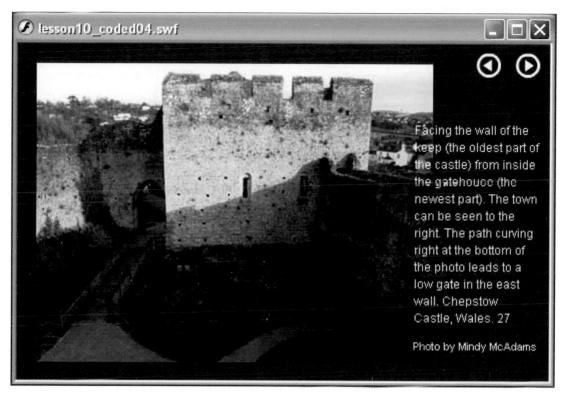

Fig. 2.10.09 While the caption and credit shown in Figure 2.10.08 look all right, the photo in Figure 2.10.09 indicates a lack of planning. When you are building this kind of reusable slideshow, make sure you have clearly recorded the maximum width (and maximum height) for photos that the slideshow can accommodate—and make sure the person editing the photos has those numbers! Also, the caption on the right is too long—two words are cut off at the end. This is a common problem; the way to avoid it is to provide clear rules for the length of the caption and credit information.

If you want to add a soundtrack to this slideshow, you can do so now by following the instructions in Lesson 8. For example, you could add a music loop with the attachSound() method, or a narration with the loadSound() method. Just write the appropriate script from Lesson 8 to Frame 1 in the "actions" layer of your slideshow FLA. You could also add buttons to control the sound.

Exercise 10.5: Add an Individual "Photo Loading" Message

In this exercise, you will add a chunk of ActionScript to detect whether the photo has loaded and to let the user know what's going on.

Even though the individual photo files may not be very large, it's always possible that the user will have a slow connection, or your server might be sluggish at times of heavy use, or there might be a general Internet bottle-neck. In those cases, when the user clicks one of your two buttons to get a new photo, there will be a delay. To be considerate of the user, your new script will check the status of the photo file's loading process and provide a text message. This way, the user knows nothing is broken if the photo does not appear immediately.

This script is similar to the script used in most Flash preloaders, which are explained in more detail in Appendix A.

1 Start with the same FLA file you used in the previous exercise. Save it with a new filename if you want to preserve the earlier file.

2 In the "actions" layer of your **Timeline**, click *once* on Frame 1 to *select* it. Open the **Actions** panel (it is assumed you are in "Expert Mode"). The new ActionScript should go *below* the function "get_photo."

3 In the **Actions** panel, place your cursor *below* all the other script and press Enter/Return to make a blank line. Add these *new lines* there:

```
function photoPreloader() {
    percent_loaded = (loader_mc.getBytesLoaded() / ¬
    loader_mc.getBytesTotal()) * 100;
    if (percent_loaded < 100) {
        pl = Math.round(percent_loaded);
        // below is the preloader text message
        loadstatus_txt.text = "Photo loading: " + string(pl) ¬
        + "%";
    } else if (percent_loaded > 1) {
        delete _root.onEnterFrame;
        loadstatus_txt.text = "";
    }
}
```

Note: When you see the ¬ sign, you must continue typing *on the same line* in the **Actions** panel. *Do not type* the ¬ sign; it's only there to let you know the line continues.

This function reads the status of that empty movie clip with the *instance name* "loader_mc" to see whether something (a photo, in this case) has loaded completely (100 percent) into the movie clip. Whenever something is *less than* 100 percent loaded, this script writes into a Dynamic text field with the *instance name* "loadstatus_txt" (which does not exist yet in your movie, but you are about to create it, in the next step).

The final section of the script guarantees that the photo has started to load. Sometimes there's a lag between photos, during which time "getBytesTotal" equals zero; that can foul up the whole script (because then it would seem that 100 percent of zero had been loaded). With *this* script, if the amount loaded is greater than 1 and also less than 100, the loading check continues.

4 To make this script work, you must create one more *Dynamic text field*. Make sure you are on the "text" layer in your **Timeline** (click that layer). Create a new text field just as you did in Exercise 10.4, Step 3—but this time, give it the *instance name* "loadstatus_txt" (without the quotes), to match the preloader script you just wrote. Position the new text field near the *upper left corner* of the **Stage**.

5 Ideally, this kind of message would never appear on top of the photo. The script *should* ensure that it never does (because when the photo is 100 percent loaded, it changes the text in the field to " "—that is, blank). But just to be safe, you can *move* your "text" layer *below all the other layers*. Just *click and hold* on the layer name in the **Timeline**, and *drag* it to the bottom of the stack.

Note: Regardless of the layer position of your "loadstatus_txt" text field, if the upper left corner of the text field is *within the photo display area*, you will see an annoying ripple effect in the corner of your photos at the moment when they appear—even if you never see the preloader text! To prevent this ugly effect, *select* your text field and set the X and Y (**Properties** panel) for that field to numbers *less than* the X and Y of your empty movie clip, "loader_mc." For example, if "loader_mc" has 20 for both its X and its Y, and "loadstatus_txt" has 10 for both its X and its Y, the effect will be prevented.

---

6 What makes your new function work? Right now, nothing does. A function does not execute unless it is called. You want this preloader script to run repeatedly each time a new photo is loading. That means you need to call the function from inside the "get_photo" function, because that is the function that causes a new photo to come into this movie.

Add this line of script immediately *before* the closing curly brace in the "get_photo" function (just *below* the line beginning with `credit_txt.text`):
`_root.onEnterFrame = photoPreloader;`

You used the `_root.onEnterFrame` event handler in "Input Text, a Tour of What You Can Do," in Lesson 9, in a way very similar to its use here. This event handler can execute a function at the frame rate of your movie (for example, 15 times per second). In this case, the event handler is running "photoPreloader" at that rate of speed. The `_root.onEnterFrame` event handler continues to run until it is deleted, which happens *inside* the "photoPreloader" function when the photo is fully loaded.

7 Save and test your movie: Ctrl-Enter (Win) or Cmd-Return (Mac). You will not see your preloader text message unless you upload and test the SWF on a Web server. After all, your photos and your SWF are on your hard drive, so there is no waiting. This version of the slideshow may seem no different from the previous one, but in live use on the Web, it is very different.

Exercise 10.6: Guarantee That the Caption File Loads

You may experience problems with the way this slideshow runs because of a time lag in loading the plain text file. (Even if *you* don't see a problem, your users might.) The way to prevent the problem is to add some frames between (a) the frame when your text file begins to load and (b) the first frame where the text information is actually *used* in your movie. You will also add a little more script to ensure that everything works as it should.

1 Start with the same FLA file you used in the previous exercise. Save it with a new filename if you want to preserve the earlier file.

2 In the **Timeline**, select Frame 15 *in all three layers* (Shift-click the frame on each layer) and press F5 *once* to extend the Timeline to that point.

3 In the **Timeline**, in the "actions" layer, move the *keyframe* in Frame 1 to Frame 15. To do this, click Frame 1 *once* with the mouse and *release*. Then *click and hold* the mouse button, and carefully *drag* the frame rightwards to the Frame 15 position in the same layer. Release the mouse button when the frame is in position.

4 Open the **Actions** panel. Select and *cut* these two lines from Frame 15:

```
myCaptions = new LoadVars();
myCaptions.load("captions.txt");
```

5 Select Frame 1 in the "actions" layer and, in the **Actions** panel, *paste* those two lines. The two lines are now the *only* script in Frame 1.

6 Create a new *keyframe* (F6) at Frame 14 in the "actions" layer. In the **Actions** panel, add these two new lines of script on that keyframe:

```
stop();
myCaptions.onLoad = nextFrame();
```

7 Finally, in Frame 15 in the "actions" layer, in the **Actions** panel, add a stop() action alone at the very top of the script (as a new Line 1). You must stop on this frame so that the movie does not loop back to Frame 1 (Figure 2.10.10).

8 One more change on Frame 15 will make it easier to change the number of photos in any future slideshows you produce, using the SWF from this file. At the top of your script, change this:

```
total_photos = 7;
```

To this:

```
total_photos = parseInt(myCaptions.totalpics);
```

Now you must add a line to your plain text file to complete this change.

9 Open your plain text file in your text editor and add this text at the top of the file:

```
&totalpics=7&
```

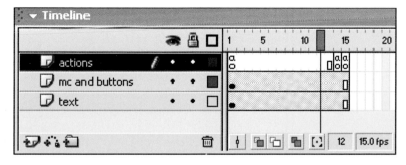

Fig. 2.10.10 You're working only in the "actions" layer; the other two layers do not change at all. The purpose of dividing the script among Frames 1, 14, and 15 is to ensure that your text file has enough time to load completely. Otherwise, the user might not see your captions.

Now the total number of photos is part of the text file outside Flash, and you can edit it without opening Flash, just like the captions and credits in the same file. (If you had more or fewer than seven photos, use the number that matches your slideshow.)

10 Save and test your movie: Ctrl-Enter (Win) or Cmd-Return (Mac). You will not see any differences unless you upload and test the SWF from a Web server.

A very professional thing to do at this point: Add some text to your text field named "caption_txt" to let users know they are waiting for something. This typed text will be *overwritten* by loaded text as soon as the user clicks either button. Alternatively, add a new layer with a blank keyframe at Frame 15 (where the slideshow now begins), and in Frame 1, add a title and some information about the content of your slideshow. If the caption file loads very quickly, however, this new information will be onscreen for only seconds—so you will also need to consider adding a button on Frame 14 to handle the "nextFrame()" action.

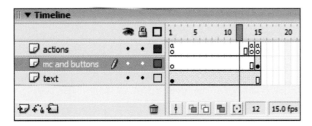

Another professional touch: Why show the buttons if they don't do anything yet? Users might click them and get no result; that would be bad. You can grab Frame 1 in your "mc and buttons" layer and drag it to Frame 15 (just as you dragged Frame 1 in the "actions" layer in Step 3). The result is shown in Figure 2.10.11.

Fig. 2.10.11 By moving Frame 1 in the "mc and buttons" layer to Frame 15, you prevent the users from seeing your buttons until they are functional.

Note: You can load an external text file in this same way for Flash packages that are not slideshows. Any kind of textual information can be formatted with variable names in a plain text file and used by Flash. For example, you could provide detailed information about locations on a map. When the user rolls over a button on the map, script on the button loads a particular item from the external text file into a *scrolling text field* beside the map graphic. The button script would give Flash the variable name of the appropriate item in the text file.

Exercise 10.7: Automating the Slideshow

In this exercise, you will delete your Next and Previous buttons and add ActionScript to make the same slideshow play automatically. You will include a new Pause button that toggles the auto-play feature.

1 Start with the same FLA file you used in the previous exercise. Save it with a new filename if you want to preserve the earlier file.

2 Select your Next button (click it *once*) and *copy* all the script. *Paste* it into a text editor outside Flash (such as Windows Notepad, or Mac TextEdit or SimpleText). You will use it later in this exercise. You might want to label it so you remember which button it came from.

3 *Delete* your Next button *and* your Previous button from the **Stage**. (The buttons are still safe in the **Library**, but as soon as you delete them from the Stage, all the script on them is gone.) *Be careful* not to delete your empty movie clip, "loader_mc"! Do not delete the "mc and buttons" layer either; you will add a Pause button on this layer later in this exercise.

4 In the "actions" layer of your **Timeline**, click *once* on Frame 15 to *select* it. Open the **Actions** panel (it is assumed you are in "Expert Mode").

5 In the **Actions** panel, place your cursor at the end of all your script and press Enter/Return to make a blank line. Add these *new lines* there:

```
function autoplay_photos() {
}
```

6 Here is where you get to *reuse the script* you saved from your deleted Next button. On the blank line in the middle (see Step 5), *paste* your saved script. Leave out or delete the *first* and *last* lines, which make the button work and are not needed here. Your new script will look like this:

```
function autoplay_photos() {
    if (n < total_photos) {
        n++;
    } else {
        n = 1;
    }
    get_photo(n);
}
```

You have scripted a new *function*, named "autoplay_photos," that does exactly what your old Next button did. Understanding this concept can be useful, so if you're writing script for the first time as you read this book, think about it for a minute or two. Clicking a button is not the only way to make things happen in a Flash movie. You knew that, of course. By now you should understand how a chunk of ActionScript will produce the same result whether it is on a button or elsewhere. Sometimes the script is just sitting on a frame, and it executes when the playhead reaches that frame. In other cases, the script is tucked inside a function, and then it will execute only when that function is called.

This movie's script includes three custom functions at this point.

7 Right now you have a lot of script on Frame 15 (about thirty lines), but nothing is going to happen if you test this movie now. That's because none of the functions are being called. The one you want to run is "autoplay_photos," so add this line *below* all the script on Frame 15:

```
autoplay_photos();
```

If you follow through the script at this point, you can see that "autoplay_photos" calls the function "get_photo," which in turn calls the function "photoPreloader." Okay, all three functions are being used!

8 Save and test your movie: Ctrl-Enter (Win) or Cmd-Return (Mac). You get to see the first photo, caption, and credit, and then . . . it's stopped. That's because after the first photo appears, no further instructions are given in your script. Look at the "photoPreloader" function: It's a dead end.

You need to make "autoplay_photos" run again and again at a comfortable pace. You must include *a timing mechanism*, and that's the next step.

9 There are *two pieces* to the timing mechanism you will use here: One piece starts the timer, and the other piece makes it quit. The trick is to make sure the timer starts counting *after* the photo is onscreen (so the user gets to look at each photo for the same amount of time). That means you'll place the next instruction inside the "photoPreloader" function, immediately *after* this line:

```
loadstatus_txt.text = "";
```

Add this new line *below* that one:

```
runAutoplay = setInterval(autoplay_photos, 3000);
```

Let's examine that new line of script:

(a) The *function* setInterval is the key to this timing mechanism. It always measures time in milliseconds, so "3000" here means "3 seconds." If you'd rather have 4 seconds, then make it "4000." (Note that setInterval does not work in versions *before* Flash Player 6, so in your Publish Settings, make sure you are saving for Player 6 or later.)

(b) The *variable name* "runAutoplay" identifies this particular *interval call* so that we can disable it, or clear it. In other words, by identifying this interval call with a *name*, we make it possible to cancel it later. Without a name, you cannot make the timed function stop.

(c) You have not forgotten the function you wrote in Step 6, named "autoplay_photos," have you? That function is what `setInterval` uses, in this case, to make the photo change after 3 seconds. It's as if you were clicking your old Next button at 3-second intervals.

10 Now you'll add the other piece of the timing mechanism—the one that makes it quit. You need to remove the timer when the next photo starts to load, in case there's a delay and that photo takes a while to show up. So you must put the new line of script at a spot where you can be sure the current photo has already been in view for the full interval (e.g., 3 seconds). That would be at the beginning of "autoplay_photos," immediately *after* this line:

```
function autoplay_photos() {
```

Add this new line *below* that one:

```
clearInterval(runAutoplay);
```

11 Save and test your movie: Ctrl-Enter (Win) or Cmd-Return (Mac). Your slideshow should play endlessly, changing the photo about every 3 seconds. (The timing is not always exact, but it should be very close to 3 seconds.)

Note: These timing functions can get out of whack if you use an excessively fast frame rate for your movie. Both "onEnterFrame" and "setInterval" can overwork an older computer's processor if the frame rate is high. It doesn't hurt the computer, but it can make things look bad in your Flash movie, because the computer can't keep up the pace. If you stick with 15 fps, though, there won't be a problem.

The complete script on Frame 15 now:

```
stop();
total_photos = parseInt(myCaptions.totalpics);
function get_photo(newnumber) {
    current_photo = "photo" + newnumber + ".jpg";
    loader_mc.loadMovie(current_photo);
```

```
            caption_txt.text = eval("myCaptions.caption" + newnumber);
            credit_txt.text = eval("myCaptions.credit" + newnumber);
            _root.onEnterFrame = photoPreloader;
    }
    function photoPreloader() {
            percent_loaded = (loader_mc.getBytesLoaded() / ¬
            loader_mc.getBytesTotal()) * 100;
            if (percent_loaded < 100) {
                pl = Math.round(percent_loaded);
                // below is the preloader text message
                loadstatus_txt.text = "Photo loading: " + string(pl) ¬
                + "%";
            } else if (percent_loaded > 1) {
                delete _root.onEnterFrame;
                loadstatus_txt.text = "";
                runAutoplay = setInterval(autoplay_photos, 3000);
            }
    }
    function autoplay_photos() {
            clearInterval(runAutoplay);
            if (n < total_photos) {
                n++;
            } else {
                n = 1;
            }
            get_photo(n);
    }
    autoplay_photos();
```

Note: You can copy and paste this script from the FLA on the Web site for this book. No need to type it all!

12 Now you will create a Pause button and add it to this version of the slideshow. The "Circle Buttons" collection from Flash's Common Libraries does not include a Pause button, but you can find one in the "Playback" collection ("gel Pause"). Drag that button onto the **Stage**, or create your own custom button if you like.

13 Select the new button on the **Stage** (click it *once*) and open the **Actions** panel. Write this script on the button:

```
on (release) {
    clearInterval(runAutoplay);
    if (running_auto == true) {
        running_auto = false;
    } else {
        running_auto = true;
        autoplay_photos();
    }
}
```

You've seen this kind of button script before, in Lesson 8. It sets a true/false "flag" so that the result of clicking the Pause button toggles between pausing the slideshow and restarting it. The *variable name* "running_auto" could be any word; what's important is that when its *value* is "true," the button does one thing, and when its *value* is "false," the button does something else.

Step 10 explained how `clearInterval(runAutoplay)` stops the timing mechanism that is started when the "photoPreloader" function completes. It's doing the same thing here, whenever the user clicks your Pause button.

Why does the Pause button *always* clear the interval? Because in one case, the button pauses the slideshow (that's the easy part), and in the other case, the button calls the function "autoplay_photos"—which ultimately starts the timer again, because it leads to "photoPreloader." You always clear the interval to make certain that the timer is never running more than once.

14 One last thing to complete this version: Because of the true/false toggle on your Pause button, you need to set that variable to true *the first time* the slideshow begins to play. To do so, add this line at the very end of all the script on Frame 15:

```
running_auto = true;
```

15 Save and test your movie: Ctrl-Enter (Win) or Cmd-Return (Mac). Your users can now pause the slideshow whenever they get the urge, and then resume auto-play by clicking the same button again.

Exercise 10.8: Adding External Sound

In this exercise, you will use techniques learned in Lesson 8 to play an external MP3 file and control it from your slideshow. You will add a button to allow the user to pause or replay the sound. Making the MP3 file play is relatively trivial; however, the button scripting requires some finesse.

1 Start with the same FLA file you used in the previous exercise. Save it with a new filename if you want to preserve the earlier file.

2 Copy your MP3 file into the *same directory* with your FLA file, your photos, and your text file.

3 In the main **Timeline**, on Frame 15, after the stop() action on Line 1, add these two lines of script:

```
x = new Sound();
x.loadSound(myCaptions.audio, true);
```

4 Now add the filename of your MP3 to your plain text file, "captions.txt." Open the text file in your editing program and add this line near the top (in this example, the audio file is named "interview.mp3"):

```
&audio=interview.mp3&
```

Adding the filename to your text file, with the *variable name* "audio," enables you to change it without opening Flash, just like the captions and credits in the same file. You can see how this line in the text file works in tandem with the new script you added to your FLA in Step 3.

Note the ampersand at the end of this line; it cuts off two trailing end-of-line characters that otherwise make the filename unusable in the Flash script.

5 Create an Audio button on the **Stage** (or grab a generic button from the Common Libraries) and write this script on it:

```
on (release) {
    if (soundplaying == true) {
        soundplaying = false;
        p = Math.floor(x.position / 1000);
        x.stop();
        audio_txt.text = "AUDIO IS OFF";
    } else {
```

```
            soundplaying = true;
            x.stop();
            x.start(p, 0);
            audio_txt.text = "AUDIO IS ON";
        }
}
```

The new *variable* "soundplaying" is created especially to control the sound file and prevent it from playing multiple times and overlapping itself. All the script affecting the sound file will check the *value* of this variable and reset it if necessary; it's a true/false toggle, just like your Pause button.

6 You will also need to create a new *Dynamic text field* near your new button, and give it the instance name "audio_txt" (without the quotes).

7 Go back to the main **Timeline**, on Frame 15, where you added these two lines in Step 3:

```
x = new Sound();
x.loadSound(myCaptions.audio, true);
```

Just below those two lines, add:

```
soundplaying = true;
x.onSoundComplete = function() {
        soundplaying = false;
        p = 0;
        audio_txt.text = "REPLAY";
}
```

These six lines of script set the initial value of the "soundplaying" true/false variable to true and determine what happens when the sound file ends— the existing Audio button is used to replay the file, if the user wants to hear it again.

8 Save and test your movie: Ctrl-Enter (Win) or Cmd-Return (Mac).

Try to test every possible way the user might operate your buttons. Does the sound ever play over itself? Does a button ever fail to function as expected? Are the button functions clear to the user? These are important questions to consider as you are building any Flash journalism package.

In this example, the button that pauses the auto-play slideshow and the button that controls the sound file operate independently of each other. If

Fig. 2.10.12 The text beside the Audio button will change to show the state of the sound file, thanks to a bit of ActionScript.

the sound and photos were synchronized, you would want to pause them together; that would require moving all the script to one button.

Exercise 10.9: Stopping on the Final Photo

In this exercise, you will make the slideshow detect the final photo and stop there (until now, your slideshow has always restarted itself after the final photo). When the slideshow stops, the Pause button will *change* to a Replay button. This entails two separate buttons that are hidden or revealed depending on which photo is on view in your movie. Each button will have a different script on it.

1 Start with the same FLA file you used in the previous exercise. Save it with a new filename if you want to preserve the earlier file.

2 Select the layer in your movie that contains your Pause button. Create a new Replay button on the **Stage,** or use one from Flash's Common Libraries. For now, don't position the button precisely, because you will move it later.

3 Select your Replay button on the **Stage** (click it *once*) and give it the *instance name* "replay_btn" (without the quotes). Tab out of the field so the name sticks.

4 Select your Pause button on the **Stage** (click it *once*) and give it the *instance name* "pause_btn" (without the quotes). Tab out of the field so the name sticks.

5 Create a new *Dynamic text field* on the **Stage** and give it the *instance name* "pauseplay_txt" (without the quotes). Make the field large enough to contain the word RESUME. Position the text field close to your Pause button. Script will make this text *change* to reflect the state of the button (Figure 2.10.13), like the text field you created for your Audio button in Exercise 10.8.

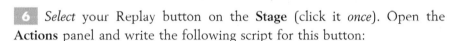

Fig. 2.10.13 The Pause button will change to a Replay button when the slideshow reaches the final photo. While the slideshow plays, text beside the Pause button will let the user know what the button does when clicked in its current state.

6 *Select* your Replay button on the **Stage** (click it *once*). Open the **Actions** panel and write the following script for this button:

```
on (release) {
    n = 0; // resets the photo sequence
    running_auto = true;
    autoplay_photos();
    switch_buttons(true, false, "PAUSE");
}
```

The first line inside the on (release) event handler resets the photo number (contained in the variable "n") to zero. The next two lines should look familiar to you by now. The fourth line calls a new *function* that will be written (and explained) in Step 8.

7 *Select* your Pause button on the **Stage** (click it *once*). Open the **Actions** panel and *change* the script currently there to match the following new script:

```
on (release) {
    clearInterval(runAutoplay);
    if (running_auto == true) {
        running_auto = false;
        switch_buttons(true, false, "RESUME");
    } else {
```

```
            running_auto = true;
            autoplay_photos();
            switch_buttons(true, false, "PAUSE");
    }
}
```

8 Your buttons are ready now, but the script that controls the Pause button and the Replay button has not been written yet. That's next. In the main **Timeline**, click on Frame 15 to select it. In the **Actions** panel, type this new script *below* what's already there:

```
function switch_buttons(pb,rb,tt) {
    pause_btn._visible = pb;
    replay_btn._visible = rb;
    pauseplay_txt.text = tt;
}
switch_buttons(true, false, "PAUSE");
```

The "switch_buttons" function is another bit of scripting that may seem complex to you, but it's very powerful, and well worth the time needed to understand it. The function expects to receive three *parameters* inside the parentheses. It will read them in order and act according to what they say.

- The first parameter can have one of two values: true or false. If it is true, then your Pause button will be visible (and functional). If it is false, your Pause button will be invisible (and nonfunctional).

- The second parameter also requires a true/false value. It affects your Replay button in exactly the same way as the previous parameter affects your Pause button: The Replay button will be visible if the value is true, not visible if it is false.

- The third parameter determines which word(s) the user sees in your text field named "pauseplay_txt." If there is an empty pair of quotation marks, then the field will be empty.

So when you see `pause_btn._visible = pb` in the function, you should understand that the value of the variable "pb" will come from the parameters inside the parentheses. The value for each parameter is sent to this function when the user clicks the Pause or Replay button.

The last line above (below the function itself) calls the function for the first time, making the Replay button invisible.

9 Now to set up the end of the slideshow. First you'll write one more function; this one tells the slideshow what to do when it reaches the last photo. Write this *after* all the other script on Frame 15:

```
function lastPhoto() {
    switch_buttons(false, true, "REPLAY");
    caption_txt.text = "End";
    credit_txt.text = "";
}
```

This leaves the final photo on the screen but changes the caption to say "End" and makes the credit text field empty. It also changes the Pause button to the Replay button, using the function you wrote in Step 8.

10 To make this new function work, of course it must be "called" somewhere in the script. Some part of your script has to check to see whether the current photo is the last photo in the set, and if so, run the "lastPhoto" function. The logical place for this to happen is within your "autoplay_photos" function, which looks like this now:

```
function autoplay_photos() {
    clearInterval(runAutoplay);
    if (n < total_photos) {
        n++;
    } else {
        n = 1;
    }
    get_photo(n);
}
```

The second half of that function is what makes your slideshow always return to photo1.jpg and play all the photos again, without stopping. Since the usual journalism slideshow does not replay automatically, you're going to make it stop with the new script.

Change the existing script so it matches this instead:

```
function autoplay_photos() {
    clearInterval(runAutoplay);
    if (n < total_photos) {
        n++;
        get_photo(n);
    } else {
```

```
                        lastPhoto();
            }
}
```

With this change, you have *moved* the line `get_photo(n)` because now you want to call that function *only if* the slideshow *has not* reached the last photo in the set. If the value of "n" is not less than (<) the value of "total_photos" (a value coming out of your plain text file), then the new function "lastPhoto" will be executed.

11 Now that everything is set up, position your new Replay button *exactly* on top of the existing Pause button. Use the X and Y fields in the **Properties** panel to be precise (that is, copy the X and Y of the Pause button into the X and Y of the Replay button). You can put the Replay button on a new layer, if you like. It will work the same way. But you do not need to be on a separate layer to do this because, at any time, you can use the Modify menu to change the "stacking order" of the two buttons (Modify menu > Arrange > Send to Back). In this way, you can switch the position of either button easily while you are editing the FLA. The visibility of the buttons in the final SWF is controlled by your "switch_buttons" function, of course.

12 Save and test your movie: Ctrl-Enter (Win) or Cmd-Return (Mac).

What should happen: The last photo, caption, and credit will appear just as the others do, but after the interval completes (e.g., 3 seconds), the caption and credit text will disappear, and the Replay button will replace the Pause button. The last photo remains on the Stage. (The Pause button will work normally before the interval ends, so the user can pause the slideshow normally.) When the Replay button is clicked, the slideshow restarts at your first photo, and the Pause button replaces the Replay button.

You have a rather sophisticated slideshow now, one that plays automatically and also allows the user to pause it or restart it. As before, the audio file still operates independently of the photo sequence, providing some versatility for you to work with. If you would like to synchronize the photos to an audio file, refer to "Synchronizing Images to Loaded Audio" in Lesson 8.

Exercise 10.10: Add Fade-In, Fade-Out Transitions

In this exercise, you will create a movie clip that fades a photo in and out, using alpha (transparency). Using ActionScript, you will make the fader work with all your externally loaded photo files. Steps 1–17 in this exercise explain how to construct the movie clip, which covers ground you have already walked in previous lessons. Steps 19–28 explain how to revise the ActionScript on your movie (from the previous exercise) to make your new fade-in/out effect work properly.

1 Start with the same FLA file you used in the previous exercise. Save it with a new filename if you want to preserve the earlier file.

2 Move your layer containing the empty movie clip, "loader_mc," to the bottom of the layer stack in the **Timeline**. If there are other objects in the layer with that movie clip, then create a *new layer*, drag it to the bottom of the stack, and *move* your movie clip to that layer.

The cleanest way to move an object that is already "in position" is to *select* it, *cut* it (Ctrl-X/Cmd-X), and then use the Edit menu to "Paste in Place" on the new layer, in the desired frame.

3 Create a new layer *above* the layer containing the movie clip, and name it "fader" (without the quotes). In other words, you must have your movie clip (the container for all your loaded photos) alone on a layer. Above it, you have a layer that will contain the fader.

4 In the "fader" layer, in Frame 1, create a rectangle with no stroke color (use the fill color only). Make the fill color the same as the *background color* of your movie. Use the **Properties** panel to make the width (W) and height (H) of the rectangle match the width and height of your movie.

5 *Select* your rectangle shape and Convert to Symbol (press F8); choose "Graphic." Name the symbol "Rectangle" (without the quotes).

6 Align the upper left corner of the new symbol with the upper left corner of the **Stage** (X and Y both 0).

7 *Select* the rectangle symbol (Figure 2.10.14) and Convert to Symbol (press F8) *again*; this time, choose "Movie Clip." Name it "Fader."

8 Now go into Symbol Editing Mode by *double-clicking* the movie clip instance on the **Stage**. Make sure you have not clicked so many times that

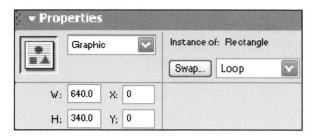

Fig. 2.10.14 When you first select the graphic symbol on the Stage, you can look at the Properties panel to make sure you have selected only that one object.

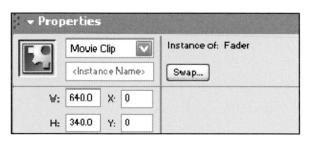

Fig. 2.10.15 After you select a symbol and Convert to Symbol again, you have not changed the first symbol (in this case, one named Rectangle). You have instead created a new symbol (in this case, one named Fader) that contains the first one.

you are inside the rectangle shape—if the rectangle fill color is dotted, you clicked too many times! Check the text to the *right* of the blue arrow (below the **Timeline** layer names in Flash MX; above them in MX 2004): *You should not see the name of your rectangle symbol there. You should see only the name of your movie clip symbol* (Figure 2.10.17).

9 In Symbol Editing Mode, extend your **Timeline** to the length (in time) that you want for the fade-in, fade-out effect. If you have a *frame rate* of 15 fps, and you want 1 second of fade-in, 1 second of clear view, and 1 second of fade-out, then you need 45 frames. Click in the Timeline at Frame 45, and press F5 *once* to extend the Timeline.

10 Create a new keyframe (press F6) at Frames 15, 30, and 45.

11 In two frames, 15 and 30, *change* the alpha of your rectangle symbol to 0 (zero). How to change the *alpha property* was explained in "Fading Photos into Each Other," Lesson 7, Step 12.

12 Put a *motion tween* on the sequence Frames 1–14 and on the sequence Frames 30–44.

13 *Name* the single layer you have in the movie clip **Timeline** "rectangle."

14 Create *two new layers* above that one. Name the top layer "actions" and the middle layer "labels."

15 In the "labels" layer, create a keyframe (press F6) at Frames 2, 15, and 30. Write the following frame labels: "startfadein" on Frame 2; "clearview" on Frame 15, and "startfadeout" on Frame 30.

16 In the "actions" layer, place a stop() action on Frame 1.

17 *Exit* from Symbol Editing Mode by clicking the blue arrow, or press Ctrl-E (or Cmd-E/Mac).

18 Save your file. Don't bother testing it, because if you did, you would never see a single photo. Right now, the stop() action on Frame 1 will hold the Fader movie clip at its 100% alpha (no transparency) position.

Now that the movie clip is constructed, the remaining work is to alter your ActionScript so that (a) the Fader fades the photo in when it should, and (b) whenever the user pauses, the photo is always at full visibility.

19 First you must *name* that Fader movie clip instance, so you can control it with script. On the **Stage,** click *once* anywhere on the movie clip to select it. Your **Properties** panel should show you that you have clicked the correct object. In the Properties panel, give it the *instance name* "fader_mc" (without the quotes) and tab out of the Instance Name field.

20 What's needed is to replace any existing script that uses "setInterval" or "clearInterval" with new script that controls the movie clip, using its frame labels. Only the lines concerning the timing must be replaced. The fader clip will now act as the timing mechanism for your slideshow.

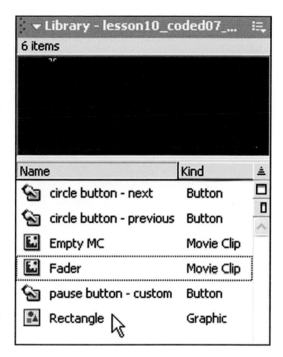

Fig. 2.10.16 Look in your Library the graphic symbol named Rectangle is still intact. The movie clip symbol named Fader contains an instance of that other symbol. The first symbol can still be used independently in your movie.

Select the frame in your main movie **Timeline** that contains the bulk of your slideshow script, Frame 15. Open the **Actions** panel. Starting from the top of the script, the first change will be in the "photoPreloader" function. Find this line:

```
runAutoplay = setInterval(autoplay_photos, 3000);
```

Delete that line and replace it with this:

```
fader_mc.gotoAndPlay("startfadein");
```

21 Next, in the function "autoplay_photos," find this line:

```
clearInterval(runAutoplay);
```

Delete it.

22 You still need to call the *function* "autoplay_photos" for every photo; now you will copy it to the Fader movie clip. So find this line in your script and *copy* it:

```
autoplay_photos();
```

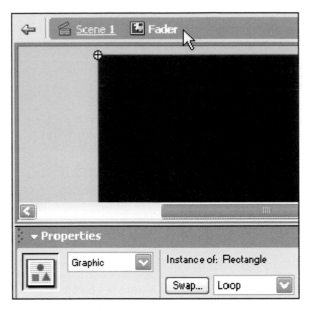

Fig. 2.10.17 Before you start creating the fader effect, make sure you are in the right place. The text to the right of the blue arrow, below the Timeline, tells you that you are inside your movie clip symbol. If any object names follow the name of the movie clip, you are too deep inside. If you are too deep, click the blue arrow to go "up" a level. The Properties panel (below the Stage) tells you that the correct object is selected, which in this case is the graphic symbol named Rectangle. Notice how helpful it is to give sensible names to each symbol you create; naming them can prevent confusion.

23 Double-click the movie clip Fader on the **Stage** to edit it. You must see the unique Timeline for your movie clip (as shown in Figure 2.10.18). If you don't see that Timeline, you are not in Symbol Editing Mode for the movie clip, and you need to get there. (Make sure you select the *correct* movie clip, and then *double-click* it, and you should be in the right place.)

24 In the **Timeline** on the "actions" layer in the Fader movie clip, select Frame 1. Open the **Actions** panel and *paste* the line of script you just copied (Step 22) beneath the stop() action that is already there:

autoplay_photos();

Then type "_parent." in front of it, so the line now looks like this:

_parent.autoplay_photos();

You are using the *same line* of script, and you are calling the *same function*. But now you are "down" inside a movie clip, and the function is "up" in your main movie. Adding "_parent" and the dot before the instruction tells Flash that it needs to look "up" in the main movie to find the function. (In object-oriented programming, an object that contains another is the *parent*; the contained object is the *child*.)

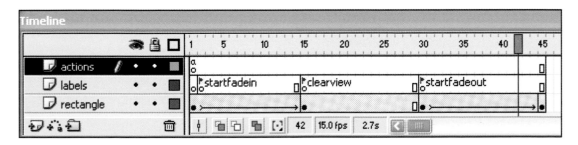

Fig. 2.10.18 The Timeline for the Fader movie clip should look like this after the frame labels are written.

Now you have a timing loop that will play all your photos (the loop *is* the Fader movie clip). As soon as one photo has completely faded out (Frame 45), the movie clip goes to Frame 1, where the script you just added there will load the next photo. It does this by doing all the same things your script did before, with the one exception in the "photoPreloader" function (the change you made in Step 20).

The stop() action on the movie clip's Frame 1 prevents your Fader clip from playing until the new line in "photoPreloader" sends the Fader clip to its Frame 2.

24 Exit from Symbol Editing Mode by pressing Ctrl-E (or Cmd-E/Mac) and return to the **Timeline** of the main movie.

25 Save and test your movie: Ctrl-Enter (Win) or Cmd-Return (Mac). The auto-play with fade-in and fade-out effects should work perfectly for all your photos.

The Pause button will not work properly yet; you'll fix that next. It will be fast and painless! The Audio and Replay buttons work exactly as they did before; no changes are needed on those two buttons.

26 Back on the **Stage**, *select* your Pause button (click it *once*) and open the **Actions** panel. Replace or edit the script to match what appears below:

```
on (release) {
    if (running_auto == true) {
        running_auto = false;
        switch_buttons(true, false, "RESUME");
        fader_mc.gotoAndStop("clearview");
    } else {
        running_auto = true;
        switch_buttons(true, false, "PAUSE");
        fader_mc.gotoAndPlay("startfadeout");
    }
}
```

This script uses the frame labels on your Fader movie clip to make the current photo *fully visible* as soon as the user clicks your Pause button the first time. When clicked again, with the movie paused (and "running_auto" being false), your Pause button tells the Fader movie clip to fade out the current photo; then the movie clip will loop back to its Frame 1, and from there the script will load the next photo in the sequence.

27 Save and test your movie. Now everything should work perfectly, including your Pause button.

If you think the photos do not stay fully visible long enough during auto-play, go into the Fader movie clip and *add frames* to the middle sequence (where there is no motion tween). Make sure you select *all* the layers—keep the keyframes lined up so your frame labels are still associated with the correct position in the fading motion tweens. For simplicity's sake, in Step 10 you set only 1 second (15 frames) for full visibility, but 2 seconds might be more to your liking.

If you would like to keep your last photo onscreen, the trick is to get the Fader clip to stop at the "clearview" frame and stay there, but only for the last photo. Also, if the user clicks the Replay button, that last photo should fade away gracefully before the loop back to the first photo. This can be accomplished with a bit of additional ActionScript.

Go into the Timeline for your Fader movie clip and make a new keyframe (press F6) on the "actions" layer at Frame 15. *Add* this script on that frame:

```
if (_parent.n == _parent.total_photos) {
    stop();
    _parent.lastPhoto();
}
```

You probably need to look at Exercise 10.9, Step 11, to remind yourself how to get access to your Replay button, which is likely hidden underneath your Pause button.

On your Replay button, *add* this line at the top, inside the button handler (after the opening curly brace):

```
fader_mc.gotoAndPlay("startfadeout");
```

And *delete* this line on your Replay button:

```
autoplay_photos();
```

That fixes it. Now the last photo stays visible until the user clicks your Replay button.

BUILDING SLIDESHOWS WITH SOUND SUMMARY

This lesson has brought almost all your new Flash skills to bear on a typical online journalism package, a photo slideshow with sound. While more advanced Flash developers might chuckle and dismiss a slideshow as a minor or easy project, that is probably not how you viewed it when you first picked up this book. Back in Lesson 7, you may have heaved a sigh at the idea of importing dozens of photos and positioning each one individually on the Stage. Now you understand that importing JPGs from outside the SWF is not only straightforward; it is also easy to automate (with n++, your little helper).

You have also learned how to import a whole set of captions and credits, as well as other information (such as the filename of your soundtrack), in a single plain text file. By replacing one set of photos and caption file with another, you can reuse the same SWF for a completely different slideshow.

This lesson has shown you a number of custom-built ActionScript functions to control your slideshow, buttons, sound, and other assets. Although the intention has not been to transform you into a computer programmer, it is hoped that through repeated exposure to similar ActionScript actions, methods, event handlers, and conditional statements, you have begun to see how providing a handy option or assistance to users usually takes no more than a few lines of script.

You have learned to check the loading progress of an external file and how to set up a timing mechanism. These are relatively high-level skills, and they are vital to creating a usable information or news package online. You have also seen, briefly, how to load external files onto a level, as well as into a movie clip. As you build on the skills acquired here, you will discover more and more uses for both of these capabilities, and you will see how the same modularity shown in the ActionScript functions here can be applied to entire Flash packages, consisting of multiple SWF files that load into and communicate with one another.

The photo slideshow with sound *is* a simple idea—but simple ideas make good building blocks for communication. What is a story, if not a sequence of bits of information? Yet some bits of information may be irrelevant to the current story; other bits will change the entire meaning of the story.

It's outside the scope of this book to explain storytelling. All online storytellers today are still finding new ways to perform that ancient human magic: Capture the imagination of your audience, and take it to a place it hasn't been before. Journalists try to tell stories that help people understand the world they live in, and of course those stories must always be truth, not fiction. But that has *never* restricted us to only "one true way" to *tell* the story.

With the tools at hand in Flash, you have a lot of options for how to tell the story you want to tell. Don't just bang it out, following an old template. Look for new ideas every day, and always try to think of the *best* way to tell the story you have to tell *today*.

CONCLUSION

In this lesson, you have learned to:

1 Plan before you build: Make a prototype or sketch layouts to avoid time-consuming design mistakes later.

2 Prepare and name JPG files to be loaded at runtime by Flash.

3 Use `loadMovieNum()` to load an external file to a level.

4 Replace one file loaded onto a level with another file.

5 Use `loadMovie()` to load an external file into an empty movie clip.

6 Replace one file loaded into an empty movie clip with another file.

7 Position an empty movie clip on the Stage so that loaded photos are positioned as you want them to be.

8 Load an unlimited number of photos, using ActionScript to move through the set of all photos.

9 Match captions and other data to photo files by number.

10 Format a plain text file, with a unique variable name for each item, for use by Flash.

11 Use the `LoadVars()` object to bring plain text into Flash from an external file.

12 Write text from an external file into a Dynamic text field.

13 Use ActionScript to check the loading status of each externally loaded photo, and delay actions until the loading has completed.

14 Show users the loading status with a Dynamic text field.

15 Avoid an annoying ripple effect that occurs when Dynamic text is inside a photo's footprint on the Stage.

16 Ensure that your external text file is fully loaded before attempting to access the contents of the file.

17 Include information about the total number of photos in the text file, so it can be edited without the need to open the FLA.

18 Script the slideshow to display the photos automatically, without the user clicking any buttons.

19 Set up a custom timer script to display each photo for a specified amount of time, using "setInterval."

20 Clear the timing sequence as needed.

21 Script a Pause button that toggles the auto-play on and off when clicked.

22 Add an externally loaded MP3 file to your auto-play slideshow, and control it with its own pause button.

23 Specify the filename of the MP3 file in the external text file, so it can be changed without the need to open the FLA.

24 Use Dynamic text to let the user see the status of a toggle button (e.g., Audio On/Off).

25 Set a true/false variable to track the state of a toggle button.

26 Use onSoundComplete to change the functionality of an Audio button.

27 Use ActionScript to determine when the final photo is shown and stop the slideshow there.

28 Use two separate buttons and the "_visible" property to offer different functionality, depending on whether the slideshow has reached the end.

29 Switch an overlapping symbol on the Stage ("Send to Back") to get access to a symbol beneath it.

30 Create a movie clip that acts as a fade-in/fade-out transition between photos in a slideshow.

31 Use a movie clip (and a little ActionScript) as a timing device.

32 Switch scripted functionality between frames and buttons.

Part III
Case Studies

Case Study 1

washingtonpost.com Sniper Shootings

URL: *http://www.washingtonpost.com/wp-srv/metro/daily/oct02/ snipershootings.htm*
Interview Date: April 25, 2003
Location: Arlington, Virginia
Interview Subjects:
- Giovanni Calabro, News Design Manager
- Brian Cordyack, Senior Designer
- Nelson Hsu, Senior Designer

> *"This was our first test of building something on the fly, and updating it as we go along, and having no idea how long the story was going to be, and trusting that we knew the technology well enough that we could fix any problems that came up."*

—*Brian Cordyack*

On Oct. 3, 2002, snipers shot and killed five people in suburban Maryland and Washington, D.C. By Oct. 9, the snipers had shot nine people; seven had died. People in the area felt deeply frightened—no one knew where the snipers would strike next. Victims had been shot in store parking lots, or in their own yard while mowing the lawn. People were afraid to go outside.

That week, three designers at washingtonpost.com began to build a Flash journalism package that would be updated in real time, on hard news deadlines. They knew that whenever the snipers acted again, large numbers of users would come immediately to washingtonpost.com for the latest information.

"We never knew when something would break," said Giovanni Calabro, news design manager, referring to the unpredictable times and locations

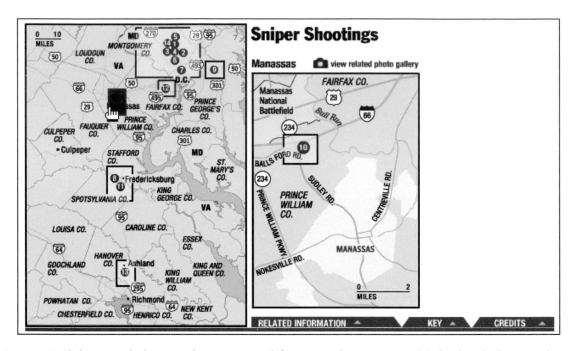

Fig. 3.1.01 Clicking a marked area on the master map (left) opens a close-up map (right) detailing the location where a shooting occurred. Printed by permission of washingtonpost.com.

of the shooting incidents. The unknown became a major consideration in planning the package.

Maps turned out to be central to telling this story, as shootings occurred across a broad geographical area, at gas stations, shopping centers, and a school. The tenth incident occurred well to the west of the first nine, broadening the area where residents no longer felt safe. A master map provides the primary interface for the package: When you click a marked location on the master map, a zoomed-in map of that location appears on the right.

"The hardest part was making this a dynamic application where we would have to do the minimal amount of work to update it," said Nelson Hsu, senior designer, the acknowledged Flash guru of the group. "Basically, what we did was create a bunch of templates, so that when a new map comes in, you throw it into this template and update the big map on the left and tell it to call this file. We did a pretty good job of making this easy to update."

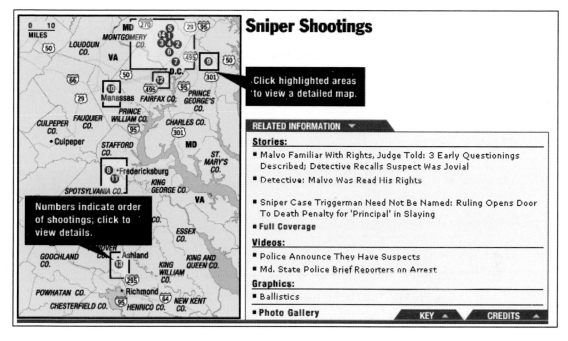

Fig. 3.1.02 Main screen of the "Sniper Shootings" Flash package: The map serves as the interface to the story. Printed by permission of washingtonpost.com.

THE MASTER MAP

The close-up maps of the crime scenes came from the print newspaper's graphics department. The reason: "They were faster at getting the information," Calabro said. *The Washington Post*'s newspaper offices are in downtown Washington, D.C. The washingtonpost.com office is across the Potomac River in Arlington, Virginia. The two newsrooms maintain close communication even under normal conditions. During the course of the sniper shootings, Calabro spoke constantly to Michael Keegan, the newspaper's assistant managing editor for News Art.

The online design department created the master map to address the need for an overview of the story, past and present. Unlike the day-to-day stories in the printed newspaper, the online version would need to contain the entire story, growing bigger with each new incident. So the complete "geography" of the story functions as the user's entry point into the Flash package; it also demonstrates the elasticity of online coverage of a news story, in contrast to a newspaper's tighter focus on what happened *today*.

The version of the master map Hsu kept on his own computer actually covered a much larger area than the one appearing in the Flash package. The final version online is "the second or third iteration" of the master map, Hsu said. The first map showed a smaller area, reflecting the early range of the shootings. As the design team realized the next shooting might be anywhere, they expanded the geographical area of the offline map as well. Hsu could edit it easily in Photoshop and create new versions as needed to replace the master map in the Flash file.

The master map is a JPG inside the FLA file. All the other maps in the package are in external SWFs, called in with the ActionScript method "loadMovieNum" (see Appendix B); they are loaded into levels, not into target movie clips.

INFORMATION ABOUT THE VICTIMS

For any close-up map on the right side, a user can click a numbered marker (a Flash button) to learn more about the shooting victim at that location. The button opens a small floating window, or panel, that can be dragged to a new position; both the master map and the close-up map remain visible beneath it. Inside the floating window, a photo of the victim appears on the left, and text appears on the right. The text can be scrolled, while the photo remains stationary.

After any shooting, it always takes some time before the victim can be named; journalists need to wait until they can verify the person's identity, and it's important to be certain that family members have already been notified by police. Before he could update the Flash package, Hsu waited for a photo and text about the victim to be sent to him from the editorial department at washingtonpost.com. Victims were not always identified on the day of the shooting.

When the information had been checked for accuracy and cleared by editorial, the designers added a new labeled frame to the movie clip that contained the floating panel. The numbered marker button on the right-side map calls the movie clip and tells it to go to that frame. The text appearing in the window is called in from a text file outside the Flash movie. (See the Tech Tip to learn how the floating panel was constructed.)

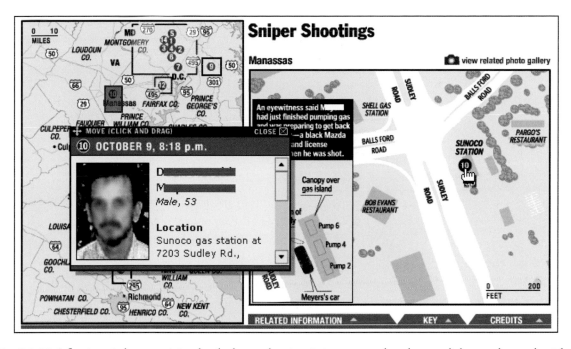

Fig. 3.1.03 A floating window containing details about a shooting victim appears when the user clicks a marker on the right-side map. Printed by permission of washingtonpost.com.

TECH TIP: A DRAGGABLE FLOATING WINDOW

In the sniper package, information about each victim appears in a small floating panel that Hsu created as a movie clip symbol. This type of movable information box is used in hundreds of Flash journalism packages.

The FLA and SWF files for this Tech Tip are on the Web site for this book (*http://www.flashjournalism.com/book*). Open the FLA to see exactly how the panel is constructed.

In this case, one instance of the movie clip is used for all thirteen victims. There are fourteen frames in the Timeline: One for each person, plus one for the first shooting, in which no one was hurt. When the user clicks a marker on a map—the marker is a button symbol—a "gotoAndStop()" script sends the movie clip to the single frame corresponding to that person (see "A Sliding Panel," Lesson 6, to learn how to put that script onto a button that controls a movie clip).

The base of the movie clip is a white rectangle. Create the rectangle, save it as a movie clip symbol (named, for example, "Floating Panel"), and continue building in Symbol Editing Mode, where you see the Timeline of your movie clip. A shadow effect can be created with a black rectangle saved as a graphic symbol and given an alpha of 50 percent; place that one underneath the white rectangle.

A dark gray strip at the top of the white rectangle contains text and two invisible buttons. One button, on the left, allows the user to click and drag the whole panel as one object. The other button, on the right, allows the user to close the window.

The ActionScript on the left button enables the dragging action:

```
on (press) {
    this.startDrag(false, 0, 0, 350, 250);
}
on (release) [
    this.stopDrag();
}
```

About the script: The four numerals constrain where the panel moves (at the edge of the Flash movie), so it doesn't go outside the main Flash window. The first two numerals (0, 0) represent the top and leftmost edges of the Flash movie. The last two numerals are relative to the size of the floating panel *and* the size of the Flash movie; they indicate where the pop-up should "hit the wall" at the rightmost and bottom edges of the Flash movie. In the preceding code, "350" represents the width of the Flash movie (550) *minus* the width of the movie clip (200); "250" represents the height of the Flash movie (400) *minus* the width of the movie clip (150). This is not the actual size of the washingtonpost.com movie; round numbers are used here for the sake of simplicity.

The ActionScript on the right button "closes" the window:

```
on (release) {
    gotoAndStop("notvisible");
}
```

About the script: Newcomers to Flash often try to make movie clips hide, or become invisible, but that's not always the best approach. Instead, you can make a part of the movie clip Timeline that is completely empty (blank frames on all layers), and then give a specific label to the first frame of that empty sequence. (The frame label here is *notvisible*.) A button on the movie clip that makes the movie clip "disappear" (or close) actually sends the playhead to the part of the movie clip Timeline where nothing is on the stage. That's what the Close button script shown does.

After the movie clip has been constructed, putting content inside the panel is fairly simple.

The photos in this case are very small (both in pixel dimensions and in file size), so Hsu chose to import the JPGs into the FLA rather than call them from outside the file. (For instructions on importing bitmaps, see Lesson 7.) Each photo was dragged out of the Library and positioned in the panel in the appropriate frame of the movie clip. If the number of victims had gotten much greater, it might have been better to load the JPGs from outside, so as to reduce the file size of the SWF.

The text in the panel, which is different in each frame in the movie clip, is called in dynamically from a single text file outside Flash. In that text file, the block of text about each person has a unique variable name. (For instructions on creating a suitable text file and calling the text into Flash dynamically, see "Add Automated Captions" in Lesson 10.)

To create the scrolling text field, follow the steps under "Scrolling Text with the ScrollBar Component" in Lesson 9.

Note about Dynamic text: Do not forget to *name* the instance of the text field before you attach the ScrollBar component. To do that, select the text field and look on the far left side of the Properties panel for the Instance Name field. Type a suitable name there, such as *personFacts*, in this case.

Note about Dynamic text fields: Do not resize the text field using the width and height fields in the Properties panel; that will distort your text. Instead, drag the handle that appears when the Text Tool is selected. If you change the size of the text field, delete the ScrollBar component and reapply it. It will not work otherwise. If you must move the text field after you have applied the ScrollBar component, first "group" the two (shift-click on each one, and then select Group from the Modify menu); if you don't, the scrollbar will separate from the text field.

The keys to making this movie clip work are the *frame label* (one for each person) and the ActionScript that executes when the movie clip Timeline stops on that frame. This technique goes back to "Buttons That Let You Jump on the Timeline" in Lesson 5, where frame labels were explained. A button in the main Flash movie opens the panel movie clip, with script similar to this:

```
floater_mc.gotoAndStop("person1");
```

That script sends the playhead to the frame inside the movie clip that is labeled "person1." In the "actions" layer for that one frame, the script changes the text shown within the scrolling Dynamic text field, in exactly the same way that captions were changed in the photo slideshows in Lesson 10.

It would be possible to construct this floating panel movie clip as a tiny version of the slideshow explained in Lesson 10, with both the photos and text loaded from outside. This version, which uses an individual labeled frame for each person, demonstrates a way to do it that may be easier to manage in some circumstances.

 FLA files for this case study Tech Tip are on the book's Web site.

PHOTO GALLERIES

Photo galleries associated with the sniper package are not Flash movies; they are external static HTML files that open in a separate browser window from a link within the Flash movie.

The designers said it would have been "more useful" to put the photo galleries inside the Flash package, but more than one photo gallery had already

Fig. 3.1.04 All photo galleries in the "Sniper Shootings" Flash package open in an HTML window outside the Flash movie. Montgomery County (Maryland) Police Chief Charles Moose, shown here, became a familiar figure investigating the case. Printed by permission of washingtonpost.com.

been built—by the washingtonpost.com photo department—before planning for the Flash package began.

The designers did not want to waste time redoing the existing galleries related to the sniper story, and for the sake of consistency within the package, they did not want new galleries to look different. So the photo department continued building HTML galleries throughout the course of the story, and the designers incorporated links to them into the Flash package (a camera icon with the text label "View related photo gallery" is actually a Flash button).

"As a result of this experience," Calabro said, "we have been adding galleries directly within our Flash pieces."

"We've moved more than 90 percent of our galleries to Flash galleries" since the shooting story, Hsu said. "It's all one template that we skin different ways." "Skinning" refers to the practice of putting a different graphical look on a screen object. It does not alter the object's functionality, but it can make an object's appearance match the other elements of a package. A Flash photo gallery, for example, might have a different background color, different buttons, or a different banner title, depending on where it is used within the Web site.

The three designers agreed that it is much easier to include a Flash photo gallery "as a separate loadMovie" in a Flash package such as the sniper story, instead of writing code to pop up a browser window for an HTML gallery (as was done with the sniper package). But more important, "the user experience is more cohesive" when the photo gallery is inside the same Flash package, Cordyack said, because the user does not have to deal with a separate window. The user would not go outside the Flash package but would remain in the same information space, where all the functionality stays the same.

If he had included photo galleries within the sniper package, Hsu said, he would build the gallery as an independent SWF (see Appendix B) and load it into a level on top of the main movie; he would not "swap it out." That way, he would protect the user's position in the main movie, and when the user closed the photo gallery, he or she would be in exactly the same place as when the photo gallery opened. This eliminates the confusion a user might feel when elements such as navigation buttons disappear.

The user would not be inconvenienced by the appearance of the photo gallery on top of the main movie, making the maps temporarily unavailable, Calabro said. "If it's a clean design, I think it's a safe assumption that if someone clicks on something, they want it," he said.

The online photo department, which is separate from the online design department, manages the work on photo galleries at washingtonpost.com. Photos in the galleries come from both *Washington Post* photographers and wire services. For the sniper story, the online photo department handled all communication with the newspaper's photo department.

In the early stages of the sniper Flash project, the online designers discussed with the online photo department how they had planned for inclusion of the photo assets. The photo staff understood that when they had a new gallery or other images, such as satellite photos of the crime scene area, they needed to notify the designers so the asset could be incorporated into the Flash package as soon as possible.

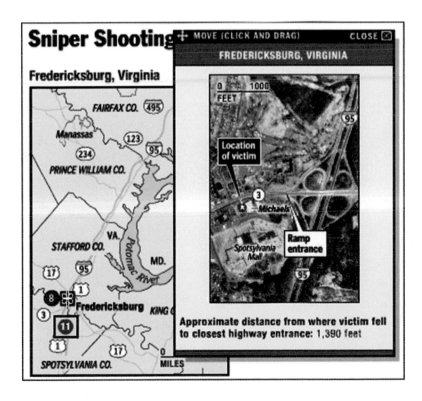

Fig. 3.1.05 For many of the shooting locations, the package includes a satellite image of the scene. Printed by permission of washingtonpost.com.

The satellite photos open in a floating window, almost identical to the one used to display information about the victims. A unique icon (also a Flash button) on the close-up maps indicates that a satellite photo is available.

GRAPHICS FROM THE NEWSPAPER

The Washington Post ran various information graphics with news articles throughout the course of the story. Like the maps and photographs that ran in the newspaper, these information graphics were available to the online designers.

On Oct. 7, police found a firearm shell casing near the scene of a shooting at a school in Bowie, Maryland. The newspaper's graphics department created several illustrated explanations about how forensics experts use bullets and related evidence to produce information that can help investigators find a suspect. The online designers at washingtonpost.com combined two separate graphics, which ran on different days in the newspaper, to create a ballistics information section within the Flash package.

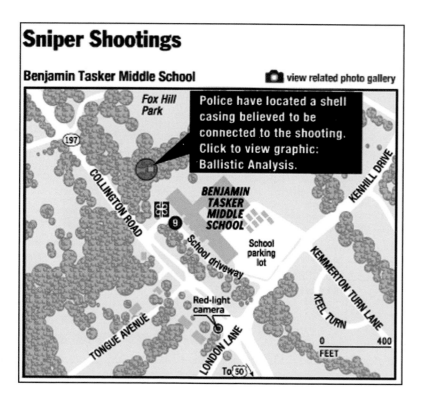

Fig. 3.1.06 From this map, showing where a shell casing was found, a user can open an explanatory graphic about ballistics. Printed by permission of washingtonpost.com.

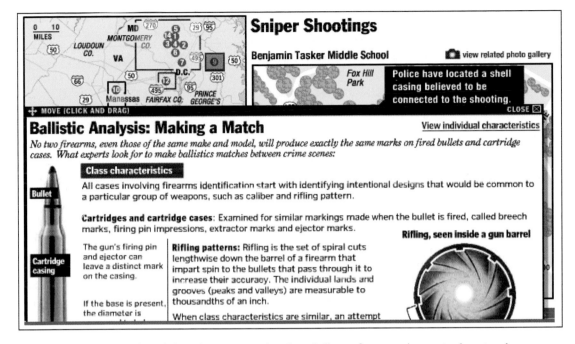

Fig. 3.1.07 The designers adapted the information graphic about ballistics from two that ran in the printed newspaper. Printed by permission of washingtonpost.com.

A link from the school shooting map (Marker 9) opens the ballistics graphic; another link to the graphic appears on the sliding menu panel labeled "Related Information" at the bottom edge of the full graphic.

The ballistics graphic comprises two "screens" (or frames); no animation is used in the explanation. "We were trying to get the most information up," Cordyack said. "If we spent all of our time animating that, then all of a sudden there's another shooting, and we're not prepared for it. Then by the time this story is over, is it worth it to go back and animate that to tell the story?"

The graphic designers continually weighed the value of changing an asset that appeared in the printed newspaper against the information value to the online users. Since this story concerned users moment by moment, sometimes the decision tipped in favor of providing information more quickly.

"You don't make something cool for coolness' sake," Calabro said. "Our jobs are to ensure that people gather accurate information. If animating helps us tell a story stronger, we will animate it. However, if putting a flat graphic up there is what you need, and it tells the story quickly and accurately, then that's all you need. This has to be a very efficient business."

MANAGING INFORMATION INTERACTIVELY

After the killing of the eleventh victim, at the Seven Corners shopping center on Oct. 14, 2002, the designers added a graphic of the shopping center, linked from the master map (Marker 12). Because they assumed many users would be familiar with the location, they wanted to include the names of the businesses in the buildings shown, to make it clear where the shooting took place. The number of labels required, though, would have produced an intimidating mass of text and pointers, cluttering the illustration. "If you put all this information on here, you run the risk of having people glaze over, because it's too much," Calabro said.

To simplify the graphic, the designers removed all the labels and devised a solution perfectly suited to Flash: They made each store building in the illustration into a Flash button. For the "Up" button state, each building looks like all the other buildings in the illustration. For the "Over" state, the building becomes red, and the labels and pointers for that one building appear. The "Down" state does nothing. (For instructions on making buttons and changing button states, see Lesson 4.)

The end result: Mouse over any building and see which stores are there. A user can get an accurate picture of exactly where the shooting occurred, relative to the stores in the shopping center.

Cordyack noted the necessity of adding an instruction to the base graphic to tell users they will see more information if they roll over the buildings. Many people will not think of trying to mouse over if that instruction is not present. The instruction comes up in a box overlying the graphic, catches the user's attention, and then quickly fades away.

UPDATING BREAKING NEWS IN FLASH

"There was a lot of pressure on us to have accurate information quickly," Cordyack said. Users throughout the Washington area checked the *Washington Post* home page frequently for news about the sniper attacks,

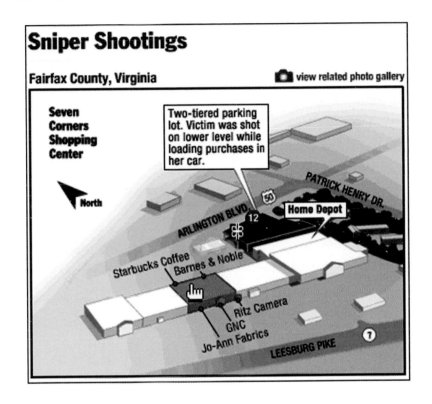

Fig. 3.1.08 Scene of a shooting: Labels appear to identify stores in a Virginia shopping center when the mouse rolls over each building. Printed by permission of washingtonpost.com.

especially during weekdays when most office workers had no access to television.

Until two suspects were arrested on Oct. 24, 2002, and the shootings ended, Calabro kept a TV set on all the time whenever he was at home, so he would know as soon as anything happened. In many cases, he could then update the graphics in the story package by logging in to the washingtonpost.com editorial computer system from home.

When a new shooting occurred, someone at washingtonpost.com would remove the link to the Flash package from the home page (because the package was no longer up-to-date) and replace it with a link to a map showing the location of the latest attack. The map of the most recent attack would be a flat graphic. As soon as enough information was available to update the Flash package, the new map would be made interactive and added into the package (via a new marker button added to the master map on the left side), and the Flash package would be linked on the home page again.

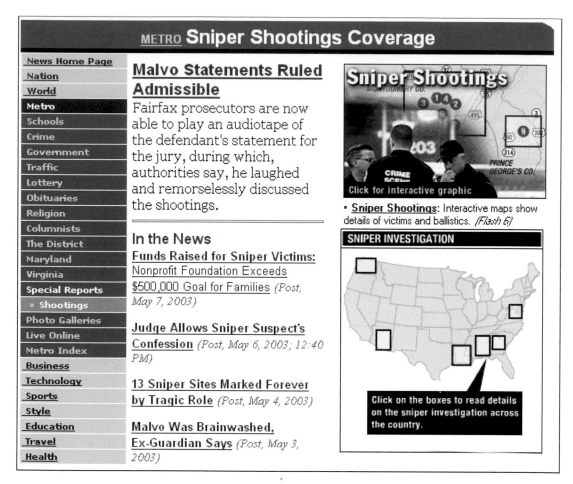

Fig. 3.1.09 The main Web page for the complete washingtonpost.com "Sniper Shootings Coverage" package (screen capture taken May 8, 2003). Clicking the image at upper right opens the Flash package. Printed by permission of washingtonpost.com.

PLANNING WITH STORYBOARDS

The three washingtonpost.com designers storyboard every Flash project. "We found that storyboarding is very helpful, because it keeps things really focused," Calabro said. "For something of this size, you need to determine at the beginning what the goals of the piece are."

For large projects, they use whiteboards for their storyboards (protecting them by writing "DO NOT ERASE" in big letters). For a smaller project, usually the designer draws the storyboard out on paper. Drawing a diagram of the package saves time in the long run, because the designer can recog-

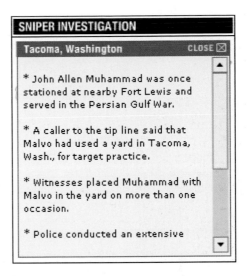

Fig. 3.1.10 Two frames from the "Sniper Investigation" package, a small follow-up Flash graphic added after two suspects were taken into custody. Printed by permission of washingtonpost.com.

Fig. 3.1.11 Clicking a marked area on the U.S. map (Fig. 3.1.10) opens a fact list related to events in that area. Printed by permission of washingtonpost.com.

nize things that will not work and eliminate them without ever building them in Flash. It's also easier to see in advance which assets will be needed, such as photos, video, or maps.

By using storyboards for the sniper project, the design team could easily speculate about any possible new developments in the story: What if the shootings moved north as far as New York? What if the snipers killed more than ten people in one day? What if different weapons were used? How would the package be able to grow if that happened?

The storyboards also helped the designers communicate their ideas to people on the editorial, photo, and production staffs at washingtonpost. com. "Going to other people with a plan is a lot better, especially under a circumstance like this—it's hitting the fan—you need to have a plan to start with. It's much easier critiquing a plan that's already started than going to a group and saying, 'What are we going to do?' We say, '*This* is what we're going to do. How does this play in with *your* ideas about how we're going to cover this?' "

As the story continued with the arrest of two suspects, then with their trials and convictions in separate courtrooms in March 2004, the washingtonpost.com "Sniper Shootings Coverage" page (*http://www.washingtonpost. com/wp-dyn/metro/specials/shootings/2002/*) continued to be updated with the latest headlines and additional graphics. The original Flash package received no manual updates after the arrests, but the "Related Information" menu panel in the graphic always displays the three most recent headlines relative to the story, thanks to a script linked to the Web site's content management system.

Case Study 2

Star Tribune Slideshow Tool

URL: *http://www.startribune.com/stories/319/*
Interview Date: May 17, 2004
Location: Minneapolis
Interview Subjects:
- Dave Braunger, Designer/Artist
- Regina McCombs, Multimedia Producer

> *"If I have to open up a linear Flash file and tweak stuff, that takes time. The tool takes it out of my hands and puts it back into the editor's hands."*

> *—Dave Braunger*

Time was the problem. Not that building a slideshow took very long, but with a total of four designers working on the online edition, their availability is at a premium.

"Plus, we were reinventing the wheel every time," said Regina McCombs. Each slideshow had a new design. So she and Dave Braunger started talking about creating a template in Flash that would allow non-designers such as McCombs to quickly build an audio-driven slideshow with any number of photos.

Braunger did not think a template—essentially a "blank" Flash document (an FLA file) that someone can copy and then fill with new photos and captions—would be the best solution.

"I was thinking they would screw it up," he admitted, evoking laughter from McCombs.

McCombs said both she and another online producer at the *Star Tribune*, Jenni Pinkley, had "a couple of days' training" in Flash, and she was confident they could work with a template. But Braunger envisioned a fool-

The lure of the Mississippi

The bridge between Bluff Siding, Wis., and Winona.

Regina McCombs / startribune.com

Fig. 3.2.01 The slideshow tool allows startribune.com producers to publish audio-driven photo slideshows without waiting for a designer to be available. Printed by permission of startribune.com.

proof tool that would allow the producers to do what they were already doing—editing the photos, editing the sound file, and writing captions and credits—and not much more than that.

"They have to comp the photos, they have to edit the audio, and at that point, you've got the finished pieces of the puzzle," Braunger said. He saw it as an editorial bottleneck: The producers finished the journalistic work, and then the project sat in limbo, waiting for the designer. "Even with the captions, we kept running back to them and saying, it's two words too long," he said. Then the designer would have to wait for the producer to re-edit the text.

"We'd been working to develop editing tools for our publishing system, for the online. We were at a point where they didn't have to hand something off and lose control of it," Braunger said. "This was an opportunity for us to say, well, best-case scenario, what do we want?"

CRITIQUING OLD METHODS

Until late 2003, producers at startribune.com were building slideshows in RealSlideshow, a simple tool from RealNetworks based on SMIL (Synchronized Multimedia Integration Language). The audio in those slideshows sounded great, but the quality of the photos always disturbed McCombs; they were overly compressed. The photographers didn't like the picture quality either. The presentations played in the Real player, which carried branding graphics from RealNetworks. Braunger and McCombs agreed they would rather not see another company's brand on startribune.com slideshows.

The word *slideshow* is used at startribune.com only when audio accompanies the presentation. If photos are displayed without a soundtrack, it's called a photo *gallery*.

"We all liked the Flash slideshows much better," McCombs said. There was another problem, though: In Flash, the audio had a persistent sibilance the producers were never able to eliminate. It wasn't in the raw AIFF files, but once the sound was in Flash, the quality declined, and the producers felt dissatisfied with the audio. McCombs said they were also unhappy about offering two entirely different experiences for the users.

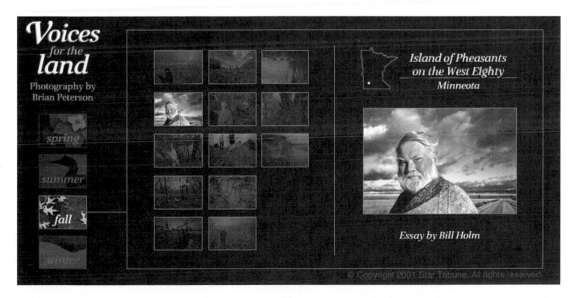

Fig. 3.2.02 Dave Braunger used much of what he learned from designing this project, "Voices for the Land," in the slideshow tool he built for the *Star Tribune*. Printed by permission of startribune.com.

"The Real tool was very intuitive, very easy to use," Braunger noted. "It's just that the final product was all compressed, distorted. On the other hand, in Flash the sound was distorted, so it was pick your poison."

A new option opened up with the release of Flash MX in 2002, which allowed producers to dynamically load external MP3 files. Because the audio never went into the FLA, it was never altered by Flash. The producers could finally control the quality of the audio.

Having experience with two different production methods under their belts, Braunger, McCombs, and Pinkley discussed what they would want from an automated slideshow tool. In part, that required identifying what they didn't like about slideshows they had already done. Braunger described a "post-mortem process we always go through on projects, saying, I wish we could have done this, I wish we could have done that."

Their basic goals for Version 1:

- Use bigger photos than before.
- Provide a cleaner loading experience for users.
- Provide better sound.
- Use timing coordinated with the audio file to drive the presentation.
- Be able to edit the captions after they have been uploaded.
- Show a photographer credit for each photo.
- Display production credits at the end of the presentation.

USE OF AUDIO

The startribune.com slideshow tool went into regular use in fall 2003. It requires one MP3 audio file per slideshow. The ActionScript in the SWF uses the loaded MP3 to advance the photos in the slideshow (see "Synchronizing Images to Loaded Audio," in Lesson 8), so the producer not only places the photos in a particular order but also selects the point in the audio file at which each photo will appear onscreen. Each transition point is entered into the tool as two numbers, representing minutes and seconds.

At least four *Star Tribune* photographers had gathered their own audio at the time of this interview. "There are also photographers who like having audio with their stories, so they will call me, or Jenni [Pinkley], and say, I'm going out on this story, do you guys want to go and get audio?" McCombs said.

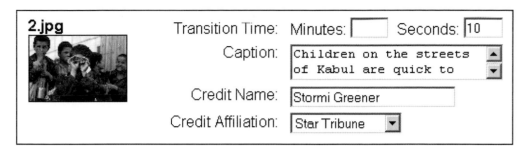

Fig. 3.2.03 A caption, credit, and transition time are assigned to each photo in the slideshow, using an HTML form. Printed by permission of startribune.com.

Probably five or six staff photographers have done that, including Jerry Holt, who shot the photos for "The Lost Youth of Leech Lake" (*http://www.startribune.com/leech/*), a story project about crime and other problems on an Indian reservation in northern Minnesota. Holt, who had lived on the reservation for six months to work on the project, later went back with Jackie Crosby (a print reporter who had worked on the online staff for eight years) and introduced her to the people he had come to know as he made pictures of them. Crosby then conducted and recorded interviews.

"More and more," McCombs said, "they [photographers] are starting to call us before they go out."

STARTRIBUNE.COM FLASH SLIDESHOW FACTS

Pop-up window and SWF size:	770 pixels × 430 pixels
Photo size limits:	500 pixels wide × 385 pixels high
Average JPG file size:	40–50 KB
MP3 file size:	500 KB or less
Average MP3 file length:	1.5–3 minutes
Average onscreen time per photo:	5–6 seconds
Streaming audio:	No
Preloading:	Yes; all JPGs are loaded into separate movie clips before the audio is started
Timing:	Uses "onEnterFrame"; each photo transition is synchronized with Position property of the sound file

startribune.com

Adding the Oom-pah-pah to the band

Brooks Stapleton and Jacob Denman hold their full-size tubas, waiting for their parts.

Darlene Pfister / Star Tribune

Fig. 3.2.04 The slideshow may have a plain white background or a super-lightened JPG as a background image. For Version 1, the PHP tool did not include an option to change the caption and credit text color (both dark gray), and so it was not possible to use a dark background. Printed by permission of startribune.com.

Sometimes a photographer contacts the online staff after the shoot. "They'll come back and say, I did this story that really should have had audio," McCombs said. One example was a story about a tuba class, which met every week. The story (*http://www.startribune.com/stories/319/4173729. html*) wasn't going to run for a while, so Pinkley went to the class and recorded students' comments and the music of tubas. "For something like that," McCombs said, "it's not really critical that you were there at the same time the photographer was."

In other cases, though, the event is finished and it's impossible to go back for audio.

Either McCombs or Pinkley edits the audio file, using Sound Forge or Cool Edit Pro (now Adobe Audition). For capturing, they always use MiniDisc recorders, "mostly the small consumer-grade models," McCombs said. The online producers' standard microphone is the Electro-Voice RE50, an omni-directional unit; they also have two Sennheiser ME66 shotgun (directional) mics and two wireless models. Photographers love the wireless mics, which the interview subject clips on and usually forgets about, she said. "In fact, they now have one of their own in their pool gear."

One of the *Star Tribune* picture editors, Vickie Kettlewell, has done some audio gathering. "The great thing about her is, she's really been trying to encourage the photographers to think about [when a story] might be great audio, or even great video," McCombs said. "We don't have as many people shooting video, but we have a couple. Some of that's timing; it's really hard to get both if you're in breaking news. Part of it is access to gear. I think more of them would shoot if they had better access to gear."

Star Tribune photojournalist Mike Zerby shot video during the war in Iraq, and CNN used some of it on-air.

The photographers like the new slideshow format, McCombs said: "The pictures are much bigger now, and the quality is very good."

The photos in the project "To Be a Doctor" seemed tiny in comparison, McCombs said. "They will be bigger in the redesign," said Braunger, who designed the project originally in 2001. The photographer, Judy Griesedieck, volunteered to go back and re-edit all the pictures for the redesign (*http://www.startribune.com/doctors/*); she also gathered much of the audio for the project, which documents the experiences of students in the class of 2004 at the University of Minnesota Medical School. McCombs produced the project and edited the sound.

In the doctors project, like the newer slideshows, captions appear beside most photos while the audio plays. "Sometimes things just need captions. They need a little more information than what's coming in that audio," McCombs said. "But we know that pulls you away from listening, when you start to read. So we try to keep our captions as minimal as we can.

"Too many times, the eye will pull you away from your ear. For most people, the eye dominates the ear. That's why I love video, because that keeps both engaged."

McCombs objects to multimedia packages where the text onscreen reproduces what the soundtrack says. "It's not giving you new information. You're wasting your medium. If people can read it, then let them read it. If they need to hear this guy's voice, then let them hear it and listen. If you're trying to give them a glimpse into this person's personality, then do that.

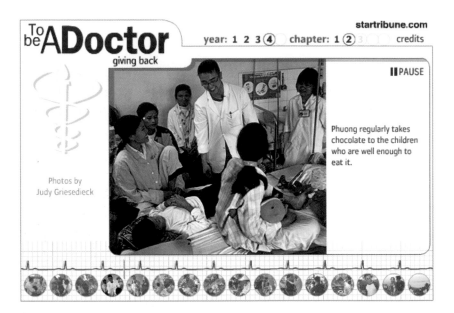

Fig. 3.2.05 The project "To Be a Doctor," originally designed in 2001, documents the experiences of students in the class of 2004 at the University of Minnesota Medical School. It preceded the development of the slideshow tool. Printed by permission of startribune.com.

If you're trying to make sure they understand exactly what he's saying, then do it another way."

If the producer needed to ensure that the content was fully accessible to users who couldn't hear audio, or who couldn't read, McCombs said she would offer the content in two different formats, as an either/or option, instead of creating redundancy: "I would say, if you want to read it, read it. If you want to listen to it, listen to it."

TRANSITIONS

The slideshows generated by the tool are straightforward, not overly "flashy." The background, either plain white or a white-saturated photo, does not compete with the displayed photos. The interface includes a Pause button and a Close button. At the end, with the final credits, there's a Replay button.

"We don't move a lot of images," Braunger said. He looked pointedly at McCombs.

"That would be because of me," McCombs said, a little sheepishly. Both she and Braunger laughed, as if recognizing a familiar topic. "It's not like I *never*

TO BE A DOCTOR photos by Judy Griesedieck

Year one
Year two
Year three
Year four
Epilogue

YEAR FOUR:
graduation

Tom Christenson is hooded by his father, Dr. David Christenson, a family practitioner in Winona.

Voice of:
Dr. David Christenson

playing   > ‖ ≪

Fig. 3.2.06 Redesigned after the medical students' graduation in 2004, "To Be a Doctor" now incorporates Version 1 of the slideshow and also some enhancements that are on the producers' wish list for Version 2. Printed by permission of startribune.com.

like them to move," she continued. "My feeling is that *if* they move, they should be going *from* somewhere *to* somewhere. To reveal. They should be revealing some piece of information."

She attributed her conviction to her background in television. "Pans and zooms just for the sake of pans and zooms are evil. They have to have a reason for their existence," she said. "The vast majority of the time you see pans and zooms on photos, they have no point. It's not serving the photograph. It's not serving the information. It's just moving. In fact, sometimes it's downright confusing, because you're looking *for* something. You're looking to see what's coming. And then nothing is ever coming."

"If the photograph is strong enough, it doesn't need fancy transitions," Braunger said. "If the photograph is what the piece is about, then the photograph should carry the information. We've always had really strong mate-

Fig. 3.2.07 Some slideshows have all black-and-white photos. The producer may decide that some photos do not need a caption. Printed by permission of startribune.com.

rial, and if you have strong material, that stuff just takes away from the viewing experience."

The photos in the slideshows cross-fade into each other, rather than fade to white (or black). Each photo is visible for about 5 or 6 seconds. "To me, that fade to black, or fade to white, indicates something ending, so it's a visual language that isn't comfortable for me," McCombs said, again referring to her experience with video.

"A straight cut between the photos could be a little jarring," she said. "I'm not opposed to transitions at all. Transitions mean something. It's a visual language we're all used to, whether we know it consciously or not. We've been trained by movies and television shows that different transitions mean different things. If you're video editing, you use a cut in one situation and a dissolve in a different situation."

Because the photos are not moving, when you change from one to the next, she said, "you're changing time and space with that, so you want to show that—with a transition."

"I think it keeps the continuity of the audio too, because it's a smooth transition," Braunger added. "You've got someone talking, and the cross-frame transition, the dissolve, makes that feel more natural: This is related, this isn't a new chapter."

"When transitions work right," McCombs said, "they almost create a third thing in the middle. When transitions are really good, you create a relationship between this photo and this other photo *in* the transition. That's your ideal, really."

PUTTING SOUND AND PICTURES TOGETHER

Whether or not she has recorded the audio herself, when McCombs creates a slideshow, she usually starts by looking at the photos. She asks to see the photographer's entire "take," knowing that usually no more than three or four shots will be filed for the newspaper's use. She will need about eighteen pictures to cover 90 seconds of audio.

Sometimes there's just not enough variety in a set of photos—shots at different distances from the subjects, close-ups of details, pictures shot with different lenses. "In some ways, I'm asking them to shoot things they never would have shot" for traditional photojournalism, McCombs said. "Some love to shoot details; others don't."

Sometimes the time for a shoot is very limited, and the photojournalist must concentrate on getting the single shot for the newspaper. In those cases, if she has advance notice, McCombs may go out with a second camera.

After looking at the pictures, McCombs listens to the audio and starts to capture "anything I think I might use." The captured audio will end up being much more than what's used in the final product, but the process requires the producer to sort, discard, and select. Capturing discrete sound bites is a way to start breaking it up. While capturing, she makes notes about the content of the sound bites and her thoughts, beginning to structure the slideshow in her mind.

"I think, okay, that's my open. Okay, that's my close," she said. "Then I'll think about the middle." A slideshow uses many of the same storytelling techniques as video, requiring her to consider the pacing, the climax, and even character development.

After the audio is on the hard drive, she looks at the pictures again. "It's a back-and-forth process," she said. "Sometimes I can't use something [from the audio] because I have no pictures to go with it."

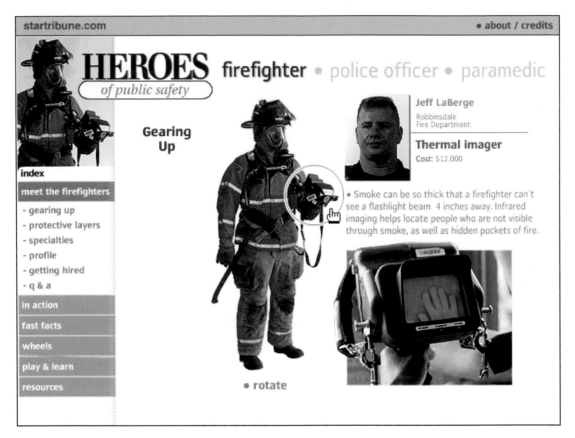

Fig. 3.2.08 A September 11 anniversary package, "Heroes of Public Safety" (2002) was "a breakthrough project for us, because it was the first time we were able to sit at the table and be viewed as peers" by the print newspaper staff, Braunger said. "They were very generous with us. If we needed anything, they were more than willing to help us. We were involved in planning meetings from the very beginning." Cooperation between the online and print journalists has been improving ever since, McCombs said. Printed by permission of startribune.com.

The first rough version of the audio file might be as long as 6 minutes, with the bites just tacked together, without transitions. In the end it must come in under 3 minutes, and probably closer to half that. She likes to use natural sound if she has it, but she rarely uses music, because of the rights issues: "It's more of a hassle than it's worth."

The number of photos available always has a direct effect on the final length of the audio file, McCombs said. No photo can stay onscreen too long. "If a picture is up for 20 seconds, people are just going to be *gone*."

BUILDING THE SLIDESHOW TOOL

Braunger worked eight to twelve months on the slideshow tool, fitting it in between regular design projects for the *Star Tribune* Web site. He made multiple attempts, only to start over again at the beginning. He completely abandoned two different versions of the slideshow tool at advanced stages of development.

"I'd get one that would work, but the transitions wouldn't be smooth. I'd be like, this is ridiculous. I have a 1.5-gighertz G5 [computer], why can't this transition smoothly? And if it's not transitioning smoothly on this, I can't imagine what it's going to do on a common everyday machine. So—scrap it."

One snag that held him up concerned the way he originally loaded in the JPGs. So that the photos never get out of sync with the audio, he needed to preload all of them. His script loads each JPG in turn into a new empty movie clip and sets the alpha of the clip to zero. "After a few of these, you get a white box on top of your photos, covering the area where they overlap," he explained. When he was loading the photos on the Stage at exactly the position where the user would eventually see them, the mysterious white box presented an insurmountable problem. It covered the currently visible photo. Solution: Load the JPGs "offstream." That is, load them to the side of the Stage, where no one can see them. They are still stacked on top of one another, and the white box appears, but it no longer matters. When the next photo needs to be onstage, the script simply changes the movie clip's X and Y coordinates to bring it into position.

When he got the Flash application working as he wanted, it was a one-frame movie with one layer and lots of ActionScript. The Stage is vacant, except for three empty movie clips: one for sound, one for pictures, and one named "check" to keep tabs on the other two. "That was always the plan," Braunger said. "Everything had to be made so they [the producers] never had to open up a SWF."

ActionScript creates a new Dynamic text field for each caption and positions it based on the width of the photo, making it possible "to use vertical images gracefully," Braunger said. The width of the text field is also computed by the script, based on the amount of space available to the right of the photo.

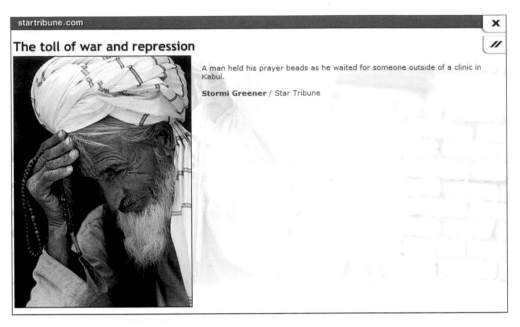

Fig. 3.2.09 The width and position of the caption and credit automatically adjust to the width of the photo. Printed by permission of startribune.com.

A copy of the SWF needs to be in the same folder on the Web server with the photo files (JPGs named in numerical sequence), the background image, the MP3 file, and the text file, which contains all the information about the individual slideshow. (This method of producing a slideshow is explained in Lesson 10.) Each startribune.com slideshow is complete within its own folder. During the testing phase for the Flash file, the producers would simply drop their files into a folder, and Braunger would troubleshoot them. He would manually add variable names in front of each caption and credit in the text file.

When Braunger was satisfied that all the functionality of the Flash file worked reliably, the next step was to integrate it into startribune.com's online publishing system, which is used for all the stories on the Web site. In-house they call it the "PHP tool"; its official name is NewsEase 2.2, and it's internal to the *Star Tribune*. Everything from the newspaper goes through NewsEase on its way to the online edition. PHP is an open-source programming language used on many Web servers, so as you might guess, the NewsEase system is programmed in PHP.

NewsEase is a content-management system (CMS) for a news Web site; many news organizations have their own proprietary CMS. What most such systems have in common is an HTML-form interface that allows a producer or editor to type text into fields, click a Submit button, and thereby publish the text to the Web site. The "management" part of these systems ensures that stories and other items are assigned identification numbers or names, which work with the Web site's archiving and search tools.

Braunger doesn't know PHP, and he didn't work on creating NewsEase, so he had to depend on one of the startribune.com programmers, Jack Weber, to write the connecting script between his Flash application and the NewsEase system. "One of the hardest things was to get the programmer time for that," McCombs said.

Late in 2003, "we kind of shoehorned the slideshow feature into" NewsEase, Braunger said. The PHP programmers were at work on an upgrade to the CMS, and when the upgrade was finished, the slideshow tool was better integrated. McCombs called the upgrade "a pretty huge overhaul" of startribune.com's publishing system.

Thanks to the CMS, producers such as McCombs can log in from anywhere and fill in a standard Web form to set up a new slideshow. When they click a button, a new folder is created for the slideshow; all the files for the slideshow are uploaded to the Web server; the SWF is copied into that folder; and a text file is created, containing not only the captions and credits but also the transition timing data.

TECH TIP: DYNAMIC BORDERS, TEXT FIELDS

Dave Braunger's script for the startribune.com slideshow tool includes some neat tricks not used in the scripts in Lesson 10. Two of the functions it performs: (1) It dynamically draws a one-pixel border around the photo. (2) It dynamically creates and positions a new text field for each photo. Either function can be plugged into another script; the examples on the Web site for this book demonstrate how they can be added to one of the slideshows from Lesson 10.

To draw a border around a photo, it's necessary to "read" the width and height of the loaded JPG file from the width and height of the movie clip it has been loaded into, and store those two numbers as variables:

```
loader_mc.photoWidth = loader_mc._width;
loader_mc.photoHeight = loader_mc._height;
```

Note that the photo must be fully loaded before these two statements execute. If it's not, the width and height will be incorrect.

The parameters (or properties) of the border to be drawn (line thickness, in pixels; line color, in hexadecimal; and alpha percentage) can also be defined and assigned to variables:

```
linethick = 1;
linecolor = 0x000000; // Flash requires this format for colors
linealpha = 100;
```

Here is the script that draws a border around the outside edge of the photo, inside the movie clip that's holding it:

Table 3.2.01

```
1  loader_mc.lineStyle(linethick, linecolor, linealpha);
2  loader_mc.moveTo(-1, -1);
3  loader_mc.lineTo(loader_mc.photoWidth, -1);
4  loader_mc.lineTo(loader_mc.photoWidth,
   loader_mc.photoHeight);
5  loader_mc.lineTo(-1, loader_mc.photoHeight);
6  loader_mc.lineTo(-1, -1);
```

What the script does:

1 The ActionScript *method* "lineStyle()" is used to draw lines dynamically. It typically appears in the format seen here: First, the *instance name* of a movie clip, followed by a dot. Next, the *method* itself. Finally, the *parameters*, separated by commas and enclosed in parentheses.

2 Here's where the line begins to be drawn. The line will originate at the X,Y coordinates of −1, −1 *inside* the movie clip. That makes it 1 pixel to the left of, and 1 pixel above, the upper left corner of the photo inside the movie clip.

3 The line is drawn from the starting point (see No. 2) to the X coordinate equal to the variable "photoWidth" (see script) and the Y coordinate of −1. This is the top edge.

4 The line continues (right edge) to the X coordinate equal to the variable "photoWidth" and the Y coordinate equal to the variable "photoHeight" (see script).

5 The line continues (bottom edge) to the X coordinate of −1 and the Y coordinate equal to the variable "photoHeight."

6 The line continues (left edge) to the starting point at the X,Y coordinates of −1, −1 and stops there. This completes the border around the photo.

In the SWF for Braunger's slideshow, the text field doesn't exist on the Stage until it is created by ActionScript. This enables the script to position each caption and credit close to the rightmost edge of the current photo, and also to adjust the width of each caption and credit, depending on how much space is available to the right of the photo.

If you provide the total width and the total height available for both photo and caption, and assign each one to a variable, you make the slideshow script more flexible, so you can easily reuse it in a different design later.

```
availWidth = 490; // total width of display area on Stage
availHeight = 340; // total height of display area on Stage
```

(Note that these two values match the example for this book, and not the startribune.com slideshow.)

Assuming that you want the caption always to appear at the same vertical position in the SWF, provide that value and assign it to a variable:

```
captionVertPosition = 80;
```

Assume too that you want the caption always to appear at the same distance to the right of any photo, so provide that value and assign it to a variable:

```
captionHorizDistance = 20;
```

In Lesson 10, you learned how to load a text file (containing all the caption and credit information) into a Flash movie. After that file had loaded, the script found the text for the current photo and displayed it in text fields that were already on the Stage:

```
caption_txt.text = eval("myCaptions.caption" + newnumber);
credit_txt.text = eval("myCaptions.credit" + newnumber);
```

In this case, there are no text fields on the Stage. The script will create a new text field and position it inside the movie clip, alongside the photo. As the script loops through all the photos and matches up the captions and credits, first you will copy each caption and credit into variables, where they will be stored until the new text field is created:

```
caption = eval("myCaptions.caption" + newnumber);
credit = eval("myCaptions.credit" + newnumber);
```

Here is the rest of the script:

Table 3.2.02

```
1  loader_mc.createTextField("caption_txt", 10,
   (loader_mc.photoWidth + captionHorizDistance),
   captionVertPosition, (availWidth - loader_mc.photoWidth),
   availHeight);
2  loader_mc.caption_txt.html = true;
3  loader_mc.caption_txt.wordWrap = true;
4  loader_mc.caption_txt.multiline = true;
5  loader_mc.caption_txt.htmlText = _root.caption;
6  loader_mc.caption_txt.htmlText += "<br>";
7  loader_mc.caption_txt.htmlText += _root.credit;
8  loader_mc.caption_txt.setTextFormat(_root.captionStyle);
```

What the script does:

1 Here you use all those variables that were set in advance, to ensure consistency in the look of the captions: availWidth, availHeight, captionVertPosition, and captionHorizDistance. You also reuse photoWidth, which was already "read" from the width of the movie clip. The ActionScript *method* "createTextField()" uses a format similar to the "lineStyle()" method shown in the preceding script: First, you see the *instance name* of a movie clip (loader_mc), followed by a dot. Next, the *method* itself. Finally, the *parameters*, separated by commas and enclosed in parentheses. The first parameter gives the new text field an instance name (caption_txt). Then some simple math sets the position, width, and height of the text field based on the space available. The parameters expected for "createTextField()" are, in order: instance name, depth (a level), X coordinate for this text field, Y coordinate for this text field, width of this text field, height of this text field.

2 Sets the text field "caption_txt" to accept HTML formatting.

3 Sets the text field "caption_txt" to accept automatic word wrapping.

4 Sets the text field "caption_txt" to multiline rather than single-line format.

5 Places the caption text (taken from the external text file and stored in the variable "caption") into the text field and allows HTML formatting (such as <b> for boldface).

6 Places an HTML tag at the end of the caption, to start a new line.

7 Places the credit text (taken from the external text file and stored in the variable "credit") into the text field, on the new line; allows HTML formatting.

8 The variable "captionStyle" represents a detailed specification for the appearance of the text in the caption and credit, not shown here. For more information, see "TextFormat (object)" in the Flash Help files. It's key to apply this formatting *after* the text is already in the field.

FLA files for this case study Tech Tip are on the book's Web site.

THE FORM INTERFACE

When an online producer has finished editing the photos, the MP3 file, and the background image, she opens a Web page and enters information into a form to "Create a new story" within the content management system. When the form is submitted, it will generate a normal Web page on the site, from which the slideshow pop-up window is launched. The "story" in this case is nothing more than a short description of the slideshow.

Having this page in the system makes it possible for users to search and find the slideshow using keywords, the title, or the name of the photographer or reporter. Without this page, the slideshow would be invisible to the CMS.

Next, the producer clicks the option labeled "Create a new slide show" in the PHP tool and selects the story just created, to associate the two within the system. On the same form page, the producer types the number of photos to be included in this slideshow and the credit information that will appear at the end of the slideshow.

The JPGs must always be named in the same format, and numbered 1, 2, 3, etc., as part of the filename. The background image and the audio file also must have standardized filenames. Uploading the files requires the producer to point to each one on the hard drive where they are stored.

The PHP tool uploads all the files, then provides a new form where the producer will write the caption and credit for each photo, and also select the credit affiliation (such as "Star Tribune") from a drop-down menu. The interface is easy to understand, especially because it shows a thumbnail of each photo beside the box for its caption, credit, and affiliation. In a fourth field for each photo, the producer types the number representing the transition time; this is not the length of the cross-fade but rather the time position (in the audio file) at which this photo will fade in.

Fig. 3.2.10 The slideshow tool allows the producer to write in end credits. Printed by permission of startribune.com.

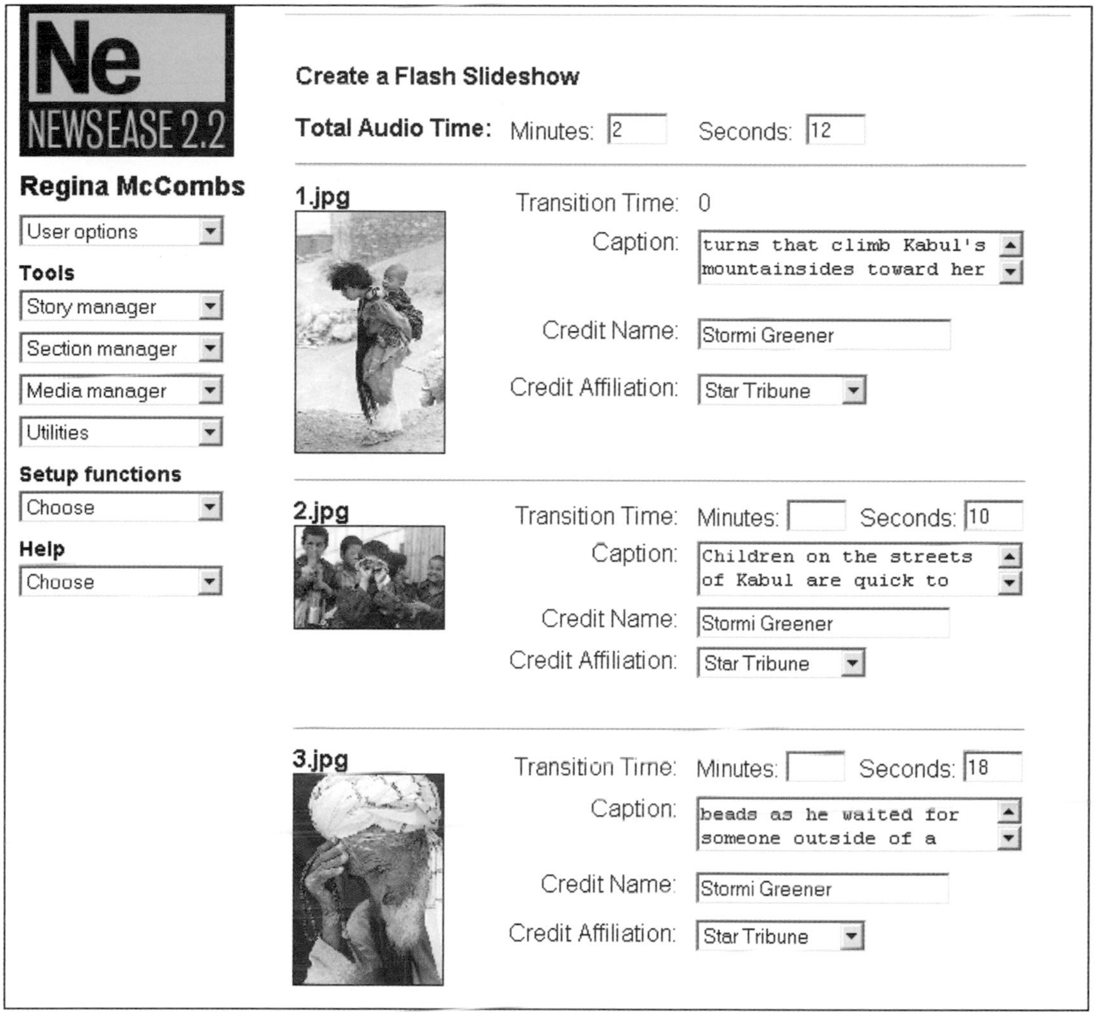

Fig. 3.2.11 The slideshow tool has been integrated into the site's content management system, called NewsEase2.2. Printed by permission of startribune.com.

When the producer submits the form with all the caption information, the CMS creates a new plain-text file that contains all the typed text, formatted in exactly the way the Flash SWF expects to find it. The entire package of files (excluding the "story" page) is neatly contained in its own numbered folder on the staging server, where the producer can test it and proofread all the captions and credits. If she needs to edit something—for example, if a caption is so long that part of it is cut off—she goes back to the PHP tool and clicks the option "Edit a slide show."

After checking it, the producer makes the slideshow "live" by clicking a button, which moves the folder to another Web server.

Braunger was working on Version 2 of the slideshow tool at the time of this interview, but without a sense of urgency. "This [Version 1] is working," McCombs said. "We're pretty happy with it."

In redesigning the "To Be a Doctor" package (relaunched in July 2004), Braunger incorporated some of the new wish-list items:

- A "voice of" text box that lets the user know who's speaking.

- A progress bar made up of tiny squares (one for each photo) that shows the current position of the slideshow relative to its total length.

He was rewriting all the loading scripts for the JPGs and the MP3, incorporating new functionality made possible by ActionScript 2.0. One reason was that everything runs faster in Flash player 7, he said. Loading issues always represented the biggest problem in the slideshow.

"It's not as bulletproof as I'd like it to be," Braunger said.

Case Study 3

ElPaís.es March 11 Attacks

URL: *http://www.elpais.es/*
Interview Date: June 18, 2004
Location: Madrid
Interview Subject: Rafael Höhr Zamora, Infografista

> *"Knowing what is newsworthy is the essence of a journalist. Sometimes if there is only text, you have nothing. But if you have a graphic, then there is something. Sometimes when you see it, then you see how this is news."*

—*Rafa Höhr*

Note: This interview was conducted through an interpreter. The author knew some Spanish, and the interview subject knew some English, but the interpreter translated almost everything. The material in quotation marks was either said in English by Rafa Höhr or understood (in Spanish) by the author.

When the bombs exploded at 7:39 a.m., Rafa Höhr was in bed. Soon afterward, his phone rang. Come into the office. Now. Something has happened.

After fighting to get into a taxi, he ended up sharing one with strangers. The trains had been stopped. There was a general evacuation of the subway system. Cell phones did not work. Madrid had entered a state of emergency—not an unfamiliar experience for Spaniards, who have suffered multiple bomb attacks by the homegrown terrorist organization ETA over the years. March 11, 2004, would turn out to be different, but that would not be apparent for several hours.

When Höhr arrived at *El País*, the daily newspaper where he works as one of two *infografistas*, or infographic artists, on the Internet staff, no one was really sure yet what was happening. Some journalists were in the office; others were sent downtown to the bombing sites at three train stations. The

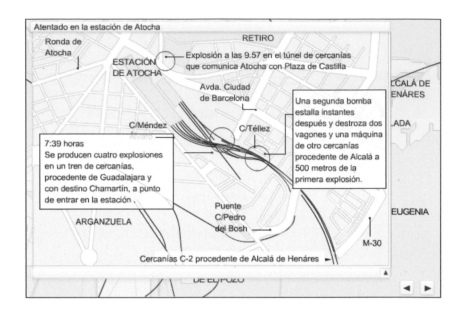

Fig. 3.3.01 An early version of the interactive map went online around midday, March 11. Printed by permission of elpais.com.

Fig. 3.3.02 A different version of the interactive map replaced the first one later in the day on March 11, when more details were known. Printed by permission of elpais.com.

Internet news desk buzzed with activity. Four Internet reporters were in the field; one who lived near the Atocha station was working from his home, sending in reports. Ironically, when Höhr finally managed to get to the newsroom, it was about 10 a.m., his usual starting time.

The print side would publish a special midday edition of the newspaper, so everyone scrambled to pull together the facts for a very early deadline (the regular deadlines are in the evening). The Internet desk was already adding information to the Web site whenever the journalists were able to verify anything new. Even getting an accurate count of the dead and injured proved difficult. The biggest question, though, was *who* had put the bombs on the trains?

When the special print edition hit the newsstands in the afternoon, it remained uncertain who was responsible for the attacks—the ETA (Euskadi Ta Askatasuma, or Basque Homeland and Freedom; founded in 1959, this organization has taken responsibility for numerous car bombs and other terrorist acts in Spain) or a group connected to Al Qaeda.

The first graphic to go online, Höhr recalled, was a screen-grab from CNN+, the Spanish-language TV partner of *El País*'s parent company, Grupo Prisa (*http://www.prisa.es*). Normally, he said, the Web staff looks at television during a breaking news situation, because there will be video on-air before pictures come in from the newspaper's photographers. Legal agreements between the corporations allow elpais.es to reproduce screen-grabs from CNN+ on the Web site. (CNN+ is not simply a translation of CNN International; its programming is original, with Spanish-speaking anchors and reporters.)

The other Internet artist had recently left *El País*, and the paper was in the process of hiring a replacement, Höhr said. Luckily, he wasn't alone; the print side has a dozen *infografistas*, and they typically work comfortably together with the Internet staff. Two of them, including the section head, were in the office already when he arrived that day.

Unfortunately, when the artists went into the paper's database of archived graphics, diagrams, and maps, they came up empty-handed: They had no art for the Madrid trains or train stations. All they had were maps of the city and the train system. "We should have had something, but there was nothing," Höhr said. Everything would have to be drawn from scratch.

Höhr would not leave the office until 3 a.m. on March 12—and he would be back again later that day.

A SUBSCRIPTION WEB SITE

Not many news Web sites have been able to move successfully from a primarily free-of-charge Web site to a subscription-only model. One of the

EL PAIS

DIARIO INDEPENDIENTE DE LA MAÑANA

www.elpais.es   FRIDAY, MARCH 12, 2004

ENGLISH EDITION WITH THE INTERNATIONAL HERALD TRIBUNE

Massacre in Madrid

Latest death toll puts dead at 192 and injured at 1,400 in the worst attack in the history of the country

"March 11, 2004 now occupies a place in the history of infamy," Prime Minister José María Aznar said yesterday

UN Secretary General Kofi Annan condemned the attacks, saying he feels "profound horror and indignation"

The scene of Thursday's attacks, the worst in the history of Spain. / PABLO TORRES GUERRERO

192 dead, more than 1,400 wounded

United against terror, political leaders speak out

G. HEDGECOE / A. EATWELL
Madrid

The bloodiest terrorist attacks in Spanish history paralyzed Madrid and the rest of the country Thursday, suspending the campaign for Sunday's general election and sending the nation into three days of official mourning. Although initially blamed on the Basque terrorist group ETA, authorities have not ruled out the possibility that Al Qa'ida was behind the attacks.

The blasts occurred almost simultaneously at three Madrid railway stations, killing at least 192 and injuring 1,421 in a massacre that many people described as Spain's September 11.

Candidates of both Spain's principal parties running for government in the general election, Mariano Rajoy of the ruling Popular Party (PP) and José Luis Rodríguez Zapatero of the Spanish Socialist Workers' Party (PSOE), agreed to bring their campaigns, which have revolved heavily around the issues

A distressed rescue worker at Santa Eugenia train station. / C. ÁLVAREZ

of terrorism, security and the territorial unity of Spain, to a premature close.

"The election campaign is over," Rajoy said. "It is the moment to put aside our differences and unite the will of every Spaniard against terrorism."

Government representatives swiftly put the blame for the

bombs, which were placed in Atocha, Pozo and Santa Eugenia stations and exploded just before 8am, on ETA yesterday morning. However, throughout the day doubts circulated regarding whether or not the Basque group was in fact responsible.

Late Thursday night, a British newspaper reportedly received a letter in the name of Al Qa'ida claiming responsibility for the attacks.

"We have succeeded in infiltrating the heart of crusader Europe and struck one of the bases of the crusader alliance," the letter, which called the attacks 'Operation Death Trains,' stated.

The letter bore the signature of the Abu Hafs al-Masri Brigades, an Al Qa'ida-linked group which also took responsibility for the bombings of two synagogues in Turkey in November and the devastating attack on the UN headquarters in Baghdad in August.

Continued on page 2

A. E. / S. U. **Madrid**

"March 11, 2004 now occupies a place in the history of infamy," Prime Minister José María Aznar said in an address in which he offered consolation to the families of the victims and hope for the "defeat" of terrorism. He was joined in his sentiments by other political leaders nationwide, with Socialist candidate José Luis Rodríguez Zapatero calling for "democratic unity — because through unity we will defeat terror."

Noting that "terrorism is not blind," Aznar said the intention of the attacks was "to kill as many people possible for the mere fact they are Spanish." Continued on page 3

Zapatero promises change, dialogue and "no more lies"

ELECTIONS   P4 & 5

Fig. 3.3.03 Page one of the English-language print edition of *El País*, March 12, 2004. Printed by permission of elpais.com.

best-known exceptions in the United States is *The Wall Street Journal*, which moved its site to paid subscription in fall 1996. Many others have tried it, but most returned quickly to offering content without charge. The reason: News is available free at so many sites, the users simply go elsewhere. Numerous news sites charge for access to their archives, but for most major dailies, the recent articles and features (whether from the printed paper or created for the online edition) are free. Free content may go back one month, one week, or one day; the time frame varies from site to site.

The Web site of *El País* began operation in May 1996 and went to a subscription-only model in November 2002. The move was announced weeks in advance, and as part of the change, the site was completely redesigned, new Web-only content was included in the operating plan, and a sophisticated new archives search tool was launched. A one-year subscription to all content is €80; half a year is €50.

Free content includes the home page, editorials and opinion columns (including the editorial cartoon), advertising, and selected features. Only paid subscribers can read today's full articles. Only paid subscribers can see the information graphics created especially for the online edition. (All graphics and photos are meticulously keyword tagged and stored in the digital archives, so subscribers are also able to review them at will.)

In June 2004, the paid subscribers to elpais.es numbered about 32,000, giving the Web site annual revenues of more than €2 million.

In Spain, newsstands on nearly every corner of the cities and dotted throughout the smaller towns sell a broad array of newspapers—including sports dailies, which outsell everything else. Subscription to (and home delivery of) a daily newspaper remains a rarity. People go to the newsstand and buy whichever papers they want to read that day. The newspapers' practice of including different "supplements" or inserts (about entertainment, sports, books, business, etc.) each day feeds this shifting loyalty; people buy the paper that contains an insert they like to read. Unlike the insubstantial inserts in many North American newspapers, the Spanish supplements are fat with original content and, of course, advertising.

Other major dailies in Madrid, such as *El Mundo* (*http://www.elmundo.es*) and *ABC* (*http://www.abc.es*), continue to allow free access to most content on their Web sites. But as the newspaper of record in Spain, *El País* holds a unique position. When the online subscription model was announced, the

Spanish government agencies and ministries, as well as major companies that have research departments, got on the phone immediately and wanted to subscribe—because they could not afford to lose access to the online edition, Höhr explained.

El País is tabloid in format but not in content; color is used only on the first and last page, and for advertising. It's a "gray" newspaper, a serious newspaper. The information graphics that appear in the newspaper are always black and white only. Its launch in 1976, after the death of the dictator Francisco Franco, and its politically progressive outlook identified it with a new era in Spain. It is also the largest news daily in Spain, with a circulation of more than 500,000 daily and almost 800,000 on Sunday.

Höhr said he hates to admit it, but the perception persists that in a serious newspaper, the words are more important than the pictures. Yet there's a bright side to that, he said: While *El País* does not devote much space to images, the editors make certain all the images used are top-notch, whether they are photos or graphics, online or in print.

Grupo Prisa, the parent company of *El País*, owns sports newspapers, business dailies, and other print publications in Spain, as well as broadcast and print subsidiaries in Bolivia, Chile, Colombia, Costa Rica, Mexico, Panama, France, and the United States, with a significant presence in Spanish and Latin American radio. Its holdings also include major book and music publishing concerns. Its PrisaCom unit focuses on digital content.

MARCH 11

The Internet news desk at *El País* is never left unstaffed. At night, at minimum, there are two writers and a documentation specialist, or researcher. A total of thirteen journalists cover the desk around the clock in the newsroom, and six more online journalists work at PrisaCom. The Internet desk, with eight workstations, is in the middle of the *El País* newsroom, next to the layout desk, across the aisle from infographics on one side and the National desk on the other, not far from photo.

As he explained where Internet journalists were on March 11, Höhr doodled a diagram on a large sheet of paper, showing both Web and print reporters in the field, in the street, people in the office, all calling in brief pieces of information throughout the day. "It's a bit like sailing a boat," he

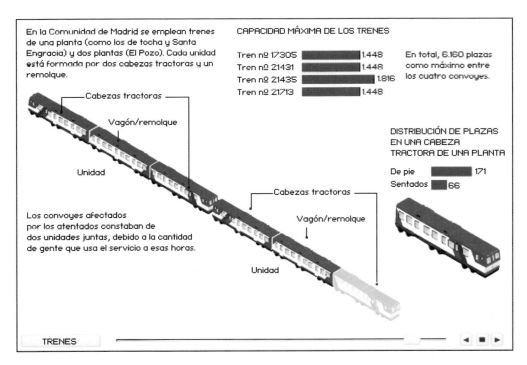

Fig. 3.3.04 Some similarities are evident between the online graphic that appeared on March 11 (shown here) and the graphic that ran in the printed newspaper on March 12 (Fig. 3.3.05). Printed by permission of elpais.com.

Fig. 3.3.05 This is part of a double-page graphic that ran in the printed newspaper on March 12. Printed by permission of elpais.com.

said. "The Internet desk knows where it wants to go, so they have a lot of people looking out to make sure they catch the wind properly."

He needed to create an accurate map of the bomb locations for the home page as soon as possible, to replace the TV graphic. "First, a GIF," he said—not a SWF. "You don't need anything more." The people coming to the Web site at that point would want to know what happened, and where, and how many victims (which was not known yet); just answers to the most basic questions. So the GIF map went online in the late morning, as he remembers it, and as soon as that was done, he could begin work on the Flash graphic.

The first SWF that went online was almost identical to the GIF map, only larger. (The GIF was 350 × 200 pixels. The SWF was the standard size used by elpais.es: 600 × 400 pixels.) It included no animation, no buttons—just a map. Providing a larger version of the map was the sole reason for replacing the GIF, Höhr said. A GIF at 600 × 400 would be too slow a download; the SWF came in at 48 KB (not exactly lightweight) because he didn't spend the time, then, to simplify the map file from Adobe Illustrator.

While Höhr worked on the SWF, the Internet editors were also putting the first photos online. The photo spot on the home page used a script to rotate images placed in a queue, so users would likely see a new photo each time they checked the page.

As the journalists confirmed more details, they created photo galleries and added more documentation. The photo galleries were built in HTML rather than Flash to make the photographs easily available to the rest of Grupo Prisa's news entities through the in-house database system. In other words, simple HTML galleries provide the most efficient way to share the photographs among group members in a breaking news situation. The database also allows the other group members to share video and *El País*'s Flash graphics.

The next version of the SWF has three zoomed-in map overlays, each of which drops down like a window shade over the larger map, which shows all of Madrid. When the animation plays, first the larger map zooms in just a bit, and then three red squares appear to mark the three affected train stations: Atocha, El Pozo, and Santa Eugenia. Black squares represent the stations in between. When the user clicks a red square, the overlay drops down to show a close-up of that area, with the major streets labeled.

Each train's path animates as a red line, which moves in toward the station and then ends abruptly, with a small red burst and a circle where bombs exploded. Four trains were affected. A text box appears near each bomb point, giving the time of the explosion and the few other details that were available.

Users have two options for navigation in this version: Instead of clicking a red square, they can use prominent Next and Previous buttons in the lower right corner to play the animation.

When this SWF went online in the afternoon, a lot of people were still hitting the Web site, Höhr said, so he was still very concerned about the file size, which was down to 46 KB (after some cleanup on the map file from Illustrator), even though animation and more graphics had been added.

THE NATIONAL ELECTIONS

On March 12, the English-language edition of *El País* carried a two-page interview with José Luis Rodríguez Zapatero, leader of the (then) opposition Spanish Socialist Workers' Party (PSOE), and now the prime minister of Spain. He said the ruling party (the Popular Party, or PP) had led Spain on a path "to a new approach to Atlantic relations, which has no ideological, historical, or political grounding in our country," one that "lacks any sense at all, and is simply based on the current government's affinity with the [U.S.] Republican Party, which is as conservative as the PP. They are probably the two most conservative parties to be found anywhere in the democratic world."

His remarks were representative of a conversation Spain was suddenly having, out loud and in public, which had not been prominent before March 11. Increasing criticism of the ruling PP's support for the war in Iraq, along with criticism of the government's continued blame of ETA for the M11 bombings, became impossible to ignore.

The national elections were set for Sunday, March 14. The expectation before the bomb attacks—and even right up to the counting of votes on election day—was that the PP would retain power in the Congress of Deputies (the larger of two houses in the legislature), and thus continue to run the country. The conservative PP had won a small majority in 1996 and

Fig. 3.3.06 An animated arch shows the change in party representation in the Congress of Deputies for each election since 1977. Blue shows the seats held by the Popular Party. Red shows the seats held by the Spanish Socialist Workers' Party (PSOE). Shown here are election results in 2000. Printed by permission of elpais.com.

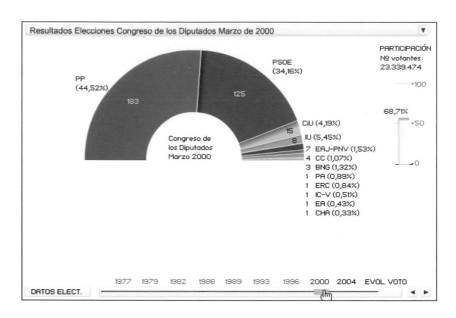

Fig. 3.3.07 Shown here are election results in 2004, three days after the March 11 attacks. (Compare with Fig. 3.3.06.) Printed by permission of elpais.com.

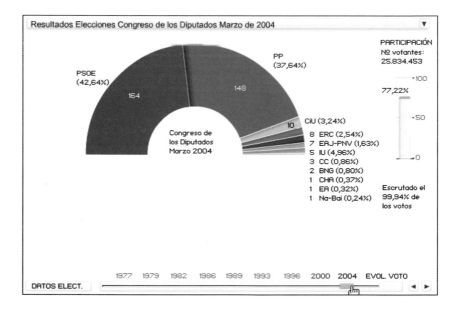

a landslide victory in 2000. When Spain went to sleep on Wednesday night, March 10, no one doubted that the PP would win a large majority again on Sunday.

On Friday, March 12, the newsroom felt strange, out of balance. "It was as if you were playing chess," Höhr said, "and someone came and lifted the game out of your hands." It seemed obvious that the PP would lose many seats. Overnight, the game had changed completely.

Höhr's editor, Mario Tascón, thought it would be interesting to compare the performance of the Madrid stock exchange with other events on March 11. So Höhr asked the Internet desk for a list of key events and statements from the previous day. They had already compiled a chronological list, which they gave to him.

His next step: Phone the central newsroom at PrisaCom and talk with a journalist for CincoDias.com, the Web site of a major business newspaper owned by Grupo Prisa. The journalist sent Höhr a line graph representing the stock market activity on March 11, with the value marked at the time of each statement. Höhr animated the graphic in Flash (with a simple moving mask) to advance the graph line from morning to afternoon, stopping each time a new block of text appears at the top. At each stopping point, the users also see the time, the market value, and the count of dead and injured people from the attacks.

A precipitous drop in the graph (76 points, to 8075) just after noon followed a statement published at 11:50 a.m. from the leader of the Basque separatist party Batasuna, in which he denied responsibility by ETA and attributed the attacks to members of the "Arab resistance."

To a Spaniard, the graphic is as clear as simple addition: At that moment, the people lost trust in the sitting government. All morning, the government had been pinning the blame on the ETA terrorists. When a Basque leader said ETA was not involved, the Spanish people concluded their government had lied to them. Of course, the graphic says none of this explicitly. Around 2 p.m., the government repeated its view that the attacks were the work of ETA, according to the graphic.

In public demonstrations on Saturday, people carried signs that said: "Before the vote, we want the truth."

On Sunday, the voters ousted the PP and put the PSOE in charge of the Spanish government—a result considered impossible less than a week earlier.

On March 16, elpais.es published another Flash graphic by Höhr, a kind of retrospective on the connection between the bombings and the election result. It uses an analog clock with spinning hands, a short block of text,

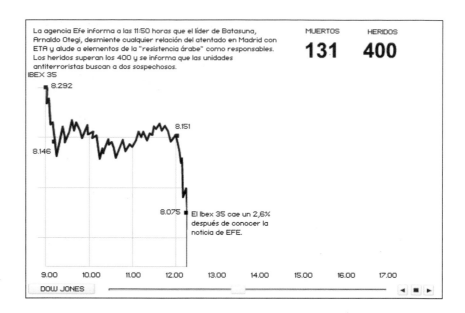

Fig. 3.3.08 An animated graphic posted on March 12 compared the activity of the Madrid stock exchange with the timing of statements from various officials. It also showed the official accounting of the dead and injured (upper right corner) as the numbers increased during the day. Printed by permission of elpais.com.

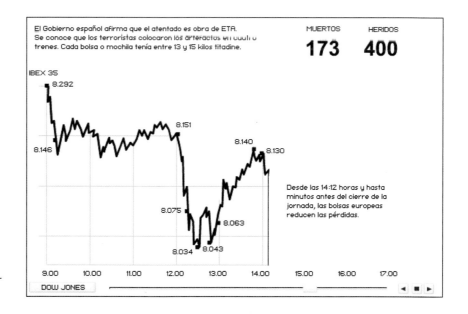

Fig. 3.3.09 As the user moves forward through the animation, the graph advances to a later time, and a new statement appears. Printed by permission of elpais.com.

and a series of photos to summarize the claims and counter-claims of the four days from Thursday to Sunday. It makes clear that the old government, led by the Popular Party, repeatedly named ETA as the group responsible for the attacks, even as other evidence was brought forward.

JUEVES 11 DE MARZO

12.00. La policía descubre siete detonadores y una cinta con versos del Corán en una furgoneta abandonada cerca de la estación de cercanías de Alcalá de Henares.

Fig. 3.3.10 In a graphic published on March 16, a clock (upper left corner) showed when key clues about the bombings came to light, interspersed with official statements concerning what was known. Printed by permission of elpais.com.

MARCH 12

The entire contents of elpais.es were made available free to everyone on the day after the attacks. A note at the top of the home page announced this and linked to the related coverage from the morning's printed newspaper and the Web-only content—including a completely new version of the animated map graphic that had gone online late in the day on March 11.

Höhr had worked until 3 a.m. drawing trains and getting his facts confirmed. Not that he was making or taking phone calls himself —"I have only two hands," he said—but other journalists were getting the information he needed and passing it to him.

In the new SWF, each of the three close-up maps had its own animation, and each map filled the entire 600 × 400 window, instead of sliding down as an overlay. There was more text, because now the journalists had more information, so Höhr wanted to use all the space available in the window.

Explaining another difference between the two SWFs, he said the secondary information early in the day on March 11 was about the stations: Where were the trains? By the end of the day, the secondary information was about the location of ten bombs on four trains. So a major addition to the new graphic is a panel overlay that shows all the trains, with the affected cars

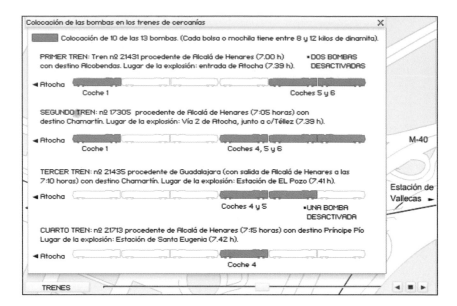

Fig. 3.3.11 The second version of the map graphic included more data about the ten train cars that had carried bombs. Printed by permission of elpais.com.

colored red; a frame near the end of the animation explains differences among the four trains involved. There's nothing to click in the trains panel because it wasn't known (and still is not known) how many victims were in each car. The panel contains all the information the journalists had about the trains at that time.

An accurate total of how many had died was still pending. Survivors had been taken to several different hospitals (by the final official account, 190 people died as a result of the attacks, and more than 1400 people were injured). The morning newspaper on March 12 had only the barest information about the victims, the names and phone numbers of the hospitals, and the location where the dead were being identified.

When Höhr returned to work, he began working with that information to expand it. The result was a graphic that explains the process for identification at IFEMA, a large conference and fairs center in the northeast of Madrid, where all the dead were taken. It clearly shows where the families of the missing should enter the huge complex, and in six frames provides details of how volunteers and professionals would meet the family members and help them find out whether the person they sought was among the victims.

He also produced a simple timeline in Flash that showed "the most bloody attacks" in Spain and the world since 1974, using text and photos.

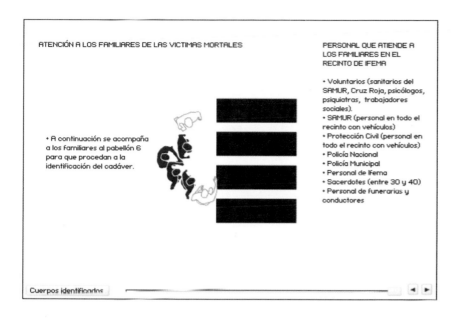

ATENCIÓN A LOS FAMILIARES DE LAS VICTIMAS MORTALES

PERSONAL QUE ATIENDE A LOS FAMILIARES EN EL RECINTO DE IFEMA

• Voluntarios (sanitarios del SAMUR, Cruz Roja, psicólogos, psiquiatras, trabajadores sociales).
• SAMUR (personal en todo el recinto con vehículos)
• Protección Civil (personal en todo el recinto con vehículos)
• Policía Nacional
• Policía Municipal
• Personal de Ifema
• Sacerdotes (entre 30 y 40)
• Personal de funerarias y conductores

• A continuación se acompaña a los familiares al pabellón 6 para que procedan a la identificación del cadáver.

Cuerpos identificados

Fig. 3.3.12 Another animated graphic from March 12 explained the procedures used at the location where the victims' bodies had been taken for identification. Printed by permission of elpais.com.

A DIFFERENT WAY TO EXPLAIN

The differences between print and online graphics seem very obvious to Höhr. Motion, for example. He pointed out that while animation helps to tell the story, adding movement to a graphic also entails risk—the risk of making a mistake. "You need more information," he said.

In the March 12 newspaper graphic of the attacks on the trains in Madrid, the reader sees only the train on the track, with a circle marking the point of the explosion. In the online animation, when the train moves (as a red line), the artist must know for certain which track the train came in on; in the Atocha station, there were four possible tracks for one of the trains.

Experience has taught Höhr that in some cases he should not add motion until all the facts have been confirmed. He recalled a story where police chased a group of terrorists in a car through Madrid. During part of the chase, the police lost sight of the car. The print graphic showed points in the city where police spotted the terrorists' car; the online animation showed the car speeding through the streets, connecting the dots. Users later called in to say the route was impossible: The animation showed the car going the wrong way on a very busy one-way street.

It's important to know when to raise a fuss to get all the information you need, Höhr said. Insufficient information results in an inferior graphic. He emphasized that there are many professional journalists—not only the artist—behind each graphic in print and online.

An online graphic that explains and informs might not even resemble the graphic that worked fine in the newspaper. Höhr's M11 investigation animation is an example. The newspaper's graphic was a tall, narrow tree diagram, or flowchart, that shows very small photos of the people arrested or suspected of having some part in the bomb attacks (Figure 3.3.13). Each suspect's name appears beside the photo. Suspects are grouped together in boxes connected by arrows; each box has a label to identify the role of that group, such as people who allegedly financed the attacks. The problem this chart would pose online, Höhr said, is that in trying to make sense of it, the user would have to scroll up and down many times. On the printed page, in contrast, the whole chart remains visible.

Fig. 3.3.13 A vertical tree diagram from the printed newspaper showed relationships among groups suspected of involvement in the March 11 attacks. The design of this chart is ill-suited to online use because the user would need to scroll up and down many times and try to mentally connect information at the top of the graphic to information at the bottom. Printed by permission of elpais.com.

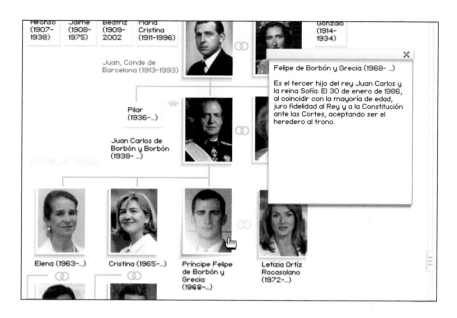

Alfonso (1907-1938)　Jaime (1908-1975)　Beatriz (1909-2002)　María Cristina (1911-1996)　　Gonzalo (1914-1934)

Juan, Conde de Barcelona (1913-1993)

Pilar (1936-...)

Juan Carlos de Borbón y Borbón (1938-...)

FAMILIA REAL

Felipe de Borbón y Grecia (1968- ...)

Es el tercer hijo del rey Juan Carlos y la reina Sofía. El 30 de enero de 1986, al coincidir con la mayoría de edad, juró fidelidad al Rey y a la Constitución ante las Cortes, aceptando ser el heredero al trono.

Elena (1963-...)　　Cristina (1965-...)　　Príncipe Felipe de Borbón y Grecia (1968-...)　　Letizia Ortíz Rocasolano (1972-...)

Fig. 3.3.14 A vertical tree diagram from the Web site showed the family line of Prince Felipe of Spain. Rafa Höhr created this graphic for the Web and then adapted it for use in the printed newspaper. Printed by permission of elpais.com.

This is not to say it's impossible to use a tree diagram on the Web. Höhr pulled up a chart showing the paternal family line of Prince Felipe de Borbón y Grecia, who had recently married (with all the press attention inspired by any royal wedding). Its tall and narrow format mirrored the printed M11 suspects graphic, and it required scrolling up and down. However, there were no complex relationships to sort out. King Fernando II (1452–1516) and Queen Isabel I are at the top of the tree; Prince Felipe is at the bottom; the kings and queens in the middle are familiar to Spaniards. Höhr pointed out that not only was the M11 chart less strictly linear than the royal family chart, but it was also packed with unfamiliar names, making them more difficult to remember.

Höhr's online M11 investigation graphic eliminates the tree model altogether. Instead, he shows groups of suspects being arrested or held by police in dynamic poses, from a bird's eye view, and indicates relationships between groups by drawing a line on the "floor" connecting them. Users do not see all the lines at once, but they can go backward and forward in the animation to review the connections. Groups of suspects disappear from the picture when they were not involved in the part of the plot explained in that frame, or the lines under their feet disappear when they are not part of the current explanation. The relationships are made manageable to users by division, and yet each group is visually distinct and memorable.

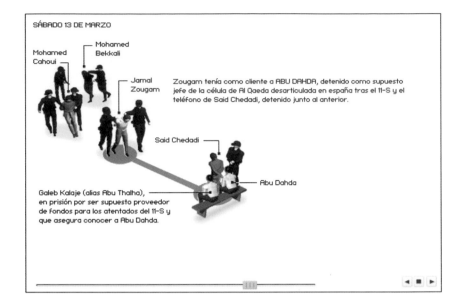

Fig. 3.3.15 Instead of a tree diagram, the Web graphic used animation to show the relationships among groups of suspects in the March 11 attacks. Printed by permission of elpais.com.

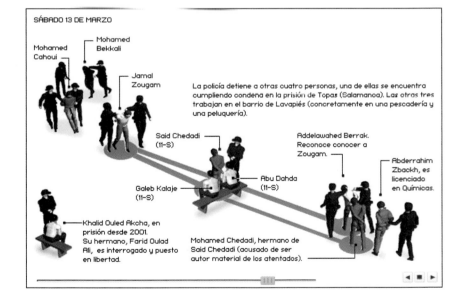

Fig. 3.3.16 As the user moves forward through the animation, new people appear in the illustration, new blocks of text appear to explain how the plans were allegedly carried out, and new orange lines are drawn, connecting one group to another. Printed by permission of elpais.com.

The graphic also includes maps, a model of a gym bag containing an unexploded bomb, and a diagram of a building where explosives were prepared. As more information is revealed, Höhr intends to incorporate it into this same animation.

TECH TIP: A CONTROLLER BAR

For a continuous animation that stops at several points to allow the user to read various text blocks, it can be nice to provide a controller, or "scrubber," that lets a user move backward and forward to review the animation. Rafa Höhr uses the same controller on almost every animation he builds. It makes sense to save time by reusing the same script and graphics for a controller, so he has more time to work on original graphics. That means the script must be portable, or easy to insert into a new movie.

The script shown here is a modified version of Höhr's script.

There are two ways you might choose to handle the main animation in the movie. You can enclose it in a movie clip (as Höhr does), or you could create a separate SWF and load it into a movie clip at runtime (explained in Appendix B). On the Web site for this book, you will find examples of both versions (the controller script is the same for each version); but here, only the first version is discussed.

To begin, you will need a continuous animation with several stopping points on the timeline, a stop in Frame 1, and a stop at the end. You can download a suitable file from the Web site for this book and use that, if you don't have one of your own. The simplicity of this controller requires a fairly simple animation. If internal movies clips or jumps on the Timeline are included, the controller may malfunction.

To put your finished animation inside a movie clip:

1 Create a new, empty FLA with the same width, height, color, and frame rate.

2 Create an empty movie clip in the new FLA (Insert menu > New Symbol).

3 *Select* all the layers in the other movie (shift-click the first and last layer names in the Timeline).

4 *Copy* all the frames (right-click/Win or Ctrl-click/Mac on any frame, and use the menu to select "Copy Frames").

5 Return to the new FLA. *Select* just Frame 1 inside the empty movie clip Timeline.

6 Right-click or Ctrl-click (Mac) to get the menu; select "Paste Frames."

7 Exit from Symbol Editing Mode (Ctrl-E/Win or Cmd-E/Mac).

8 Use the Align panel to center the movie clip on the Stage.

9 Save your new movie.

Note: For the script shown here to work, you must give the *instance name* "anim_mc" to the empty movie clip containing your animation.

There's one more step to adapting the animation: On each frame in the animation (now inside the movie clip) where you have a "stop()" action, *add* this line of script:

```
_root.direction = "curframe";
```

Before building the controller, create three buttons and place them on the Stage, *outside* the movie clip: Back, Stop, and Next. Write the following script on the buttons.

Back button:

```
on (release) {
    _root.direction = "backward";
}
```

Stop button:

```
on (release) {
    _root.direction = "curframe";
    anim_mc.stop();
}
```

Next button:

```
on (release) {
    if (anim_mc._currentframe == anim_mc._totalframes) {
        anim_mc.gotoAndStop(1);
    } else {
        _root.direction = "forward";
        anim_mc.play();
    }
}
```

Most of this script should look familiar to you, except the variable name "direction." Note that this is merely a variable, not a regular part of ActionScript. Later, you'll see how the three values of this variable ("forward"; "backward"; "curframe") are used to control the animation.

Next, you will make the graphics for your controller. It does not need to be fancy. All that's required are a handle (a small rectangle) and a bar (a long, narrow rectangle), in contrasting colors. If you make the handle 20 pixels wide and 12 pixels high, and make the bar 400 pixels wide and 10 pixels high, all the script shown here will work without modification. In other words, the dimensions of the handle and the bar *really count* a lot!

Build the controller:

1 Convert the handle to a movie clip symbol.

2 Delete it from the Stage.

3 Convert the bar to a movie clip symbol. This one will be the controller clip.

4 Go into Symbol Editing Mode for the controller bar.

5 Add a new layer in the Timeline, *above* the bar.

6 Drag an instance of the handle movie clip from the Library to the new layer inside the bar clip.

7 Position the handle at X, 5 and Y, 0.

8 Name the handle instance "marker_mc" (without the quotes).

9 Write the script shown below *on the handle clip* (as if you were writing script on a button).

10 Exit from Symbol Editing Mode (Ctrl-E/Win or Cmd-E/Mac).

11 Name the controller bar instance "scrub_mc" (without the quotes).

Script on the handle movie clip instance:

```
on (press) {
    this.dragging = true;
    this.startDrag(false, 5, 0, 375, 0);
    this.onMouseMove = function() {
        updateAfterEvent();
    }
}
on (release, releaseOutside) {
    this.dragging = false;
    this.stopDrag();
    delete this.onMouseMove;
}
```

If you compare this script with the one in the Case Study 1 Tech Tip, you'll see the same "startDrag()" and "stopDrag()" functions that were introduced there. They are doing the same work here. What really makes this little handle movie clip useful is the true/false variable named "dragging," which will be read by the final chunk of script, below.

Create a new layer on the main movie Timeline and name it "actions" (without the quotes). Your whole movie is only one frame long. You may have your "anim_mc" on one layer and your "scrub_mc" on another layer, or you may have both on one layer. As always, it's the best professional practice to put your script in its own layer, where it will be easy to find and edit later.

Script on the "actions" layer in the main movie Timeline:

Table 3.3.01

```
1   function checkWhatsUp() {
2   if (_root.direction == "forward") {
3   anim_mc.gotoAndStop(anim_mc._currentframe + 1);
4   }
5   if (_root.direction == "backward") {
6   anim_mc.gotoAndStop(anim_mc._currentframe - 1);
7   }
8   if (scrub_mc.marker_mc.dragging == true) {
9   _root.direction = "curframe";
10  anim_mc.gotoAndStop(1+Math.floor(anim_mc._totalframes *
    (scrub_mc.marker_mc._x-5)/375));
11  } else {
12  scrub_mc.marker_mc._x =
    5+Math.floor((anim_mc._currentframe-1) *
    370/(anim_mc._totalframes-1));
13  }
14  }
15  _root.onEnterFrame = checkWhatsUp;
```

What the script does:

- Lines 1–14 are a single function. Line 15 causes that function to be executed at the frame rate of the movie, which should be 15 fps, in most cases. (If you use a very high frame rate, the "onEnterFrame" event will work poorly on some users' computers.)

- Lines 2–4: If the value of the variable "direction" is "forward" (that is, if the user clicked your Next button), then move the movie clip "anim_mc" forward one frame (+1).

- Lines 5–7: If the value of the variable "direction" is "backward" (that is, if the user clicked your Back button), then move the movie clip "anim_mc" backward one frame (−1).

Note that whenever the value of the variable "direction" is something other than "backward" or "forward," the script in lines 2–7 has no effect. That is why in some cases (for example, when the animation is *stopped*) you have set the value of "direction" to "curframe."

- Lines 8–10: If the value of the variable "dragging" is true (that is, if the user is dragging the handle in the movie clip "scrub_mc"), then *move the movie clip* "anim_mc" according to the given equation, which uses the number of frames in "anim_mc" (through the ActionScript property "_totalframes") and the usable width of the controller bar (375 pixels in this case) to translate the position of the handle clip ("marker_mc") into a frame number in the "anim_mc" clip.

- Lines 11–13: If the value of the variable "dragging" is not true (that is, if the user is not dragging the handle in the movie clip "scrub_mc"), then *move the handle* according to the new equation, which varies in several ways from the previous one. This equation moves the handle, whereas the other equation moved the playhead of the "anim_mc" clip.

To make sense of the math, keep in mind that the controller bar is 400 pixels wide, but 5 pixels at either end are not used, leaving 390 pixels that count. The other important measurement is the 20-pixel width of the handle ("marker_mc"). Assuming the handle's registration point is in the upper left corner, that puts the handle at X, 375 (not X, 400) when it is at its rightmost position on the bar. The handle's leftmost position is X, 5.

This script and controller will work with a movie clip of any length, but if you change the width of the bar or the handle, you'll need to change the numbers in the script too.

 FLA files for this case study Tech Tip are on the book's Web site.

THE CHALLENGE OF UPDATING

The online graphic concerning the investigation into the March 11 attacks was already at Version 10 in June 2004. Höhr's hard drive looks like a diary, with all his work carefully filed by date and version number. He has kept every file he created in the past five years, when he began using Flash. Every two months or so, he burns them to CDs as a personal archive. He has seventeen versions of one animation that shows the movements of the hijacked planes in the eastern United States on September 11, 2001.

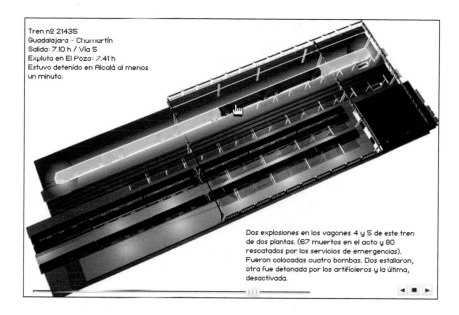

Tren nº 21435
Guadalajara - Chamartín
Salida: 7.10 h / Vía 5
Explota en El Pozo: 7.41 h
Estuvo detenido en Alcalá al menos
un minuto.

Dos explosiones en los vagones 4 y 5 de este tren
de dos plantas. (67 muertos en el acto y 80
rescatados por los servicios de emergencias).
Fueron colocadas cuatro bombas. Dos estallaron,
otra fue detonada por los artificieros y la última,
desactivada.

Fig. 3.3.17 A 3D animation of the train platform at the Alcalá de Henáres station showed how the backpacks containing bombs were quickly planted in ten cars on four trains, while all four waited there together. Rolling the mouse cursor over any train (top) provides additional text information about that train. (Graphic published March 29, 2004.) Printed by permission of elpais.com.

It's important to keep them, he said, because you don't really understand how much you've done, and what it is that you've done, until you see it after some time has passed.

When he began Version 1 of the M11 investigations graphic, Höhr knew he would be adding to it over time, so he tried to design it with updating in mind. Sometimes it's not clear how long an online graphic will need to be kept current, he said; updating it may not be so easy, depending on how it was constructed. Another problem he faces: Managing the amount of time needed to update multiple online graphics. He is tied to the past, he said; "it's neither good nor bad, but sometimes it drives me crazy." Yet there's no question in his mind that the M11 investigation graphic should be kept up-to-date on the Web site, as long as the investigation continues.

Another example he gave concerned a major oil spill off the northwest coast of Spain in 2002. The investigation into and cleanup of the *Prestige* tanker spill continued two years later. Sketches of deep-sea oil recovery equipment covered Höhr's desk. He plucked one page from the assortment to show his storyboard technique.

He always draws a storyboard; he says he thinks of it as "a script for a little movie." The one at hand showed about fifteen penciled scenes demonstrating how a particular device recovers oil from the ocean floor. The numbered drawings snaked around the oversize sheet (about 12 × 16 inches)

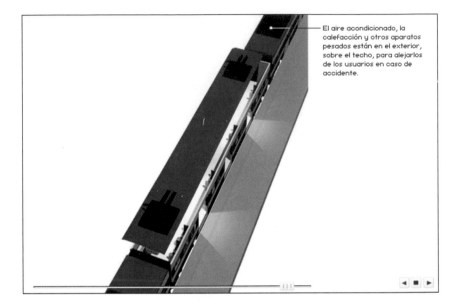

Fig. 3.3.18 Rafa Höhr used 3D software to create a model of a train car. He imported JPG images of the model into Flash and then animated them. Printed by permission of elpais.com.

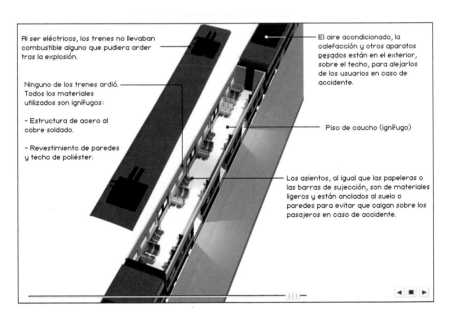

Fig. 3.3.19 This is a later frame from the same animated sequence shown in Fig. 3.3.18. Printed by permission of elpais.com.

in a Z shape, clearly in sequence, with a block of text neatly written beside each one.

Höhr pointed to the corresponding graphic in that day's printed newspaper, where the machine he was meticulously animating in 3D appeared in one very small black-and-white photo. The print artists don't always understand, he said, why he will not simply take the same approach they took—why he won't put the same graphic on the Web. The problem with the photos of the oil-recovery machines: "They don't add anything. There's no life to them." By animating how the machines do the work, Höhr's illustration will explain to the user. The motion is information.

He quickly added that there are plenty of things that move that *don't* need to be animated in an online infographic, but the story of the *Prestige* oil spill cleanup is an important one for *El País*, which gave it two full pages in the newspaper that day in 2004. He made a similar point about the use of 3D graphics. To show the amount of oil leaking from the sunken tanker, 3D is not necessary; a simple bar chart makes it clear.

If he has the time, Höhr likes to create 3D illustrations, using Carrara Studio, a software package from Eovia. For the later M11 graphics, he built 3D models of the trains and their interiors, which he also shared with the print graphics desk. He can export a file format such as TIFF, which the print artists can import into Illustrator. For use in Flash, Höhr exports JPGs from Carrara.

The print artists sometimes ask Höhr to create a 3D model for them, which they can then use as a base graphic in Illustrator. If a graphic calls for a difficult angle, "sometimes it's faster to work in 3D," Höhr said. (That is, if an artist is already familiar with the 3D program, it can be faster.) This demonstrates another way the *El País* print and Internet graphic artists work together.

An important part of the job of an Internet *infografista* is knowing when to animate, and when not to; when to use 3D, and when not to; when to use the graphic that ran in the newspaper, and when to create something different. The news value of the story, the nearness of the deadline, and the "legs" of the story (that is, how long the story will be of interest) all figure into the decisions Höhr makes every day.

Case Study 4

CBC Radio 3

URL: *http://www.cbcradio3.ca/*
Interview Date: May 12, 2004
Location: Vancouver
Interview Subject: Rob McLaughlin, Executive Producer

> *"You shouldn't be saying, 'Look at that cool Flash,' because that's not what this is about. This about people's art, people's stories."*

> —*Rob McLaughlin*

Within the Canadian Broadcasting Corporation, a group of about twenty-five people is known as "Radio 3." They run a few award-winning Web sites and an overnight nationwide radio program on Saturdays. This is not your granddad's CBC (whether or not your granddad is Canadian); everything Radio 3 does is woven together with new music, and your granddad probably wouldn't like most of it.

Among the Web sites, there is one—at the eponymous domain cbcradio3.ca—through which Radio 3 defines and pursues its vision. Vision and radio? Yes. And a generous sampling of some of the largest, most intriguing photographs on the Web, accompanied by a soundtrack of independent songs, all bundled into a seamless Flash interface.

Every week, Radio 3 launches a new "issue" of what could be called a magazine (it does have page numbers). The staff just calls it "the site."

"Most Web sites operate on a constant publishing schedule," said Rob McLaughlin, an executive producer at Radio 3. "They think that's the power of it, when maybe they're missing the power of other things. We've always said this is like a program, or a television show—we say it's a radio show, and we meet deadlines, and we publish weekly."

Fig. 3.4.01 Cover. Issue 02.13, Nov. 28, 2003. Printed by permission of CBC Radio 3 and Pete Soos. Photo by Pete Soos.

The deadline is midnight Friday (in the summers they go bi-weekly); the staff usually publishes six new stories a week, plus a portfolio of thirteen pictures by a single photographer. Each issue has a new soundtrack of twenty songs, which also constitute the playlist of next Saturday's final two hours of on-air radio programming. Two of the stories are usually about Canadian musicians or bands, and each of those has its own soundtrack as well.

There's a lot of music here, and more every week.

ORIGINS

You might assume that Radio 3 is a network. After all, CBC Radio One is a network, for news. CBC Radio Two is a network, mainly for music, most of it classical. Radio 3's programming, however, airs on CBC Radio Two, starting at 7:30 p.m. Saturday and ending at 4 a.m. Sunday. You can't punch up Radio 3 on the air at any other time.

In summer 2002, that programming was being delivered as several different shows, each with a different name. "There was nothing that was called Radio 3," McLaughlin said. "We had a department, but that's all we had. There was no connection between the three Web sites, or the programming.

Fig. 3.4.02 "Presstube": Animation by James Paterson (full-screen video). Issue 02.36, May 14, 2004. Printed by permission of CBC Radio 3 and James Paterson. Animation image by James Paterson.

We said there has to be a way to bring this all together in a way that makes sense. That's when we started planning for Radio 3 dot-com."

It was a branding issue, McLaughlin acknowledges, but also a content issue, because Radio 3 wasn't only about music. "The people who are interested in stories about the country they live in *also* listen to music. The people who listen to music, and make music, are *also* interested in the stories about their country. It doesn't matter if you're a jock, or a science guy, or into politics, whatever—everyone listens to music. So why don't we make something that has music as the thread throughout that speaks to a lot of different types of people? We would brand it as one thing and have this mass appeal."

To understand why CBC Radio 3's identity centers on its Web site, you have to go back to about 1998, when a plan hatched to create a third over-the-air network broadcast service aimed at new audiences. According to McLaughlin, people inside CBC worked on the plan for about two years, only to see it abruptly quashed when a new president took the helm of the corporation and new priorities came forward. Those involved in the Radio 3 network plan thought there must be another way to do what they had wanted to do, and they decided to try to reach the same new audiences using the Internet instead. They launched three Web sites in June 2000:

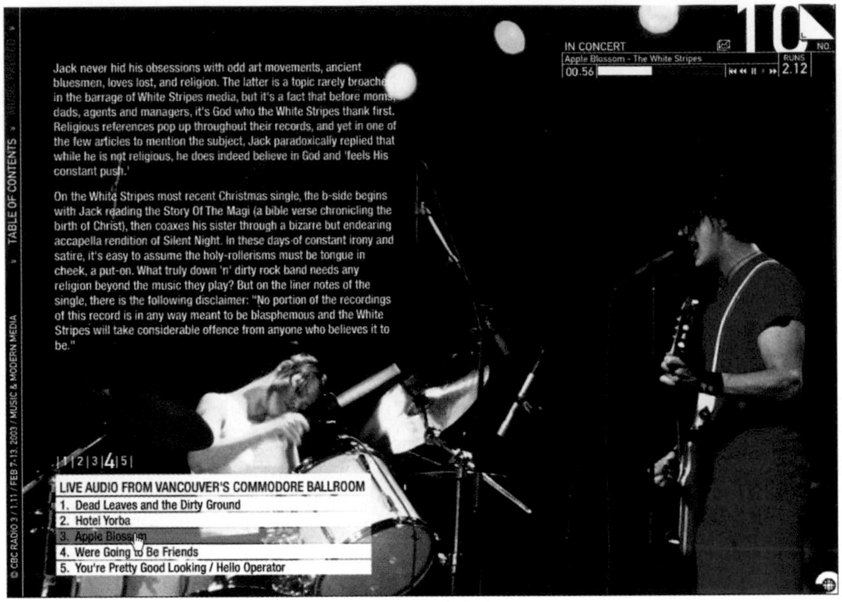
TABLE OF CONTENTS
© CBC RADIO 3 / 1.11 / FEB 7-13. 2003 / MUSIC & MODERN MEDIA
IN CONCERT
Apple Blossom - The White Stripes
00.56
RUNS
2.12
NO.
Jack never hid his obsessions with odd art movements, ancient bluesmen, loves lost, and religion. The latter is a topic rarely broache in the barrage of White Stripes media, but it's a fact that before moms, dads, agents and managers, it's God who the White Stripes thank first. Religious references pop up throughout their records, and yet in one of the few articles to mention the subject, Jack paradoxically replied that while he is not religious, he does indeed believe in God and 'feels His constant push.'
On the White Stripes most recent Christmas single, the b-side begins with Jack reading the Story Of The Magi (a bible verse chronicling the birth of Christ), then coaxes his sister through a bizarre but endearing accapella rendition of Silent Night. In these days of constant irony and satire, it's easy to assume the holy-rollerisms must be tongue in cheek, a put-on. What truly down 'n' dirty rock band needs any religion beyond the music they play? But on the liner notes of the single, there is the following disclaimer: "No portion of the recordings of this record is in any way meant to be blasphemous and the White Stripes will take considerable offence from anyone who believes it to be."
1 | 2 | 3 | 4 | 5
LIVE AUDIO FROM VANCOUVER'S COMMODORE BALLROOM
1. Dead Leaves and the Dirty Ground
2. Hotel Yorba
3. Apple Blossom
4. Were Going to Be Friends
5. You're Pretty Good Looking / Hello Operator

Fig. 3.4.03 The White Stripes: A story about the band, with five complete live concert tracks. Issue 01.11, Feb. 7, 2003. Page 4 of 5. Printed by permission of CBC Radio 3 and Andy Scheffler. Photo by Andy Scheffler.

- 120seconds.com came first, and was built entirely in Flash.
- Newmusiccanada.com has become home to 4700 Canadian artists with 23,200 tracks of music (as of July 2004). The content is managed by the artists themselves.
- Justconcerts.com delivers live concerts and also studio sessions from famous and obscure Canadian artists, all recorded by CBC.

Back at the beginning, the 120 Seconds site, with an all-Flash interface, won several awards. The path to the Radio 3 site began there. "We were having a lot of success around these things we call features, which are more story-driven things that we produce. These were getting noticed a lot," McLaughlin said. He pointed to "Belgrade 2001" (120 Seconds Archives: Aug. 25, 2001), a collection of stories about people who had stayed and persevered in the former Yugoslavia. That package came out of a Radio 3 team's accompanying a team of CBC news producers to Belgrade, when Radio 3 had been producing Flash features for about a year.

The Belgrade package holds up even today: Big photos, outstanding audio, and a personal, not-the-network-news quality to the reporting. Even Radio 3's first feature, "Ad-Nauseam" (120 Seconds Features: July 13, 2000), is comfortably viewable, although it's not as immersive as the later work.

Radio 3 attracted attention too for its man-on-the-street interviews around Canada on September 11, 2001 (120 Seconds Archives: Sept. 12, 2001). "We went to the street and did streeters, that's all we did. We put them up, and we had audio with it; we put it in Flash, and used a little bit of tempo and pacing," McLaughlin said. What made it different from a lot of other September 11 coverage: It connected the event with people in Canada, who were also affected, even if they were just sitting in the Vancouver airport that morning. The praise for this package still resonated for the staff a year later, when the Radio 3 site launched.

The Radio 3 group wanted to somehow bring together the Web features and the stories they produced for radio. "There was a disconnect between the radio programs and what we were doing online," McLaughlin said. "We needed to find a way to have common story meetings, to tell stories on *this* platform"—he tapped his computer screen—"that are the same stories as *that* platform, but knowing full well they need to be different."

STORIES

Saturday night on the radio program, you'll always hear more than music. "We thread a seam of stories through it—stories about crossing the border, worst jobs, ghost stories, whatever," McLaughlin said. Not all stories from the radio show go online, and a story might appear in either medium first, and then later, in a different form, in the other. Some stories are online only.

"For a story about a guy who owns the only all-metal record shop in Canada ["Defending the Faith," April 16, 2004], we might do the interview, write that [for the Web] first, then go, take the tape, and turn it into a radio thing afterward," McLaughlin explained. It depends on the story.

He admitted it's a challenge for Radio 3 producers to think about what is the best way to do the story every time. "*Every time,*" he repeated. "For every story. It's much harder to do, it's much harder to say how to do it, because you have to enter the conversation about *what it is,* first." Making a comparison to broadcast, he continued, "If you're booking the 7:15 interview on the morning show, it's the same thing every day: You read the greens [scripts], you get them to the host, the host reads them, you know how to chase it—you learn how to do it in your sleep. Whereas we don't know even how it's going to look, or work, and everything needs to be worked

Fig. 3.4.04 National elections, 2004: On each day of the election campaign, Radio 3 posted a new video featuring a non-politician talking about an issue of importance to him or her. Speakers included a filmmaker, a magazine editor, an immigrants-rights advocate, and a law school professor. Issue 02.40, June 11, 2004. Page shown: Day 22 of 36. Speaker shown: Gail Sparrow, former chief of the Musqueam Indian Band/Day 19. Printed by permission of CBC Radio 3 and Gail Sparrow.

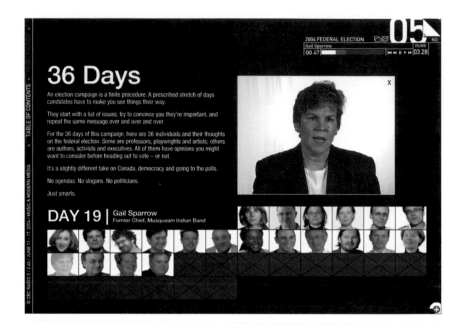

through—so *everything* is a conversation about what are we doing, and how are we going to do it."

When hiring, Radio 3 looks for people "who have skills we absolutely must have, and then try to teach them the things that they're missing," McLaughlin said. "Sometimes it's easier to teach someone mic skills, and how to get good tape, than it is to teach them how to work with Flash. So we have more people from non-content backgrounds than we have from content."

The staff at Radio 3 is a mix of radio producers, journalists trained in print journalism (who have also done a lot of radio journalism), a handful of people who went to art or design school, plus "some who are hosts, some who can write ColdFusion, some who can keep the computers running," McLaughlin said. Even the ColdFusion programmer has produced a story for the Web site.

A staff member will not be left alone in his comfort zone, doing only what he knows how to do best. An example was someone with an art school background who produced a story that included a 2000-word essay, a photo shoot, and recorded interviews. "He just made all that stuff happen, said, 'I need someone to this, I need someone to do that'—and that's how we operate," McLaughlin said. "You need to understand what pieces go into

Fig. 3.4.05 "The Way of the Jaks: 20 Odd Years in Skateboarding." Issue 02.34, April 30, 2004. Page 4 of 11. Printed by permission of CBC Radio 3 and Chris Jones. Photo by Chris Jones.

it, you need to be able to deconstruct your product, so that you can make interesting stuff."

At first glance, the Radio 3 site may seem to be templated. That is, maybe each page of each story is basically the same design: a big photo, a block of text, page numbers for navigation. But the more stories you look at, the more variations you'll find. If you are reading about some motorcycle riders who each year go to a particular bar out in the wilderness to see who can do the most impressive burnout, for example ("Laying It Down," July 2, 2004), you might notice a line of text next to the page numbers that's not part of other stories. "Watch the burnouts," it says. It's a link that launches a full-screen video showing the contest in action. Not many stories have a separate video feature, but here, that's what worked best. If a story needs something out of the ordinary, then the story design can be adjusted.

McLaughlin gestured outside his office door to the desk clusters of Radio 3, where men and women, most younger than 35 years old, worked at their computers surrounded by posters, assorted plastic toys, stacks of music CDs. They wore sandals, sneakers, hiking boots; some shirttails hung out. One wore a ball cap and a baseball glove; he tossed and caught a baseball as he talked to someone. They didn't look like Toronto bankers, but they were not excessively pierced or tattooed, either.

"If you look at the people in our office, I'm interested in what they find interesting," McLaughlin said. "So all they have to do is pitch ideas they think are interesting." During the regular Monday story meeting, those who have ideas they want to pitch get together with two or three others and step away for 20 minutes. "You brainstorm, you pitch your peers—the idea is that if everybody else gets excited about it, you pitch to the larger group," McLaughlin said. "Now, it works great in theory, but in practice, it doesn't work that way, because people are afraid to tell other people that their ideas aren't as great as they should be." To compensate, there is a parallel process where people pitch outside that weekly meeting as well, and freelancers—with their own ideas—might also contribute to the decision-making.

"Of course, the executive in charge does decide on final story selection," said McLaughlin (who *is* the executive in charge, unless he's on vacation). "Some of the criteria we use are: Has this story already been told? Is there a new take on the story? Is there another way to tell this story that hasn't been tried yet?" That's really no different from any other editorial operation, he pointed out. So what sets Radio 3 apart, in the end, is the staff of producers who are seeking out stories that interest them. A story about a group of senior citizens rollerblading might be a good story for Radio 3, McLaughlin said, but a story about a group of senior citizens holding a dance might not be.

Everything produced for the Web site is governed by union rules; all freelancers are automatically covered by all the terms and conditions of the existing Canadian Media Guild collective agreement. "Last fiscal year, we contracted 350 freelancers," McLaughlin said. Canadian freelance photographers shoot most of the photography on the Web site. All of the music writing is done out of house; Radio 3 staff members produce all the other non-music content.

One way or another, the story pitch leads to a go-ahead or a no-go. The person who pitched a story that wins approval owns that story and directs everything necessary to make it happen, whether on-air or online. Some stories take a day to produce; some take weeks or months. "Each producer is assigned a deadline depending on the content of the story," McLaughlin said.

"People here three years ago had 'designer' on their business cards. Now most people here have 'producer.' Because you don't need to write anything. I don't need you to know how to design. I don't need you to know how to Flash," McLaughlin said. "I need you to understand what it takes to make this stuff happen."

MISSION

At CBC, there's a lot of discussion about "new audiences." McLaughlin explained it this way: "A 'young person' at CBC is under 55. A 40-year-old is super young. So we don't really talk about 'youth'; we talk about new audiences." In spite of that, Radio 3 has been viewed by many inside the corporation as being a radio network for youth. "We've struggled to break free of that," McLaughlin said. "When we think of things, we actually don't think of 'youth' at all."

The words they do think of are "emerging artists, emerging culture," he said. "There's a newness to it, somewhere, that needs to happen. The interesting thing about the Web is that you can tell a lot of the same stories that have been told on radio and television a million times, and it seems new here, because it hasn't been done yet."

Naturally, there's a national aspect. The Canadian Broadcasting Act (1991, c. 11) specifies that CBC programming should be "predominantly and dis-

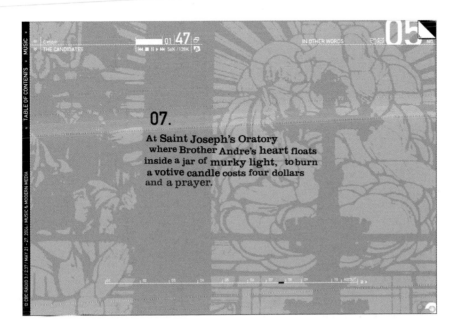

Fig. 3.4.06 Poetry: A horizontally scrolling poem by Chris Hutchinson is set against a stylized backdrop of the city of Montreal. Issue 02.37, May 21, 2004. Printed by permission of CBC Radio 3 and Chris Hutchinson.

tinctively Canadian, reflect Canada and its regions to national and regional audiences, while serving the special needs of those regions, [and] actively contribute to the flow and exchange of cultural expression." (In 2002–2003, the yearly operating cost of CBC/Radio-Canada per citizen was $29 Canadian, according to the corporation's annual report. Radio 3 constitutes a tiny speck in the CBC constellation of television, radio, news, documentary, and music.)

"We wave the flag a lot," McLaughlin said. "We [also] do stories about things outside the country. We've done lots of stories about the world—written by Canadian freelancers."

Stories about emerging artists and emerging culture "might just mean things are happening in the world that people haven't noticed yet. We tell them in new ways. I don't want to just do old things, I don't want to have someone just interview someone. I don't want to do things that are personality-driven all the time," McLaughlin said. "Radio is a personality high—'I am . . .'; 'Joining me now is . . .'; 'After this I'm going to talk to . . .' You'll notice there has never been a face on the cover [of CBC Radio 3]. I don't want people to associate what we do with a face."

The size of Radio 3's audience might be less important than the people that audience represents. "Our audience has a certain value to CBC because

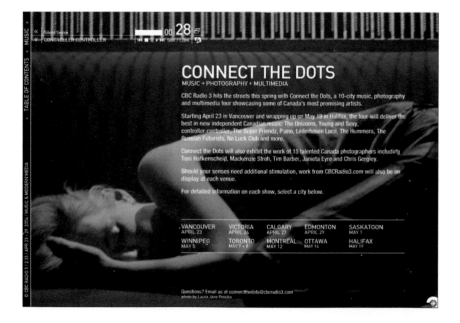

Fig. 3.4.07 "Connect the Dots," 2004: CBC Radio 3 put on a ten-city arts tour featuring gallery exhibits of the work of fifteen Canadian photographers and live performances by numerous independent musicians. Issue 02.33, April 23, 2004. Printed by permission of CBC Radio 3 and Laura Jane Petelko. Photo by Laura Jane Petelko.

it isn't in so many other places. Some people will see that the work we're doing here will mean a lot more five years from now," McLaughlin said.

SOME OF THE AWARDS WON BY CBC RADIO 3

Webby Award for best broadband site, 2003 (*http://www. webbyawards.com*)

New York Festivals Gold WorldMedal for best online radio site, 2004; Grand Award for best radio programming format, 2004 (*http://www.newyorkfestivals.com*)

Art Directors Club Gold Medal for best online magazine or periodical, 2004 (*http://www.adcglobal.org*)

Communication Arts Interactive Award, 2003 and 2004 (*http://www.commarts.com/CA/interactive/*)

"Audience is not just numbers, it's voice—and awards, and peers, and what other people in your family, the company, think of you," McLaughlin said. "We're trying to work in ways that can help people understand how the work we do here, and the work we do Saturday night, can fit into *their* show—or how a *version* of that could fit into their show."

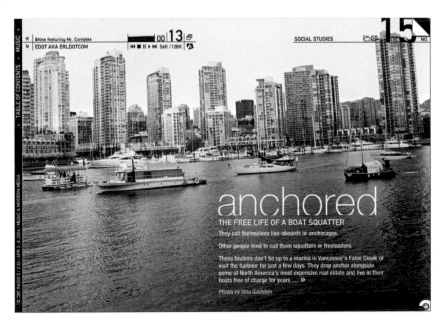

Fig. 3.4.08 "Anchored" tells the story of people who live on their boats off the shores of Vancouver. Issue 02.30, April 20, 2004. Page 1 of 15. Printed by permission of CBC Radio 3 and Dina Goldstein. Photo by Dina Goldstein.

McLaughlin pointed to a photo essay about people who live on boats moored in a creek in Vancouver, next to some of the most expensive real estate in the world ("Anchored," April 2, 2004). "They don't pay taxes, they're squatters," he said. "This story would matter to anyone. It's not just an online thing. And people say, 'Oh, yes, we should tell these stories as well. This would *cross over.*'

"That will win for us in a lot of ways. In the last four years, we've worked hard to figure out what stories for us *are*, and now that we're having success, people in the company are saying, 'Those are great stories, I see why people like what you do—can we have a little of that, please?' " This, McLaughlin said, is part of how Radio 3 justifies itself and what it does within the corporation.

To the staff at Radio 3, he said, "Public broadcasting isn't a numbers game." But all the same, he added, "Our numbers are growing, and that's a good thing."

PHOTOGRAPHS

You'd expect a radio Web site to have music, of course. But Radio 3 also packs the site with engrossing, often quirky photographs, and they are much bigger than those used on most news Web sites. Every page of every story delivers a new image—at 1014 × 716 pixels. The image size is optimized to fit within the 1024 × 768 version of the Radio 3 pop-up window. (As a comparison, many photo sites limit the size to 600 × 400 or even 500 × 300 pixels.)

The photos that accompany story text come from various sources; for a story about people's contemporary experiences with ghosts, for example ("Ghost Stories," May 7, 2004), Radio 3 used historic photos of séances taken in the early 1900s by a doctor in Winnipeg. Sometimes Radio 3 producers go out and shoot photos themselves; sometimes they hire a photographer.

The photo portfolio that accompanies each issue (usually a series of thirteen images) is wholly separate from the stories. The producers do not take photos from the portfolio and use them in stories; the photos for any story are selected or shot specifically for that story. The photo portfolios are not commissioned; in most cases, Canadian photographers pitch a series they

Fig. 3.4.09 Table of Contents, Issue 01.21, April 18, 2003. Individual photos in the featured portfolio are listed in the center of the right column. The layout of the contents page stays the same, but every issue brings a new photo. Printed by permission of CBC Radio 3.

have already completed. The diverse portfolios selected represent the tastes of the Radio 3 staff. The Table of Contents provides a list of the portfolio photos by title, providing one option for viewing them. Most users probably encounter the portfolio photos more randomly. If a user is "paging through" the site with the plus/minus dog-eared corner in the upper right of each page (which Radio 3 calls the Folio) or just tapping the left or right arrow key, the photos from the portfolio series intervene between the stories. The stand-alone photos "give space between content, like ads in a magazine," McLaughlin said. As part of a public broadcasting corporation, Radio 3 does not run paid advertising on any of its Web sites.

The procedure Radio 3 uses for handling photos is to edit them in Photoshop, save them as BMPs, and import them into Flash "nine times out of ten"—not load them at runtime, McLaughlin said. That is, they are not external JPG files; they are inside the FLA (see Lesson 7 for more information). The compression levels vary depending on the photo, but the producers try to go low. A *Quality* setting of 30 percent in the Bitmap Properties dialog works fine for many of the photos, if detail is not important; 70 percent is the highest setting Radio 3 will use, with few exceptions.

Often there is only one photo in a SWF—in other words, each page in a Radio 3 story is a single SWF. This is not always so, but usually the story is constructed this way, with the story navigation (a row of numerals) loading each SWF in turn into a movie clip (see Appendix B for more information). All SWFs for a single story are kept together in a folder on the server. A story such as "Anchored" (April 20, 2004), with 15 pages, would consist of fifteen separate SWF files, each one well under 80 KB. The logic is twofold, according to McLaughlin: (1) Because the Radio 3 site is intended for broadband users, the download of a single page should be very fast. (2) If there's any waiting time between pages, the user sees a loading progress bar. In 2003, 64 percent of Canadian households had Internet access, and nearly half of those (48 percent) had broadband, according to Statistics Canada (*http://www.statcan.ca*).

TECH TIP: PHOTOS THAT FILL THE SCREEN

CBC Radio 3 uses a combination of JavaScript and clever Flash techniques to show photos at super-large sizes. The users' experience will vary slightly depending on their screen resolution. The Radio 3 browser window recognizes three basic resolution options: (1) 800 × 600 pixels; (2) 1024 × 768 pixels; (3) larger than 1024 × 768 pixels.

The site was designed "to fit wall-to-wall at either 800 × 600, or 1024 × 768," McLaughlin said.

Both the HTML window and the SWF are automatically sized to match the user's screen resolution; this requires three steps. The first step is to open the pop-up window for the current issue at the full resolution of the user's screen. This is accomplished with a script on the Radio 3 page named "index.cfm"—the page that opens when you go to the main site (*http://www.cbcradio3.ca*). To see the JavaScript, view source on that page. It uses the browser's "screen.width" property to read the width of the user's screen resolution (for more information about this use of JavaScript, see *http://www.pageresource.com/jscript/jscreen.htm*). It also uses two other properties, "navigator.appName" and "navigator.appVersion," to detect which Web browser is being used. (It's outside the scope of this book to explain the JavaScript in more detail than this, but the script is not difficult for someone who already knows JavaScript.)

The second step is in the new pop-up window, which is named "main.cfm." You can view source on that page to see a relatively standard JavaScript detection for Flash, which was explained in Lesson 3 in this book. Remember that you already have a pop-up browser window at full-screen, because of the previous step initiated by "index.cfm." On "main.cfm," the script is determining what width and height the SWF will be inside that window. There is a lot of script repeated from the earlier script, because the size of the SWF *also* depends on the screen width.

There are four possible sizes given for the SWF, depending on what the JavaScript detects about the user's platform, the Web browser, and the screen resolution.

Table 3.4.01

SWF width × height	SCALE parameter in OBJECT code
1014 × 716	PARAM NAME=scale VALUE=scale EMBED
950 × 673	PARAM NAME=scale VALUE=exactfit EMBED scale=exactfit
790 × 558	PARAM NAME=scale VALUE=scale EMBED
675 × 525	PARAM NAME=scale VALUE=exactfit EMBED scale=exactfit

Radio 3 producers extensively tested these sizes, and the script that contains them, to ensure that the site opens and displays properly on just about any computer, regardless of its configuration. Even so, McLaughlin said it's still not perfect.

No user will ever see the SWF open at a size larger than 1014 × 716 (which fits perfectly at 1024 × 768 resolution), and so if someone has a higher resolution, the SWF will be centered on the screen, with a black border extending out to all four edges. That feat is accomplished by enclosing the JavaScript in a regular HTML table, which centers the SWF on the screen:

```
<div align="center">
<table width="100%" height="100%" border="0" cellspacing="0"
cellpadding="0">
<tr>
<td align="center" valign="middle">
        <script language="JavaScript">
        All the OBJECT code goes here.
        </script>
</td>
</tr>
</table>
</div>
```

The other tricks necessary to make the table work perfectly are to set the background color of the Web page to black (#000000) and to set all page margins to zero, as explained under "Using a Pop-up Window (Case No. 2: SWF and HTML Together)," in Lesson 3.

The actual dimensions of the FLA are 790 × 558.

You should be wondering: Why don't the photos look blocky or "pixelated" when the SWF appears at a larger size? This is an especially good Flash trick. Radio 3 saves all the full-screen photos as BMP files at a resolution of 1014 × 716. The producers import the BMP to the FLA and convert it to a symbol, which is also 1014 × 716. But when they position an *instance* of that symbol on the Stage, they resize it to match the Stage size of 790 × 558. When the SWF is "blown up" to 1014 × 716, the photo is at its true size, and no distortions occur.

It does mean that users with 800 × 600 resolution are downloading files that are larger than they would need to be for maximum quality at that resolution, but Radio 3 wanted to provide an optimum experience for a resolution of 1024 × 768, which more users have—without shutting out the users with 800 × 600.

Don't forget that the producer uses the Bitmap Properties dialog (see Lesson 7) to adjust the Quality setting for each BMP individually, and often the percentage goes as low as 30.

 FLA files for this case study Tech Tip are on the book's Web site.

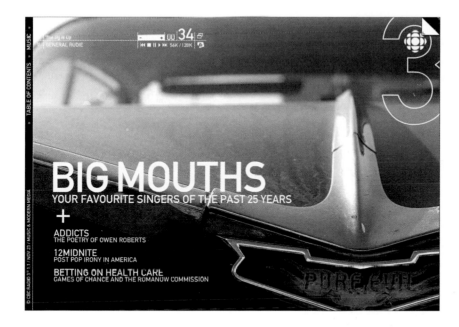

Fig. 3.4.10 The cover of the premiere issue of CBC Radio 3 on the Web. Issue 01.01, Nov. 23, 2002. Printed by permission of CBC Radio 3 and 12Midnite. Photo by 12Midnite.

SITE DESIGN

At the time of this interview, Radio 3 was planning on a redesign for fall 2004. The look of the site had changed very little since its launch in November 2002. "What has changed a lot is what's inside," McLaughlin said.

The most obvious differences in design can be seen between the first and second issues (01.01 and 01.02). Originally, the staff intended to produce a new motion intro to the site every week. By Week 2, they had decided against it: Too much effort spent for too little effect. The Table of Contents background was blank on Issue 01.01, but every issue thereafter used a full-screen photo background. The Page One editorial layout was redesigned, and the second (right side) player was added when Radio 3 decided to include full-screen video with some stories.

Fig. 3.4.11 The "right side" player can also play video and animations—any content a SWF can contain, in fact. Here it is buffering a video file; also shown is the user's ability to "scrub" the video by dragging the progress bar. Printed by permission of CBC Radio 3.

The right-side player allows "scrubbing" (dragging a progress bar to move forward or back in the content); the files it plays are externally loaded SWF files, whether they are video or just audio. Video is imported in the Flash-native FLV format at 320 × 240 and simply blown up to full-screen by increasing the size of the movie clip. The frame rate used is always 31 fps, which McLaughlin explained as a solution to a problem with slowness in the Flash player version 6 on the Mac OS.

Fig. 3.4.12 The Radio 3 "right side" player loads and plays SWF files. For music stories, these are typically music-only, with a tie-in to the Just Concerts site. Printed by permission of CBC Radio 3.

Fig. 3.4.13 The Radio 3 "left side" player loads MP3s dynamically. Each week a new playlist of twenty songs is added; the player provides a direct connection to the New Music Canada site. Printed by permission of CBC Radio 3.

Fig. 3.4.14 The Folio control appears at the top right of every page. It works with Radio 3's back-end database to move the user forward and back through an issue's contents. Printed by permission of CBC Radio 3.

Content in the right-side player is not managed by the Radio 3 site's database; it's built into the story. The left-side player, by contrast, uses a playlist in the database to load streaming external MP3 files from the separate New Music Canada site, where content is uploaded and managed by the bands themselves. The left-side player runs independently of any story, providing a soundtrack for the site as a whole. When a user opens a story that contains a right-side player, the story pauses and hides the left-side player. It will reappear when the user leaves that story and the right-side player is no longer visible.

The site's content management system (CMS), which was built in-house with ColdFusion, provides an HTML form interface that the Radio 3 staff uses to update the site each week. It handles the story content, playlists, and all related files. The database is used to generate the full table of contents for each issue dynamically; it also works with the Folio control that appears in the upper right corner of every page and allows the user to "page through" any issue (either by clicking on the Folio, or by pressing the arrow keys on the keyboard). The Folio control uses the database information to determine which page to load next, whether the user opts to move forward or back.

By entering the folder location and filename of each story into the form, and assigning a page position to each one, the producers build the whole issue without the need to manually create any links at all. The "page" and "issue" metaphors for the site are thus integral to the way the database manages the content, including the way it handles the Archives.

The Archives have changed significantly, thanks in part to keywords stored in the database for each story. The original version of the site had a less satisfactory search function in the Archives, and also a cramped display of results; these were changed after almost a year. The new search function works better than most, searching titles, summaries, and an extensive keyword list for each article. It returns results in a very readable two-column listing.

Interestingly, however, the text the user sees onscreen in any story is Static text that is part of the SWF. In other words, the story text onscreen is independent of the database. It just works better that way, McLaughlin said,

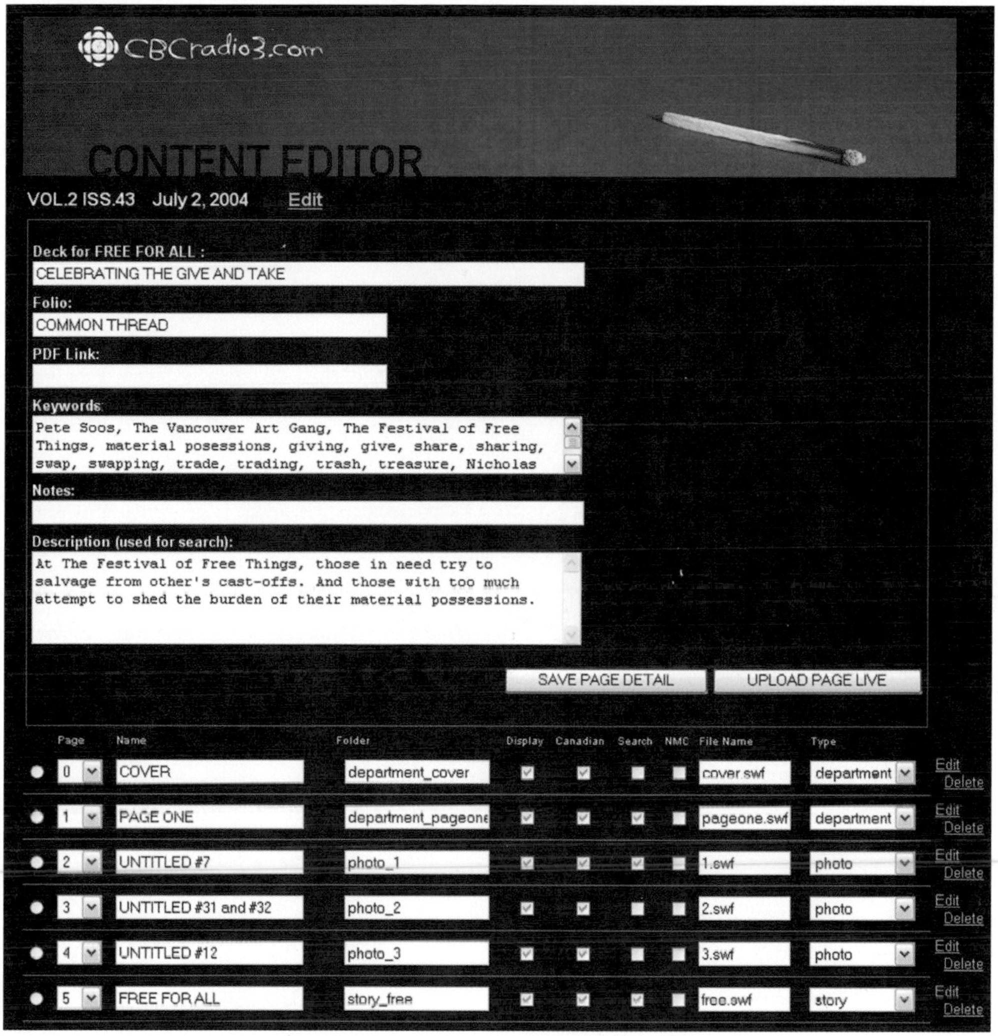

Fig. 3.4.15 The Radio 3 content management system uses a straightforward Web form and ColdFusion on the back end to simplify the construction of each week's new issue. Printed by permission of CBC Radio 3.

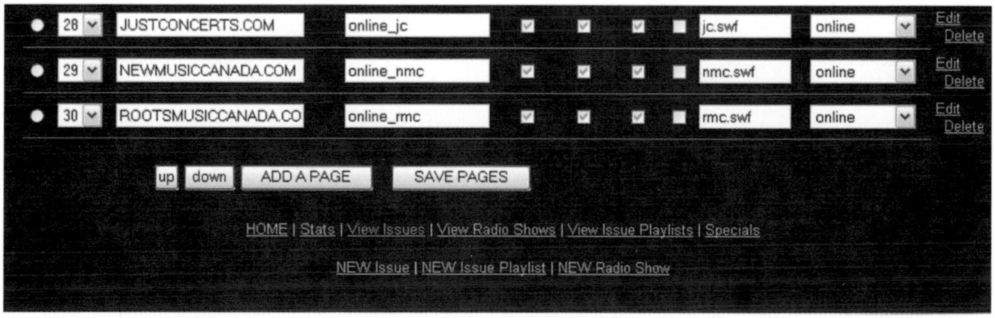

Fig. 3.4.16 Links at the bottom of the CMS form page allow a producer to start a new issue or a new playlist. Printed by permission of CBC Radio 3.

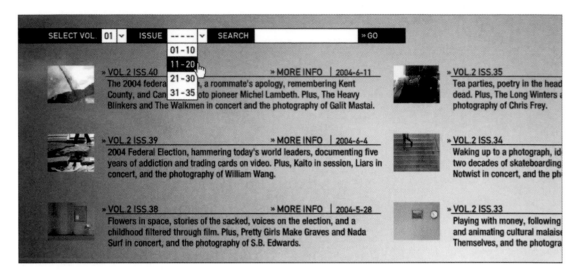

Fig. 3.4.17 Radio 3 Archives: If the user knows the volume and issue number, it's easy to find past issues of the site. Printed by permission of CBC Radio 3.

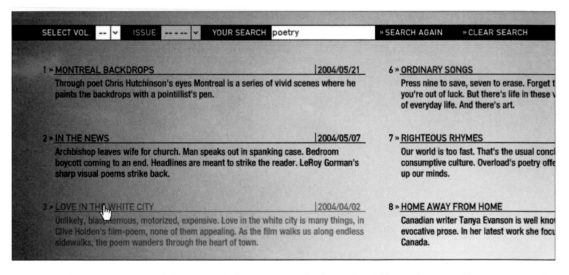

Fig. 3.4.18 Radio 3 Archives: The full-text search function brings back very readable results. Printed by permission of CBC Radio 3.

with the producers able to see and control their text in the FLA during production. Most online publishing operations today, as a rule, separate content and design for the sake of efficiency, but for Radio 3, the practice of handcrafting each page in each story justifies breaking the rule. The summary and keywords in the database enable the Archives search, but it's not a true full-text search, according to Nicole Goodman, Radio 3's Cold-Fusion programmer. Producers add the summary and keywords into the CMS form after the story production has been completed.

Goodman, who has been at Radio 3 since January 2000, explained she has also been working to make individual Radio 3 stories more accessible to external search engines, using some ColdFusion techniques to make the story titles and keywords searchable in ways that would allow a fully functional Radio 3 story page to open directly from a search-results link in Google.

As for the actual construction of the Web site, producers build the SWFs for each story and the photo series. Only the table of contents and the left-side player music are generated automatically by the database.

An identical SWF named "main" is the shell for each issue; it contains several empty movie clips (see Lesson 10 to learn how these work). All the content—players, pages, the Folio control, the Table of Contents control—is loaded into these movie clips as needed. None of the content is ever loaded onto levels; McLaughlin said working with levels can get to be too confusing when there might be multiple producers working on a project. Each content item is a separate SWF file, and all files for an issue are stored in that issue's unique folder on the server.

The CMS does not include version protection or a check-out function. "It's a small shop," McLaughlin pointed out. "I can open the door and yell—and there *is* a lot of yelling—'Do you have that file open?'" Members of the staff know whom to ask if they want to go into a story and make a change. If someone needs to check who owns a story, there's an Excel spreadsheet on the network that anyone can read; it shows what everyone is working on. Two producers are responsible for keeping the spreadsheet up to date. "All the organization is in people's heads," McLaughlin said.

MUSIC PLAYLISTS

The CMS manages the relationship between the Radio 3 site and the New Music Canada site in two ways, Goodman explained in a phone interview. The twenty-song playlist that drives each issue's left-side player is constructed in a Web form that lets the producer browse the bands and MP3s on the New Music Canada site; these are in an entirely separate database.

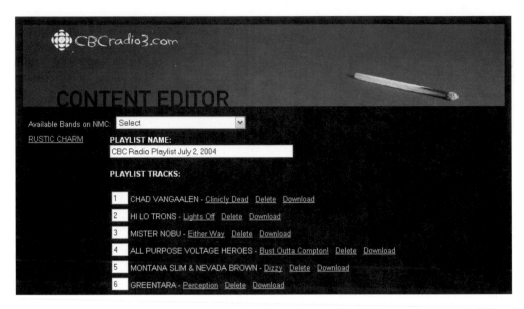

Fig. 3.4.19 The twenty-song playlist for an issue's "left-side" player is built in the content management system, even though the songs come from the separate New Music Canada site. Printed by permission of CBC Radio 3.

For each slot in the playlist, the producer opens a menu and selects a song title. When all twenty have been selected, the playlist is ready to run automatically for the issue with which it is associated. Online users who open a past issue always hear songs from the playlist that originally accompanied that issue; the playlist becomes part of the issue. Users can open the playlist and select any song by clicking a button on the player; they can open a band's page (and hear more songs by that band) on the New Music Canada site by clicking another button on the player.

The MP3s streaming in the left-side player are coming straight from the New Music Canada site and its server. Since all the music on that site is managed by the bands themselves, it's possible that a song on a playlist (from this week or from a year ago) might be deleted. If that happens, an e-mail is sent automatically to a Radio 3 editor as an alert; the editor can go in and substitute another song.

For the weekly radio show, a Radio 3 producer uses that same twenty-song playlist to download the MP3s, then edits them in Cool Edit Pro to create the mixdown (a single file including all tracks, effects, and other material) for the final two hours of the show. The mixdown file is submitted to another computer system that feeds into CBC's master control, which puts it on-air.

Separately, Radio 3 creates a complete playlist for everything that goes on-air Saturday night (a total eight and a half hours)—and this demonstrates a convenient integration between the Web site and the radio program. Users who want to receive the complete playlist can sign up for a free e-mail newsletter online. The database generates the list of all artists and tracks, which a script transforms into a newsletter format each week and sends out to subscribers. The same playlist (in a different format) is also sent to SOCAN (the Society of Composers, Authors and Music Publishers of Canada), which ensures that the artists are paid for use of their work.

A brief text summary of the radio programming appears on the Radio 3 site under the link "CBC Radio 3 On Air Playlist," but there is no listing of all tracks available on the site; a user must sign up for the newsletter to get that. Music in the first six and a half hours of the radio program does not necessarily have any relationship to the New Music Canada site; it might be tied into the Just Concerts site, or it might be something else altogether.

There is no separating the Saturday night radio programming from the Radio 3 Web site, and while the various Web sites produced by Radio 3 have their own identities, they are also undeniably related to one another and linked together. In September 2003, the radio programming was relaunched as CBC Radio 3; for the first time, the entire eight and a half hours had one name and one brand, consistent with the Web site.

Is Radio 3 a radio network or a Web site? If the producers had to choose one, then maybe Radio 3 could not be what it is.

Case Study 5

MSNBC.com The Big Picture

URL: *http://bigpicture.msnbc.com/*
Interview Date: May 13, 2004
Location: Redmond, Washington
Interview Subject: Ashley Wells, Senior Producer, Broadband Productions

> *"You can't overstate what* making stuff move *does to people. When stuff moves, they pay more attention."*

> *—Ashley Wells*

The first time people see The Big Picture, a peculiar expression comes to their faces. They're not sure whether they *like* it, but they are definitely impressed. It's moving, it's talking, it's video—and it's *big*.

There are two video "screens" in this Flash package. The main one, much larger, is at the top; the small one is in the lower right corner. The two can play simultaneously (and often do). Users can switch what appears in the big window, choosing from a playlist at the left side. While the video content plays, text content changes dynamically in a box below it. This is not really like anything else on the Web today. It's part of how online media are evolving.

The coordination among the elements of the package impresses most users, but Flash developers notice particularly the way it all fits together as an application. The Big Picture can be stuffed full of different types of content (video, slideshows, games, animated maps), but no matter what's playing, the interface works the same way.

Ashley Wells built a demo for The Big Picture in summer 2002, to pitch the idea to top editors at MSNBC.com. The two video windows are there, and the playlist at the left; it looks very similar to the final product. The demo, however, was designed to be a container for pre-existing content, with a TV-anchor/guide in the small video window helping the user make sense of it all. It provided a way to aggregate all the animated graphics,

Fig. 3.5.01 "Civil Rights Today," the fifth Big Picture, was launched in July 2004. Printed by permission of MSNBC.com.

video, and other non-textual content that MSNBC.com had already produced for an ongoing story. This tidy package would be linked on any text stories about the same topic.

The way it turned out, The Big Picture instead became a new vehicle for original content produced specifically for The Big Picture.

THE IDEA

Wells wanted to do something new back in 2002. "Something that you don't have to read. The Internet is capable of a lot, and it shouldn't be a rehash of what print is," he said. "I think some things are easier explained visually."

He pulled up an "interactive" from that time, a voice-driven animation about the Enron business scandal (*http://www.msnbc.com/modules/enron/*).

"My job as an interactive producer was to add the context to things," he said. The package, titled "Enron 101," uses Sim City–like illustrations and pop-up text blurbs, along with a narration, to explain the story in three segments. "We can take something that is pretty complex and boil it down," Wells said.

He acknowledged that some people working in offices turn their sound off, and some people just don't absorb information presented in this way. "If they don't have audio, and they don't want to watch things that move, then the whole rest of our site is for them," he said. "There are going to be people who want to do that, and that's fine."

Wells showed another interactive, one about September 11 titled "The Darkest Day" (*http://www.msnbc.com/modules/wtc_terror_experience/*), which looks very different from "Enron 101." Two of its six sections are

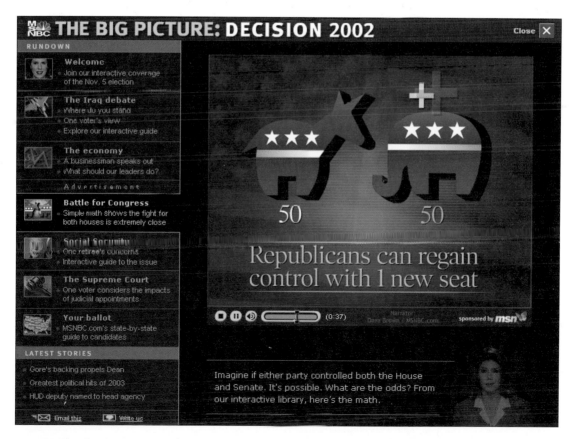

Fig. 3.5.02 The first Big Picture, "Decision 2002," focused on the U.S. midterm elections. Printed by permission of MSNBC.com.

slideshows with audio from people on the scene; two are animated maps that show the paths of the hijacked planes. It organizes a complex story in a compact package. "The Big Picture is just an evolution from this," Wells said. "Certain topics lend themselves to this kind of treatment; others don't."

Another pre–Big Picture interactive Wells likes to show is "Airport Security/Can You Spot the Threats?" (*http://www.msnbc.com/modules/ airport_security/screener/*), which invites users to watch an airport-security monitor and try to detect weapons or explosives hidden inside carry-on baggage. By scoring a user's performance as if in a video game, the package demonstrates what a security official faces on the job.

Wells aspired to combine elements from all three of these examples into one integrated package. "Everything I was doing was in Flash, because Flash was the convergence of code and design in a way, finally, that one person could participate in both," he said. "As Flash became more complex and robust, what we could do with it naturally increased." He wanted The Big Picture to incorporate real interactivity with sound and motion.

VERSION 1

Decision 2002 (Midterm Elections)

http://www.msnbc.com/modules/bigpicture/elex/

Conflict with Iraq (2003)

http://www.msnbc.com/modules/bigpicture/iraq/

75th Oscars (2003)

http://www.msnbc.com/modules/bigpicture/oscars/

VERSION 2

Academy Awards (2004)

http://www.msnbc.msn.com/id/4277322/

Civil Rights Today (2004)

http://www.msnbc.msn.com/id/5439480/

Wells prefers to build and pitch a demo when he's seeking approval for a new kind of project. "Making a demo makes you think it through," he said. He and Ken Oelerich, a senior designer, created The Big Picture demo in Flash, but it loaded a combination of old projects and still images to stand in for other content that did not yet exist. In the lower right corner, it showed a still image of NBC's Tom Brokaw, so Wells could explain the role of the talking anchor/guide. The demo conveyed the concept well enough to allow Wells and Oelerich to take it into a senior editorial meeting attended by section heads and the editor-in-chief.

"We came in with this [demo], and we go, 'Here's what we want to do, here's how it would work, what do you think?' And they're like—'Awesome,' " Wells said. "That's typically how people react when you come up with an idea and you've thought it through enough to make a demo."

With top-level management behind the project, all that remained was to wait for a suitably significant news topic to come along. (The demo used the Enron story, but that was played out by the time all the approvals came through.) The U.S. midterm elections seemed like a natural fit, and the first Big Picture made its debut in October 2002.

"At some point, we said we should brand it, so people can call it something—particularly sales, so they can sell it," Wells said. He wanted it to have "a TV name" that could be used for any topic.

A funny thing happened on the way to the first Big Picture, though: A lot more original content was created for it, and not much repurposed content found its way into the package.

"The reason it didn't turn out [like the demo] is because it's not executable [that] way," Wells said. Pre-existing modules could have been loaded, as they were in the demo, but "it doesn't stick together as a cohesive whole. That was one of the premises: How do you take a bunch of things that are inherently different and make them similar, so they are consumable in the same kind of medium?"

EVOLUTION

When they began building the first Big Picture, neither Wells nor the people he worked with had done any video in Flash. They had not tested or even tried it. Very recently, they had upgraded from Flash 4 to Flash MX; they had not used Flash 5. Working with video in Flash for the first time threw

Fig. 3.5.03 In the first Big Picture, some pre-existing content was inserted into the presentation but popped up in a separate window ("Decision 2002"). Printed by permission of MSNBC.com.

Fig. 3.5.04 The second Big Picture concerned U.S. preparations for the war in Iraq. Printed by permission of MSNBC.com.

Fig. 3.5.05 The third Big Picture previewed the 2003 Academy Awards. Printed by permission of MSNBC.com.

up serious challenges, but the team managed to include some interactive features, such as instant polls that invite users to agree or disagree with remarks made (in a video clip) by a U.S. senator, and then see how others have voted. Several interactives launch in external windows, not fully integrated into The Big Picture itself.

For the second Big Picture, which concerned the U.S. buildup to the war with Iraq that began in 2003, "We tried to be more interactive than the first one. It didn't take as much development time, but it took more editorial time, more writing and research," Wells said.

Wells intended to reuse whatever he could from the first Big Picture, but some changes were in order, inspired in part by tracking data that showed how people had used the first version. "We implement new features as we go, and once we get that stuff out of the way, we start getting more ambitious with content," Wells said.

The interactivity in "Conflict with Iraq" again uses instant polls, but in this case, the user does not see how others have voted until the final segment of the package. It's possible to skip ahead and just see the results, without voting yourself. Or you might register your opinion at the end of each segment and then view the results, comparing your opinions with those of all the other users who have voted.

For the third Big Picture (2003 Oscars), the producers made hardly any changes in functionality. The voting model remained the same as in "Conflict with Iraq," but in this package, users voted for the best actor, actress, and picture. Interactive additions included a trivia quiz and an animated game called "You Be the Producer," a stand-alone interactive inserted seamlessly into the package.

It might appear that by the third Big Picture, all the bugs had been worked out and the format could be used on a regular basis, with producers simply plugging in content and publishing a new package whenever a sufficiently important topic emerged. Not so. A year passed before the fourth Big Picture "because we didn't have the resources to do these after the war started," Wells said. Everyone at MSNBC.com focused on producing content to keep up with the march to Baghdad, the subsequent battles, and coverage of the U.S. occupation of Iraq.

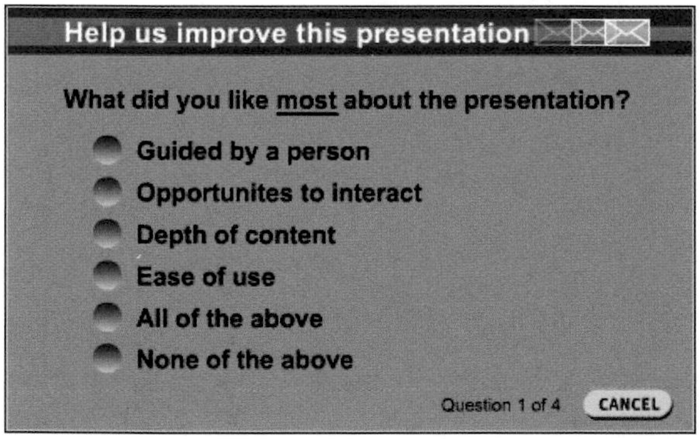

No one revised or updated the "Conflict with Iraq" Big Picture after its launch. "We see them as a show that would air on TV, a one-time thing," Wells said. "There are parts of it you can update, but what you don't want to do is get into the business of having to re-do entire segments, because then you're stuck with maintaining it indefinitely." Only a limited number of people have the skills required to create even one entire segment, and "they have to move on to the next thing" rather than updating a completed package, he said.

The fourth Big Picture would entail an extensive redesign, aimed at creating a format that's both easier for producers to work with and more engaging for users.

Fig. 3.5.06 On closing the presentation, users were invited to provide feedback about their experience ("75th Oscars," 2003). Printed by permission of MSNBC.com.

Fig. 3.5.07 In a segment of "Conflict with Iraq," three videos were coordinated with a fourth video showing the anchor, or guide, who posed questions to the panel of experts. Users could also choose to ask additional questions, which were supplied onscreen. Printed by permission of MSNBC.com.

PRODUCTION

The complexity in assembling all the content for each Big Picture segment depends on what is in the segment. "When it's just a standard slideshow, that's not very hard," Wells said. "When it's an interactive segment, and you've got to change the Timeline, combined with the picture edits, and making *this* video timed with *this* video"—he pointed to the large window and then to the small window—"it's not something Flash does naturally. You have to have design skills, coding skills, video editing skills, and there aren't that many people here who have that combination."

One segment in the Iraq package ("Weapons Panel: Can Inspections Work?") presented a special challenge because four separate videos are onscreen at one time. "It took probably two days just to edit this segment together, once we had everything in place—all the video, all the design elements," Wells said.

With three people working full time on nothing but one Big Picture, it would take at least two weeks to build the entire package. In the first week, Wells said, "There's the research, writing, and reporting phase, where you figure out what the content's going to be, you go research it, do phone interviews or video, or whatever you need." In the second week, the pieces would be put together.

Some of the video comes from NBC and MSNBC, while some is shot specifically for The Big Picture. "Often we can get raw tape from NBC News, and we can use it any way we want," Wells said.

"What's difficult about making these is, first and foremost, you need talent to be the track of it. Someone like Lester Holt, who's one of our big cable anchors, doesn't have time to record these very often," he said. The scripts for each segment must be fully written before the script for the anchor/guide can be written. An anchor will read and tape the entire anchor script at one time. Both anchors who have appeared in The Big Picture (Holt and Dara Brown) are based at MSNBC's Secaucus, New Jersey, studios. While the anchor is taping in New Jersey, Wells watches via an Internet video window on his computer on the other side of the country; if necessary, he can direct the anchor to read part of the script over again. A typical taping session with an anchor takes about 30 minutes.

Both anchors appear in the "Conflict with Iraq"; in all the others, Brown appears alone. (She also reads the video headlines for the regular MSNBC site every day.) The reason for having two anchors on Iraq was partly just to try it, but also because Holt was anchoring that story for the network; he had become MSNBC's on-air face for the Iraq buildup.

Until recently, the Secaucus studio sent the physical videotape out to the Redmond office where Wells edited it on his Avid system. They don't transmit the video over the network, because the uncompressed files are so large. Now Secaucus sends it via satellite feed.

The second week is spent getting photos to fill the gaps where the video doesn't fill, or vice versa; inserting motion graphics at the front of each segment (making them look very TV-like); inserting and testing any interactive features; completing all the segments. Finally, each segment is synchronized with the anchor/guide video.

Not long before this interview, MSNBC.com reorganized its producer teams, which had been structured around the type of work they did (interactive, graphic design, photo editing). Under the new structure, one team handles daily production while another team manages special projects; the broadband team takes care of large-scale projects and new formats.

"We will create the format, and then we'll create the content that goes in it," Wells said. "I have a journalism degree, and the two guys who work for me do too. It just so happens that most of the time, Greg [Perez] is a designer. Most of the time, Jim [Ray] is a developer. In theory, at some point, we'd pass that format off, once it's easy to maintain and update, to other people who have the skills to put the content in."

This view shifted significantly with the civil rights Big Picture, Wells said later. "Greg, Jim, and I were all segment reporter/producers, researching, reporting, writing, and voicing our own work," he wrote in an e-mail. "Some of that work is field work. For instance, I flew to Boston to shoot my interviews on school re-segregation."

The focus now, he said, will be on "original, made-to-be-interactive journalism" and not as much on tinkering with the shell or the player. The model will be that one person pitches and then owns a story, or a segment. "We have become a small, almost self-contained team of true multimedia journalists," Wells wrote in July. Their work does go through an editor, who provides guidance as needed, signs off on scripts, and copy edits text.

Production expenses must be considered for every Big Picture. "If we work on one presentation for a month, and it gets 400,000 unique users, that may sound like a lot to most people, but it's not that much for our site," Wells said. "Having three well-paid people who only did that for an entire month—it has to pay for itself, or we don't do it.

"We're going to make these mostly either when there's an obvious news event, or when someone's sponsoring it," he said. (Hyundai sponsored the Big Picture for the 2004 Oscars; General Electric sponsored the fifth Big Picture, "Civil Rights Today.") A sponsor with enough cash can name a topic, but "they cannot tell us what is going to be included in the content." MSNBC.com might also turn down a sponsor if a news topic Big Picture, such as the elections, were already in the pipeline. Neither can a sponsor have approval prior to launch. "That's what you sign up for, when you sponsor something that's about news," Wells said. "We're starting to develop a calendar of upcoming shows so that sponsors can choose to support a scheduled topic, but not name the topic themselves."

BACK-END EDITING

MSNBC.com uses an HTML-form–based interface to manage certain interactive features on the site; the form input is used to generate stand-alone XML files. The same editing tool works hand-in-hand with The Big Picture. The Flash file is scripted to read an external XML file; the information taken out of that file is then stored in ActionScript arrays and used to populate various Dynamic text fields in the SWF. Editors don't need to know how that works, though; if they need to edit copy for The Big Picture, they just use the same tool they use for other interactive content.

"Sometimes, when I wasn't around, someone wanted to add a bullet point or change a text piece," Wells said. "I didn't want them to call me at home at midnight to do that. This way, they can do it themselves."

While Wells has written many of the audio scripts for The Big Picture, other people have written most of the text that appears in the packages. This is changing, though. Writing the "contextual text" for each segment is now part of the script-writing process. The broadband team developed a three-column script format for the fourth Big Picture. Column 1 contains the audio script; Column 2 contains thumbnails of the visuals; Column 3 contains contextual information directly related to the script in Column 1.

All the text visible in The Big Picture (except the display type and the small silver UI buttons) comes from one XML file.

Visualize an HTML form, like one you might fill in when you're buying something on the Web. In the form used for text in The Big Picture, the first form fields are the segment names, stacked in the order that corresponds exactly to the playlist buttons on the left side of The Big Picture. All the text on a playlist button appears in one of these form fields, with HTML formatting for boldface and other styling. A producer can reorder the playlist buttons by assigning a new number to one button in the form.

As for the rest of the form, its fields reflect everything that is onscreen when that playlist button is selected in The Big Picture, including the filename of the segment SWF to be loaded and the thumbnail image that goes on the selected button. By selecting a different playlist form field from the list, the whole form changes to display the content for that playlist item, and a producer can edit all the text and filenames associated with that playlist button.

When the producer submits the form, it writes a new XML file, replacing the one already on the server.

Comments submitted by users are stored in a separate XML file. During the early days or weeks of a Big Picture's life cycle, Wells reads the day's comments and manually selects representative ones to pull in, relative to the Flash Timeline position.

In the bottom center text field of The Big Picture, the text changes to pop up additional facts, comments, and links while a segment is playing. Each

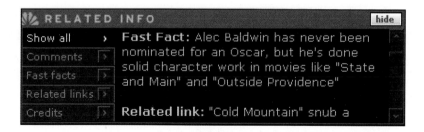

Fig. 3.5.08 The content
in the box at bottom
center is synchronized
with the currently playing
segment, so the text
changes as the segment
moves forward ("Academy
Awards," 2004). Printed
by permission of
MSNBC.com.

chunk of this text in the XML file includes a variable that associates it with a particular frame number in the SWF. An "onEnterFrame" event handler in ActionScript continually checks the current frame number and displays the appropriate text at the appropriate time. The chunks of text are also scripted to be associated with a particular category, because the user can click a button to choose to view only text from one category.

If you've never used a content management system to upload or edit text for a Web site, this may seem impossibly difficult. In actual use, though, it's the opposite: It allows a producer simply to type into fields in a form, and then click a Submit button, to create or change any of the text in a complex Flash package.

VERSION 2

In February 2004, Wells and a small team prepared to launch the first new Big Picture since the 2003 Oscars package. The topic would be the 2004 Academy Awards, but it would not be a simple matter of pouring new wine into an old bottle.

"We redesigned the entire shell to include functionality based on what we'd learned [about how it performs], and also to fit the redesign of our site [msnbc.com had become msnbc.msn.com], and to ease some work-flow issues," he said.

Wells spent a week redoing the interface and making it easier to replicate for future Big Pictures. "For three weeks, I worked every weekend day; I worked probably 12 to 16 hours a day, and on the very last day, before the deadline, I was here for 48 hours straight without going home or falling asleep," he said.

One of the biggest differences between the 2004 Oscars package and the previous Big Pictures is the way video is handled inside the FLA (see the

Fig. 3.5.09 The fourth Big Picture previewed the 2004 Academy Awards, but it was completely redesigned from the previous year's Oscars package. Printed by permission of MSNBC.com.

Tech Tip for details). Wells also doubled the frame rate in the FLA, from 10 fps to 20 fps, and increased the size of the larger video window to 560 × 420 (from 480 × 370).

Other significant changes included the appearance and functionality of the playlist (the stack of gray buttons on the left side); the control bar (which allows users to pause, replay, or "scrub" the content in the big window); and the pop-up hints that appear when triggered by either users' actions or something occurring for the first time. Each of these has been constructed as a Flash "component" (like the ScrollBar described in Lesson 9), which makes them easy to use again and again. Instead of scripting them afresh for each new Big Picture, or even copying them from an older package, the components can be dragged and dropped into the movie and customized by typing parameters in the Properties panel.

The pop-up hints look and act like Windows tool tips. They not only fade up and disappear after a specified amount of time onscreen; they can also be modified (in the Properties panel) to show a pointer or to include a thumbnail image.

The control bar's modifiable parameters include its width, which buttons are shown with it, where the sub-segments are divided, and whether it includes hints. In comparison, the control bar in the first three Big Pictures looks like a preschool toy.

In addition to the hints, the control bar component uses another component that Wells built for the 2004 Oscars package: the user interface (UI) button, which can be configured to show any text on the button, or to display one of a set of icons representing stop, play, pause, fast-forward, and other standard functions. Each UI button is drawn dynamically, so just about everything about it can be modified in the Properties panel, including its color, height, and the font family.

The control bar component thus incorporates the inde-pendent UI button component and the hints component. Wells sees this as a way of making future Big Pictures not only much easier to build but also more stable and robust.

In May 2004, Wells had just finished creating a component for the playlist, which could be used for slideshows, audio players, or other interactive fea-tures—not only The Big Picture. In the new playlist component, everything is drawn dynamically, just as for the UI buttons. "You can determine what color it is, whether it has a simple icon or a thumbnail image; you can

Fig. 3.5.10 Items in the playlist can be moved to create a new viewing order for the full presentation ("Academy Awards," 2004). Printed by permis-sion of MSNBC.com.

Fig. 3.5.11 Helpful notes, which mimic Windows tool tips, pop up at various places to tell the users how things work ("Academy Awards," 2004). Printed by permission of MSNBC.com.

Fig. 3.5.12 The control bar used on the first three Big Pictures bears almost no comparison to the new component control bar. Printed by permission of MSNBC.com.

control the text that goes in it; you can determine whether the segments are draggable or not," he said.

The next step was to build the boxes at the bottom of The Big Picture as components: Your Comments (left); Related Info (center); and the Guide (right). Jim Ray completed the new Related Info box component for inclusion in "Civil Rights Today"; it uses tabs across the top rather than buttons in a stack, to provide more flexibility in new packages.

With these components, Wells said, "you can come up with other interfaces that do other things, really quickly, without having to be an expert."

Fig. 3.5.13 If users do not want to view all the types of related information in the text box at bottom center, they can select one of four other options ("Academy Awards," 2004). Printed by permission of MSNBC.com.

The control bar, UI button, hints, and playlist are all what Wells calls "UI components"; there's something else he calls a "content component," and an example is the voting option at the end of each nominee segment in the 2004 Oscars Big Picture. This component allows an editor or designer to set up a graphic voting feature for any five choices, with an optional "Who's Out" box in the sixth position. The component is used every week for MSNBC.com's "It List" feature (*http://www.msnbc.msn.com/id/4043608/*); it has also been used to invite users to rate Tiger Woods's golf opponents and to rank possible choices for the U.S. Democratic vice-presidential candidate. In all these cases, the user votes and then gets to see how all other users have voted so far. Wells explained that his help is not required when an editor decides to use the voting component: "They just type in the text and ask the photo editor for the photos."

Fig. 3.5.14 Users are invited to post their comments ("Academy Awards," 2004). Printed by permission of MSNBC.com.

Not everything in The Big Picture will be "componentized," though. The popular "Red Carpet Fashion" segment from the 2004 Oscars package is unlikely to become a component "because at most, you'll build that once a year," Wells said.

TECH TIP: MULTIPLE VIDEOS

"The huge, gigantic, abysmally bad disadvantage to video in Flash, still, is twofold," Wells said. "One, when you put video in here, like the anchor video, you cannot *hear* her as you scrub through the Timeline. If you're trying to synchronize things, then you have to be a lip-reader. Or hit Ctrl-Enter and publish again and again and again until you get it right. That is a production nightmare."

What he referred to is the way video on the Timeline normally works in the FLA (see Appendix C): The producer cannot hear the audio track while working in normal editing mode, even though it's possible to scrub back and forth through the visuals.

"The other disadvantage: Any time you put two videos in the same FLA, they would both lose sync almost immediately—and they'd be *way* off, and there's no way to correct it." That is, the video and its own audio would not stay synchronized, even though they had been imported as a single file.

In the first three Big Pictures, the producers had to plan around this problem whenever they used any video in addition to the anchor/guide. "We did some pretty weird things" to compensate, Wells said. "It was very fragile."

The solution—and the way Wells has handled video in Flash beginning with Oscars 2004—is to separate the audio from the video before bringing them into Flash, import silent video as an FLV, import the audio track as a WAV, and then place the two on separate layers in the FLA Timeline, starting on the same frame. This eliminates both disadvantages. (Note, however, that audio and image could *still* go out of sync if an individual user's computer processor is slow.)

"Because of this trick we found, we don't have to worry about audio ever getting out of sync," Wells said, "and we can use as much video as we want."

All the video is edited in Avid. "Our whole intake system here runs on Avid, so it's easy for me to pull one and put it on my machine," Wells said. The video, originally captured from broadcast tape, must be in its final edited form before being output as two separate files

Fig. 3.5.15 Video from nine films plays simultaneously, but with only one soundtrack ("Academy Awards," 2004). Printed by permission of MSNBC.com.

one video only, the other audio only. Wells outputs video at a frame rate of 20 fps (to match his FLA) and a data rate of 300 Kbps. He uses the Sorenson Squeeze Compression Suite to output the video File as an FLV (a file in the Flash-only format that can be viewed in Editing mode in the FLA).

Note that both the video and the audio are on the main Timeline of the segment—not inside a movie clip. Each segment is an external SWF (see Appendix B), which is loaded into the main movie when the user clicks a button on the playlist. In any segment of a Big Picture, pretty much everything is directly on the Timeline, so that the control bar component—which is in the main SWF—can successfully run the show. (The Tech Tip in Case Study 3 explains how this works.)

For the first three Big Pictures, Wells had to put the anchor/guide video into a separate SWF and import it to the segment's Timeline, which increased the complexity of controlling the segment while it played.

Wells takes the audio file into Sound Forge and normalizes it there, "because audio coming out of Avid is quiet, for some reason," he said. "So you might have a WAV file playing in your Big Picture that didn't come through Avid, and it would be much louder than what the anchor was saying, and you don't want that." The early Big Pictures suffered from some great variations in the sound, he admitted.

The new, improved method makes for a Timeline with a large number of layers (each imported video is dropped onto a new layer), but it's relatively simple to control, because it's completely Timeline based.

The file size of the SWF may be gigantic, but Wells doesn't even know how big it is. He doesn't care, because he's concerned only about the Bandwidth Profiler (see Appendix A). "That thing is key, and most people don't know how to use it," he said. Given Flash's native streaming ability, and the fact that tracking data showed most users who watched the 2004 Oscars package had an average bandwidth of 500 Kbps or better, his concern centers on managing the download so that users are watching something relatively low-bandwidth at the beginning of any segment—like motion graphics created in Flash—and the higher-bandwidth content has time to download in the background.

When he's testing the movie in Flash, Wells sets the Bandwidth Profiler to 300 Kbps (Flash MX 2004: View menu > Download Settings; Flash MX: Debug menu > Customize) and keeps his eye on the red line. Typically, the user will be waiting for content if the profile goes above the red line on any frame early in the movie. The control bar on the main Timeline is scripted to manage the preload for any new segment, reading a variable Wells scripts into the segment to determine how many frames to load so that, under typical conditions, the user will not need to wait once the segment has started to play. (Some Flash authors script to detect percentage loaded, while others prefer to monitor the number of frames loaded.)

After the current segment is fully loaded, the control bar will spawn a new movie clip offstage (and out of sight) and begin to load the next segment, using the playlist to determine which segment that will be. If a user watches all the segments in order, there will never be any waiting after the show begins.

FLA files for this case study Tech Tip are on the book's Web site.

TRACKING USE

Wells puts great stock in collecting data about how people use any Big Picture. "It's worth it, if we spend three weeks doing something, to know how successful it was," he said. While MSNBC.com collects various usage data for the site overall, and for individual stories, Wells wanted more details about The Big Picture. His solution: Use the system that handles user polls on the site. By saving data continually while the user is in The Big Picture and then, when the user closes out of The Big Picture, writing it to the polling system as if the user had just completed a poll on the site, the package can capture usage information about everyone who opens it.

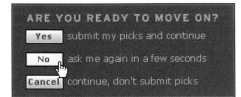

No personal information about the user is captured—only information such as which segments the user opened, whether the user watched the entire segment or quit before it finished, and how long the user spent with The Big Picture overall.

Fig. 3.5.16 At several points in the presentation, users were invited to rearrange the nominees for an Academy Award in rank order. Before it moves ahead to the next segment, the package gives the user a chance to finish deciding ("Academy Awards," 2004). Printed by permission of MSNBC.com.

While 27 percent of all users who started the 2004 Oscars package quit after less than 1 minute, 20 percent spent 5 to 9 minutes, 9 percent spent 10 to 14 minutes, and 11 percent spent 15 or more minutes, according to Wells (the full package lasts about 20 minutes if a user just sits back and lets it play).

"You can only interpret this in comparison to other things we know about our site," Wells said. He paused dramatically, clearly pleased with the implications, before he finished: "Ten to 15 minutes is what the average user spends on our site in an entire month."

The way the tracking data are saved, technically (consult the Flash Help files if you want to understand this thoroughly), is that while the user is in The Big Picture, some ActionScript is continually writing to a *shared object*, which is much like a Web browser cookie. Cookies are stored on a user's machine and can be read only by the Internet domain that wrote them; the idea is that a returning user can be identified as someone who has visited a site previously. In Flash, the shared object can be used to save a game score and position on your machine, for example, so that you can restart the game at the same point if you return to the site later.

The other piece of the puzzle is something Flash calls the Local Connection object, which allows two separate SWF files to communicate with each other. When a user opens the Web page for The Big Picture, even though the package itself is not open yet, there's an SWF embedded in that page. To spawn the Big Picture window, the user clicks a button in the embedded SWF. The local connection is thus established between the Web page (which remains open) and the SWF in the pop-up window, which is The Big Picture.

When the user quits The Big Picture, the information stored in the shared object is sent back to the first SWF (the one on the Web page that spawned the Big Picture window), which can then write it to the MSNBC.com polling system. All the Flash shared object can do is save information written by the SWF itself, and the SWF cannot find out anything about the user except a few facts about the system it is running on (for example, the operating system and the Web browser being used).

Still, the data collected this way can be valuable. Data can be extracted from the polling system in the aggregate, and statistically accurate samples can be derived.

"No one else around here has this kind of data for what they do," Wells said. "No other feature on our site has such detailed analysis of how it worked."

One key finding from the 2004 Oscars package data concerned an advertisement that was programmed to run as soon as the first segment ended. The user might choose to watch any segment first, but as soon as that first one concluded, the ad began to play. The ad took over the Flash presentation and could not be stopped or skipped; once it began, the user had only two options: Let it play to the end, or quit The Big Picture entirely by closing the pop-up window. The playlist was frozen and would not function while the ad was on.

Half of the people who saw the ad closed the window and left. Wells poked the data on a printed page with an accusing index finger. "There's my evidence," he said. "We can't disable the playlist."

Fig. 3.5.17 The Web page that launches the Big Picture window gives users a choice of four segments as a starting point. Half of all users chose one other than the default, which was "Critic's Take" ("Academy Awards," 2004). Printed by permission of MSNBC.com.

For the 2004 Oscars package, 60 percent of all users used the playlist. For the previous Big Pictures, that figure was about 40 percent. About one-fifth changed the order of the segments in the playlist, an option that was possible for the first time in the 2004 Oscars package. "The playlist was more effective this time, I think because it was designed more like an interface," Wells said. "It was more obvious; it was bolder. And that was one of the things we set out to do. We wanted to make this more discoverable."

Another finding of interest: People will choose what they are most interested in, given the ability to do so. On the Web page from which the 2004 Oscars Big Picture is spawned, four entry points are offered: "Our Critic's Take"; "Rank the Nominees"; "Red Carpet Fashion"; "Independent Films." Nearly half of all users chose an entry point other than "Our Critic's Take," the default. Fashion was the most popular after the default; independent film was last, selected by 8 percent of all users who made a choice.

"The independent film one was a segment we put a lot of our own personal production time into, because we found it interesting. It was about the business of movies, and it was very journalistic. Fashion was not at all journalistic," Wells said. "The journalistic one was the least popular. Damn."

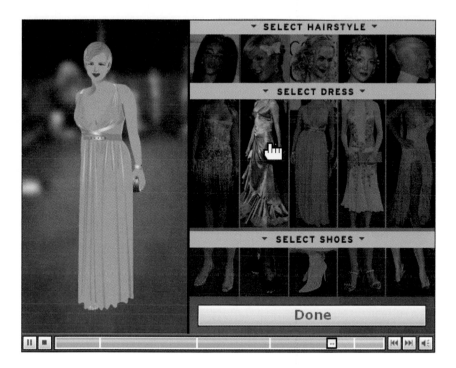

Fig. 3.5.18 The fashion segment of the 2004 Oscars package proved very popular with users. Printed by permission of MSNBC.com.

This got Wells thinking about how to promote segments from The Big Picture outside the package. "On stories about independent film, you could tease The Big Picture there. Or, how do you take just that segment and put it in the video player, where more people will see it? Since it's a stand-alone SWF file, how do you use it somewhere else, in addition to The Big Picture?"

Recalling his original idea to repackage pre-existing interactives and video inside The Big Picture, he said, "Now it's flipped: Make stuff for The Big Picture and see where else you can put it."

Another unexpected spin-off from The Big Picture has been the transfer of Web content to television. MSNBC TV now does a weekly segment about the MSNBC.com "It" List, chatting about who's in and who's out, according to users who vote on the Web site.

In the 2004 Big Picture about the Academy Awards, MSNBC.com gossip columnist Jeannette Walls did a video standup about fashion, where still photos of actresses attending the previous year's ceremony were interspersed with Walls's commentary about what they wore. "The TV producers saw this and said, 'We want to air that on television,'" Wells said.

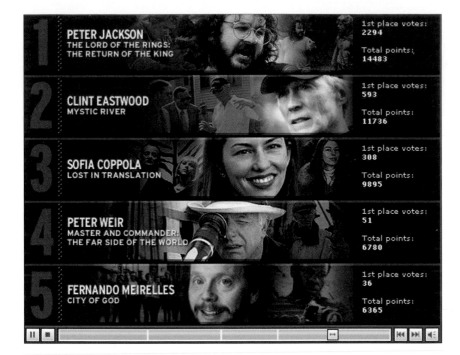

Fig. 3.5.19 Users' picks for the major awards were tallied and shown on the site at the end of the relevant segments ("Academy Awards," 2004). Printed by permission of MSNBC.com.

"So, what a weird paradigm," he continued. "Usually online is repackaging. We're actually making stuff that they can broadcast." It turned out that the television network could not use the fashion segment "as is" because the Web site's rights to use the still photos did not permit reuse by the network, but the point holds up: Now MSNBC.com is talking with the cable network about MSNBC TV airing versions of the Big Picture segments, possibly even a half-hour TV version of each Big Picture.

Case Study 6

Agence France-Presse: Tour de France

URL: *http://www.afp.com/*
Interview Date: June 23, 2004
Location: Paris
Interview Subjects:
- Marlowe Hood, Project Manager, Medialab Development Department, AFP
- Julien Demoly, Project Manager, Art Movies (*http://www.artmovies.com*)
- Russell Copping, Engineer, Medialab Development Department, AFP
- Jon Dillon, Client Relations, Medialab Development Department, AFP
- Jean Fèvre, Software Manager, Database Development, AFP
- Nicolas Giraudon, Chief, Sports Marketing, AFP
- Damian McCall, Journalist, Sports Multimedia Desk, AFP
- Gilles Ramel, Chief, Sports Multimedia Desk, AFP

"One hour before the start of the competition, it doesn't work. One hour after, it works."

—Julien Demoly

 Note: To see an archived version of the 2004 Tour de France package, in English, go to the Web site for this book.

Every summer since 1903 (except during the two World Wars), a select group of hardened men has set out on bicycles to attempt one of the toughest events in sports, the Tour de France. Across more than 2,000 miles in twenty-three days, punishing mountain climbs, sprints, and team and solo time trials grip the entire nation of France and cycling fans around the world. In 2001, Agence France-Presse (AFP) attempted to pack the entire event into a database-driven Flash application with live updates during each stage of the race. Flash would allow Web users to see and interact with the race information in real-time. The development schedule gave AFP two months.

Fig. 3.6.01 When the
Flash graphic first opens, a
vector animation of three
cyclists riding plays while
the maps and data are
loading. Printed by permission of Agence France-
Presse.

"We had no idea, really, of the overall functionality of large Flash animations," said Russell Copping, an AFP engineer who worked on the launch
of that first application.

With some luck and the right people in the right places, AFP pulled it off.
A news agency measures success through its clients, which choose the products they want to pay for. "We were absolutely ecstatic to have five or six
clients that first year. Right off the bat, they paid top dollar," said Marlowe
Hood, project manager. "We had *Le Monde, Figaro*; we had major titles in
the French press; we had a couple of sponsors as well." In 2003, with the
U.S.'s Lance Armstrong riding for a fifth consecutive victory, AFP sold
the Tour de France package to North American clients for the first time.
The next year, with Armstrong riding for a record-shattering sixth win, AFP
added ESPN.com to its client roster.

"The elusive 'plug-and-play' product," said Jon Dillon, who manages client
relations for AFP's development department. He explained that for many
years, AFP had a number of "raw" sports databases that it would license to
clients such as CNN, which then devoted technical and design resources to
creating their own front-end interface to display the information appeal-
ingly to online users. Not every client has those resources, though—and so
the idea was to build something AFP could sell as a complete package, "a
site in a box, basically," Copping said.

AFP's first discussions focused on the European football (soccer) leagues,
involving a huge number of players, teams, and matches on a ten-month

schedule each year. The French league alone has twenty clubs (teams); each country has its own league. "Finally, we scrapped the whole thing," Hood said. It was just too complicated for a first front-end project.

On the opposite end of the complexity scale, AFP tried an in-house development project for Formula 1 racing, with a staff graphic artist acting as lead developer. (Formula 1 entails only one race at a time, and in 2001, for example, only seventeen races.) The resulting application looked absolutely great, but the scripting was too buggy to permit its deployment.

With the Formula 1 season already under way, in March 2001, AFP's development department zeroed in on the upcoming Tour de France for its first Flash database product. The news agency had the database already; although it was not offered for sale to clients, it had been used in-house for several years. Raw results are fed into the database during each stage of the three-week race, and AFP journalists file reports from the race via the wire service. All that AFP needed was a plug-and-play front end, or interface, that would let Web users view and interact with the data.

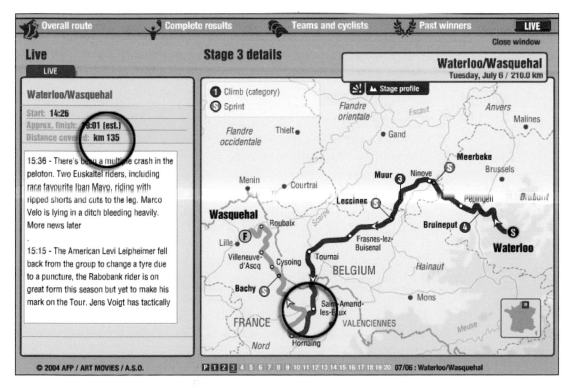

Fig. 3.6.02 The position of the *peloton* is marked in red when the graphic is in "live" mode. The distance covered (circled at left) is updated as the map line is updated (screen capture: July 6, 2004). Printed by permission of Agence France-Presse.

Hood concluded that AFP could not produce the project entirely in-house; they did not have the necessary skill sets. "We had a budget for two [people] to come for a six-month development. So I thought, we'll get one real crackerjack Flash graphic artist and one engineer, and they'll work together," Hood said. "I must have interviewed two dozen, maybe three dozen people, and it just didn't click. I couldn't find a way to put the team together."

PRODUCT DEVELOPMENT

Agence France-Presse resembles other newswire services, but it has strong connections to the French government, and part of its mission has always been to keep the government informed about what's going on in the world. Today, international sales account for a larger percentage of the bottom line than do sales in France, but that was not always so. The agency made a major expansion into the English-language market starting in 2002, increasing its English-speaking staff fivefold.

"Our principal client used to be the state," Hood said, and representatives of the French government remain on the board of directors, as do representatives from the major print media of France. But budget concerns pushed the agency to make itself more responsive to market demands in the late 1990s, and in 2000 AFP created a department devoted to developing new products with an eye on expanding its client base.

"We never had a development department before," Hood said. "We never even had a marketing department." Now a staff of international and commercial marketing experts and development staff work closely together, both to repurpose existing content for new platforms (such as mobile devices and the Internet) and new markets, and to create entirely new products. "The multimedia development department is the development nerve center within AFP, period," Hood said.

The Medialab unit, within the development department, started out with the recognition that to come up with successful new products, a mixture of skills is necessary. "We had three journalists, two engineers, a business development person with a strategic marketing background, and we had Jon [Dillon], who had a lot of sales experience with AFP," said Hood, a career journalist. "As we invented new services and products, being able to evaluate them from all those different perspectives at once was something we had not been able to do before."

Hood was the head of AFP's English-language graphics department when Medialab was formed. AFP wanted to look into providing animated online graphics to its clients, and Hood felt ready for a change, so he became a project manager for the new department.

Today AFP sells a subscription Flash graphics service in English, French, German, and Spanish, which is also translated into Chinese. Hood planned a full integration of AFP's animated and fixed graphics staffs by the end of 2004. "We'd like as many as possible of our graphic artists to be ambidextrous—that is, to be able to do both," he said. At the time of this interview, the animated graphics service consisted of two full-time Flash artists, and usually a third working full-time on contract; plus one full-time editor for each of the four European languages. On the fixed graphics desk, there were two full-time editors for each language.

Clients who subscribe to the animated graphics service are guaranteed ten graphics a month. "With a small team, that's about all we can comfortably guarantee," Hood said. A subscription to that service does not include special applications like the Tour de France or Euro 2004 packages, or AFP's Flash photo slideshows, which are also developed by Medialab under Hood's direction.

The development of the Flash slideshow product illustrates part of Medialab's role in the news agency. A cultural separation between journalistic, technical, and administrative groups within AFP sometimes led to time and money being expended on product development within one group without consultation from the other two. More than once, a project already in development turned out to be unworkable after representatives from an outside group got a look at it; assumptions about what an outside group could do proved to be dead wrong. Projects were scrapped after significant resources had been invested—a scenario today's more budget-conscious AFP tries hard to avoid, in part by using the development department as a clearinghouse for new ideas.

For the Flash slideshow, the lack of communication was as much geographic as cultural: "At one point I think we had five [slideshow projects]—one was developed in Washington; two or three here, one developed by a photo service, one by an engineering service; one in Hong Kong," Hood said. "So think of all the hours going into that development."

AFP did eventually choose and deploy one of those five slideshows, with minor modifications, early in 2003. The development department "got all the parties together in one room, and there was finally agreement on which was the best one. There may have been one black eye," Hood joked. "I think the hatchets have been buried by now."

After four years, Medialab has proved itself. "We have a settled place in the agency," Hood said.

THE INTERFACE

After interviewing dozens of Flash designers, Hood began to doubt that AFP would get its 2001 Tour de France application. "And then Julien Demoly from Art Movies walked in the door, and it turned out they had developed their entire expertise on bending Flash 4 and Flash 5 toward databases," he said.

Art Movies, a four-person company with an office on the Left Bank in Paris, had built a Flash application for *Le Monde*'s Web site for the 2000 U.S. elections, using real-time data to update the Flash graphic throughout the night of Election Day (and long into the next day, as Paris time is six hours later than U.S. East Coast time). It made the perfect calling card at AFP, because the real-time updating envisioned for the Tour de France application was what no one else seemed able to deliver. A large part of the reason lay in a Macromedia strategy to push a server product called Generator, which was later scrapped, to handle interaction between Flash and a database. That solution wouldn't work for AFP; its product had to be independent of the server so that AFP's clients could install it and make it work on their own Web servers.

In May 2001, in other words, getting a stand-alone SWF file to call and read external data required a creative quantum leap in scripting finesse. The elections application proved that Art Movies had already made that leap.

Users can receive the AFP 2004 Tour de France application in any of five languages: French, English, Flemish, German, or Spanish. Switching languages for everything in the Flash graphic, from button text to live commentary, is made possible by both ActionScript and the AFP database.

The package opens with a map of France; the map shows the Tour route as a snaking blue line punctuated by dot markers, designating the start and finish of each stage (or leg) of the race. Rolling over a stage changes the text in a small box showing date, distance, place name, and other data. Clicking any stage opens a zoomed-in map with terrain details and place names, on which new dot markers designate climbs and sprints in that stage. Clicking one of the sprint or climb markers at any time after the event has concluded opens a small pop-up box showing the top three finishers. These

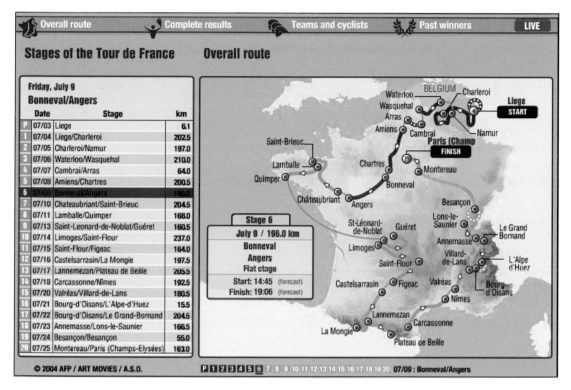

Fig. 3.6.03 Each day during the race, a different stage is ridden. Both the list of stages (left) and the overall map (right) highlight the current stage in red (screen capture: July 9, 2004). Printed by permission of Agence France-Presse.

lists represent a crucial part of the real-time updating the AFP journalists perform during each stage: As soon as the winners for a climb or sprint are posted, the journalists enter them into the AFP database, and the Flash graphic refreshes itself to show the new data.

Other features of the zoomed-in stage maps are a stage profile, showing a topographic view with altitude and distance for each segment, and a thumbnail inset of the larger map, with a rectangle outline indicating the area shown in the zoomed version. Clicking the inset returns the user to the full map.

"It's hard to exaggerate the place that the Tour de France has in the French collective imagination," said Hood, a native of California. It struck him sharply for the first time when he was standing with a few French journalists, watching the race on a TV in the AFP newsroom. "I was looking at the body language of my colleagues and noticing the way they reacted; they were picking up on all kinds of strategic and tactical maneuvers that were invisible to me," he said.

Fig. 3.6.04 During the race, users can look at future stages of the race by using the navigation below the main map. Rolling over a stage on the map changes the information shown in the box circled at left (screen capture: July 8, 2004). Printed by permission of Agence France-Presse.

"I realized it's like me watching a baseball game. I can see the nuances— like whether the signal is to bunt, or not—which I know how to read because I grew up watching baseball. A French person doesn't see any of that. The Tour de France has the same level of complexity. You have team events, individual events, cyclists who are there not to win but just to support somebody on their team—which can change from one stage to another. You also have sprints, you have climbing events—so there's an enormous complexity. Basically all French people grow up knowing how to read the Tour de France, in the same sense that having grown up in the U.S., I have some ability to read baseball."

The Flash application includes pop-up panels to display team data, individual cyclist data, tables of stage standings and overall standings for all teams and all individuals (users can re-sort the data by clicking column headings in the table). The pop-up panels for teams or individuals can be dragged to the side and kept open; they can also be minimized with a roll-up effect. These information modules exploit something Flash does very well: Layering a large volume of information in a compact space, without forcing the user to leave the main information display.

"Flash was a perfect instrument to display complex data," said Russell Copping, an AFP engineer.

DESIGN AND USABILITY

The team at Art Movies knew—really *knew*—they could do what AFP was asking in 2001, according to Julien Demoly, of Art Movies. "We had already tested all the configurations, tested the live loading in real-time, using text files to update data and refresh the animations," he said, referring to the elections package Art Movies created for *Le Monde*.

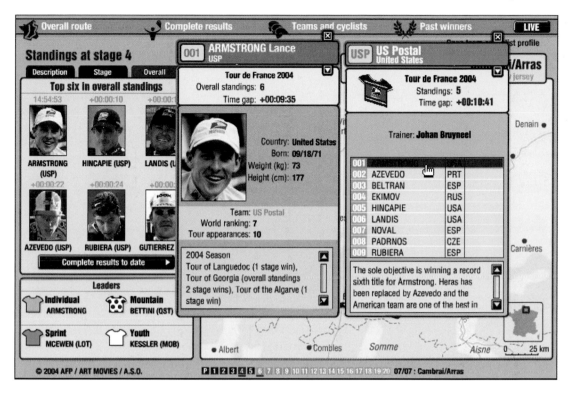

Fig. 3.6.05 Pop-up panels provide statistics about each cyclist (center) and each team (right). This is what AFP calls "warm" data; it can be finalized before the race begins. Clicking one of the six photos at the left opens the info panel for that rider (Stage 4: July 7, 2004). Printed by permission of Agence France-Presse.

Work on the Tour de France package took "two, maybe three times longer" than they had estimated, though. There was barely enough time to complete it in the two months before the race began.

The biggest challenge was not the scripting, but the ergonomics—what many online developers would call usability. "How we organize each screen, the hierarchy of the information," Demoly said. This, for him, was the most important part of creating the Tour de France package. Significant time was also spent on integration with AFP's Tour de France database and on testing the application in various Web browsers on different operating systems.

The graphic artists at Art Movies first prepared all the screen layouts for the application, using Adobe Illustrator, and got AFP to sign off on each one before they did any work in Flash. The mockups were flat, or static, and the designers had to explain the types of animation and what each button would do. Defining the second level of information (the individual stages of the race) proved most difficult: "What to show, what to provide,

Fig. 3.6.06 Photos of the top six cyclists appear for each stage of the race, as well as the top six overall. When the user clicks a photo, a panel opens to provide details about that cyclist (screen capture: July 21, 2004). Printed by permission of Agence France-Presse.

where to put it, what to call it. There are the detailed results of each stage, and how to show the data for all the teams," Demoly said.

"Then we would come back and say, 'How can we make this more visually attractive? How can we add photos?' " Hood said. AFP didn't want to see only tables of data. "That's how we got the idea to show [photos of] the six top finishers in every stage. The heavy lifting—the hours and hours we put in—was to decide how to prioritize the information, and at the same time, make it visually attractive and user-friendly."

It worked, in the end, because Art Movies had already created a coherent work-flow, a system for having a database engineer, a Flash programmer, and graphic artists share ideas. They had figured out how to integrate *les métiers*—which in English is simply "trades," but which Hood translated as "skill sets."

As for technical problems, there were very few. Trouble with the text files loading improperly on Internet Explorer on the PC, even though they loaded fine on the Mac, was eliminated simply by changing the frame rate from 24 to 12 fps.

In 2002 and 2004, Art Movies made no significant scripting changes to the Tour de France package, according to Demoly. In 2003, however, they optimized the script for Flash Player 6, changing a lot of the outdated Flash 4 and 5 techniques and implementing some new functions, such as the ability to track how long the user spends in each module, and the option to change advertisements, depending on how long the application is open.

Demoly said he saw no reason to adopt Flash MX 2004 in the near future. ActionScript 2.0 is "very, very heavy," he said. "Before doing anything, you need 20 K of code. It doesn't meet the needs of developers like us." In discussing Art Movies' concern for small file sizes and faster loading, he explained that one technique they use is to edit the fonts they embed in the Flash file so that no unused characters are included in the download.

They construct each stage map as a set of layers in the Flash file, so that only the topography, or bottom layer, is a bitmap. On top of that, they lay

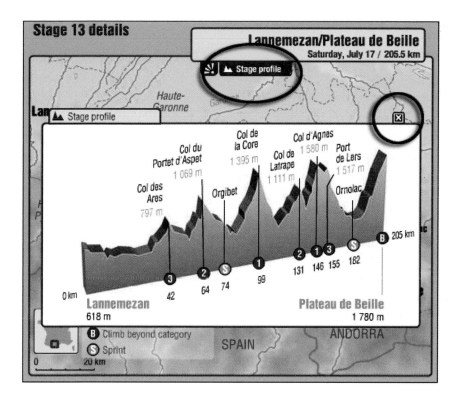

Fig. 3.6.07 At any time a stage map is onscreen, the user can open a profile of that stage by clicking the Stage Profile button (oval, left). The profile has its own obvious Close button (circle, right). Stage 13 had seven category climbs, which are named on the topographic view. The altitude of each climb is also given (screen capture: July 17, 2004). Printed by permission of Agence France-Presse.

in the rivers and boundaries as an imported file from Illustrator; on top of that, the place names are Flash text. Another layer contains 20-km segments in red for the entire stage, which are used to show the position of the *peloton* (the main group of riders) while the stage is live. Each stage of the race is a separate SWF file, ranging in size (in 2003) from 13 to 56 KB. Each year, Art Movies must create new maps for the application, as the stages change each time the Tour de France is ridden; in 2004, there were twenty stages, plus the prologue. The stage profiles are separate SWFs, each about 12 KB.

TECH TIP: REFRESHING LIVE DATA

The AFP Tour de France package is not a single SWF file that loads in text, photos, and maps. It is a collection of many different SWF files that interact with one another through ActionScript. These techniques are explained in Appendix B (loading external SWFs) and Lesson 10 (loading external text files).

One of the more unusual aspects of this package is the live updating of the data while a Tour stage is "live." Several sets of data are updated: The up-to-the-minute commentary posted by the AFP journalists in the Paris newsroom; the position of the *peloton* on the current day's map; the final results of each Tour stage; and the overall results for the race. The users see new information appear in the Flash graphic as the race progresses. How can all this be accomplished?

First, consider the structure of the event. The Tour de France lasts just over three weeks, with two rest days when no racing occurs. Each day's race is one "stage"; in 2004, there were twenty stages, plus a "prologue," which also counted in the final results. Each stage has its own set of files in the Flash package, so each stage has its own map, contained in one SWF (total: twenty-one stage map SWFs). Each stage also has its own external text file, containing the commentary written by AFP journalists during the stage.

Additional text files provide information relevant to the whole event, not just the individual stages.

If you have read Appendix B, you know how to script a button to load an external SWF. In the Tour de France package, when a user clicks a button for Stage 10, the stage map SWF for Stage 10 is loaded into the main movie. The stage map SWF includes ActionScript that then loads the text file for that stage. The Web server folder thus contains at least two files for each stage: the SWF and the text file.

When the Tour is "live," however, it is not necessary to click a button to see the map of the live stage. If the Tour package script determines that a particular stage is live today, it automatically loads and displays that stage map and the appropriate commentary text. ActionScript

Table 3.6.01 The chart shows the SWF and its companion text file.

SWFs	Text Files
main.swf	stages.txt
stagemap001.swf	stagetext001.txt
stagemap002.swf	stagetext002.txt
stagemap003.swf	stagetext003.txt

makes that determination by checking today's date and the current time, and then by comparing those with information in the loaded text files.

The script is able to determine whether the current year is the same as the year of this event, whether the current month falls within the range of months for the event, whether today's date matches the date of a stage (and not a rest day), and, finally, whether today's stage should have started by now, according to the current hour and minute (which must be converted to the current time in France).

The first text file that loads (stages.txt, in the example) contains basic data about all the stages of the Tour, including some of the critical data for comparison: date and start time for each stage of the race. It also contains the place names for the start and end points of each stage; for example, "Paris (Champs-Elysées)" is the end point for the final stage. This text file can be created days or weeks before the Tour; it will not need to be changed or updated after the event begins.

The main movie (main.swf) first ensures that the stages.txt file has loaded completely. Once that is done, the main movie can execute a function to compare today's date with all the dates in the text file (stages.txt). ActionScript gets the current date and time from the user's computer. If the comparison fails, or comes up false, then the function can just quit, meaning the Tour is not live today.

Table 3.6.02 The chart shows data in the text file stages.txt for one stage; all twenty stages and the prologue are included in the real file.

Variable Name	Value
this year	2004
stage001num	001
stage001start	Liege
stage001finish	Charleroi
stage001month	7
stage001date	4
stage001starttime	12:35
stage001finishtime	17:15
stage001dist	202.5

If a date in the text file matches today's date, then today is a live Tour day, and the script sets several variables to indicate that, including one that indicates *which stage* is live today. These variables will be used by other functions that automatically reload the commentary file and check to see whether the stage has been completed.

If today is a live Tour day, an ActionScript function will automatically load the appropriate stage map SWF into the movie clip on the right-hand side of the main movie. That SWF then calls in the commentary text file. It also reloads the SWF on the left-hand side of the main movie to ensure that all previous data are deleted.

While a stage is live, if the map for that stage is visible, a timer function continually reloads the stage map SWF. Each time the SWF reloads, it in turn reloads the commentary text file. It also checks whether the stage is complete; if it is, the script clears the timer, and the stage is not considered "live" anymore. When the stage results file is available for today's stage, that panel can be loaded on the left side of the main movie (it shows the photos of the top six riders for the stage).

Since the text file will need to be reloaded once every minute or so, it makes sense to use the "setInterval" function and not the "onEnter-Frame" event handler. (You have seen both of these before, in Lessons 8, 9, and 10.) The difference between the two is very important in a case like this. The "onEnterFrame" event handler should be used when you need to check for a new condition many times each second; it executes at the frame rate of your movie. The "setInterval' function, in contrast, can be used much less frequently, such as to check for a condition or to execute a function.

If you want to change the contents of a text field every 30 seconds, for example:

```
var elapsedtime = 0;
function timeToReload () {
    elapsedtime = elapsedtime + 30;
    timer_txt.text = elapsedtime.toString() + "seconds";
}
timerCounts = setInterval(timeToReload, 30000);
```

Note that "30000" equates to 30 seconds (time for "setInterval" is measured in milliseconds).

If you decide you want to stop the timer after 90 seconds, you must write a "clearInterval" inside the function called by "setInterval" (see "Automating the Slideshow," Lesson 10, Step 9):

```
function timeToReload () {
    elapsedtime = elapsedtime + 30;
    timer_txt.text = elapsedtime.toString() + "seconds";
    if (elapsedtime >= 90) {
        clearInterval(timerCounts);
        timer_txt.text = "Time is up!";
    }
}
```

Each commentary text file contains three important values (in addition to the comments themselves):

- The actual start time of the stage (blank until the stage begins)

- The actual finish time of the stage (blank until the stage ends)

- The current distance ridden by the *peloton* (updated throughout the stage)

Because each stage map SWF loads its own commentary text file, these three values can be checked each time a stage map is loaded, whether it loads automatically or as a result of the user clicking a button. If the start time is blank, for example, then the stage has not started. If the start time has a value but the finish time is blank, then the stage is live. If the finish time has a value, the stage is not live; it is complete.

The distance variable in the commentary text file controls the position indicator on the current day's map. By checking the value of that variable each time the text file is reloaded, the script can activate a movie clip in the map SWF to show the location of the *peloton*. The value is the distance (in kilometers) covered by the *peloton* so far. If today's stage is 200 km, and each indicator shows a 20-km increment, then there are ten movie clips to activate, one at a time. If the dis tance value is less than 20, then activate the first movie clip. If the distance value is greater than 20 but less than 40, then activate the second movie clip. When the stage is no longer live, none of the movie clips are activated.

You can probably think of some applications where this technique might be used to update a graphic even if there is no need to update live commentary.

 FLA files for this case study Tech Tip are on the book's Web site.

REAL-TIME COMMENTARY

Most of the stages of the Tour de France begin around midday, while Europeans are at work. The AFP graphic enables a cycling fan to follow the action live—without video, but with journalists' running commentary and the intermediate winners updated at each event where points are scored (climbs, sprints, and time trials).

Six journalists working in French, English, and Spanish staff the sports multimedia desk at AFP, headed by Gilles Ramel. In addition to the Tour de France, they cover the World Cup, the Euro, and summer and winter Olympic Games—not only during the competitions but also in advance, by collecting data on the teams and athletes and entering it into AFP's database. For the Athens Games, for example, they were compiling biographies of about 400 words each, plus a photo, for hundreds of the athletes, in three languages, simultaneously with covering three weeks of the Euro football (soccer) championships, followed by three weeks of the Tour de France.

Three journalists (one for each language), plus an overseer, covered the Tour de France on the desk. Damian McCall, the English-language writer on the team, explained that as he is writing, he can open a Web page and see what the others are writing—not only the two on the desk with him, but also two others filing remotely in Flemish and German. "We want to be writing more or less the same information," he said.

Their coverage relies on the television set clamped to a column above the desk; the official Tour de France Web site (*http://www.letour.fr*), and in the early part of any stage, before the TV coverage begins, France 2 radio.

"There's no journalist running after the Tour de France," or filing from the scene during the race, McCall pointed out. "The helicopter has a camera;

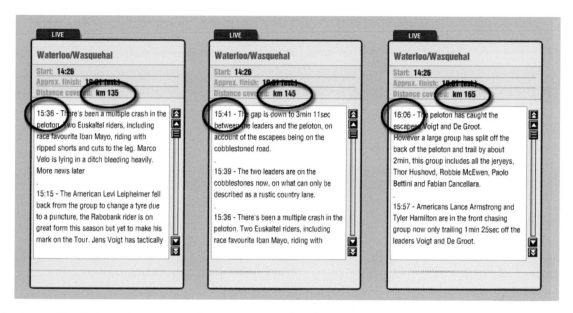

Fig. 3.6.08 The Flash graphic automatically updates the display of live commentary written by AFP journalists. Note the time stamp on each comment (circled) and also the distance covered in this stage, which updates throughout the stage (screen captures: July 6, 2004). Printed by permission of Agence France Presse.

the motorcycles have cameras. They're not writing." AFP does have journalists on the ground, but their main tasks are to show up at the start and then somehow make it to the finish in time to interview the leaders at the end of the stage.

Each new comment posted from the news desk starts with the time, in 24-hour format. The user can scroll down in the Flash graphic and read earlier comments. "We tend to write every time something happens, or every ten minutes throughout the race," McCall said. In the final kilometer of a flat stage, when the sprinters are limbering up to make a run for the line, he may file as often as every 30 seconds.

"It's really tough writing live running copy. I first did it on football matches five years ago. It's nerve-racking," he said. "Cycling is a lot calmer than football, where you're trying to cover several matches at one time." Even so, "there will be blood, sweat, and tears on at least half the stages. You will have your work to describe action as it happens."

The overseer, another seasoned journalist, walks around the desk and reads over each writer's shoulder. "That's essential," McCall said. "It's not a complete disaster if we make an error, because we can correct it. It's not like the wire, where we have to file a correction and kill the earlier version." That is, the earlier text can simply be revised and replaced. The watchful eye of the overseer not only helps keep errors to a minimum but also assists in coordination among the comments. McCall noted that even though each journalist writes his own remarks, they don't want to have extreme differences in length or content among the versions.

"We have an advantage over the journalists on the scene because we have TV," McCall said. He had edited copy filed from the Tour for two years before he first worked on the multimedia desk in December 2002. "This job is about 40 percent editing, 30 percent writing, 30 percent translation—preparing French text for the English market—rather than being a reporter," he said. "We really enjoy it."

The rights to use the data about the race are licensed from the Amaury Sport Organisation (*http://www.aso.fr*), which owns the content, results, and name of the Tour de France. AFP deploys its own photographers for the Tour, and at the end of the day, the journalists create a Flash photo gallery with twenty-four photos that have been edited and validated by AFP's photo editors.

Before the Tour in 2003, McCall worked on preparing the fact files about each cyclist, which are part of the Flash application. As a result, he would often remember personal details during the Tour. "There was one guy making a break at the finish," McCall said, "and I remembered—he's *from* this town [where the stage finished]. So he's making a break for home! We were the first ones to have that."

Covering the Tour is not just another day at the office. "You get really quite involved," McCall said. "We were all brought to tears at one time or another, just because of the shattering physical demands" on the cyclists.

CONSTRUCTION AND COOPERATION

For any sport, "there's a point of view about what you need to see for that sport," and you won't know what that point of view is unless you're a serious fan, a journalist, or an editor, who follows that sport. Russell Copping, engineer, worked as a kind of mediator between the journalists, the database designers, and Art Movies to make the first version of the AFP Tour de France package not only functional but also a good experience for its intended audience.

Copping referred to the organization of information in the Art Movies design as "zonal," meaning each module (actually an SWF loaded into a movie clip) is a unique zone within the application. One of the challenges in planning the package was that "when we decide that *these* variables are loaded in *that* zone, we can't then suddenly say, ah, I want all of the variables that are loaded *there* loaded into that [other] zone—because these are separate modules. The journalist may come back and say, 'What? You don't show this information in that page? That's unacceptable.'" So whenever Art Movies delivered new screen design mockups (created in Adobe Illustrator), Copping said, it was essential to have experts from both the journalism side and the database side sign off on them.

Another challenge: In 2001, a 56-Kbps modem was state of the art for online content delivery; most users had only 33 Kbps. "We had no idea of file-weight limits, loading times, the complexity of 209 riders, with first name, surname, team, height, weight—all of these to be entered in, pulled up quickly, looking for response times of, hopefully, under 5 minutes when you launch the animation," Copping said.

He recalled they had a report from America Online that said if a page did not load in 8 seconds, the user would give up and leave. "Our animation wouldn't load in anything under 2 minutes on a 56K modem," he said. "So we did all these things with loading animation, so you saw something right away, saying, 'It's coming, it's coming. It's loading the rider file, it's loading the map.'"

Three years later, most users did not experience those long waits, even though the script and the file sizes were essentially the same; Web access speeds had increased.

In the beginning, much of the work AFP did involved just learning how to work with a company like Art Movies, which understood Flash and its data-loading quirks, but didn't necessarily understand sports journalism or the structure of AFP's database.

Copping had plenty of experience with using traditional HTML to display information extracted from databases on the Web. "With HTML and XML, you make your rules," he said. There are structural tags, "but within that, you do what you want. The thing with Flash was, it interpreted what we did. It made the rules. You must display it and process it in *this* way."

Live updates presented additional challenges. "With our traditional graphics, the information they display is cold. It's not updated. If it's updated, they make a new graphic," Copping said. "It was a very different experience working with a graphical view which was live." For Art Movies, the idea of checking and reloading only certain files every minute was new. There is no reason to reload, for example, the information about individual cyclists during a live stage, because the first name, surname, team, height, and weight of a cyclist will not change. The live commentary, however, must be reloaded continually during a live stage.

AFP identifies files as "cold," "warm," or "hot," depending on how they might be updated. Cold files would be, for example, information about all the stadiums in the European football leagues, or the names of the stages in the Tour de France. Those files, delivered before the event begins, are not expected to change.

Team information would be considered a warm file. The members of each team in the Tour de France must be set by a certain date. But after that date, under special conditions, the team roster might be changed. There has to be enough flexibility to correct a team roster data file, but there's no need to check for new team files every minute. A "warmer" file would be a set of statistics published at the end of the day, such as the General Classification for the Tour de France, which is updated at the end of each stage. After that data file is sent, it's not at all likely to be changed again that day, but it might be changed once each day.

A hot file can be updated every minute. "For Art Movies, they build their engine to say, okay, I know when I call this module in this zone, I need to make sure I recall this file, because it can change," Copping said. Part of the functionality includes knowing when the hot file is actually hot—that is, while the race is happening—because there's no need to check the file in the evening, after the stage is completed.

"With a product like Tour de France, we actually send a file which depicts 'I'm now in live mode.' This triggers the animation to say, 'Now you must look for other files, because I'm in live mode,'" Copping said. The football (soccer) leagues are much more complex, he noted, because multiple matches are played at the same time in different stadiums; nevertheless, that application works on a similar principle.

The files are sent from AFP's servers to the client's server on a "push" basis: When the AFP database is updated, it sends out new files as necessary, and those files overwrite the files already on the client's server. The client's server never initiates a request to the AFP server. The Flash application (the

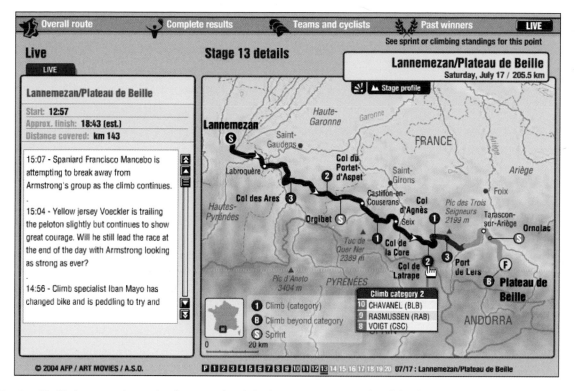

Fig. 3.6.09 Clicking on a dot marker for a completed climb or sprint pops up a list of the three winners of that event (screen capture: July 17, 2004). Printed by permission of Agence France-Presse.

SWF) resides on the client's server too, and it simply looks in the local directory for the files it needs.

"We have a live update path, so when we deliver to a client, they give us a delivery point with a set structure, and we control the whole structure," said Jon Dillon, who manages client relations for AFP's development department. "We ask them to mirror that structure and point to the index HTML page to put it online. Then every time we have a new version or a new module, we just overwrite the old one." This includes graphics files as well as data files; if an SWF needed changes, a new version could be sent to the client. "So the next time someone clicks on the thing, they receive the latest version," Dillon said. "It's automatic."

TEXT VS. XML

For all the Flash applications built from the Tour de France model, the data files are plain text, not XML—even though AFP has been using XML inter-

Individual overall standings after stage 16				
			Find	
Cyclists	**Time**	**N°**	**Team**	**Country**
1 ARMSTRONG Lance	67:53:24	1	USP	USA
2 BASSO Ivan	+00:03:48	61	CSC	ITA
3 KLODEN Andreas	+00:05:03	17	MOB	DEU
4 ULLRICH Jan	+00:07:55	11	MOB	DEU
5 AZEVEDO Jose	+00:09:19	2	USP	PRT
6 MANCEBO Francisco	+00:09:20	71	BAL	ESP
7 TOTSCHNIG Georg	+00:11:34	81	GRL	AUT
8 SASTRE Carlos	+00:13:52	67	CSC	ESP
9 CAUCCHIOLI Pietro	+00:14:08	134	ALS	ITA
10 LEIPHEIMER Levi	+00:15:04	151	RAB	USA

Fig. 3.6.10 Data from A.S.O. (organizers of the Tour de France) is fed into AFP's database, which outputs a text file that the Flash graphic can locate and "read" as soon as it's available. Individual and team standings appear in the graphic just minutes after the stage has been completed. Printed by permission of Agence France-Presse.

nally since 1997. The reason goes back to 2001, when the ability of Flash 5 to handle larger XML files left a lot to be desired. Flash MX changed all that, but Art Movies had already scripted the Tour de France application to handle AFP's data as text files.

Before the 2000 Olympic Games, AFP had maintained a separate Access database for each sport it covered. Beginning in 1998, a project led by Jean Fèvre at AFP undertook to combine all sports into a single SQL Server database, beginning with the 40 sports of the summer Olympics. In 2001, the Tour de France data remained in a separate Access database. In 2002, the data for the Tour de France were integrated into the larger database, but the change had no effect on Art Movies or its scripts in the Flash file. The reason: Fèvre and his team rewrote the scripts that extract data from the database and transform it into the text files used by the Flash application.

"They give us the format of the text file they want, and we change what was output to the text file," Fèvre said. "But for them, nothing changes. It is exactly the same thing."

For Art Movies to change the ActionScript to read XML files instead of text files would require extensive work and time—not only on the parts of the script that read the files, but also on the script that constitutes the "engine" in the master SWF, which coordinates all the files and handles checking and updating within the application after it's already open.

"To look and move forward is not a cheap experience," Copping said. "You look at the longevity of a product. You need a module that you pay for and design to run for x years."

"The database development is finished for this product," said Julien Demoly, of Art Movies, referring to the Tour de France package. "XML, I'm not sure we need it. For new developments, yes. For the old ones, I'm not sure we need to change them."

"Maybe we'd pick a sport we don't do now, such as tennis, and start from scratch," Copping said. "Then, maybe, we would go back and rework these."

For now, the original model holds up fine. Clients who bought the World Cup package in 2002 and then bought the Euro 2004 package have never complained about the similarities between them; graphically they are different, and all the data are new, but the underlying structure within the Flash application remains the same.

"It takes a long time to have facts about the product and the business model. It's not in one year that you know if a product will work or not," said Nicolas Giraudon, head of sports marketing for AFP. "If we had listened to some AFP directors, or other people, maybe these products would have been killed earlier. We tried to keep them and look where we would go with this, and now it's being successful."

The Tour de France package formed the model for four other database-driven Flash products from AFP: World Cup 2002, Euro 2004, the European football leagues, and Formula 1.

"We look back, and we look at our development costs, and we say, okay, I think we made the right choice," Copping said. The punishing two-month development experience in 2001 turned out to be a wise investment.

Afterword: The Future

What's next for Flash journalism? No crystal ball is ever 100 percent reliable, but we can consider several factors from the present and use those to help us see ahead.

Broadband: In Canada and South Korea, more than half of the homes with Internet access have high-speed access. In the United States and some northern European countries, such as Denmark, Sweden, and Switzerland, more than 10 percent of all consumers had broadband access in 2004. By 2008, the number of business and consumer broadband subscribers worldwide will triple, to more than 325 million, according to a forecast made in July 2004 by the Yankee Group, a market research firm.

Broadband means less waiting. The Internet is less of a chore, more of a habit, when it's always on and not so slow. Add to that a generation of young adults who grew up with the Web and wireless technologies.

Cell phones: News agencies such as Agence France-Presse and Reuters provide wireless news feeds that can be accessed via cell phones. As phones with color screen displays and Internet connectivity continue to replace older phones, use of these services (particularly for sports and business updates) will likely increase.

Almost 90 percent of DoCoMo's 46 million customers in Japan subscribe to its data services.

Nearly 50 percent of U.S. Internet users ages 18 to 27 had phones with Internet access capability, according to a March 2004 survey by the Pew Internet & American Life Project.

A 2004 study by consulting firm A.T. Kearney and Cambridge University found that 41 percent of 4500 mobile phone users surveyed in thirteen countries said they expect to be "regular or heavy users" of wireless data services such as e-mail, games, music downloads, photo messaging, or news updates by sometime in 2005.

Internet-enabled cell phones mean instant information, anywhere. Some of that information will be graphics. Macromedia released Flash Lite 1.1, a new version of the Flash player for cell phones, in June 2004; DoCoMo started using Version 1.0 in 2003.

Convergence: This buzz word refers to the consolidation of media organizations such as Bertelsmann, Grupo Prisa, NBC Universal, Sony, Time Warner, and Viacom into global giants that control interests in journalism, book and magazine publishing, music, movies, radio, and TV. Their ownership of multiple media encourages them to reuse and repurpose their content, as well as to cross-promote products. So "convergence" also refers to how a property, such as a best-selling book, might be promoted on a talk show on a TV network owned by the corporation that also owns the book's publisher. It refers to MSNBC.com's ability to use NBC News video online.

Finally, "convergence" can refer to journalists' skill sets, which increasingly span multiple media. It is becoming more common for journalists to move from TV to a newspaper, or from a newspaper to online media, or from a magazine to TV, during the course of their careers. It is becoming more common for a photojournalist to carry an audio recorder, and for a TV reporter to write articles for the station's Web site.

For journalists just starting out, sometimes having experience in more than one medium gives them the edge over other candidates for a job. That may not mean knowing how to use Flash; it could mean knowing how to write and use a camera, or how to edit audio. It could mean knowing how to make a story "interactive."

For the major media corporations, the more efficiently they use and reuse content, content containers, products, and personnel, the more they increase profits. You might think of it as selling the same thing in different packages—or maybe by creating new combinations, it's possible to tell more stories, to do more journalism.

Databases: In the early 1990s, the infant Web was a collection of HTML pages that had to be updated by hand, by individual Webmasters typing on their keyboards. After Jeff Bezos launched Amazon.com in 1995, the power of databases for online commerce became apparent to everyone. It took years for most newspapers to migrate their legacy publishing and classified advertising systems to new configurations that took maximum advantage of database technologies. By 2004, using databases to manage content on Web sites had become the norm for all but the smallest sites.

Once content is organized in a database, separated from containers that might confine it within a particular medium, it can be searched, extracted, and used in various formats and combinations. Sometimes it's most useful in tables, grids, and lists of facts and figures. But databases also hold entire stories, links to photographs and other assets, and associations conjured on the fly by words entered into a search engine.

Databases by themselves are rather dry. By putting a great face (or interface) on a tool that lets users find and interact with data, a designer can transform the value of the database.

News site registration: Many Web sites require users to register—providing a user name, password, and other information—before being able to read articles or view features on the site. While numerous users have happily registered for Amazon.com, eBay, and Yahoo!, some people are not as willing to register at news Web sites, even when no subscription fees are involved. News organizations would like to rely on registration data to analyze traffic on their sites, in part to use in setting advertising rates, and also to figure out what would attract more users or keep the same ones coming back.

The question news site managers are asking, then, is what will make users willing to register, willing to provide some information in exchange for information, and willing to log in each time they return to the site?

TV graphics: If you have a great-looking animated map in Flash, with all Flash text and without any bitmap elements, you can display it online at just about any size, and it will still look great. If you need a tiny version, you can open the FLA and mask the text layer, save it again, and it will look great, even at a small size. You can output a GIF or a JPG from that file and use it on a Web page where you don't need animation. Or you can output it as an MOV (a QuickTime movie) and copy it from the hard drive to videotape. Once it's on tape, you can show it on TV. It could be a map, a 3D animation, or a chart showing economic growth. The graphic could be exactly the same both on the Web and on TV.

This goes back to the idea of convergence: If a graphic can be created in a way that makes it portable—reusable in various media, on various platforms—the utility of the graphic increases.

Video: As more people get broadband access to the Internet, online video becomes more appealing, because users don't need to wait forever to see it. However, broadband does not solve the problems caused by multiple players and plug-ins: lack of control over the player interface, intrusive downloading and updating requirements, and reduced opportunities for interactivity. Using video online makes little sense if the video acts just like TV, as if the user would sit back and simply watch. We don't even use TV that way anymore.

Video, like other content, increases in value when it becomes reusable. When digital video becomes not only searchable but also combinable with other content, it gets easier to adapt it to formats that are more fragmented, and more interactive, than traditional video formats.

Ashley Wells of MSNBC.com pointed to TiVo and iPod as devices he loves to use and sources of inspiration. "You look at TiVo and you go, 'Look how clear it is to use TiVo, how simple.' iPod, the way it interfaces with the Music Store—you can rate things, you can share things. Those are all interesting concepts."

Some people surf the Web while they watch TV. Nicolas Giraudon, chief of sports marketing at Agence France-Presse, has been thinking about this for at least three years. He knows that during sporting events, fans do it to get a summary of the game and background information on players and teams. A fan in the stadium might even want to use a cell phone to look up stats during an event.

Every major news Web site had Flash advertisements on numerous pages by 2004, and yet many of those same sites hesitated to mix Flash and journalism. This seemed incongruous to Rob McLaughlin of CBC Radio 3, who speculated that maybe there are misperceptions that Flash files are too large, require some special technology, or have no place in day-to-day journalism. And yet, he said, pointing to the Flash ads: "Every major site in the world is serving their revenue stream in this format."

The future of Flash journalism is linked to television and to print media as well as to the Web. It's inseparable from the job descriptions of journalists and the pursuits of corporations that have financial interests in many areas in addition to journalism. It's not that journalism can't be done without Flash. It can. But certain kinds of journalism—certain formats, combinations, and ways of telling a story—can emerge only if certain elements are in place.

The key to a great piece of journalism is not the tool but the journalist, the person who has a vision of what the story is and how it should be told. Journalists are less and less likely to work alone. Can you share your vision of a story with other people? Can you do whatever is needed to make sure that story is told in the best possible way?

About the Flash Journalists

The people interviewed for the case studies in this book came to journalism (and to Flash) in various ways. Their stories demonstrate that you don't always know where your talents and interests will take you.

DAVE BRAUNGER, DESIGNER/ARTIST

startribune.com

Interview Date: May 17, 2004

Dave Braunger studied graphic design in college because he "was always interested in art growing up." Being less interested, though, in "the money-grubbing rhetoric of commercial design" led him to get involved with the student newspaper at the University of Wisconsin–Eau Claire. "Working at a college paper is great, because you can pretty much do anything you want," he said. "I reported, I took pictures, I networked their computers, I paginated the paper. It was a great experience that I wouldn't have gotten anywhere else."

After graduating with "an unofficial minor in journalism," Braunger took a news graphics internship with the *Star Tribune*—the nearest large newspaper to Eau Claire. (Braunger grew up in Waunakee, Wisconsin.) At the end of the internship, he spent a few months in Europe.

"When I came back, I just lucked out—they were looking for someone for the online" at the *Star Tribune*, he said. Someone who remembered him from his internship gave him a call. Asked what he knew about online then, Braunger laughed and answered, "Goose egg! As soon as I realized that was what the job was for, I grabbed a book and just copied a frameset [in HTML], so I could have something that showed some initiative."

He started work as an online graphic artist at the *Star Tribune* in December 1996. It never gets old, he said, because "nothing we do repeats itself. Give it a year, and the tools you're using are completely different."

His first Flash project was a map for the state fair in August 1997, using Flash 3. "I think I spent a couple of weeks working on it. You could click on stuff and you'd hear a duck"—he grinned broadly—"or you'd hear somebody shilling mops." The map of the fairgrounds came as a digital file from the newspaper, and the audio came from Regina McCombs, who had just started worked at the *Star Tribune*. The package also had photos—very small photos, according to Braunger.

When he started using Flash, he had no background in any kind of programming or animation. "The nice thing about where I work is, you're given an area of expertise, and it's kind of your duty to push forward and try new things," he said. "It's buying a lot of books, sitting down, ripping through a lot of examples—trial and error. It takes a lot of time." His voice conveyed no trace of regret, but rather a sense of satisfaction.

Braunger doesn't think designers should manage Flash journalism projects alone, without a producer. "We've tried that before. It absolutely does not work unless we have leadership." If the designers produce it alone, he said, "It will be really pretty—but shallow."

Advice about Flash

"You need to think outside the code, because you limit yourself so much if you think about how difficult it's going to be. The project is going to be difficult regardless of what you do.

"I've found that if you can verbalize what you want it to do, it is much easier to code that, rather than jumping in and trying to swim toward your goal. You can say, 'I want this window to change to text when I do this,' and you diagram the whole thing out, verbally, and then you go back and figure out how you can do each of those things through code—or however you're going to be doing it—within Flash."

Braunger explained that "diagramming verbally," for him, means he both draws it and writes what the drawings mean. He sketches boxes and lines on loose-leaf paper that "show how things will react to other things." Blocks of text accompany each step in the drawing. "Usually I have to talk it out in order to write it down," he said.

GIOVANNI CALABRO, NEWS DESIGN MANAGER

washingtonpost.com
Interview Date: April 25, 2003
As an undergraduate at George Mason University, Giovanni Calabro was the managing editor for the online edition of the student newspaper. The

journalists taught him news writing, and he taught them the software tools of the Web, including Photoshop.

"Journalism really struck me, when I started to work at the paper, as something I enjoyed," he said. As a result, he applied for a job at washingtonpost.com and started working in the photo department in 1998. A year later, he transferred to the design department.

At the student newspaper, he wrote HTML and designed pages. At George Mason, he took only one basic computer programming course and completed a degree in communication. (His original focus was music.) He began to "play with Flash" in 1999.

"Having a strong design knowledge really can take you far, regardless of what you use," Calabro said.

Advice about Flash

"Don't get caught up in the capabilities of the program; rather get caught up in the requirements of a story. Let the program work for the story."

BRIAN CORDYACK, SENIOR DESIGNER

washingtonpost.com

Interview Date: April 25, 2003

Brian Cordyack's introduction to journalism came from TheAngle.com, an online magazine where he worked as the graphics manager while he was a student at the University of Virginia. An English major and fine arts minor who "loved computers, art, and English," he jumped at the opportunity. Through a connection at the online paper, Cordyack got a one-week internship at washingtonpost.com in the winter of 1998–1999 that led to a summer internship there, during which he started learning Flash.

"I got to do a Major League Baseball All-Star preview in Flash," he said. "I learned so much that summer—I got really excited."

His first job out of college: Designer at washingtonpost.com, summer of 2000.

Advice about Flash

"Restraint. Use Flash when it tells the story better. If someone wants to go to design, you really need to understand color theory, perspective, all the basic fine art principles. Someone's going to take it over the top because they know which two colors work together, which two colors can really set the mood of the piece."

RAFA HÖHR, INFOGRAFISTA

elpais.es

Interview Date: June 18, 2004

Ever since childhood, Rafa Höhr has loved to draw. He claims to draw better than he speaks. But he completed a five-year *licenciatura* in journalism (*periodismo*) at the University of Seville, the equivalent of a master's degree in North America, and he thought he would be a reporter.

"To work at *El País*, you must be a journalist," he said. Everyone who comes to the newspaper without a degree in journalism, or lacking significant experience at another professional journalism organization, must complete the *El País* Master of Journalism (a one-year training program) before being offered a position in the newsroom; this policy applies to the graphic artists as well as to the staff of the Internet news desk. Höhr joined the online staff in 2000, after about ten months in a similar job at *El Mundo*, another major daily in Madrid.

Before he decided to become a journalist, Höhr considered attending a fine arts school. These have a long tradition of respect in Spain—and also a demanding entrance examination, which Höhr passed. But when someone is very young, maybe he doesn't really know what he wants to be, Höhr said, by way of explaining that he had also applied for the journalism program—and in the end, that's the way he went.

He never planned to be a news graphic artist, and received almost no instruction in graphics as part of his university program. While he was a student, though, he earned spending money by designing posters. He also took extra classes in drawing and painting that were not part of his journalism curriculum. After graduating, he went to work as a newspaper reporter and learned news graphics on the job—starting with design of the weather page.

"The Internet has been a great adventure," Höhr said. He was working as a graphic artist for a group of small daily newspapers in the south of Spain, including his hometown paper, *Diario de Cadiz*, when Mario Tascón, then director of at El Mundo Digital, called him up and asked him to come to Madrid.

Tascón had become familiar with Höhr's work through the annual Congreso Internacional de Comunicación, an important journalism conference hosted every year at the University of Navarra, in Pamplona. They also had friends in common. The conversation went something like this, according to Höhr: Tascón said, Come to *El Mundo* and do animated graphics for me on the Internet. Höhr replied, "What is Internet?"

He moved to Madrid and began working at *El Mundo* in the fall of 1999. Tascón went to *El País* not long afterward, and Höhr accepted his invitation to follow in the summer of 2000.

Advice about Flash

"Do not lose sight of the fact that this is a tool, just a tool." Although we were discussing only the Internet, soon it will also be television, Höhr pointed out. CNN+ and the local television networks make many requests for Flash maps and 3D drawings from PrisaCom, the parent company of elpais.es. So although Flash is a valuable tool, and maybe its value is growing, it's still only a tool.

"What really matters is that you are sharing news, and you have to know what that news is from the beginning, and all the way to the end. What part of the news will you be sharing; how will you relay it; what is the scope of the news; in what way will you present the information?"

MARLOWE HOOD, PROJECT MANAGER

Agence France-Presse

Interview Date: June 23, 2004

In China, working on a Ph.D. dissertation in the mid-1980s, Marlowe Hood decided to change direction and go into journalism. Through friendships with several journalists, he became familiar with their work and thought it would suit his temperament better than a life in academia.

Because he had the language skills and knew the country well, he "almost instantly" got a job as a stringer for *The Wall Street Journal* in Beijing. He covered the Tiananmen Square protests for the *South China Morning Post*, an English-language daily based in Hong Kong. He also worked for *U.S. News & World Report* in China.

After four years with the *South China Morning Post*, Hood relocated to New York, where he worked freelance, mostly for magazines and writing mostly about China. He also wrote a regular column there for the *South China Morning Post*. The move to Paris came in the early 1990s, for family reasons.

Hood took a position as head of Agence France-Presse's (AFP) English-language graphics department, even though he had no previous experience with graphics, because it was the first thing available within the news agency. As an American in Paris, Hood had limited options for staff journalism jobs (even though he speaks French fluently). Managing the graphics desk didn't require him to be an artist; it did require experience in journalism. It also required fluency in multiple languages, since AFP's infographics are not merely translated but are reworked and even redesigned for different language markets.

When AFP formed its Medialab 2000, "I was ready for a change, and they said, given your experience with graphics, we'd like you to look into animated graphics. We'd like to evaluate the possibility of sending out some kind of animated graphics," he said.

No one at AFP was working with Flash then. "No one even knew what it was," Hood said. "I went on the Internet and started looking, and I realized that Flash had already emerged as the de facto standard. It was obvious that whatever we did, it was probably going to be done in Flash."

AFP built its ability to deliver Flash content both by sending existing graphic arts staff out for training and by hiring some new people who already knew Flash. "Our real anchor in the Flash graphics service was somebody who came from in-house," Hood said.

Under Hood's guidance since 2000, AFP's development department has launched a Flash graphics subscription service; a plug-and-play Flash photo slideshow package; and a suite of sports database products that includes the Tour de France, World Cup, Euro (soccer championship), and Formula 1 racing.

Advice about Flash

With the kind of development commitment required for Flash applications such as AFP's sports database products, an organization must make choices informed by marketing expertise. "With the Winter Olympics [in 2002], we made a strategic error, developing too much Flash and other stuff, at great expense, that AFP sales people could not really sell," Hood said. "Like the Titanic, we saw the iceberg but could not turn away fast enough."

The organization must evaluate what resources it owns and what should come from outside—whether through contracts to purchase live data, such as AFP has for the Tour de France (with the Amaury Sport Organisation) or European football (with Infostrada Sports), or through a revenue-sharing agreement, such as the one with Art Movies, which develops the graphics and Flash scripting for the Tour de France package.

NELSON HSU, SENIOR DESIGNER

washingtonpost.com

Interview Date: April 25, 2003

Nelson Hsu majored in fine arts, with a concentration in graphic design, at the University of Maryland. His only experience with journalism before beginning work at washingtonpost.com was "one intro to journalism class." His interview at washingtonpost.com came about as the result of an internship elsewhere; his supervisor there recommended him to a headhunter firm, which sent his résumé to washingtonpost.com. At that time, he was torn between print and online graphics. Ultimately, online work appealed to him more because of the higher pay, he admitted.

He worked briefly as a contractor for washingtonpost.com before being hired for a full-time design position in 1999.

Like the other washingtonpost.com designers interviewed for this book, Hsu started working with Flash in 1999. He attended the annual Flash-Forward conference in New York for the first time in the summer of 2000.

"It changed my entire perspective on design," he said. When he came back to work, he started using ActionScript in earnest. Hsu usually did poorly in math classes, he said, and never took any programming classes in school, "but the nice thing about Flash is, you don't need that."

Advice about Flash

"With Flash, you can never be satisfied with what you know about it. The program is so powerful, once you get comfortable with what you know, you're going to be falling behind. No matter how much you think you know, there's always someone out there who knows more. Always keep reaching higher."

REGINA MCCOMBS, MULTIMEDIA PRODUCER/PHOTOGRAPHER

startribune.com

Interview Date: May 17, 2004

In a speech and television class in high school, Regina McCombs "had one of those moments," she said. "We were doing the TV stuff, and I thought, you mean somebody would pay me to do this? That would be cool." She studied media management and production at a small school in northern Minnesota, Concordia College, where she earned a communications degree with a minor in English. She took multiple internships, including one at a local television station, where she wrote commercials and publicity for in-house productions.

"I actually thought all along I was going to be a writer," she said. Her first job, at "a little tiny cable startup" in a suburb of Minneapolis, "was equivalent to going to small-market television," she said, because "nobody knew anything, we were all making minimum wage, and everybody did everything." McCombs wrote the station's newsletter and other promotional materials, but she also learned to edit video and did some studio camera work.

When the venture went under, she tried freelancing for a while, and then went to work as an assistant producer for a half-hour television show for what was then the American Lutheran Church Media Services Center. McCombs did location arrangement and setup, scriptwriting, and a lot of offline video editing—before the show was canceled.

From a woman she had known through that job, McCombs heard about a video editor position at the local NBC affiliate, then called WTCN, which is now KARE-TV. McCombs, now four years out of college, applied and got the job. "It was the first time I had worked in news, so that was sort of a shock to my system. But I discovered I loved it, just loved it," she said. She spent 14 years there.

She went from editing full-time to the assignment desk, and then started to shoot and do field producing, which "really is reporting, only I was never on camera." KARE was "a fabulous place to learn news photography," she said. Carrying the 35-pound camera was not a problem for her. Sometimes she "heard about it" from people in the field ("That's a mighty big camera for such a little girl"), but the male photographers offered only support and encouragement.

The switch from TV news to online journalism came while McCombs was working on a master's degree at the University of Minnesota. She called four Web operations in the Minneapolis area: the *Star Tribune*, Pioneer Planet (from the *St. Paul Pioneer Press*), AOL Digital Cities, and Microsoft Sidewalk. "I just wanted informational interviews, really, just to see what I should study, and three of them asked me in for job interviews. I took it as a sign from God," McCombs said. She had been thinking about possibly moving to online in ten years or so. "I could see the day coming when I would want to do something different."

She concluded that AOL and Sidewalk didn't interest her, because "they didn't seem very newsy." She was interested in the *Star Tribune* job, but it went to an internal hire. So McCombs stayed at KARE and kept going to school. About six months later, the *Star Tribune* called her back and offered her a job.

"That was probably the single hardest decision I have ever had to make, because I really wasn't unhappy [at KARE]," she said. "It was a great place to work. It's the Number One station [in its market] and well respected for the photography."

McCombs started working at the *Star Tribune* in summer 1997. "I always tell people that instead of changing markets, I changed mediums."

As a multimedia producer, McCombs has multiple roles. "Sometimes I'm the news gatherer—reporting, shooting, whatever. I may not be doing any kind of producing. Other times, I'll produce a project that has almost no multimedia, just text and a lot of graphics." Her strong point, she said, is "thinking about the whole thing."

While she's no expert in Flash, she said, "I think it's really important that I know it as much as I do, partly because I can understand a lot of what Dave [Braunger] says. I can talk about it. That's true in television producing too; you have to understand everybody's role, and what it takes to get the job done, so you can figure out timing and that kind of stuff."

Advice about Flash

"One of the things we talk a lot about is how we can put all the elements together, and not have a flying window here and a flying window there. How can you do something in one [part] that doesn't repeat exactly what the other one is doing? What are you trying to achieve with this story? What are you hoping people will get out of it? And how do you help them find it and get around it? You've got to think about the overall structure. You have to think about the story as a whole, not just a bunch of clumps.

"Too much of online news, still, is what we call a Christmas tree, where you have this newspaper story that you just hang these things on—not an integrated story in any way, shape, or form."

ROB MCLAUGHLIN, EXECUTIVE PRODUCER

CBC Radio 3

Interview Date: May 12, 2004

Even though his father was a news director at a TV station in Prince Albert, Saskatchewan, while Rob McLaughlin was growing up, he did not intend to go into journalism. "I had no idea what I was doing with my life," he said. As an undergraduate at the University of Saskatchewan, he studied politics and liberal arts. "I took the LSAT at one point and never went to law school. I tree-planted for three years. I traveled the world, I was a fishing guide for a while, I worked as a farmer—I did a lot of things in my early twenties that I'm very happy for today."

Eventually, McLaughlin earned a second bachelor's degree, this time in journalism, at the University of King's College at Dalhousie University, in Halifax, Nova Scotia. He started studying journalism "to be a crack newspaper reporter and right the wrongs of the world," but he grew disillusioned when he realized how long it would take "before I got to do what I wanted to do." While still a student, he discovered Web work and "got excited about it, the power of the hyperlink and stuff like that." He also realized he had a good eye for design.

While still a student, McLaughlin "met the right people" at a conference and as a result landed a job as an editorial assistant at the *Edmonton Journal*, based on his Web skills, in 1996. "I got to sit in the newsroom, got to go to all the editorial meetings, got to see how things were decided, and learned the process of how a newspaper is run every day. That was kind of valuable," he said. But after $2\frac{1}{2}$ years, he wanted to get out of Web work. "I was sick of it, and it didn't have the respect that it needed," he said.

He left the newspaper and started doing freelance radio work, but soon he was offered a higher-paying job doing Web work again, for CBC Radio in Winnipeg. He took the job. As a result, he "fell into cahoots with people here [in Vancouver] at Radio 3," who were making an application to start a third network; he began working with them in 1999. Then in 2000, the Radio 3 group hired him, and he moved to Vancouver.

The first time McLaughlin worked with Flash was in 1998. "I remember taking that stupid tutorial with those three symbols, and you make the ball bounce; I remember doing that, and it didn't happen." He laughed.

In 1999, during the Pan-American Games in Winnipeg, he was working on a small Web site. "I built this whole crazy thing that was a site to give info about the events, but I built it all in Flash. And it was good—things moved, and it had little sound clips, and everything like that. I had a lot of fun building it." That was his first project in Flash. He worked with one other person. "We kind of figured out the program together," McLaughlin said. "I remember sitting on my little Mac in my kitchen at home, zooming in and zooming out, and I remember my wife, who wasn't my wife then, saying, 'This is all so cool, things are moving!' "

Advice about Flash

"It has less to do with Flash and more to do with the journalism. The mistake that people make when they, journalists, jump to using a technology like Flash is they try to do too much. They worry more about how the headline animates than what the headline is, what it says. Trust the journalism, and let that do the work for you."

ASHLEY WELLS, SENIOR PRODUCER, BROADBAND PRODUCTIONS

MSNBC.com

Interview Date: May 13, 2004

In both high school and college, Ashley Wells worked in TV and print. "I wanted not only to get into the different mediums but everything about them, from the layout and design to writing, editing, picture taking, and video. So I would just do anything," he said. He grew up in Phoenix, Arizona, and went to Pepperdine University in Malibu, California, "because it's beautiful, warm, and sunny, and you could go surfing."

An internship at KCAL in Los Angeles led to a job in that station's tape coordination center in 1997. Later, when the station wanted a Web site, "they looked at me and thought: Young guy—must know about computers. And they go, 'Why don't you run the Web site?' " Wells asked if he could also produce on-air segments about technology, and the station management agreed. "I had to very quickly learn HTML because I didn't already know it. I learned it through Dreamweaver, making stuff and then looking at the code," Wells said.

In 1999, KCAL flew him to New York to cover PC Expo, a huge trade show at the Javits Center, and Wells took the opportunity to visit to his cousin, who was the art director for NBC Nightly News. "He was kind of my mentor the whole way, saying, 'Learn this, get into that,' " Wells said. "So he introduced me to a guy who worked for MSNBC.com, who kept in touch with me for a while." Months passed, and then one day the contact sent an e-mail saying MSNBC.com was about to start doing "interactive television" for Nightly News, and did Wells want the job?

"If you work in the TV world, you want to get to the network at all costs. That means you're successful," Wells said. "It was a contractor job, no salary, paid by the hour, no benefits, and I had to move all my stuff out there on my own." He paused and shrugged. "It was okay. I didn't have much."

Working in Secaucus, New Jersey (where the cable TV staff of MSNBC is based), Wells created graphic information to complement on-air stories, but the audience for Web TV never materialized. "The more I did stuff for Web TV, the more I'd make them in a way that could be used on the normal Web site," he said. "More and more I started working toward that, because I realized that's where the [page] impressions are." Ultimately MSNBC disbanded that Web TV effort, and Wells moved into a salaried job with MSNBC.com.

Still based in Secaucus, he created his first Flash project in spring 2000: a calendar for the presidential primaries and caucuses. "I don't know why, but I just thought it would be cool if it moved. It was really stupid, you had to move it back and forth by clicking buttons, and it would all animate. At that time, that was cutting edge. People said, 'This is awesome! It moves like TV!' And they linked to it off the cover [of MSNBC.com]." It was his first time "on the cover."

That summer, Wells was on a team of four people from MSNBC.com who went to both of the political party conventions, in Philadelphia and Los Angeles. "I created a Flash format that was little vignettes of video. It was almost like a Big Picture, except way less technically complex," he said. It used Windows Media Player in tandem with Flash, and the team would shoot and edit about six video segments a day. "For me, it was like television. We had a lot of fun. No one looked at it. No one had the technology at the time, or the bandwidth."

Wells had tired of living in New Jersey by then; the Northeast culture didn't suit his taste. "I thought, if I'm going to be where the action is, I gotta get out of Secaucus," he said. He was also concerned that if he stayed there, where there were so few people, he'd "never move up the ladder." So he lobbied for a transfer to the main MSNBC.com offices in Redmond, Washington, and made the move in October 2000.

Advice about Flash

"With Flash, you can learn the technology and you can also practice journalism in the same space. If you have a vision and you can sell it—I mean personably, go to other people and say this is a great idea, and here's why—and then build it, you increase your chances for success, because you're the complete package. You have more control over your destiny than if you're just the idea person and you have to rely on a bunch of developers to do it for you, because they may have different ideas."

Appendix A

Preloaders

When you design a Flash movie that makes the user wait, you want the user to realize that something's coming. Ideally, you will give the user an idea of how long the wait will be. That's what a typical preloader does. Most preloaders use dynamic text to show what percentage of the movie has loaded. If the percentage is rising quickly enough, most users will hang in there. Many preloaders also use a graphic, such as a bar, to illustrate how much has loaded and how much remains.

Here you'll see how to create a basic preloader with dynamic text and a loading bar. This one looks at the complete SWF and tracks it until it is 100 percent loaded; the SWF then begins to play. Other preloaders might track the movie up to 50 percent and then start it playing. Another option is to track the number of frames loaded, and start the SWF playing after it has passed a certain frame.

 FLA files for this appendix are on the book's Web site.

BUILDING A BASIC PRELOADER

You will need two things on the Stage to make this preloader script work: a Dynamic text field with the instance name "bytes_txt" (without the quotes), and a movie clip symbol with the instance name "preloadbar_mc" (without the quotes). If you need a review of Dynamic text, see Lesson 9. Be sure to embed the font; all you need in this case are the numerals 0–9 and the percent sign (%). Set the text to align right (not left).

For the movie clip, create a rectangle with fill color only (no stroke) with a width of 200 pixels and a height of 20 pixels. Convert this to a movie clip symbol (press F8). This will be the progress bar that grows from left to right as the movie loads.

Position both your text field and your movie clip on the Stage where you want them to appear. Note that everything concerning the preloader happens in *one frame*; normally this is the first frame of your movie.

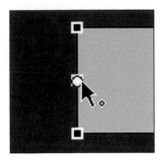

Fig. 3.A.01 Select the Free Transform tool and then select your rectangle so you can move the transformation point to the left side, center. As the rectangle grows, it grows outward from this dot. If the dot remained in the center, the rectangle would grow both to the right and to the left.

The growth of the progress bar will be controlled by ActionScript. When the movie starts, the bar should be almost invisible—or very, very short. To ensure that it grows properly, *select it* with the Free Transform tool, and move the transformation point (the white dot) to the far left, centered vertically (Figure 3.A.01). Then go into the Properties panel and resize the rectangle. In Flash MX 2004, there is a lock icon to the left of the W and H properties. Click it to unlock the two properties; this allows you to change the width but keep the height at 20.0, which is what you want to do here. Change the width to 1.0 (Figure 3.A.02).

ActionScript will do the rest of the work. Create an "actions" layer in the Timeline and write this script on Frame 1:

Table 3.A.01

```
1 stop();
2 function preloader() {
3 if (getBytesLoaded() >= getBytesTotal()) {
4 play();
5 clearInterval(loaderInterval);
6 }
7 preloadbar_mc._xscale = (getBytesLoaded()/getBytesTotal()) *
  100;
8 bytes_txt.text = Math.round(getBytesLoaded()/getBytesTotal() *
  100) + "%";
9 }
10 loaderInterval = setInterval(preloader, 100);
```

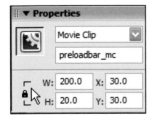 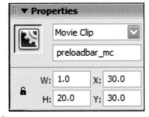

Fig. 3.A.2 To make the rectangle start out as a very narrow line, change its width to 1.0 in the Properties panel. In Flash MX 2004, you must first unlock the width and height. If you don't, the height will change in proportion to the width.

What the script does:

Line 1: Stop the Timeline here. The preloader function will tell it when it can begin to play.

Lines 2–9: The "preloader()" function.

Lines 3–6: If the value of the bytes loaded so far (getBytesLoaded) is greater than or equal to (>=) the value of the total size of the movie (getBytesTotal), then start playing the movie, and clear (delete) the "setInterval()" that is running this function.

Line 7: Change the horizontal scale of the movie clip "preloadbar_mc" to match the value of the equation. The equation will yield the percentage of the movie that has been loaded at this tenth of a second. When the equation yields "100," the bar will be 100 percent of its true width.

Fig. 3.A.03 You can dress up your preloader bar by putting it inside a frame and adding Static text, as shown here.

Line 8: Change the text in the text field "bytes_txt" to match the value of the equation, and add a percent sign at the end. The equation will yield the percentage of the movie that has been loaded at this tenth of a second.

Line 10: Creates a new "setInterval()" that executes the "preloader()" function 10 times per second. The timing is set by the numeral 100, which indicates how many 1000ths of a second should pass between each function call (100/1000 equals 1/10).

USING THE BANDWIDTH PROFILER

Flash provides a way to analyze how an SWF downloads, and a savvy developer can use this information to tweak the structure of the FLA and provide a better experience for the user. The example used here is a SWF with 401 frames and a file size of 197 KB. It contains four bitmaps, each one a symbol, each of which is tweened. Using the Bandwidth Profiler is not necessary for most SWFs of less than 100 KB.

Whenever you go into Test Movie mode (Ctrl-Enter/Win or Cmd-Return/Mac), you can open the Bandwidth Profiler from the View menu. This displays a graph that represents the progress of your movie and the amount of data that will be downloaded as it plays at a particular bandwidth, or transmission speed.

By managing what appears in the early frames of your movie, you can eliminate a long wait, and even eliminate the need for a preloader, in some cases. For example, you might put a paragraph of text on Frame 1. The text will appear almost immediately, and the user will contentedly read it, while Flash is automatically preloading everything else. This is something you can test with the Bandwidth Profiler (View menu > Simulate Download).

If you know what bandwidth most of your users will have, you can select that speed (View menu > Download Settings), and the height of the red line in the graph will change accordingly (Figure 3.A.06). Anything sticking

Fig. 3.A.04 The panel at the left side of the Bandwidth Profiler provides a lot of information about your movie. One of the most important bits of information is the "Preload" number, which indicates how many frames the Flash player is going to load before it starts playing the movie. Before those frames are loaded, your user could be staring at a blank screen.

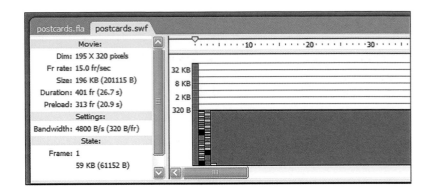

Fig. 3.A.05 This shows the Bandwidth Profiler for the same SWF, but one thing was changed—25 blank frames were added at the beginning of the Timeline. Notice how this has changed the graph. In the panel, notice the difference in the "Preload" number.

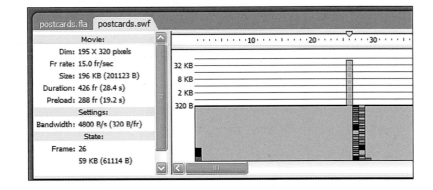

Fig. 3.A.06 By changing the Download Settings in the Bandwidth Profiler, you can simulate the speed of the user's Internet connection and see how long your movie takes to begin playing.

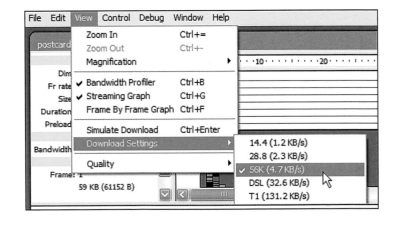

up above the red line means the user must wait. At the "56 Kbps" setting, the red line is at a height of 320 bps. At the "DSL" setting, the red line is at a height of 2.2 Kbps. You'll see how this makes a difference if you press Ctrl-Enter (Win) or Cmd-Return (Mac), which will simulate the user's experience. How long are you looking at a blank screen?

In cases where your users could have any bandwidth speed, it might work better to put something small—small in bytes, not pixels—on the first frame

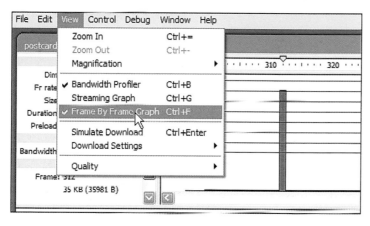

Fig. 3.A.07 You can change the graph view to represent the amount of data in each frame, by selecting "Frame By Frame Graph" instead of the default, "Streaming Graph." In the example, the last of the four bitmaps loads in Frame 312. That's why 313 frames need to be preloaded at 56 Kbps.

Fig. 3.A.08 When the Download Setting is "56 Kbps," Flash will preload 313 frames before the movie beings to play.

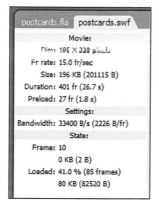

Fig. 3.A.09 When the Download Setting is "DSL," Flash will preload only 27 frames before the movie beings to play.

of a movie and let Flash manage the download itself, instead of creating a preloader.

It's outside the scope of this book to document thoroughly how the Bandwidth Profiler can be used to optimize Flash movies. This introduction aims only to acquaint you with the possibilities. As your Flash movies become more complex, and larger, you will want to experiment more with the Bandwidth Profiler.

Appendix B

Loading SWFs into SWFs

Why would you want to load one SWF into another one? If you have read Lesson 7, you probably understand why sometimes it's best to keep photographs outside the SWF as separate JPG files and load them in as needed. Loading external SWFs follows a similar logic, but the technique adds even more flexibility to your Flash work.

Imagine a Flash movie about motorcycle maintenance and repair. The opening graphic shows a motorcycle in side view. As you mouse over the wheels, the handlebars, the engine, and so on, text boxes pop up and invite you to click for more information. Any time you click, you go into a very deep instructional section, which replaces the large motorcycle graphic. Click the engine, for example, and a 3D diagram blows apart and explains how the cylinders work. A video shows a mechanic changing the spark plugs and adjusting the carburetor.

The designer could include all this video and animation inside the original SWF, but that would require a very long initial download.

Another option is to build each information section as its own stand-alone SWF file, which never downloads unless the user clicks the corresponding part of the motorcycle.

Most professional Flash developers build larger graphics and applications this way. In the case studies in this book, almost all the examples described use this technique.

 FLA files for this appendix are on the book's Web site.

TWO METHODS TO CHOOSE FROM

You will have a container SWF and one or more subsidiary SWFs. The subsidiary SWFs have no special or unusual characteristics; you can load any SWF into a container SWF.

The container, though, uses ActionScript to load (and unload) the subsidiaries. You have a choice of two methods to use. Both methods were explained in Lesson 10, in the first two exercises there:

```
loadMovieNum("photo5.jpg", 10);
loader_mc.loadMovie("photo5.jpg");
```

You can write the second option in a different way:

```
loadMovie("photo5.jpg", loader_mc);
```

This alternative way of writing the script might make it clearer to you how the two methods parallel each other.

The choice of method depends on whether you want to load the subsidiary SWF into an empty movie clip symbol, or into a "level" (which is *not the same* as a layer in Flash). Each method has slightly different results, which might affect the way you choose to design your subsidiary SWFs.

With either method, the background of the loaded SWF is always transparent.

The container movie always sets the frame rate and background color for loaded SWFs. It also sets the width and height, so if you loaded in a larger SWF, the edges of the loaded one would be cut off.

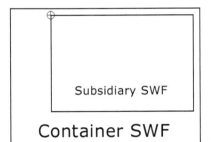

Fig. 3.B.01

Fig. 3.B.02 Inside the container SWF, the position of the empty movie clip symbol (Fig. 3.B.01) on the Stage determines where the upper left corner of the subsidiary SWF will be (Fig. 3.B.02).

Using an Empty Movie Clip

Open the FLA that will become your container SWF, or create a new FLA. Its *width* and *height* should be greater than or equal to the width and height of the subsidiary SWFs you want to load into it.

Create an empty movie clip and position it on the Stage where you want the *upper left corner* of the subsidiary SWF to be (Figure 3.B.01). Creating an empty movie clip was explained in "Playing Two Tracks at the Same Time," Lesson 8, Step 1. You can put the movie clip on any layer, but keep in mind that objects in higher layers will cover content inside the subsidiary SWF.

Give the movie clip an *instance name*, such as "loader_mc" (without the quotes). Instance names were explained in "A Sliding Panel," Lesson 6, Step 18.

Now everything is ready for your script, which you can write onto a frame or a button, or you could put it into a function that is called when some event occurs. You'll need to know the name of (and path to) your subsidiary SWF (for example, "second.swf") and your movie clip instance (for example, "loader_mc").

```
loadMovie("second.swf", loader_mc);
```

Fig. 3.B.03

Note that the name of the loaded SWF is enclosed in quotation marks, but the instance name of the movie clip is not.

You can have many different empty movie clips on the Stage and load different SWFs into each one (Figure 3.B.03). Just make sure each empty movie clip has a unique instance name.

If you need to communicate to a subsidiary SWF from the container, use the movie clip instance name, as if that were the name of the SWF. For example, this script in the container will stop the Timeline of the subsidiary SWF:

```
loader_mc.stop();
```

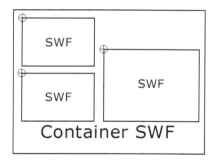

Fig. 3.B.04 If there are multiple empty movie clips on the Stage (Fig. 3.B.03), a different SWF can be loaded into each one of them (Fig. 3.B.04).

If you need to communicate in the opposite direction—to the container SWF from the subsidiary—use "_parent" (the relationship of the container to the subsidiary is *parent* to *child*, in the terms used in object-oriented programming). For example, the following script in the subsidiary will hide a button (instance name: "open_btn") in the container SWF:

```
_parent.open_btn._visible = false;
```

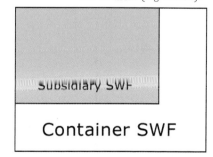

To remove the subsidiary SWF and leave the movie clip empty again, use this script:

```
unloadMovie(loader_mc);
```

Using Levels

The biggest differences between this method and the one above are: (1) With levels, the upper left corner of the subsidiary SWF will always align with the upper left corner of the container SWF (Figure 3.B.05); and (2) the subsidiary SWF will be on top of everything in the container SWF. In

Fig. 3.B.05 When the subsidiary SWF is loaded into a level, the upper left corner of the subsidiary SWF will always be at the same position as the upper left corner of the container SWF.

short, you have less ability to control the position of the loaded SWF when you use this method.

You will also need to keep track of the levels you use on your own. There is no panel to show you which levels are in use and which are free; levels are not like layers.

Open the FLA that will become your container SWF, or create a new FLA. Its *width* and *height* should be greater than or equal to the width and height of the subsidiary SWFs you want to load into it.

You can write the following script onto a frame or a button, or you could put it into a function that is called when some event occurs. You'll need to know the name of (and path to) your subsidiary SWF (for example, "second.swf"). If you have used no other levels, you can choose any number (for example, 5) for the level into which this SWF will be loaded. The main movie is level 0 (zero).

```
loadMovieNum("second.swf", 5);
```

Note that the name of the loaded SWF is enclosed in quotation marks, but the level number is not.

If you load another SWF into a level with a different number, the SWF on the higher level will cover the one on a lower level. If you load a new SWF into the same level, the old SWF will be replaced (Figure 3.B.06).

If you need to communicate to the subsidiary SWF from the container, use the level number in the format "_level5" (without the quotes). For example, this script in the container will stop the Timeline of a subsidiary SWF in level 5:

```
_level5.stop();
```

If you need to communicate in the opposite direction—to the container SWF from the subsidiary—use "_level0" to address the container (note that this could get complicated if you "nest" many SWFs). For example, this script in the subsidiary will hide a button (instance name: "open_btn") in the container SWF:

```
_level0.open_btn._visible = false;
```

To remove the subsidiary SWF and leave the level empty again, use this script:

```
unloadMovie(_level5);
```

Fig. 3.B.06 If additional subsidiary SWFs are loaded into higher levels (e.g. 10, 11, 12), they will overlap the SWFs on lower levels. If a new SWF is loaded into a level already occupied by a loaded SWF, the new one replaces the old one.

HIDING AND DISABLING BUTTONS

An important consideration when loading SWFs is *the presence of buttons* on lower levels or layers in the container SWF. Those buttons will remain functional—unless you use script to disable them. If they are not disabled, the hand cursor will appear when the user mouses over the buttons. This can be quite confusing if the user cannot see the button anymore; it will not be clear why the hand cursor has appeared. For this reason, the script shown earlier (setting the visibility of a button to *false*) can be quite useful.

As an alternative, you might prefer to disable the button and leave it visible. For a SWF loaded to a level, that can be accomplished with this script:

```
_level0.open_btn.enabled = false;
```

For a SWF loaded to an empty movie clip, it can be done with this script:

```
_parent.open_btn.enabled = false;
```

However, if the user can still see the button (that is, if the button is not covered up by a subsidiary SWF), this may be more confusing than completely hiding the button. So consider the difference between the properties "_visible" and "enabled," and decide which one will work best in the given situation.

Note that whenever a button's visibility has been set to *false*, the button is automatically disabled also.

Appendix C

Video in Flash

Video files are large, and editing video can consume a lot of time. The real challenge is compressing the video—not putting it into Flash. Okay, everybody wants to do video. But you have been warned.

Once you have a video file, open Flash's File menu and select "Import." Then, depending on the file format of the video file, you may be given an option to "embed" or "link to" the video. The correct choice is "embed," unless you are going to export your Flash movie as a QuickTime file (typically, you would not do that).

If you import a video file to the Stage, a dialog box will ask if you want to add a huge number of frames to the Timeline. Click Yes. If you import to the Library, you'll get that question later, when you drag the video to the Stage.

Regardless of whether you choose to import the file to the Stage or to the Library, it will show up in the Library. You can always delete it from the Stage and drag it out of the Library again without importing it a second time.

Once the video is on the Stage, you can drag it into position, use the X and Y coordinates in the Properties panel, or align it (using the Align panel) as if it were a symbol.

That's all there is to it. In either Flash MX or Flash MX 2004, the video is now inside your Flash movie and ready to play. You can drop regular Stop and Play buttons onto it (see Lesson 5), and they will control the video. You can also add opening credits, closing credits, or even subtitles on separate layers in the Timeline.

EMBEDDING VIDEO

When a video file is embedded in an SWF, it becomes part of the SWF, and there's only one file to manage. With Flash MX 2004 Professional, there are some new options for streaming external video files, which must be in the Flash-specific FLV format.

The FLV format often yields the best results for video quality and file size, but to create an FLV, you must have some software in addition to Flash itself. Both streaming and the FLV format are discussed in more detail later in this Appendix.

In Flash MX and later versions, you can import a traditional digital video file in AVI, MOV, or MPG format. The formats supported depend on your having either QuickTime 4 or DirectX 7 (or later versions) installed; most computers have one or both. Almost any video editing software will output at least one of the supported file formats.

You can expect the video file to be quite large. As an example, an MOV file of 1 minute 38 seconds came out of Adobe Premiere LE at 64 MB. It had a frame rate of 15 fps, to help keep it "small." After importing the MOV into Flash and publishing an SWF file, that SWF was 7.6 MB. (A video with no audio track would be smaller.) While that's a great reduction in size, the file is hardly lightweight. The screen dimensions of that video are 320 × 240, which is really about as large as you can go with online video in most cases.

In Flash MX 2004, when you import a video file in AVI, MOV, or MPG format, you will have the option to edit the video or just import it. In most cases, the file should have been edited already, and you will simply import it. Next, you can adjust some quality settings, which will affect not only video quality but also the file size of the final SWF. If you select a slower connection speed, such as "56 Kpbs modem," the quality of the video will be very poor, because the video codec will apply a severely high level of compression.

Note: Flash may refuse to import a video file from a CD or DVD, even if the format is compatible. If you run into this problem, copy the file to your hard drive and then import it from there.

In Flash MX, when you import a video file in AVI, MOV, or MPG format, you do not have the option to edit the video, but you can adjust some quality settings, which will affect both the video quality and the SWF file size.

You'll need to adjust the quality settings differently for different videos, so be prepared to spend some time experimenting. There is no "standard" setting to rely on. You can't see the results of the settings until you output the SWF.

Once the video file is in the FLA, you can place it on the Stage and add the usual Flash objects such as text and buttons on layers above it. You can also add animations on top of the video. Do not try to put anything into the same layer with the video. Make sure to extend the Timeline of any additional layers to match the length of the video layer.

FLV VIDEO FILES

Importing a file in the FLV format will result in the smallest possible SWF, as far as embedded video is concerned. For example, the 64-MB MOV file described above was converted to an FLV file (using Sorenson Squeeze, Version 3, an additional software package), and the file size of the FLV was 8.5 MB. After importing the FLV into Flash and publishing an SWF file, however, that SWF was 4.5 MB.

The quality of the final video was no worse than the 7.6-MB SWF that embedded the MOV directly.

This difference in file size indicates the importance of the FLV format. While you can import an AVI, MOV, or MPG directly into Flash, your SWFs will be smaller if you convert the video file to the FLV format and then import the FLV to Flash.

So, how do you create an FLV file?

• You could buy one of the Sorenson Squeeze video compression products (*http://www.sorenson.com/*). The lowest-priced option is Sorenson Squeeze for Macromedia Flash MX, a stand-alone package that converts a variety of regular video file formats to FLV. This will work with Flash MX (6) as well as with MX 2004 (7), and it's much easier to use than some other video compression software.

• If you have Flash MX 2004 Professional, you also have the Flash Video Exporter. (It comes on the CD and you must install it separately, so make sure you do. Macromedia also calls it the FLV Export plug-in.) This allows you to export FLV files directly from some video editing software applications (for an up-to-date list of supported applications, see the

Macromedia Web site). Macromedia released a free upgrade to the Video Exporter in 2004, so depending on when you purchased your software, you may also need to download and install the upgrade. The exporter will work only on a computer that has Flash MX 2004 Professional installed on it, so if your video editing software resides on a different computer, you may not be able to use the exporter.

If you do have Flash MX 2004 Professional, probably the least expensive way to produce FLV files is to buy QuickTime Pro (*http://www.apple.com/ quicktime/download/*); the Flash Video Exporter works with it on both Windows and Mac computers. When a video file is open in QuickTime Pro, select "Export" from the File menu; in the dialog box, open the Export menu and select "Movie to Macromedia Flash Video (FLV)" and then click the Options button; the Flash Video Exporter will open.

Some novice Flash users confuse the Sorenson codec with the external software used to create FLV files; the Sorenson codec is always used in Flash to import or export video, but it does not always create an FLV. (A codec is the algorithm used to compress the video data.) If you did not deliberately create an FLV file and import it into Flash, then you don't have the smallest resulting file.

STREAMING AND PROGRESSIVE DOWNLOAD

Flash MX 2004 Professional offers various alternatives to importing video directly into Flash; these work *only* with the Professional version.

One option, which requires no special Web server features, employs the Media Playback component, which you'll find in the Components panel (Window menu > Development Panels > Components). Drag the component to the Stage and use the Component Inspector panel to insert the filename (or URL) of an external FLV file. Enter the frame rate and length of your video. Resize the Media Playback component (using the Properties panel) so the video is full size. Save and test your movie. Instant video!

Note: Check for updates at the Macromedia Web site. You may have an outdated version of the Media Components or the Flash Video Exporter. New ones can be downloaded from *http://www.macromedia.com/devnet/mx/flash/video.html*

You can load external FLVs without the Media Playback component by using ActionScript to load and play the files. For documentation about this, search in the Flash Help files for "external FLV files." Handling video this way offers some advantages for longer video files, because cached memory is employed to store the files in segments and access them dynamically, but it's outside the scope of this book to discuss this option further.

By loading an external FLV in this manner, you're enabling a progressive download of the file. To the user, the file appears to be streaming. But true streaming is accomplished by the Web server, not by the SWF or the video file. Macromedia suggests using the Flash Communication Server for streaming video; this is an option for larger organizations that produce a lot of video content.

HELP! MY VIDEO IS UGLY!

It is not Flash's fault if your video looks bad. Squishing a gigantic quantity of motion and sound into a file small enough to send via digital transmission media requires a lot of math. As you know, math cannot see or hear your video. When you choose settings to compress your video file (in your video editing program, even before it gets to Flash), you are setting up the math, and you might do a bad job of it.

This is meant not to discourage you but rather to urge you to have patience with yourself, your video, and your software. Each video is different. Video with lots of motion and color and changing scenery requires certain math to look good, while video in which not much moves might use different math. Sound is also a very significant factor. If you apply exactly the same settings to two different videos, one may come out wonderful and the other may look or sound terrible.

Record the settings you select for each attempt. Keep a notebook. If you're going to be producing a lot of video online, you will get better at it more quickly if you learn from your past mistakes.

RESOURCES AND TUTORIALS

Video in Flash MX

"Using video in Macromedia Flash MX"
http://www.macromedia.com/support/flash/images_video/flash_video/

"Using embedded video in Macromedia Flash MX"
http://www.macromedia.com/devnet/mx/flash/articles/flashmx_video.html

"Tips for deploying video in Macromedia Flash MX"
http://www.macromedia.com/devnet/mx/flash/articles/fmx_video_tips.html

Video in Flash MX 2004

"Getting Started with Flash Video"
http://www.macromedia.com/devnet/mx/flash/articles/getstart_flv.html

"Video Learning Guide"
http://www.macromedia.com/devnet/mx/flash/video/video.html

Very Useful Keyboard Shortcuts

Note that on an iBook (and possibly some other notebook computers), the function keys (F keys) work as described here *only if* you press and hold Function *while* you press the F key. However, on most computers you can press the F key alone and get these results.

F5	Add frame(s). You can click once on a frame that is 10 or 15 frames to the right of the last existing frame in a layer, and then press F5 to add that many frames with a single click. To lengthen an existing sequence (e.g., a motion tween), click *inside* that sequence and press F5 as many times as the number of frames you want to add.
Shift-F5	Remove frame(s)—any kind of frame. (In some cases, you will find it better to right-click on the Timeline and choose Remove Frames from the pop-up menu.)
F6	Add *keyframe*(s). Click on a frame and press F6 once to add a keyframe. See Lesson 2 for the difference between a keyframe and a standard frame. Do not use keyframes unless they are needed.
Shift-F6	Clear *keyframe*. This does not delete the frame, but by converting the keyframe to a "normal" frame, it removes all information from that frame and makes it match the sequence preceding and following it.
F7	Add blank *keyframe*(s). Click on a frame and press F7 once to add a blank (empty) keyframe. The difference between this and F6: When you press F6, everything in the previous frame is preserved. If you want those things to disappear, you need a *blank* keyframe (F7).
F8	Convert to Symbol.

F9	Open the Actions panel.
F11	Open the Library panel.
Enter (Win)/ Return (Mac)	Play the current *Scene*. (This will *not* play movie clips within the scene.)
Ctrl-Enter (Win)/ Cmd-Return (Mac)	Generate a *.swf* file and play the entire Flash movie in its own window.
Comma (,)	In the Timeline, move back one frame. Press multiple times to view the movie frame by frame.
Period (.)	In the Timeline, move forward one frame. Press multiple times to view the movie frame by frame.

Flash Reserved Words List

A "reserved word" is simply one that must not be used as a variable name, and it's usually also good to avoid using it as a value. In other words, use a reserved word only as Flash expects it to be used.

Flash Player 2	on
Flash Player 3	ifFrameLoaded
Flash Player 4	add, and, break, case, continue, default, do, else, eq, ge, gt, if, le, lt, ne, not, or, switch, tellTarget, while
Flash Player 5	delete, for, function, in, new, onClipEvent, return, this, typeof, var, void, with
Flash Player 6	instanceof
Flash Player 7	catch, finally, throw, try
ActionScript 2.0/Flash Player 6	class, dynamic, extends, get, implements, import, interface, intrinsic, private, public, set, static
Special functions and constants	call, duplicateMovieClip, eval, fscommand, getProperty, getTimer, getURL, getVersion, gotoAndPlay, gotoAndStop, int, length, loadMovie, loadMovieNum, loadVariables, loadVariablesNum, mbchr, mblength, mbord, mbsubstring, NaN, nextFrame, nextScene, Number, ord, play, prevFrame, prevScene, print, printNum, random, removeMovieClip, set, setProperty, startDrag, stop, stopAllSounds, stopDrag, substring, targetPath, toggleHighQuality, trace, unloadMovie, unloadMovieNum

Reserved for future use	abstract, boolean, byte, char, const, debugger, double, enum, export, final, float, goto, int, long, native, package, protected, short, synchronized, throws, transient, volatile

Chart by Darron Schall. Used by permission.
http://www.darronschall.com/weblog/archives/000102.cfm

Index